D1474125

STATUTORY DEFAULT RULES

EINER ELHAUGE

Statutory Default Rules

How to Interpret Unclear Legislation

HARVARD UNIVERSITY PRESS

Cambridge, Massachusetts, and London, England   2008

Library of Congress Cataloging-in-Publication Data
Elhauge, Einer.
  Statutory default rules : how to interpret unclear legislation / Einer Elhauge.
    p. cm.
  Includes bibliographical references and index.
  ISBN-13: 978-0-674-02460-1 (alk. paper)
  ISBN-10: 0-674-02460-5 (alk. paper)
  1. Law—United States—Interpretation and construction. 2. Statutes—United States I. Title.

KF425.E44 2008
348.73'2—dc22   2007014164

Contents

Acknowledgments

I am grateful to the large set of persons who have given their time to give me insightful comments on a draft of this book, which includes the anonymous peer reviewers, Omri Ben-Shahar, Steven Calabresi, Frank Cross, Mariano-Florentino Cuellar, John de Figueiredo, Richard Fallon, Allen Ferrell, George Fisher, Ronald Levin, Frank Michelman, Martha Minow, Richard Posner, Todd Rakoff, Mark Ramseyer, David Rosenberg, David Shapiro, Max Stearns, Bill Stuntz, Adrian Vermeule, and participants in workshops at Harvard Law School and Northwestern University School of Law.

I am also thankful to the even larger set of persons who have previously provided comments on the articles that form the basis for many portions of this book, which include "Does Interest Group Theory Justify More Intrusive Judicial Review?" 101 Yale *Law Journal* 31–110 (1991); "Preference-Estimating Statutory Default Rules," 102 Columbia Law Review 2027–2161 (2002); and "Preference-Eliciting Statutory Default Rules, 102 Columbia Law Review 2162–2290 (2002).

I also wish to acknowledge the generous financial support I have received for this project from Harvard Law School and the John M. Olin Center for Law, Economics, and Business at Harvard Law School, the able research assistance of Michael Fertik and Won Shin, and the sensational institutional support I have received from my Dean, Elena Kagan.

Finally, I am especially thankful to my family for their patience while my work on this book took precious time away from them.

STATUTORY DEFAULT RULES

CHAPTER 1

Introduction and Overview

The Legal Dilemma

You are a conscientious judge, and you have a problem. The case before you presents an important question of statutory interpretation. Having listened dutifully in law school, you understand that the primary issue before you is to determine the meaning of the statute. Unfortunately, you also know that there is no consensus about how to do that. You try formalism on for size, and thus at first focus only on the statutory text and a dictionary that was published as close in time to the statutory enactment as you can find. But you are well aware of the extensive critique that says that formalistic approaches exclude much of the evidence that is relevant to determining what the legislature meant. Formalism also sometimes leads to results that seem absurd or contrary to what the legislature could have possibly desired. Moreover, even after applying the full panoply of approved formalistic techniques, you are forced to admit that the statutory meaning remains unclear in your case. You have narrowed the range of possible interpretations to a few options, but cannot really say with any confidence that one of them is *the* meaning of the statute.

So you consider turning to legislative history, as most judges do, to try to figure out the legislative intent or purpose that should help resolve the ambiguity in meaning. But you are also aware of the equally extensive critique that has been leveled against this practice. You know there is really no such thing as a shared intent or purpose in a multimember legislature. Each legislator has his own complex mix of reasons for voting for the legislation, and some of them may have less to do with legislative substance than with the fear of losing campaign donations, or with the legislator's loyalty or opposition to party leadership. You also know that legislative history has the considerable problem that the legislature never voted on it, and that it may thus reflect the views of those legislators who authored the relevant statements or committee reports, rather than the views of the legislature as a whole. In any event, after looking at all the legislative history in your case, you find that it points in somewhat conflicting directions, and does not really provide a clear answer to how the statute should be interpreted. Instead, you again have a range of possible answers, and no clear grounds for choosing one over the others.

You do not give up in despair yet. For we have canons of statutory construction to deal with such cases of ambiguity. But then you remember what the literature on them says: for every canon, there is a counter-canon that leads to the opposite interpretation. For example, one canon says a statute that lists specific applications excludes unlisted applications. But it seems in direct conflict with a counter-canon, which advises that a statute should be interpreted to extend to unlisted applications when doing so furthers the general statutory purpose indicated by the listed applications. And there appear to be no consistently followed rules about which canons to invoke in particular cases. Perhaps you even recall your law professors telling you with a resigned shrug, or a nihilistic smirk, that judges seem to invoke whichever one leads them to the result they favor in the particular case.

Even if you could figure out which canon to choose among any opposing pair of canons, there is a bewildering range of nonopposing canons one could possibly invoke, and the priority among them is unclear. For example, should one invoke the canon against interpreting statutes to create constitutional doubts before, or after, one invokes the canon that a statute that lists applications means to exclude unlisted ones? Not only do the legal materials fail to specify the order in which to apply most canons, they don't even provide generally accepted criteria for making case-by-case judgments about how best to prioritize the canons.

Many of the traditional canons are also normatively controversial, and you are not quite sure what justifies invoking a canon that embodies a general substantive slant you doubt the legislature shares. And you also can't help but notice that many of the relevant canons are themselves linguistically ambiguous, at least in their application to your particular case. Absent some larger theory about when and why to apply canons, they don't seem to resolve the case.

What is an honest, well-intentioned judge to do when traditional legal methods of interpretation give out in this way?

Filling the Legal Gap with Judicial Judgment

The dominant answer given in modern American law schools is that when the legal materials fail to specify the statutory meaning, you as judge have no choice but to exercise your own normative judgment about which statutory interpretations would be best, so you might as well be up front about it. Most substantive courses leap rather reflexively to this approach, treating the necessary judicial judgment as an interstitial lawmaking power akin to making common law. Other courses and scholars, especially those focusing on issues of statutory interpretation, may instead stress that the judicial judgment could or should be made at a more systematic level: judges can choose (or develop) general canons of statutory construction that further worthy public values. Such systemic judicial judgments could be made either at the level of substance—choosing canons that generally embody normatively attractive results—or process—choosing canons that lean against groups that are deemed to have excessive political influence. Some such canons operate at a high level of generality about what results are normatively attractive. Proposals that favor interpretations that promote statutory coherence rest on the premise that furthering this goal is generally normatively desirable. Proposals that favor interpreting ambiguities to minimize legislative change or the scope of statutes rest on the different proposition that change or regulation is generally undesirable. Given the diversity of positions and proposals about which substantive results or process claims are normatively desirable, analysis under this modern approach turns on which of them are deemed most normatively attractive by judges.

The resulting approach requires judges to adopt sharply bifurcated roles. Under it, judges are to act as honest agents for the legislature to the extent they can divine its meaning using traditional methods of legal interpretation. But once those methods give out, judges must instead shift to becoming independent lawmakers, furthering the normative views or canons they themselves find most attractive.

Not everyone seems disturbed by this result. Some seem to fairly celebrate it, trumpeting the virtues of judicial judgment. They argue that the judicial process is more nimble than the legislative process, more aware of changed circumstances and able to update statutes, and more focused on fact-specific applications and thus able to tailor statutes to them. They may also argue that the judicial process better protects certain fundamental values or traditions, in part because of its system of precedent and common law development. To them, judges are more likely to reach desirable results if they act as partners of the legislature rather than as its agents. Such scholars are thus not disturbed that the legal materials give out, and may in fact stress the indeterminacy of traditional legal methods in order to expand the scope for such desirable exercises of judicial judgment.

Others do find this result disturbing. In particular, many formalist scholars stress the perils of allowing judges to make judgments that deviate from prevailing political views. They seek to avoid what they consider more open-ended methods of interpretation precisely to constrain the exercise of such judicial judgment. But even this position shares the same premise that once the traditional legal methods have given out, such exercises of judicial judgment are unavoidable. Other scholars may find the situation lamentable, but have no faith that formalistic methods can do anything to lessen the problem. To them, this is simply an imperfection we must resign ourselves to accept, given the inevitable imprecision of legislative language, and the necessity of having judges resolve the legal disputes that such imprecision creates.

In short, whether or not judicial judgment is desirable, it is widely viewed to be a proposition of logic that unclear legislative instructions require shifting from an honest agent model to exercises of judicial judgment. Cass Sunstein states the prevailing view well when he says: "[T]raditional sources offer incomplete guidance and . . . their incompleteness reveals the inevitable failure of the agency conception of the judicial role." Thus, he concludes, the argument that the failure of the agency model requires judges to exercise substantive judgment about which interpretive principles or gap-filling devices to employ "is a conceptual or logical claim, not a proposition about the appropriate distribution of powers among administrative agencies, courts, and legislatures. It depends not at all on a belief in the wisdom and decency of the judges."[1]

Must the honest agent model be put aside once legislative instructions are unclear? My first task in this book will be to convince you that the answer is no. One can instead extend the honest agent model to cases of statutory uncertainty by adopting a set of statutory default rules that maximizes political satisfaction. My honest agent approach does not regard judges as robots that mechanically execute clear legislative instructions, nor as psychics who can always divine legislative intent. But it also rejects the view that judges are partners in lawmaking, or free to maximize their own ideological preferences where statutes are unclear. Instead, an honest interpretive agent should, when statutory meaning is unclear, adopt statutory default rules that probabilistically tend to maximize political satisfaction. Given the uncertainty left by unclear statutory language, no system of interpretation can ever hope to always correctly ascertain political preferences, but the right set of default rules can minimize the expected political dissatisfaction.

My second task will be to show which set of statutory default rules would fulfill this goal. If I can accomplish those two tasks, I would be more than happy. But I am going to get a bit greedy and also try to demonstrate two more things: that current interpretive practices actually embody those default rules, and that this approach to statutory interpretation is better than relying on judicial judgment.

Interpreting Statutes to Maximize Political Satisfaction

Statutes are hardly the only kind of legal text that courts must interpret. Contracts and corporate charters are also often unclear in ways that both cases and scholarship acknowledge cannot be resolved by traditional legal interpretation. Yet in the areas of contracts and corporate law, cases and scholars do not assume that, when the meaning of the legal text is unclear, the only way to resolve the matter is by having judges exercise their own substantive judgment. Rather, the modern view is that, when contracts and corporate charters are unclear, courts should apply whichever default rules are most likely to accurately reflect or elicit the preferences of the parties who agreed to such contracts or charters. If, for example, a contract has not specified when payment for a product will be made, the default rule is that payment is due when the product is delivered. This is not because the courts think the parties "meant" or "intended" this default rule. It is because courts believe that most contracting parties would want that rule. Accordingly, the preferences of contracting parties will generally be maximized if this default rule is used when contractual meaning is unclear.

This does not mean that we can simply apply the default rule approach that is used in contract and corporate law in some wholesale way to statutes. For business contracts and corporations, the normal premise is that the participants would prefer the default rule that maximizes the economic pie, on the assumption that any distributional effects would be reflected in (and thus offset by) the price of the contract or corporate securities. This permits the general assumption that all parties share a preference for the most efficient default rules—though, to be sure, which default rules are efficient may turn on personal characteristics of the parties, such as their aversion to risk.

With statutes, we have no warrant for assuming that the legislative participants share the same set of preferences, and certainly no general grounds for assuming they prefer the most efficient default rules. One point of the political process is precisely to decide how much to pursue efficiency versus other social goals. Thus, if the issue is what the statutory outcome should be, we need to inquire into the set of political preferences possessed by a particular legislative polity to devise the appropriate default rules. In short, compared to corporate and contract law default rules, statutory default rules about outcomes are more likely to be tailored to the preferences of the particular participants in question. The key question will thus be how to go about doing such tailoring, and how to deal with the inevitable uncertainty about which preferences are enactable.

For nonbusiness contracts, people may care about things other than their economic gain, so choosing efficient default rules is more questionable, and the contracting parties' preferences about default rules may show a variability similar to those of legislative polities. But now we come to a second big difference between contracts and statutes. Persons normally are not bound by old contracts they did not enter into, so in contract law there is no question that the contracting parties would want the default rule that tracks their own preferences. In contrast, legislative polities are governed not only by the statutes they enact but also (indeed mainly) by old statutes enacted by prior legislative polities. Statutory analysis (unlike contracts) thus raises the question: should courts track the preferences of the enacting or current legislative polity?

Finally, consider the possibility that the choice of default rule might itself provoke the parties who created the relevant text to clarify it. For contracts and corporate charters, any clarification made in response to a default rule of interpretation must come ex ante, in the initial contract or charter, before persons develop vested rights. But for statutes, the correction can come either ex ante, in the initial statutory drafting, or ex post, through subsequent statutory amendments or overrides that can overturn the vested rights created by statutory interpretations. This will prove to be another important way by which statutory default rules differ from contractual default rules.

In short, many of the most interesting points about statutory default rules arise from their differences from contractual and corporate default rules. Nonetheless, the practice of using default rules in contracts and corporate law does show that unclarity about the meaning of legal texts, or about the intent or purpose of those who agreed to them, does not logically compel a reliance on judicial judgment. Moreover, it illustrates that an honest agent model need not rely on claims that courts have correctly ascertained textual meaning or purpose. Instead, it can take the form of default rules that reflect probabilistic judgments about which interpretations are most likely to maximize the satisfaction of the preferences of those who agreed to the relevant legal text.

This book takes a similar approach to statutory interpretation. It rejects the common assumption that the honest agent model must give out once the legislative instructions are unclear. Instead, it argues that judges can still act as honest agents when resolving indeterminate statutory meaning. Courts need simply, as they do in contracts and corporate law cases, adopt default rules that are designed to maximize the preference satisfaction of the parties who agreed to the text being interpreted.

But who are the parties who agree to statutes? It is tempting to say the electorate, or at least a majority of voters, but that would be untrue. The electorate generally does not vote on statutes. Rather, some of the electorate vote for legislators and executives, who in turn vote on legislation. What matters is thus how their elective choices are mediated by the particular political system used to translate those choices into statutes. The particular system may well alter the distribution of influence; for example, the U.S. Senate gives disproportionate influence to citizens from states with below-average populations.

Nor, however, would it be accurate to say that the relevant preferences are those of the legislators and executives themselves. They cannot enact whatever maximizes their personal utilities or even their sincere ideological views, for they are constrained by the need to get reelected, and thus cannot deviate too much from the preferences of the electorate. A majority of legislators may also be unable to take action if members of the key legislative committee are opposed, or if the executive is willing to veto and a supermajority to override does not exist.

For statutes, then, we cannot aim to maximize the preferences of particular individuals or majorities in the electorate or government. Instead, the relevant preferences must reflect the complex ways by which actual legislative procedure weighs and aggregates preferences to determine which statutes to enact. To refer to these preferences, I will use the term "enactable preferences," by which I mean the set of political preferences that would be enacted into law if the issue were considered and resolved by the legislative process. As I hope this makes clear, the term "enactable preferences" does

not clear

not refer to polling data, nor to any other indications of the electorate's general political preferences that were not manifested in their choice of elected officials. It also does not refer to legislator utility, nor to strategic private aims that legislators may harbor but could not actually enact into law.

This book argues that, when statutory meaning is unclear, judges can still act as honest agents by using statutory default rules that are designed to maximize the satisfaction of enactable preferences. I will sometimes refer to this as maximizing the preferences of the "legislative polity" because clear sentence structure often requires a subject. However, this term should be understood as an abstraction that reflects the particular political organization by which the relevant society weighs and aggregates choices into the power to make statutory enactments. Because both terms are a mouthful, I will also sometimes refer to the relevant concept as "maximizing political satisfaction," but by now you know that what I mean by this is the satisfaction of enactable political preferences. Maximizing political satisfaction means the same thing as minimizing political dissatisfaction, which is an alternative way of framing the goal that I shall use when it is clarifying.

Of course, one way to assure that political preferences are enactable is to force them to be enacted into clear statutory meaning before acting on them. And, as I will show, there are certain circumstances where that is precisely the default rule that maximizes political satisfaction. But this is not generally true because, unless and until the legislature acts, the interpretation that governs is whatever the courts say the statute means. Interpretations that deviate from the best estimate of enactable preferences thus would generally increase political dissatisfaction.

I will not, however, stop with the argument that it is logically possible to implement an honest agent model, even in cases of statutory uncertainty, by adopting statutory default rules that maximize political satisfaction. I will further argue that judges *should* adopt such statutory default rules because it is the political process for enacting statutes—not judicial judgment—that is supposed to determine what is normatively desirable within constitutional boundaries. Thus, the political preferences reflected in the portions of statutes whose meaning is understood should be equally reflected in the statutory interpretations that govern when that meaning is unclear.

This is not to deny that courts should consider other possible traditional judicial goals like advancing statutory coherence, stability, or certainty. But the proper basis for such consideration is not that these goals are ends in themselves, but rather that advancing them generally increases political satisfaction. Interpretations thus should not further those goals when other evidence indicates that doing so would deviate from enactable preferences. This goes more generally for the diverse array of public values that various proponents have argued should govern statutory interpretation. As worthy as the proposed public values generally are, they deserve consideration only to the extent that they help maximize the satisfaction of enactable preferences.

But which statutory default rules are best designed to maximize political satisfaction? And does using such statutory default rules really add anything to simply choosing the most likely meaning of the statute?

Identifying the Statutory Default Rules That Maximize Political Satisfaction

What I am about to say is quite counterintuitive, so I don't expect you to believe me yet. It turns out that an approach of maximizing political satisfaction often dictates adopting statutory default rules that do *not* reflect the enactors' most likely meaning or preferences. It is the major burden of this book to show why this is so, and the argument is sufficiently complex that it requires me to develop this point in four separate stages, each of which occupies several chapters. At each stage, I aim to do more than just make the normative case that the relevant default rule maximizes political satisfaction, I also aim to establish my descriptive thesis that these default rules better explain actual interpretive doctrine. That is, I aim to not only identify which statutory default rules courts should use, but to show they are actually using them already, though often either under a different name, or without any name but implicitly through a pattern of practice.

1. Current Preferences Default Rules

My first major point will be the default rules that overall best maximize the political preferences of the *enacting* legislative polity turn out to track the preferences of the *current* legislative polity when the latter can be reliably ascertained from official action. By "official action," I mean either agency decisions interpreting the statute or subsequent legislative statutes that help reveal current enactable preferences even though they do not amend the relevant provision.

This argument for current preferences default rules may be the most counterintuitive of my claims. Why wouldn't the enacting legislative polity want its *own* political preferences followed? The key to the answer is that the question here is not what result the enacting legislative polity would most likely want for the *particular* statute; if that were the question, then it would be true that the legislature would want its own preferences followed. The question here is instead what *general* rules for resolving uncertainties about statutory meaning—including uncertainties in older statutes that are being interpreted and applied during the time that the enacting legislative polity holds office— would most maximize the political satisfaction of the enacting legislative polity? In choosing such general statutory default rules, I will show, the enacting legislative polity would prefer *present* influence (while it exists) over *all* the statutes being interpreted, rather than *future* influence (when it no longer exists) over the *subset* of statutes it enacted.

The current preferences default rule approach explains many actual cases that rely on subsequent legislative action. More important, we shall see that it explains the *Chevron* doctrine that judges should defer to agency interpretations of unclear statutes, because agency action is generally a fairly good indicator of where current enactable preferences lie. Further, this approach explains the otherwise confusing pattern of exceptions to that deference that exist under *Mead* and other doctrines. These exceptions turn out to track cases where agency decisions are less exposed to the sort of political influence that makes them likely to reflect current enactable preferences. The current preferences approach can also explain why deference is denied to those agency interpretations that plainly conflict with prevailing legislative preferences, and thus could not be enactable. This approach explains, among other things, why the Court denied deference to a Clinton agency decision that cigarettes could be regulated as a drug, and to a Bush agency decision that drugs used in physician-assisted suicide could be criminalized as a controlled substance.

Explaining *Chevron* and its numerous exceptions is no minor matter, because this is the single canon of statutory interpretation that is most frequently applied in the modern administrative state. Thus, the current preferences default rule approach not only merits theoretical priority, but is the most important practically because it explains the biggest set of statutory interpretations.

2. Enactor Preferences Default Rules

What, however, should courts do when current preferences cannot be reliably ascertained from recent official action, perhaps because there is no relevant agency decision or legislation on the topic? In those cases, courts should use enactor preferences default rules that maximize the preference satisfaction of the enacting legislative polity.

Enactor preferences default rules come closest to paralleling the meaning that the enacting legislative polity would most likely have attached to the unclear text. But we shall see that even here the inquiries differ, mainly because the sources of information for making probabilistic estimates of political *preferences* are broader than those for ascertaining the *meaning* the enactors likely attached to a particular text. The probabilistic goal of maximizing political satisfaction thus provides an alternative way to justify and understand many common interpretive practices, which have been heavily critiqued as means of ascertaining statutory meaning. For example, this approach can explain the judicial practice of making broad-ranging inquiries into legislative history when the statute is unclear, even if one agrees with the critique that such inquiries cannot accurately reveal any shared legislative intent. It also provides a stronger justification for the practice of allowing statutory interpretations to vary over time with changes in factual circumstances. Even when those changes cannot really alter any fixed statutory meaning, they do often alter which statutory results we think would maximize the satisfaction of a fixed set of enactor preferences.

Perhaps more surprisingly, I will show that, given sufficient uncertainty about which preferences are enactable, minimizing the dissatisfaction of those preferences often dictates adopting *moderate* interpretations, even when more extreme interpretations are more likely to reflect enactable preferences. For example, suppose a statute has three plausible interpretations, and the likelihood that each will reflect enactable preferences is 40% for the right-wing option, 35% for the left-wing option, and only 25% for the moderate option. It turns out a default rule favoring the moderate interpretation will minimize expected political dissatisfaction, even though it is the least likely to reflect enactable preferences. Thus, even enactor preferences default rules often deviate from just choosing whichever interpretive option is most likely to reflect the preferences of the enacting polity.

The discussion will also shed light on the current controversy about how to treat presidential signing statements. Given the power of the presidential veto, such statements can indicate what was actually enactable. They thus should influence interpretation when they have been signaled early enough to be reflected in the legislative drafting. But they should not be given weight when they came too late for the legislature to take them into account in deciding what to enact, because then they may not accurately reflect a constraint on what was actually enactable. In short, the problem with most presidential signing statements is not with their presidential nature, but with their late timing.

3. Preference-Eliciting Default Rules

Suppose that both current and enactor preferences are unclear, making it highly uncertain which interpretive option either would prefer. Then, I will show that, under certain conditions, political satisfaction can be maximized by choosing preference-eliciting default rules. Such rules intentionally *differ* from the most likely political preferences, in order to elicit a legislative response that makes it clearer precisely where enactable preferences lie. The elicited legislative response may either come in more explicit statutory drafting by the enactors (anticipating the future application of an eliciting rule) or in post-interpretation statutory overrides by the current legislature.

Preference-eliciting default rules will, however, enhance political satisfaction only when the chosen interpretation is more likely to elicit a legislative response, by a margin sufficient to outweigh a weak estimate that another interpretation is more likely to match enactable preferences. In other words, a necessary condition for applying a preference-eliciting default rule is the existence of a significant differential likelihood of legislative correction. Where that and other conditions are met, a preference-eliciting default rule can create statutory results that reflect enactable preferences more accurately than any judicial estimate of current or enactor preferences possibly could.

Like current and enactor preferences default rules, preference-eliciting default rules are not merely a matter of theory. To the contrary, they explain many apparent anomalies and inconsistencies we see in the actual application of legislative canons. The above-described conflict between various canons and counter-canons, for example, can be resolved by understanding the necessary conditions for applying preference-eliciting default rules rather than current or enactor preferences default rules.

Preference-eliciting analysis also explains various canons that favor politically powerless groups. This includes the recent Supreme Court decision in *Hamdan,* which interpreted statutes to favor the adjudication rights of Guantanamo detainees. Given the lack of political clout these detainees had, it was entirely predictable that this decision would, as it did, elicit a statutory override, which made clear precisely where enactable preferences lay on the trial rights of detainees in the war on terror.

4. Supplemental Default Rules

Finally, what should a court do when it can neither meaningfully estimate nor elicit the preferences of the relevant legislative polity? I will show that, in such cases, a set of supplemental statutory default rules exists that is and should be applied. In some of these cases, the political preferences of a *subordinate* legislative polity will be clear, and political satisfaction can thus be maximized by having the supplemental default rule track them. This explains many canons that interpret ambiguous federal statutes to incorporate or protect state law or autonomy. In the remaining cases, the judiciary must resolve the statutory ambiguity with the default rule that (within the politically plausible range) the judiciary deems best. But this does not mean every judge is left to her own devices. Instead, canons of construction in such cases serve mainly to limit judicial variance by requiring judges to follow common law or constitutional principles. Limiting such variance is desirable because it minimizes uncertainty even if it does not reduce the magnitude of likely judicial error in estimating enactable preferences.

5. The Resulting Order of Application

I will show that our existing set of statutory canons can all be explained as different parts of this system of default rules that maximize political satisfaction. Further, understanding the underlying theory allows one to better prioritize the canons and understand their pattern of application. For example, the priority outlined above explains why *Chevron* deference (a current preferences default rule) should be employed before looking at legislative history (an enactor preferences default rule). It also explains why both should be employed before using the canons that serve a preference-eliciting function, such as the rule lenity, and why all three should be applied before using supplemental default rules, such as the canon against preempting state law.

Let me summarize. When statutory meaning is ambiguous, courts should first determine whether current enactable preferences can reliably be inferred from official action. If so, courts should apply a current preferences default rule. If not, then courts should apply an enactor preferences default rule, whose content may vary over time with changing factual circumstances. If neither enactor nor current preferences seem very certain, a preference-eliciting default rule should be used in those categories of cases that meet the necessary conditions, including—most important—a significant differential likelihood of legislative correction. Where neither estimating nor eliciting preferences is feasible, then supplemental default rules should be used that track the preferences of political subunits or (where those are unavailable) that reduce judicial variance by avoiding constitutional difficulties or deviations from common law principles. As we shall see, understanding this prioritization of default rules, and the conditions for applying them, explains many otherwise puzzling anomalies in the doctrine of statutory *stare decisis*.

The Nature and Scope of My Descriptive and Normative Claims

Throughout this book, I will be making both the normative claim that the statutory default rules I just described are desirable, and the descriptive claim that they largely fit U.S. legal doctrine. Even if I convince you of my normative claim, you might balk at my descriptive claim on the ground that what I describe matches neither what judges say they are doing in their opinions nor what judges subjectively think they are doing. But this is not what I mean by my descriptive claim. Rather, I mean that my theory fits and predicts the legal doctrine.

Indeed, by the end of this book, I hope to have persuaded you that designing default rules to minimize political dissatisfaction explains and justifies many judicial practices, doctrinal distinctions, and canons of construction far better than do existing interpretive or substantive theories. This books' approach also helps resolve what might otherwise appear to be little more than open-ended conflicts among statutory canons and cases. But rather than fitting the self-description of these practices by judges, many of the insights will come from using default rule theory as a way of redescribing existing phenomena in statutory interpretation, which under current descriptions have been entirely mired in intractable debates about how best to ascertain statutory meaning. These redescriptions can better justify, cabin, and make sense of these judicial practices. This improved understanding of the reasons underlying statutory constructions, and the justifiable grounds for their seemingly inconsistent application, also renders them more determinate, and thus more constraining on judges.

I mean my normative and descriptive claims to stand separately. If you disagree with my normative thesis, my descriptive claim would remain that my theory best explains the actual contours of current statutory interpretation by U.S. judges. Likewise, if you disagree with my descriptive thesis, my normative claim would remain that statutory interpretation should be governed by the above set of statutory default rules.

While my descriptive claim is limited to U.S. judges because those are the cases I have here studied, there is no reason to be so Americentric or juricentric about the normative claim. The same statutory default rules that are normatively attractive in the United States should be just as attractive in other nations. Nor are judges the only ones who issue binding statutory interpretations. In the modern administrative state, it may well be that most interpretations are rendered by agency officials. One virtue of this book's approach is that it offers needed guidance on the largely unexplored issue of how agencies should interpret statutes. Such guidance is particularly necessary under formalist theories that avoid the problem of what judges should do with uncertain statutes mainly by invoking the rule that they should defer to agencies, a tactic that provides little assistance with the begged question of just how agencies should interpret the same statutes.

With one vital exception, my analysis indicates that agency officials should use the same set of default rules as judges when they interpret statutes. The vital exception arises from the fact that, if the agency itself is making the decision, then deferring to agencies can hardly provide the basis for a current preferences default rule. Rather, agencies are the interpreters who can and should consider more general evidence of current enactable preferences, without limiting their inquiry to the inferences ascertainable from official action. Agencies generally do this naturally because of their responsiveness to political forces. However, agencies are often too formalistic and intent-focused, probably because they are trying to mimic existing theories of statutory interpretation that were designed for courts. What is appropriate for courts is not appropriate for agencies if a different statutory default rule would better maximize political preference satisfaction. And that is the case here because agencies are more likely than courts to be knowledgeable about (and responsive to) general evidence of current enactable preferences. Thus, where statutory meaning is unclear, the current preferences default rule applied by agencies should involve their own open-ended inquiry into current enactable preferences, before they inquire into matters like enactor preferences.

For that matter, the independent nature of my normative claim extends to legislatures themselves. That is, my normative claim indicates not only that adjudicators should adopt statutory default rules that maximize political satisfaction, but that, if adjudicators fail to do so, legislatures should enact codes of statutory construction that specify those statutory default rules. My analysis thus provides a recommended content for any codes of statutory construction that legislatures decide to adopt. Generally one would expect that self-interest would naturally drive legislatures to adopt codes of statutory construction that maximize the satisfaction of enactable political preferences. Congress has generally not bothered to adopt codes of construction that are very substantive, which itself is an indication that they are fairly happy about the extent to which current judicial interpretive practices already maximize their enactable preferences. But state legislatures have adopted more substantive codes of construction on many issues, which will provide valuable evidence on which statutory default rules are most likely to maximize political satisfaction.

In some cases, however, legislators might try to enact codes of construction that maximize careerist self-interest over the satisfaction of enactable preferences, or that favor their own interests or views over those of future legislatures. In such cases, the theory of this book provides a ground for limiting codes of construction that endeavor to opt out of the statutory default rules that maximize political satisfaction. We shall see that those limits might even be deemed constitutionally mandatory, depending on how one interprets the legislative and judicial powers under the relevant constitution. In any event, these limits affect my own recommendations about the best content for such codes of construction. Further, any code of statutory construction is itself a statute that must be interpreted, and courts will need default rules to do that, which should and have been fashioned to further the same goal of maximizing political satisfaction.

While my normative and descriptive claims stand separately, my claim about U.S. judicial doctrine also draws strength from the combination of descriptive and normative claims that is the peculiar province of law professors. One of the tasks of legal scholarship is to explain legal doctrine in a way that can provide guidance to future courts. It has thus always been important to establish that any proffered theory has not only normative attraction but also a sufficient fit with extant doctrine. For example, suppose one concluded that my descriptive claim was not as accurate as the alternative claim that judges simply interpret statutes in whatever way furthers their personal ideological preferences. Even if this alternative offered a viable positive account of the sort that would be acceptable in political science and rational choice theory, such a normatively corrosive position cannot offer an attractive legal theory for guiding future courts. A valid legal theory must instead have some normative justification to merit adoption.

Conversely, a perfectly valid normative argument that has no connection to existing doctrine may offer a useful blueprint for legislative reform, but has no claim to being a theory of legal doctrine. Without any grounding in the authority of existing doctrine, such a normative theory cannot offer guidance to an agency, trial court, or intermediate appellate court. Its utility would even be limited before a jurisdiction's high court, partly because of the presumption in favor of *stare decisis,* but even more so because that court must rule case by case in reviewing lower courts that will generally be following existing doctrine. This structure tends to limit high court decisions to altering the margins of existing doctrine, and makes it difficult for even a high court to accomplish a wholesale shift to an entirely different normative foundation.

Thus, while legal theory often includes pure positive or normative theory, what distinguishes it from those endeavors is that it also focuses on determining which of the possible normative justifications is most consistent with the descriptive landscape of current doctrine. The best legal theory might thus be neither the most descriptively accurate nor the most normatively attractive, but rather the theory that provides the best combined fit of descriptive explanation and normative justification. Accordingly, even if I do not convince you that my theory of statutory default rules offers the best descriptive and normative theory when such matters are considered separately, I still hope to convince you that it offers the best legal theory of current doctrine on statutory interpretation when one considers the combination of descriptive fit and normative attraction.

Objections and Implementation Issues

Perhaps by now you are brimming over with objections or with questions about how precisely one would implement such default rules. I cannot hope to satisfy such concerns at this introductory stage before I have explained my theory in greater detail, but I can at least assure you that I am going to get to them in the last part of this book.

One objection might be that the theories here diverge from some excellent political science literature that models statutory interpretation and provides empirical data designed to validate those models. A modest response is that such theories, even if more accurately reflecting what courts do, depend on corrosive premises that could not, for reasons noted above, offer a sound basis for a legal theory. But there is actually a far more direct response. As I will show in Chapter 15, these models turn on various assumptions. If one alters those assumptions to conform to the default rule theory offered in this book, we shall see that my default rule theories actually provide a *better* explanation for the results of various empirical studies about statutory interpretation. In short, properly understood, those empirical studies provide strong confirmation of the descriptive accuracy of the default rule theories in this book.

The final part continues by considering the fundamental objection that my theory seems quaint, if not naive, because it assumes enactable political preferences are worthy of respect. This premise might seem contrary to an extensive body of scholarship showing that the political process frequently deviates from the views of the electorate. Given this deviation, what is wrong with judges trying to improve the political process by, say, interpreting statutes against the special interest groups that enjoy disproportionate political influence? Under such an approach, one might argue, judges do not impose their substantive views on statutory interpretations, but simply help the electorate express its true views.

This is a powerful objection and will require an extended response. One modest response is that this line of argument does not really provide any grounds for lessening deference to enactable preferences in those cases where statutory meaning happens to be unclear. If enactable preferences do not merit respect, then why obey them when statutory meaning is clear? Thus, if persuasive, this line of argument may justify reforming the political process or adopting constitutional change, but does not really justify a theory of statutory interpretation.

The more fundamental response will be that this line of argument is wrong to think that one can separate process from substance. The claim that interest group theory shows that some groups have disproportionate influence turns out to inescapably depend on controversial normative baselines about what degree of influence each group should have. Allowing interest group theory to guide interpretation thus does not truly differ from having judges apply those normative judgments directly. Nor, if one believes that interest group theory does show that some groups have disproportionate influences, does that theory demonstrate that the judicial process is less subject to those influences. Similar problems beset claims that collective choice theory shows that legislative preferences are too prone to cycling and path dependence to merit judicial deference. Both theories thus fail to demonstrate that defects in the political process make judicial judgment—about substance or process—preferable to maximizing the satisfaction of enactable political preferences.

The final part next considers the objection that a better alternative would be default rules that interpret all statutory uncertainty to protect reliance interests or to reduce the effect or change caused by the statute. None of these alternative default rules would be preferable to those that maximize political satisfaction. A pro-reliance default rule would not only reduce political satisfaction, but encourage excessive reliance. The anti-effect and anti-change default rules would systematically sacrifice political satisfaction to further a dubious norm in favor of the status quo. They amount to efforts to elicit legislative preferences, but are not limited to the conditions where such an effort is likely to enhance the satisfaction of enactable political preferences. Nor are they constitutionally mandated, contrary to what some other scholars have argued.

The final part ends by considering operational and jurisprudential objections. I conclude that the jurisprudential objections parallel those historically raised against the legal realist analysis that judges were implicitly using policy in resolving legal uncertainties, and should be rejected for much the same sorts of reasons. A more serious concern might be that judges lack the competence to employ open-ended case-by-case standards that assess testimony by political scientists on how best to estimate or elicit political preferences. The answer to this concern is that my approach requires no such thing. Rather my approach simply offers a better way of explaining the set of existing doctrinal rules that judges have been applying to accomplish those ends.

Nor, I hope to show you, is it a persuasive objection that judicial decisions about which rules best advance those ends may be uncertain and often inaccurate. That problem exists for any sort of judicial decision, and here judges can take uncertainty about political preferences into account by using eliciting or supplemental default rules. Moreover, judges cannot avoid making decisions one way or the other about how to resolve uncertainties in statutory interpretations. If, for example, courts ignored the consequences of their decisions for the likelihood of legislative override and ultimate satisfaction of political preferences, that does not mean those consequences would not follow. It would merely mean courts would be making decisions that have those consequences without thinking about them. There is no reason to think that judicial incompetence is so great that judges make worse decisions when they estimate the consequences of their decisions than when they ignore them. That would be true only if judicial estimations were actually worse than random, which hardly seems plausible.

In any event, claims of judicial incompetence can be persuasive only if it is possible for courts to shift the relevant decision to a more competent branch. But that is not a claim that can be made against statutory default rules that maximize political satisfaction, for their aim is precisely to either estimate political preferences where enacted clarification has not yet occurred, or (with preference-eliciting canons) to shift the decision to the legislative branch, which can best maximize the satisfaction of enactable political preferences by identifying what they are.

The Scope of Statutory Default Rules and Their Feedback Effect on Inquiries into Meaning

I began this chapter by assuming a case where statutory meaning was unclear under existing methods of interpreting that meaning. After all, it is only when statutory meaning is unclear that the need for statutory default rules arises. But, as I shall argue in one chapter, we might instead reason in reverse: using the theory of statutory default rules to found a theory of meaning. That is, I shall argue that the best grounds for concluding that a meaning is "clear" is by asking whether the legislature signaled a desire to opt out of the default rule process. Opting out by adopting a fixed meaning will make sense, even though it results in some deviations from political satisfaction, where the legislature fears that judicial inaccuracies in applying the default rule methodology would on balance produce greater deviations from political satisfaction. I shall further suggest that a legislature should be understood to have desired such an opt out whenever (1) it uses precise statutory language, rather than words (like "reasonable") that delegate the development of standards to courts or agencies, and (2) the statutory language is being applied to a contingency that the legislature actually considered, or that was common enough to be within the normal range of contemplation when it enacted the statute.

But my theory of default rules stands entirely independent of this theory of meaning, and throughout the rest of the book I shall remain relentlessly agnostic about what the proper theory of meaning might be. For those who hold other theories of meaning, this means the importance of statutory default rules clearly varies with how determinate those methods for divining statutory meaning are. Suppose you find the various arguments in the debate about how to interpret statutory meaning sufficiently persuasive to believe that judges and scholars could reasonably subscribe to different theories. Then statutory default rules should be especially important, for in many cases those theories point in opposite directions. But suppose you are a partisan for a particular theory of meaning—say, a dedicated formalist or a thoroughgoing purposivist. Even then, I would hope you would confess that reasonable persons applying that same theory would often reach different conclusions in the same case. That is, each theory for finding statutory meaning has many unclear applications that cannot be resolved by the theory itself.

To those who find our legal methods for ascertaining statutory meaning wholly indeterminate, the choice of default rules actually resolves more cases than the choice of interpretive method—at the extreme, all cases. But even if one has a high degree of faith in such methods, choices about which statutory default rules to use will resolve many interesting cases in whatever residual remains unresolved by such methods. The proportion of such residual cases will be particularly large in the U.S. Supreme Court, which only takes cases that have split the lower courts, because cases that do not involve statutory uncertainty are less likely to create such splits. So even if statutory default rules do not dominate interpretation in the lower courts, we can expect them to dominate interpretation at the Supreme Court.

We might also expect to see a feedback effect running in the reverse direction. The better our statutory default rules, the less courts may feel impelled to insist on strained claims that current legal methods establish a particular statutory meaning or legislative intent, even in cases that were probably unanticipated by the enactors. The judges most likely to feel the need to strain to find unambiguous meaning are those who—quite properly—believe that statutory interpretation doctrine should constrain judges to effectuate legislative preferences. A theory of statutory default rules that is designed to provide such a constraint should increase their willingness to rely on those default rules. This should, in turn, reduce the number of cases that are resolved with rather implausible claims that the statute has a determinate meaning.

In short, judges can be honest interpretive agents for the political process without always claiming that the process has generated a clear statutory meaning they can decode. To the contrary, the political process should prefer to appoint interpretive agents who, rather than insisting on resolutions of uncertain statutory meaning that are arbitrary or heavily tinged by (perhaps unspoken) judicial preferences, resolve those statutory uncertainties with default rules that are designed to maximize the satisfaction of political preferences. Further, we shall see that the proposed default rules provide a new way of understanding many judicial doctrines that are currently cast as strained claims about what the legislature "intended."

By the same token, the more constraining our statutory default rules, the less those who celebrate judicial judgment over political judgment may feel an impetus to strain to find uncertainties in statutory meaning. For instead of authorizing the exercise of judicial judgment, the proposed default rules would constrain judicial judgment to further the satisfaction of political preferences. In short, a well-developed theory of statutory default rules can help avoid strained efforts in both directions on the issue of when statutory meaning or intent can be ascertained. So let's see whether we can develop such a theory in the following chapters.

CHAPTER 2

Why Courts Should Maximize Enactable Preferences When Statutes Are Unclear

What's so great about maximizing enactable preferences anyway? Sometimes, it might lead to results a judge deems bad, regardless of what the polity thinks. Other times, judges might think the enactment process fails to reflect what the polity really wants. To tackle this issue, let's divide it into two subsidiary questions. First, should judges follow political preferences, rather than judicial judgment, when the two diverge? Second, are enactable preferences the best way to measure political preferences?

Following Political Preferences Rather Than Judicial Judgment

Clearly, the polity would prefer to have its own preferences, rather than judicial judgment, govern in any case where the two diverge. That follows from the definition of preferences. It is thus equally clear that, if judges are best viewed as honest interpretive agents of a representative democracy, they should aspire to adopt interpretive practices that maximize the polity's preferences.

But should judges act as honest agents for the polity? Why shouldn't judges do the "right" thing no matter what the legislative polity thinks?[1] The reasons are several. To begin with, the whole reason we have a political process for enacting statutes is to determine what the "right" thing is. The process does so by assuring that, within constitutional bounds, political preferences are reflected in statutory results. If we preferred a judicial process, the enactment of statutes could be constitutionally delegated to judges. Instead, we have delegated statutory enactment power to the political process.

This indicates that statutory results are supposed to reflect political preferences, absent some constitutional constraint.

We must also realize that statutory interpretation is a collective act, not an individual assessment. The scholarly project here is advising judges about how best to make interpretations that will be collectively binding on us all. The judges who disagree with any scholar's proffered normative assessment about what "the right thing" is have no reason to adopt that scholar's advice about the best statutory default rules. The other judges might adopt the advice, but then the question becomes why these judges should be able to impose that contested normative assessment on citizens who disagree with it. The fact that judges disagree about normative matters raises a further problem. Why should statutory interpretation turn on the happenstance of which normative views happen to be held by the judge one draws? Normative theory provides a powerful tool each of us can use to help decide individually which statutory results are undesirable. But it cannot usefully provide an independent basis to make collective decisions (through judges) about how to interpret the results of a collective process that itself is supposed to decide what is normatively desirable. My above arguments cannot convince those who claim a privileged insight that means their views should prevail no matter what the polity thinks. But such persons have no business accepting (or being given) the role of a public servant who acts on behalf of us all.

The root problem is that we all harbor different conceptions of what the right thing is. Each person's ideal system would adopt his conception, but everyone cannot be a dictator on conceptions of the social good. The best we can do is join a democracy that accurately and equally weighs our different conceptions. True, a democracy will sometimes want to limit what it can do, and even more often want to limit what its political agents can do. But then we are in the realm of constitutional law rather than statutory interpretation, and this book throughout assumes we are operating in whatever area is left open by constitutional constraints. In choosing among those statutory results that are constitutionally permissible, the legislative polity will want those results that minimize its expected political dissatisfaction.

Why should any of us accept the statutory results of such a democracy, even when they violate our conception of justice and the social good? Because, in exchange, others accept statutory results we regard as good but they would regard as bad. We might justify such a trade-off on consequentialist grounds: if everyone accepts this social compact, the expected good consequences outweigh the bad for each of us. After all, what is the alter-

native to accepting the statutory results of democratic choices that sometimes violate individual conceptions of the good? The alternative is accepting the statutory results of *non*democratic choices that violate individual
conceptions of the good more often—unless, that is, the society does not accept statutory results as authoritative at all, and that way lies not just chaos,
but the frustration of our collective ability to pursue anyone's conception of
the good.

Nonconsequentialist theories of democracy support the same conclusion.
Theories that center on respecting the majority's will would obviously conflict with judges adopting statutory interpretations that conflict with majority preferences. The same follows if one rejects majority will in favor of
democratic theories that stress the principle of self-governance.[2] The reason
is that being a participant in a self-governing democracy necessarily means
giving up a claim to privileged insight into what advances the public interest. It means committing instead to having the public interest determined
through some political process of preference aggregation or principled deliberation, which constitutes the collective means by which the polity governs
itself. Yet another tack is taken by Jeremy Waldron, who persuasively argues that democracy is necessary to provide equal respect to all persons,
given their reasonable disagreements about what is just and desirable.[3]

What democratic government cannot mean is producing a government
where everyone's conception of the good is furthered, because that is impossible. All it can produce is the best that is possible: a government that
minimizes the expected dissatisfaction of the polity's differing conceptions of
the good. But it can do so only if interpretive agents apply default rules that
advance this goal, rather than misuse their interpretive powers to further
their own conceptions of the good. An interpreter who insists her conception of the good must take precedence breaches the fundamental social contract that leaves such matters to be resolved democratically.

One might argue that judges as a class are simply likely to make better social policy decisions than the political process. One version of this argument
stresses that judges are better qualified by virtue of greater intelligence, information, wisdom, training, or time devoted to analyzing the issues. Another
version stresses that judges are less corrupted by personal self-interest. Such
claims are similar to the more general claim that there may exist Platonic
guardians (here judges), who could make better decisions than a democracy.[4]

An initial problem with this claim is that, on contested issues of social policy, we have no independent basis (assuming we are within constitutional

bounds) to determine which decisions are better or worse, other than the outcomes of the accepted political process. To choose an outcome that the political process has rejected is necessarily to reject the conclusions of a sizeable part of the population. Where such widespread disagreement exists, what independent basis is there to conclude that one view (the one that happens to be held by the relevant judge) is the right one? And if we have such an independent basis, then why do we have a political process at all, rather than just having judges legislate by applying those independent standards to any new issues of social policy? This claim presumes an independent standard for deciding what policy is best. But unless that independent standard comes from the relevant constitution, assuming such an independent standard is inconsistent with the general decision to delegate such matters to resolution by the political process, rather than by judicial application of that supposedly independent standard.

Even if we *did* have some independent basis for determining when the political process was wrong about which outcomes are better, the claim that judges would make better decisions is dubious. In part, this is because the claim that individual judges are likely to make better decisions than individual voters or legislators is quite contestable. This is a claim that implicitly usually imagines a judiciary full of Learned Hands, who compare favorably to the average legislator. If one makes a more realistic assessment of the full range of state and federal judges, it might indicate far less of a talent gap between them and legislators. Moreover, the claim of superior judicial insight suffers from the embarrassment that judges disagree among themselves about the best policy, and tend to disagree along the same lines as everyone else does.[5] This leaves us to wonder just which of the judges we should consider superior, and what justifies assuming that majority rule produces sound results on appellate court panels more often than it does among voters and legislators.

But judges are certainly smart folk, and we need not dispute the claim that on average they make better decisions than individual voters or legislators. A deeper problem with this argument for preferring judicial judgment over political preferences is that it rests on a fallacy of composition. That fallacy is the assumption that decisions produced by an aggregation of voters are as likely to be right as the decisions of individual voters. Contrary to this assumption, it has been mathematically proven that, as long as the average voter does better than random at choosing the right decision, then aggregating their views in majority votes produces results that are far more accurate than their individual judgments.[6] Indeed, the odds of choosing the right outcome approach 100% as the number of aggregated votes gets large. Suppose, for example, that each individual voter is barely better than random at choosing the right option; that is, is 51% likely to make the right choice, and 49% likely to err. Then, the odds that a majority of 10,000 voters will make the right decision are an astonishing 98%.[7] If we assume the legislators elected by those voters are somewhat more accurate, say 60% likely to make the right choice, then it only takes 101 of them to make their majority vote 98% accurate. Those precise numbers hold only if the probability of one voter voting correctly is independent of other voters doing so, but this condition is not violated simply because the voters all have some common influence on them.[8] Further, as long as voters are somewhat independent of each other, aggregating their votes still increases their accuracy, though the aggregation benefits decline; reducing the degree of independence simply has the same effect as reducing the number of voters.[9]

Consistent with this mathematical proof, several empirical studies indicate that aggregations of many inexpert views tend to produce more accurate results than the judgments of individual experts.[10] And they find this is true on issues where the matter is something whose accuracy can be independently determined, like how many beans there are in a jar. Thus, both mathematics and empirics indicate that, even if judges are far better at making decisions than individual voters and legislators, the aggregated votes of the latter are likely to be better than the judgments of judges, who decide with no or little aggregation.

To be sure, the above point does not hold if the odds that the average individual voter or legislator will make the right decision are actually *worse* than random. In other words, it doesn't hold if voters or legislators hold views that make them systematically more likely to make the wrong choice than the right one. But such a systematic bias in the wrong direction would be plausible only if voters or legislators were applying the wrong criteria for deciding which outcomes are best. Thus, this critique must ultimately rest not on a claim that voters or legislators are less competent than judges at assessing which policy advances the best results, but on a claim that the former hold the "wrong" views about which results are best. And once we have moved from issues of competence to issues about what the right goals are, it is very unclear why we should think judges are better than voters or legislators at deciding which results are good.

Other difficulties beset the claim that judicial decisionmaking is preferable because it is more shielded by self-interest. To begin with, it would be a little naive to think that judges do not have their own interests on many issues. And while voters do have interests, it is unlikely that the act of voting is motivated by self-interest, because voting is personally costly, and any individual vote is highly unlikely to affect the outcome. The lack of any real incentive to vote to advance personal self-interest suggests that voting in large democratic bodies must mainly be motivated by altruistic desires to improve social policy.[11] Thus, political preferences are less likely to reflect voter self-interest than voter views about what constitutes sound public policy. And legislators will be policed by their accountability to an electorate for whom the act of voting is largely disinterested.

Even if voters are more likely to be acting out of self-interest than judges, it is not clear why that should be deemed bad.[12] Assuming voters have a better than random chance of guessing whether their own interests are improved by a certain decision, their aggregated judgments of self-interest are likely to produce results that further the interests of the citizenry, certainly more likely than judicial decisions shielded from considerations of interest. Indeed, shielding judicial decisions from considerations of interest may produce harmful results precisely because it leaves judges undisciplined by feedback about the extent to which they are harming the interests of the citizenry. It is easier to go completely off the tracks when lawmakers are free to pursue their ideological views without being reined in by the citizens whose interests they are affecting. This may explain the remarkable fact that only nondemocracies have ever suffered famines.[13]

In any event, the larger problem in the present context is that any claim of judicial superiority proves too much. If judges make better decisions than the political process on issues when statutes happen to be unclear, then they also do so when statutes are clear. So this argument is not a theory for deviating from political preferences just on questions of statutory interpretation. It is a theory that, if true, would suggest we should not have any political process for enacting statutes at all. It is thus not really a theory of statutory interpretation within our current system of political supremacy on statutory matters. It is rather a call for a radical overhaul of that system.

Further, this claim founders on the fact that the political process is what selects judges for their posts. So if we think that the political process makes such poor decisions, then it also follows it would make poor decisions about whom to select as judges. And if judges were understood to have plenary legislative authority, the political process would have incentives to select judges based on the same criteria that it now uses when it enacts legislation.

None of the above analysis bars the political process from deciding that, on some specific issues, judges might make better decisions than the political process. Indeed, it is often clear that what the political process meant or preferred was to delegate a matter for ongoing judicial resolution. The antitrust provisions prohibiting "restraints of trade" and "monopolization," for example, are commonly understood to involve such a delegation to courts to develop the rule of reason (and per se applications of it) in a common law fashion.[14] Open-ended statutory terms like "reasonable" or "unfair" also seem to indicate a desire to delegate, though usually the delegation is to an agency rather than to judges. In any event, when the statutory language does indicate a desire to delegate to judges, then exercising substantive judicial judgment does satisfy political preferences. Carrying out such a politically desired delegation thus differs from exercising judicial judgment even when such a delegation was not politically preferred.

Measuring Political Preferences as Enactable Preferences

The second question remains: why should political preferences be measured by the extent to which they are enactable? Part of the answer is simple consistency. When statutes are clear, no one doubts that judges must follow that clear meaning, which by definition reflects an enactable preference. If unclear statutory language were not interpreted to maximize enactable preferences, then the statutory results that governed the unclear portions of statutes would reflect preferences that conflict with the preferences reflected in the clear portions.

No doubt, in each society there are grounds to critique the process by which enactments are made. But each society must have accepted some set of reasons to justify compelled obedience to the enactable preferences that are reflected in clear statutes. Those same reasons, whatever they are, are equally applicable when considering which default rules should govern unclear statutory language. Any critique of those reasons would, if valid, indicate judges should not defer to statutory enactments either. Thus, such a critique cannot provide a sensible basis for a doctrine of statutory interpretation. It provides, rather, a general justification for constitutional limits on political decisions, or for reforming the process by which political decisions are made.

Nor does the necessary task of statutory interpretation provide any warrant for judges to impose their views of how democracy might be "perfected," by interpreting statutes to reach results that would be enactable only if one lifted certain procedural obstacles that, while constitutional, the judge finds objectionable. If a society has imposed legislative obstacles (like the concurrence of separate legislative houses and an executive) to alter the extent to which political preferences can be translated into statutory enactments, then considering those legislative obstacles should also alter the extent to which political preferences can be translated into statutory interpretations. If there is some unconstitutional defect in the process used to enact statutes, then that process must be invalidated for statutory meaning and ambiguity alike. If the alleged defect is constitutionally valid, then it is up to the society to determine whether it should reform that process to remove the defect. But as long as enactable preferences, measured by the actual legislative process, legitimate compelled obedience to the statute itself, the same set of preferences should govern statutory interpretations that command the same obedience.

In any event, judges' normative views about substance and process are not really separable. As we shall see in Chapter 16, one cannot determine whether process "defects" give a minority or majority group too little political influence without determining how much influence that group normatively ought to have. Thus, if judges were to conclude a group was legislatively underrepresented, and then favor it in statutory interpretation, that would amount to judicial imposition of the substantive normative views that led to the underlying conclusion.

Measuring political preferences by any method other than the accepted process for enacting statutes also raises another problem. Namely, once one frees judges to deviate from that accepted process, there is a huge range of possible methods of aggregating political preferences. Absent a relevant constitutional constraint, judges would have no legal basis for choosing any particular alternative method. Any choice they made would instead have to reflect their own contestable normative views about the best way to aggregate political preferences. Nor can the problem be avoided by just inquiring into the "majority" preference because, as we shall also see in Chapter 16, there are often many possible majorities, and which one is chosen will depend on how the enactment process in structured.

Further, if judges decided to favor any process other than the accepted process for enacting statutes, then they would necessarily be critiquing the process by which clear statutory language is enacted. A theory based on such a premise could not truly be said to be a theory of how to *interpret* the results of the legislative process, but rather would be a theory for *critiquing* that process and reforming it, no matter how clear its results might be. However persuasive such a theory might be, it thus does not fall within the bounds of the current project, which is developing a theory for interpreting the statutes produced by a legislative process that is presumed to be acceptable, indeed binding.

In short, the question here is what is the best theory of statutory interpretation—not whether to commit statutory enactments to the political process, nor how best to structure that process. However debatable our choices about the latter issues might be, once they have been resolved to make that commitment and structure a particular process, they do not offer viable grounds for deviating from the preferences that are enactable, given the particular process that has been chosen. Those are the preferences we have decided should determine the choice of enacted statutory language. Those preferences thus should determine interpretations of any unclear language produced by that process, given the underlying choice to advance those preferences.

Political Satisfaction versus Coherence, Continuity, or Other Public Values

Some argue that, rather than satisfying political preferences or exercising judicial judgment, courts should interpret statutes to further various important public values.[15] Ronald Dworkin has been particularly influential with his argument that interpretation should maximize statutory coherence, which is the extent to which the entire set of statutes can currently be justified by a coherent and principled set of general political convictions. David Shapiro makes a sophisticated argument that courts should instead interpret statutes to maximize continuity with the past. Amanda Tyler favors interpreting statutes to further both coherence and continuity.

But what should courts do when advancing coherence conflicts with preserving continuity? Making a statute more consistent with other statutes might require overruling statutory precedent, thus reducing continuity. Or coherence might require broadly interpreting a new provision in a way that increases the change from prior law. Without some common metric, like maximizing political satisfaction, it is hard to know how to weigh such norms when they conflict.

More important, do we really want courts to adopt the most coherent or continuous interpretation even when it exacerbates inequality, increases inefficiency, curbs liberty, or harms the public health and safety? Positing some sole goal, like coherence or continuity, as having supreme significance seems plausible only if we forget all the other things we care about. One response might be to add all the other public values we care about, and tell judges to interpret statutes to further all of them. Cass Sunstein takes this approach, including an impressively broad array of public values.[16] But even his broad array excludes such basic norms as equity, efficiency, liberty, and fairness. He also makes controversial judgments, including that coherence and continuity should take a back seat to the other public values he favors.

The problem is not with Sunstein, one of the most insightful scholars of modern times, but with the basic approach. No matter what set of public values are offered, if that set fails to include everything we care about, then it will blind us to many of the relevant factors. If it does include everything we care about, then we have simply defined the same set of factors that affect political satisfaction.

Perhaps the bigger problem is that, again no matter what set of public values we posit, their meaning or weight is contested in every case of interest. If an interpretation indisputably furthered coherence without harming any other interest, then we would have no conflict with my approach, because such an interpretation would also maximize political satisfaction. The same goes for interpretations that uncontroversially furthered any other goal, like efficiency, without harming any other interest we care about. In the cases where the difference in approach matters, either people disagree about whether a given interpretation actually advances coherence or efficiency, or the public values conflict with each other. How, though, are judges supposed to decide whether a given interpretation is more coherent than it is inequitable? Or that its greater efficiency exceeds its decreased continuity? Weighing such incommensurable values requires making some open-ended judgment, and thus brings us back to the problem with judicial judgment.

This surely does not mean that goals like coherence, continuity, equity, or efficiency are unworthy. But judges need some overarching metric for weighing them against each other, which none of these proposals provides. Maximizing political satisfaction provides a principle for deciding how much weight to give to such norms in any given case, and for prioritizing them when they conflict. Moreover, even if judges did have some independent method for weighing these norms, that would simply beg the question: why (unless constitutional issues are raised) should we allow judges to give such norms a different meaning or weight than the polity would?

For each application of a posited public value, there are two possibilities. One is that the application would maximize political satisfaction, in which case it offers no grounds for deviating from my approach. The other is that the application deviates from the norms that maximize political satisfaction. Those are the cases of interest because that is where the approaches diverge. If the judge chooses to further the posited public value rather than the interpretation she believes would maximize political satisfaction, then she is allowing political preferences to be trumped by a judicial judgment that favors that norm over others. My argument remains that judges have no warrant (absent a constitutional limitation) for imposing substantive norms that increase political dissatisfaction. Such public values thus should not be permitted to trump the goal of political satisfaction, but rather should be considered only to the extent relevant to determining how best to further that goal.

In short, while each posited public value is surely relevant to determining what maximizes political satisfaction, the latter remains the ultimate standard. It should thus determine both what counts as furthering that posited value, and how much furthering that value counts.

Dworkin uses a clever premise that might be thought to evade any conflict. Namely, he assumes that legislators share his hierarchy of preferences, which makes general political convictions more important than specific ones. If so, then a conflict never arises, because his approach would maximize the satisfaction of political preferences. But the empirical accuracy of Dworkin's premise seems dubious. Politicians probably have far stronger convictions about concrete results than about abstract principles, and where the two conflict would prefer modification of the latter.

Consider Dworkin's main case, where a politician believes in the general principle of preserving species even at great national sacrifice, but an interpreter relies instead on the legislator's more specific conviction that a dam should be completed even though it will endanger a species. Dworkin calls this interpretation a "crude . . . mistake, which no one would be tempted to make." He reasons that this legislator has made a "mistake of fact" about whether the dam will endanger a species. Thus, the interpreter should apply the general principle with the corrected "fact." I'm not only tempted to make what Dworkin calls a crude mistake, but am convinced that doing so is no mistake at all. The reason is that the more plausible conclusion is the legislator made a mistake not "of fact" but of principle, or (more likely) that the interpreter made a mistake in what *principle to attribute* to the legislator. The legislator may have accepted an abstract principle, without realizing all its consequences, but now that she realizes it would entail a concrete consequence she knows she finds unacceptable, she would modify the general principle to create an appropriate exception. Likewise, where a legislator believes that "reasonable" efforts should be made to preserve a species, is it a "mistake" for an interpreter to rely on the legislator's specific belief that stopping this dam would be reasonable, rather than on the interpreter's own assessment that in fact stopping the dam would be unreasonable? To Dworkin it would be, because this legislator has made a mistake "in fact" about the reasonableness of the dam. But it seems more plausible to conclude that what must be mistaken (and modified) are any general abstract criteria of reasonableness, which by definition failed to fit the legislator's specific concrete conclusion about this dam's reasonableness.[17]

One can test this proposition by examining the interpretive codes provided by legislatures within the United States, and seeing what they indicate should govern in any conflict between general and specific legislative conclusions. Such examination reveals that every legislature to speak on the issue has indicated that it prefers to have courts follow its more specific intent and provisions, rather than its general intent and principles.[18] No legislative statute directs courts to rely instead on evidence of the legislature's general intent. This seems the best available evidence on which default rule legislatures prefer. This default rule is also consistent with U.S. Supreme Court precedent, which adopts the anti-Dworkinian presumption that a conflict between specific and general legislation should be resolved in favor of the specific.[19]

Dworkin's preference for abstract general principles over concrete specific legislative conclusions thus, as he himself applies it, both deviates from actual legislative preferences and allows judges to interject their own value-laden judgments. But the problem is not limited to his particular methodology for determining statutory coherence. Legislation is often produced by political compromises or interest group pressures that do not reflect a common policy. Even without interest group influence, collective methods of aggregating democratic preferences can result in decisions that do not make a rational pattern, for reasons explained in Chapter 16. And even without either problem, separate enactments can simply reflect different concrete political reactions to distinct events at varying points in time, which may not fit into one overarching policy. All this means that a series of statutes will often reflect legislative preferences that fail to manifest a single coherent policy. More important, efforts to impose such a coherent policy on a set of enactments will inevitably require judicial value judgments about which reading makes the statutes work "best" together.

None of this means it is irrelevant whether various pieces of legislation form a coherent policy. All other things being equal, legislators normally prefer a policy that is coherent to one that is not. But the issue of statutory coherence must be subordinated to the general issue of what maximizes political satisfaction. A judicial or scholarly preference for coherence should not be permitted to trump evidence that legislators have different views about the desirability of coherence, or are more willing to trade coherence off against other goals. Nor, if legislators do prefer coherence, should their standards for what constitutes a coherent policy be replaced by different judicial or scholarly standards on policy coherence. More generally, coherence arguments do not justify resolving statutory ambiguities in a way that conflicts with conclusions about what, given all the evidence (including coherence with other statutes), is most likely to maximize the satisfaction of enactable preferences.

Indeed, ironically, the political satisfaction model probably advances statutory coherence much better than judicial judgment. Why? Because one of the principal implications of using default rules that maximize political satisfaction is that judges should defer to agency actions that are likely to reflect current political preferences. Given their expertise and experience in considering the full range of statutory provisions that bear on any industry, such agencies are likely to be far better at figuring out how best to achieve statutory coherence than judges that parachute into a statutory area for one case, every few years, on some particular provision in isolation.[20] Further, what constitutes coherence, and how heavily to weigh it against other factors, are not politically neutral questions, and agencies are also more likely to achieve the sort of statutory coherence that maximizes political satisfaction.

Preference Satisfaction versus Fostering Deliberation

Another view to consider is that judges should foster legislative deliberation, not preference satisfaction.[21] Many theories of deliberative democracy are so demanding in the knowledge, process, engagement, and good faith they expect from all actors that it seems clear they are not satisfied by any actual democracy. These theories would be equally critical of all the clear enactments our political process produces, and thus cannot really provide a basis for a theory of statutory interpretation However, less demanding theories might seek to encourage the forms of deliberation that, on our good days, we sometimes actually get on enactments. This view could form the basis for its own alternative statutory default rule, but in practice, it is normally invoked at the margins to justify certain exercises of judicial judgment over others.

A focus on deliberation is not inconsistent with the approach taken here, for my analysis does not depend on any assumption that the enactable preferences being satisfied are exogenous to the process of political deliberation. If deliberation helps reveal truer or deeper preferences, it is likely to produce more ultimate preference satisfaction. Those who favor such an approach should also favor reliance on deliberated political preferences, as indicia of what the enacting or current legislature would have wanted, and should favor preference-eliciting default rules even more strongly because they encourage explicit deliberation. A deliberative model is thus broadly consistent with the approach taken here, although the terminology differs, as would some applications.

However, in my view a primary focus on legislative deliberation overestimates both its capacity to mold preferences and the likelihood that any molding will improve, rather than worsen, preferences. Individual voter preferences are no doubt molded by the surrounding society, but governmental efforts to mold preferences are less successful, and the molding of preferences through legislative discussion is rarer still. And unless voter preferences are changed, the actions of legislators accountable to voters are unlikely to change.

To the extent that deliberation does mold preferences, that molding often proves unsalutary. Political discussion frequently divides rather than joins us in seeing a common view of the public interest. Consider common laments about the mean-spirited nature of political discourse and the sort of debate we see daily on cable news programs. Or, if you are an academic, consider certain faculty meetings.

Even when deliberation unites, that may be harmful. Unlike merely informing voters, which can improve their individual accuracy without reducing their independence,[22] deliberation is designed to make voters take each other's views into account. That makes voters less independent of each other, which in turn reduces the degree to which aggregating their votes improves the accuracy of majority votes. Thus, even if deliberation increases the odds that any individual voter will vote correctly, it can paradoxically decrease the odds that a majority vote will be correct. For example, as noted above, 10,000 voters who are individually 51% accurate, or 101 legislators who are individually 60% accurate, will by majority vote be 98% accurate, if they vote independently. Suppose deliberation increases the likelihood that each individual voter or legislator is correct to 80%, but also eliminates all independency of voting, because deliberation makes each voter or legislator agree with the others. Because the group is now no more accurate than the individual, a vote after such deliberation will be unanimous, but only 80% accurate. Thus, in this example, deliberation made each voter 29% more accurate and each legislator 20% more accurate, but perversely reduced the odds of a collectively accurate result by 18%. Much of the literature favoring deliberation conflates individual accuracy with collective accuracy, and thus misses the disjunction between the two that deliberation can create.

This concern is not merely theoretical. Empirical studies indicate that group deliberation often leads more informed people to defer to less informed ones, and generally leads participants to become more polarized.[23] If most members of a group begin mildly convinced that starting the Iraq War would turn out to be a good idea, then deliberation is likely to leave the group highly enthusiastic about starting the war. Deliberation also systematically makes juries award higher damages than the median juror would have awarded without deliberation, with 27% of jury awards exceeding what any single juror would have awarded without deliberation. Indeed, one of the initial proponents of deliberation-based theory, Cass Sunstein, has acknowledged that empirical tests show that deliberation makes groups more erratic and extreme in their judgments. Studies suggest that making the group more diverse can mitigate these adverse effects of deliberation, but provide no affirmative basis for generally preferring deliberation over preference aggregation.

In short, for both mathematical and empirical reasons, fostering deliberation can decrease the likelihood of achieving the right results. This presupposes there is a "right" outcome, but the premise of deliberation theory is usually that deliberation helps individuals make better decisions.[24] Even if we assume the goal of deliberation is not to reach the right results but rather to treat opposing views more fairly or with greater respect, that too is undermined by the evidence that deliberation tends to make results more polarized and extreme. If the goal is neither better results nor greater fairness or mutual respect, then it is hard to see what deliberation adds to aggregating preferences. None of the above means some forms of deliberation might not be helpful sometimes, but there is little basis to exalt deliberation as generally preferable to preference aggregation.

At Least an Important Goal

Suppose you are unconvinced by this chapter, and persist in thinking that the goal of maximizing political satisfaction must sometimes be trumped by judicial judgment, or at least by the goals of statutory coherence or fostering deliberation. Nonetheless, the analysis of this book cannot be escaped, for even such interpretive theories do not deny that political preferences should play some role in resolving statutory ambiguities. Those who admit any weight to political preferences must thus consider which statutory default rules would maximize satisfaction of those preferences. To such persons, these default rules would not be dispositive, but they would merit whatever weight is given to political preferences within their own interpretive framework. To those who are convinced by this chapter, the default rules that maximize political satisfaction will be even more important—resolving all unclear statutory language to the extent that constitutional constraints do not bind.

PART I

Current Preferences Default Rules

CHAPTER 3

The General Theory for Current Preferences Default Rules

Suppose courts are currently interpreting the unclear meaning of a 1950 statute. Should they maximize our current political preferences? Or should they maximize the preferences of the 1950 polity that enacted the statute? Taking a statute-specific perspective, most have assumed that the preferences of the enacting polity must govern, because it enacted the statute being interpreted.[1] Others have argued that current preferences should trump, because the current interpretation will govern the current polity, not the past one.[2]

We seemingly face an unavoidable choice to frustrate either current or past preferences, in any case where they conflict. But the seeming unavoidability of that choice arises from the statute-specific perspective that past work has taken. Such a statute-specific perspective narrows our focus to asking how the enacting polity would have wanted the particular statute at issue interpreted. This makes a conflict between past and current authority inevitable, and so framed, the issue seems unresolvable in any thoroughly persuasive way.

We can resolve this conflict by broadening our perspective. Instead of asking the statute-specific question, let us ask the following: what *general* default rule would the enacting polity want to interpret *all* statutory unclarity? The answer, surprisingly enough, is that the preferences of the *enacting* legislative polity would overall be maximized by a general default rule that tracks *current* enactable preferences, at least where those current preferences can be determined no less reliably than the enactor's preferences. The conflict between the enacting and current polities thus evaporates, because even the enacting polity would prefer a default rule that tracks current enactable preferences.

This probably seems counterintuitive. One would naturally think that the enacting legislative polity's political preferences would necessarily be best maximized by a general default rule that stuck to its own preferences. But that is not true. Take our example above. A default rule that stuck with enactor preferences would mean that the 1950 legislative polity would enjoy foreseeing that its preferences will resolve statutory uncertainties when 1950 statutes are interpreted in the future. A default rule that tracks current enactable preferences, in contrast, would mean that the 1950 legislative polity would enjoy having its preferences resolve statutory uncertainties for all statutes, enacted in or before 1950, that are being interpreted in 1950 while that polity exists. *Present* influence over *all* statutes might well be far more desirable than *future* influence over a *subset* of statutes.

We can generalize the point. If we were asking only which default rule maximizes the enacting legislative polity's preference satisfaction for the statutes *it* enacts, then clearly it would prefer an enactor preferences default rule. But here we are asking which general default rule for resolving uncertain meaning in all statutes maximizes the political satisfaction of the enacting legislative polity. In choosing between general default rules, the enacting legislative polity would realize that an enactor preferences default rule would maximize its preference satisfaction in the *future* over the *subset* of statutes it enacted. A current preferences default rule, in contrast, would maximize the enacting legislative polity's preference satisfaction *during* its time of governance over *all* existing statutes, including those enacted by *previous* legislative polities.

So the question is the following. Which would more likely maximize the satisfaction of the political preferences held by the enacting legislative polity: (1) an enactor preferences default rule that makes future statutory interpretations of the subset of statutes it enacted correspond to its preferences, or (2) a current preferences default rule that makes present statutory interpretation of all statutes correspond to its preferences? The answer depends on both the accuracy and strength of preference determinations in the present versus the future.

When Current Preferences Are More Reliably Ascertainable

Consider first the situation where an interpreting court cannot come to any reliable estimate of the enactor preferences, but can reliably estimate current enactable preferences. This is not a fanciful case, given that current preferences are often better known because they are contemporaneous, and that interpretation often involves issues not thought of in the past, or on which any record of past thoughts has been lost. Imagine, for example, a statutory ambiguity about which there simply is no relevant legislative history.

Where enactor preferences cannot reliably be estimated, then even the political preferences of the enacting legislative polity would clearly be maximized by a default rule that tracked current preferences. Because its preferences are unclear, the enacting polity loses no real influence over future statutory interpretations. But a current preferences default rule increases the enacting polity's satisfaction with statutory interpretations (about older statutes) that are made during the enacting polity's time of governance. Thus, in this sort of case, the enacting legislative polity would plainly prefer to gain influence over interpretations during its time of governance, rather than retain an illusory influence over future interpretations. The answer here depends solely on the relative accuracy of preference estimation, and is thus independent of whether the enacting legislative polity has stronger preferences regarding future or present events.

Consider next the more prevalent situation, where a court can estimate both the enacting and current preferences, but can estimate current preferences more accurately. Again, this improved accuracy is a powerful reason why even the enacting polity would prefer that courts track current preferences. The enacting polity gains more satisfaction from having its preferences accurately estimated during its time in office than from the prospect that they will be less accurately estimated in the future. This holds unless the enacting polity's preferences about future events are enormously strong: not just stronger than its preferences about the era which it governs, but stronger by a sufficient margin to outweigh the decreased accuracy. But for which era are preferences likely to be stronger? To isolate this issue, let us now consider the case where courts can ascertain enacting or current preferences with equal accuracy.

When Current and Enactor Preferences Are Equally Ascertainable

Suppose an enacting polity's likelihood of having its preferences accurately ascertained by interpreting courts is equal during its time of governance (concerning interpretations of all statutes) and in the future (concerning interpretations of statutes it enacts). Given equal accuracy, whether to prefer a current or enactor preferences default rule turns on whether the legislative polity is, in the general run of cases, likely to have stronger preferences about either (1) all interpretations during its time of governance or (2) future interpretations of the subset of statutes it enacted. Which preferences seem most likely to be stronger?

Generally, an enacting polity's preferences will be weaker regarding future events than regarding events during its time in governance. Part of the reason for this is the standard tendency of individuals to discount future events when making individual decisions. But for political decisions, the reasons go far beyond that premise. Most important, only some of those holding the enacting polity preferences will still be around when the future interpretation occurs. In many cases, so many decades have passed since enactment that all the participants in the legislative polity have likely changed. In other cases, there exists some overlap. But as long as a significant percentage of the legislative officials or voting population has turned over, the same legislative polity will no longer exist, and thus enactable preferences will have changed. Even without any change in the identity of officials or voters, their political views are likely to change over time, in part because their life situations will change in ways that mean they will benefit from different statutory results. Because their political preferences will change over time, they would frustrate their preferences if they instructed courts to stick to the old ones.

The enacting polity's preferences for a given statutory result are thus likely to be stronger during its time of governance, because then those who hold those preferences are those who experience that result. Accordingly, the enacting polity would generally prefer influence over current interpretation of past statutes more than influence over future interpretation of its statutes. For example, the enactable preferences that hold sway in 2008 are more likely to be maximized by statutory results that correspond to those preferences in 2008 than they would be by statutory results that correspond to them in 2108.

Moreover, there are many more pre-2008 statutes being interpreted in 2008 than there are statutes enacted in 2008 that will be interpreted in the future. The set of older statutes that will be applied, at the time when the enacting legislative polity governs, will cover the full range of statutory results that affect the satisfaction of its enactable political preferences. The set of statutes the 2008 legislature enacts will be smaller in number, and cover a more narrow range of statutory results that might impact its future preference satisfaction.

Thus, where enactor and current preferences can be ascertained with equal accuracy, even the enacting legislative polity should (in cases of statutory ambiguity) prefer a general default rule that tracks the enactable preferences of the current polity. Every enacting legislative polity would prefer such a default because it would maximize the political power of each polity at the point in time when it exists.

The supposed tension between enactor and current preferences thus dissolves. Or at least, any claim that the enacting polity would favor an enactor preferences default rule is at best uncertain. Thus, if one continues to see a tension, one must now weigh (1) an ambiguous interest of the enacting polity against (2) the very clear interest of the current polity in having a default rule that tracks its current democratic wishes. And that tradeoff now looks decisively favorable to the current polity.

A current preferences default rule also has a nice side benefit. It reduces the legislative time that would otherwise have to be spent updating statutes. Without a current preferences default rule, legislatures would have to expend more time updating unclear statutes in order to avoid undesirable interpretations, because courts and agencies would no longer be doing that task for the legislatures. Having to expend such legislative effort would crowd out other legislative activities, such as updating clear statutes that have become undesirable in ways that courts and agencies cannot correct, or enacting new statutes to address new problems.

In short, if enactor and current preferences are ascertainable with equal accuracy, each legislative polity should care more about those preferences governing present interpretations of all statutes than having them govern future interpretations of the subset of statutes it enacts. Thus, even if judges view themselves as honest interpretive agents only for the enacting legislative polity, they should adopt a default rule that tracks current enactable preferences, where current preferences can reliably be ascertained. If judges also feel some agency obligation to act in the interests of the current polity, then a current preferences default rule is even more clearly desirable.

Two facets of this conclusion bear emphasis. First, this default rule does not condemn judges to some crude model of political polling. A current preferences default rule will track only reliable official indicia of enactable preferences, not transient political views that are never shared by the political actors necessary to enact statutes. Second, a default rule that maximizes the satisfaction of enactable political preferences is *not* the same thing as the default rule most legislators might prefer. Normally, those amount to the same thing, because a polity's enactable preferences are manifested in its choice of elected officials. But sometimes they might differ. This difference proves relevant in considering various objections to the general proposition that the enacting legislative polity would prefer a current preferences default rule.

Objection 1: A Preference for Having Something to Run Against

One might hypothesize that legislators prefer statutory decisions that run contrary to their current political preferences, because that gives them something to run against in the next election. This is an intriguing possibility, but the hypothesis is probably untrue, and even if true would not justify a different default rule.

To be sure, some political scientists claim that legislators run for reelection by announcing public positions, not by achieving actual legislative results.[3] However, it is highly rare for statutory interpretations to be of sufficient general interest to make taking a position about them useful in a campaign. After all, the statutory unclarity at issue was not sufficiently salient to resolve at the time of enactment. The statutory interpretations that resolve them later usually share this lack of political salience, operating for decades below the legislative radar without being legislatively reconsidered. It is thus unlikely that having judges adopt contrary statutory interpretations would have a significant positive effect on reelection rates. It is even less likely that this reelection effect would be so strong that legislators would prefer interpretations that, by definition, run contrary to their own political preferences.

In fact, other political science literature indicates that such contrary interpretations should have a negative effect on reelection rates because voters vote retrospectively, based on their somewhat hazy perception of the governmental benefits the voters received in the past, rather than based on benefits the candidates promise to deliver in the future.[4] Thus, even if voters would not blame legislators for the statutory interpretations that run contrary to current preferences, legislators would be negatively affected by the fact that the electorate generally would have a worse experience than it could have had during the past term.

More generally, empirical studies indicate that actual legislative conduct is influenced by both the legislators' ideology and the interests of their constituents.[5] To the extent this conduct reflects the revealed preferences of legislators, these empirical studies undermine the notion that legislators would prefer statutory results that conflict with the preferences of both themselves and their electorate. Legislators may be strategic about reelection, but the ultimate purpose of getting reelected is to accomplish their preferred policy goals.

It is thus empirically dubious that legislators would prefer statutory results that contradict their own political preferences, just to give them political fodder for their next campaign. Even if this hypothesis were empirically accurate, it would not justify abandoning a current preferences default rule. Officials may have strategic preferences for contrary interpretations, but the goal is not maximizing the personal utility of legislators, it is maximizing the satisfaction of the polity's enactable preferences.[6] A statutory result that runs contrary to legislators' political preferences—and is preferred precisely because it is so unpopular that it creates an attractive election target—could hardly be said to be enactable.

More generally, statutory default rules should not try to maximize careerist objectives or strategic private aims that legislators may harbor, but could not actually enact into law. The legislative polity has no interest in having judges interpret statutes in ways contrary to the polity's current enactable preferences, just so legislators can advance their personal interest in retaining office. Nor would legislators have any legitimate interest in having statutory decisions thwart the political preferences of themselves and their constituents, just to strategically advance their personal career interests. To argue that statutory default rules should conform to such careerist objectives would be like rejecting efficient default rules in corporate law, on the ground that market imperfections mean that the managers who write corporate charters prefer inefficient default rules that increase their agency slack. The default rules that advance legislator and manager interests are not the same as those that advance polity or shareholder interests.

Although judges should serve as honest agents when interpreting statutes, the principal to whom judges are ultimately responsible is the legislative polity that has the power to enact statutes. To be sure, it is the legislative polity as mediated through a particular choice of representatives, and by the political processes necessary for statutory enactments. But the fact of that mediation does not mean that the strategic private interests of those representatives are what judges should maximize, any more than a corporate officer with a corrupt board could be said to have a fiduciary duty to aid the board in its corruption.

Objection 2: A Greater Stake in One's Own Enactments

Another objection is that legislators have more of a personal stake in the statutes they themselves enacted, in part because those are the statutes for which they can claim political credit.[7] Thus, perhaps legislators care more about seeing ambiguities in those statutes interpreted to match their preferences in the future, than they do about seeing present statutory ambiguities interpreted to match the enactable preferences of the current polity that elected them. Again, I doubt this hypothesis is true, and it would not change the conclusion even if it were.

Choosing a current preferences default rule does not, after all, void the statute. It thus would not deprive legislators of any future credit for being associated with the statute. Nor would it deny legislators the satisfaction of having their preferences followed on any matter they had thought enough about to make clear in the original statute. The default rule would merely cover interstitial matters that were not clearly resolved in the original statute. On such marginal matters, it is doubtful the legislators would have strong, enduring preferences that they care strongly about having satisfied in the future. It is even more doubtful that their preferences on future resolution of such marginal matters (in the few statutes they enacted) would be stronger than their desire to see their preferences govern marginal matters in all statutes that are interpreted during their time in office. In short, legislators may have a personal stake in the statutes they enacted, but probably not in the statutory ambiguities they enacted.

Even if legislators did have such a stake, the goal is not to maximize the utility of legislators but to maximize the satisfaction of the polity's enactable preferences. Thus, the fact that legislators may have some personal stake in credit-claiming or pride of authorship would not justify putting aside the interpretive default rule that would maximize the satisfaction of the legislative polity's enactable preferences. And because the enacting legislative polity does not have the same stake in credit-claiming or pride of authorship, it is even less likely to have a large disproportionate interest in the future resolution of statutory ambiguities it created. Or at least that interest is unlikely to be so huge that it transcends the polity's interest in actually experiencing statutory results that conform to its preferences on all statutory matters.

The mere fact that a legislative polity made certain enactments might, at first blush, seem to suggest that that polity must have a special interest in the topics covered by those enactments. But what an enactment actually signals is that polity's relative interest in *changing* the preexisting law on that topic. It does not indicate that the polity has a greater interest in that topic than other topics. For example, in 2002, the U.S. legislative polity was greatly concerned about accounting abuses that had led to overvaluations of corporate stock. The 2002 polity thus enacted the Sarbanes–Oxley Act to try to curb such accounting abuses. This may well mean the 2002 polity was more interested in changing accounting law than in changing any other body of law. But that hardly means that the 2002 polity had a greater interest in accounting law than it had in topics like civil rights, antitrust, crime, or environmental law.

Whether a polity wants to *change* the law turns not on its absolute level of interest in the topic, but on the extent to which it is dissatisfied with prior enactments. Indeed, the more important the issue, the more likely some satisfactory enactment already exists to deal with it. Thus, the polity may well be more likely to care about the topics covered by past enactments.

Even if the enacting legislative polity did have a greater interest in the topics on which it made enactments, that hardly means it has a greater enactable interest in the particular issues within that topic that led to statutory ambiguities. To the contrary, the existence of statutory ambiguity generally results either from an unforeseen issue, an intentional failure to decide, or so little interest in the issue that the legislature was unwilling to incur the decisionmaking costs of resolving it. None of those signals that the enacting legislative polity has an especially strong enactable interest in the issue. Whatever special interest the enacting polity had in changing the law would likely be resolved by the statutory meaning, or, if unresolved, indicate the sort of legislative stalemate that signals an absence of enactable preferences.

We must also realize that while certain issues are likely to attract more intense interest than others, that is as likely to be true for future legislative polities as for the enacting one. Statutory interpretations that deviate from future enactable preferences are not likely to stick (and thus really matter) on any issue where the legislative interest is intense. Instead, they are likely to stick mainly for those sets of issues where legislative interest is sufficiently weak that the issue cannot be put on the legislative agenda. Preference-estimating rules thus matter mainly in this marginal area, and issues in this area are unlikely to have provoked strong interest in any legislative polity, enacting or future.

Consider, for example, the civil rights and voting acts of the 1960s. If ever there were a set of statutes where the enacting legislative polity might be thought to have a special interest, these would appear to be them. The 1960s did finally signal the creation of a political coalition strongly interested in changing civil rights law, and this was a topic of intense interest. However, the topic of race relations has been, and will continue to be, of intense interest to every polity. One must also distinguish interest in the topic of civil rights from interest in the issues raised by statutory ambiguities left in the 1960s civil rights statutes. The latter do not necessarily signal an issue about which the 1960s polity had a particularly strong enactable interest. More likely, the issues that were left ambiguous in its enactments signaled either that its views were not that strong on that issue, that it had not foreseen the issue at all, or that its views were sufficiently divergent that they had no enactable preference on the issue. If there were some issue on which the 1960s Congress had an intense enactable interest that it somehow failed to express, that issue is likely to be of intense interest to the future polity as well, and a statutory interpretation that deviated from those future enactable preferences would not stick anyway. A preference-estimating default rule is thus likely to matter mainly for issues minor enough not to excite much legislative interest, or for issues on which the polity has no enactable view.

Suppose I am wrong in the above. Suppose, that is, that a legislative polity does generally have a greater interest in how courts resolve ambiguities in one of its enactments than in how courts resolve ambiguities in some other polity's past enactment. Even then, that would not mean that this greater degree of interest is so large that it would offset the fact that a current preferences default rule would give the polity influence when it exists rather than in the future, and give it influence over the interpretation of ambiguities in many more statutes.

Surely it seems implausible that the 2002 polity would trade greater influence over the future interpretation of its enacted accounting statute for less influence over the current interpretation of statutes on both accounting and all the other statutory topics that affect it in 2002. But what about the harder case of the 1960s polity? Given its strong interest in its civil rights statutes, might it prefer influence over the future interpretation of those statutes to influence during the 1960s on statutory interpretation concerning all topics? The answer is likely to be no, even if the 1960s polity were *solely* interested in race relations. The reason is that interpretation of a host of statutes besides the 1960s civil rights acts affected race relations during this era: including interpretation of past statutes on taxation, education, health care, benefits programs, government contracting, criminal law, and voting and employment, not to mention the Civil War–era civil rights statutes whose updated interpretation proved crucial. Thus even a 1960s policy that cared only about race relations would prefer a current preferences default rule. And as vital as race relations are, the 1960s polity surely had many interests other than race relations, including all the nonracial issues in the above list, as well as issues in administrative law, antitrust, banking, securities, intellectual property, and all the other statutory topics that governed that polity.

The issue is not whether the 1960s Congress would prefer an enactor preferences default rule for its civil rights legislation, while preserving a current preferences default rule for all other legislation. Every legislature would prefer an enactor preferences default rule for the statutes it enacts (giving it greater influence in the future) while getting the advantage of a current preferences default rule for all older statutes (giving it greater present influence). But allowing a legislature to choose one rule for its statutes, and another for the statutes of other legislatures, would unfairly aggrandize that legislature's power relative to past and future legislatures. The question instead is what general default rule the legislature would choose for all statutes—past and present.

Thus, even in an era as charged as the 1960s, there is little reason to think Congress would not prefer a current preferences default rule wherever statutory meaning is unclear. However, while the great interest in civil rights provides a good test of my theoretical claim, I should caution that the above analysis does not necessarily mean that most provisions of the civil rights statutes are, or should be, governed by a preference-estimating default rule at all. One might instead read the capacious terms of the most important civil rights and voting acts, much as we read similarly capacious terms of the antitrust statutes, as indicating a statutory delegation to courts to develop the law in this area in a common law manner.[8] My point here is that if courts were to reject this view, and instead turn to a preference-estimating default rule, then even the 1960s polity should prefer a default rule that tracks current preferences where they are reliably ascertainable from official action.

Suppose, contrary to the above, one could identify certain extraordinary legislative polities that have a greater interest in the future resolution of the ambiguities left in their enactments than in the current resolution of statutory ambiguities on all topics. Even then, the former interest necessarily wanes the further away it is in time, as less and less of the polity is around to experience the statutory results. At some future point, then, even such extraordinary legislative polities would prefer a current preferences default rule. Moreover, I doubt there are administrable criteria for distinguishing such extraordinary cases. The lack of any such criteria would make it hard for courts to resist deciding based on whether they approve of the preferences that existed at the time of enactment, because preferences that one shares are naturally going to seem more "extraordinary" than others. Indeed, once one took this tack, there would be no sharp distinction between ordinary and extraordinary, but rather a continuum in the degree of extraordinariness that, at a different point for each degree, would yield if the statutory interpretation were so far in the future that the discount for the lack of effect on the polity would outweigh the degree of extraordinariness in its interest. Thus, even if such extraordinary cases existed, tailoring the default rule for the degree of extraordinariness seems far less preferable than choosing a general default rule to govern all such cases. And if we have to pick a general rule to cover ordinary and extraordinary polities alike, it clearly should be a current preferences default rule.

Objection 3: Legislators Prefer Durable Legislation

A final objection focuses on the durability of legislation. Much rational choice literature assumes that an enacting legislature would want its legislation to be as durable as possible. But most of this literature depends on the assumption that all the legislature cares about is whether future interpretations of the statutes it enacted reflect its preferences.[9] Once one realizes that the question is instead what general default rule to choose for interpreting all statutes, it becomes plain that the legislature would care not just about the future implications this choice has for interpreting the statutes it enacted, but also about how the default rule affects the interpretation of all statutes during the time when the legislature sits. This requires the more nuanced inquiry noted above, rather than any general assumption of a preference for durability.

Landes and Posner have offered a theory about durability that requires a somewhat more complicated response. In their theory, legislators "sell" legislation to the highest bidding interest group, and the willingness of interest groups to bid would be undermined unless the legislators can offer durable legislation.[10] This theory means both the future and present effects make the enacting legislature want durability, because a future lack of durability would lead to a present decrease in interest group bids, which Landes and Posner posit is all legislators try to maximize. One might try to extend this argument to conclude that legislators would prefer a durable default rule that tracks enactor preferences, rather than a current preferences default rule that allows for changing interpretations over time.[11]

But the Landes and Posner theory concludes only that judges should stick to the original statutory meaning, which reflects the bargain between the legislators and interest groups. In the cases at issue in this book, the statutory meaning is uncertain, and thus a particular resolution of that uncertainty was never bid for, nor resolved, by the original bargaining. Because of that uncertainty, the statutory issue can have no durable resolution until a court interprets it. To the contrary, the prospect of future application of a current preferences default rule would seem to increase the incentive of interest groups to bid more at the time of enactment to secure a defined favorable statutory meaning. Moreover, even if a current preferences default rule lowered the effective price that elected officials can charge for new legislation, it would increase the effective price they can charge for influence over official indications of current preferences that would alter the interpretation of older (and more numerous) statutes.

So the empirical premise is dubious that legislators, even if they cared only about maximizing interest group bids, would prefer an enactor preferences default rule. It is also empirically questionable whether judges have any real motive to help legislators maximize interest group bids. Indeed, the assumption that the interest groups would prefer greater durability is itself dubious. Instead, more recent work by Professor Ben-Shahar has demonstrated that, because the benefits of durability are impounded into the cost of obtaining a durable legal outcome, greater durability can be irrelevant or harmful to the parties benefited by that outcome.[12] The assumption that legislatures necessarily prefer durability also seems inconsistent with the reality that they often deliberately use temporary legislation.[13]

Even if legislators would prefer an enactor preferences default rule because it maximizes interest group bidding, that would hardly make that the socially preferable default rule. Although interest group theory does not by itself provide any normative grounds for judges to try to dampen interest group influence, as Chapter 16 will show, it is equally true that nothing in interest group theory provides any reason to think judges should go out of their way to *increase* interest group influence or bidding. The goal should not be to maximize the strategic preferences of legislators, but rather to maximize the enactable preferences of the legislative polity.

On the other hand, enactable preferences could not be maximized unless statutory interpretations, once arrived at, were sufficiently durable to induce some behavioral reliance. This helps reinforce the important limitation, which I shall elaborate throughout, that only official action that provides a reliable indication of a change in current enactable preferences suffices to change an interpretation under a current preferences default rule. But these concerns provide no reason for a court's first interpretation of a statutory ambiguity not to track current enactable preferences. Nor do they provide a persuasive reason to bar a court from ever changing its first interpretation to track reliable official indications of changed enactable preferences.

Indeed, the irony is that a current preferences default rule may well *increase* the durability of legislation. This is because the alternative of consistently interpreting statutes in ways that conflict with current enactable preferences will trigger more frequent new legislation, which will create larger changes to older statutes. Statutes interpreted rigidly are less likely to survive into the future. An interest in durability thus may well favor a current preferences default rule. At worst, it does not clearly cut against it.

When Enactor Preferences Are More Reliably Ascertainable

We have one more case to consider: the situation where the interpreting courts can ascertain enactor preferences more accurately than current ones. Like its converse, this is hardly a fanciful case. The enacting legislative polity, after all, actually passed a statute on the subject at issue. Coalitions were built around that topic, and discussions about it ensued. The current legislative polity may be easier to gauge generally, because contemporaneous with the interpreting court, but have less clear preferences on the precise area at issue.

This is an important countervailing concern. Even if each legislative polity cares more about current interpretations of all statutes than future interpretations of its subset of statutes, it can derive little satisfaction from seeing statutory interpretations conform to mistaken estimates of its enactable preferences. Thus, we would expect to see (and do see) that courts follow current preferences only when they can reliably be ascertained, normally because memorialized in some official action. Concerns about reliability thus reinforce concerns about stability and reliance in arguing for this limitation. They do so not because these concerns trump the goal of political satisfaction, but rather because that goal itself requires reliable estimates of political preferences that are sufficiently stable to affect behavior.

If evidence about enactor preferences is obscure or ancient, courts might well not demand as high a standard of reliability for proof of current preferences before they apply a current preferences default rule. If enactor preferences are totally uncertain, even a somewhat loose estimate of current preferences is likely to increase political satisfaction. If the enactment occurred so long ago that the enacting polity likely has little preference at all about the future event, then once again relatively loose estimates about current preferences may suffice. Because even such a loose estimate of current preferences increases satisfaction regarding present events that the legislative polity experiences, it is more likely to maximize political satisfaction than a more accurate estimate of that polity's preferences concerning events a century in the future that they do not care about at all.

This analysis does not mean, as some have suggested, that an old statute with a defined meaning can be condemned and overruled as obsolete by a court.[14] My analysis is, rather, based on the more limited ground that, when deciding what default rule to use to resolve unclear statutory meaning, the enacting legislative polity itself would discount any preferences it has regarding the far distant future. Thus, the enacting polity would prefer a default rule that tracks the preferences of the current polity, in part because the latter rule will track the enacting polity's own views about more ancient statutes being interpreted during its own era.

In theory, one might adopt a full sliding scale to deal with this issue. Under this approach, interpretations should conform to current preferences if they can be ascertained with no less accuracy than the preferences of the enacting polity. But if current preferences can only be ascertained less accurately than enactor preferences, a court would weigh this greater inaccuracy against an implicit discount rate applied to future events. In practice, such a full sliding scale seems unworkable. Instead, courts understandably stick to a general rule of tracking current enactable preferences when official action renders them reliably ascertainable, though with somewhat greater willingness to find current preferences ascertainable the more obscure or ancient the enactor preferences.

Certifying Issues to the Legislature and Dealing with Unlikely Legislative Action

One might wonder why courts following a current preference default rule would not instead certify the statutory issue for resolution by the current legislature, much as federal courts now certify state law issues to state supreme courts.[15] Although such certifications would require explicit statutory authorization, just as certifications to state supreme courts do, such a scheme certainly seems conceivable. Indeed, even without such an explicit scheme, the U.S. Supreme Court effectively does "certify" statutory issues by putting them on its docket. This notifies Congress of the need to resolve the issue itself, if Congress doesn't want it resolved by the Supreme Court instead. In response, Congress often has amended its statute to resolve the issue, and the Court has generally applied that amendment to pending cases.

However, the fact is that Congress generally fails to act, even when it knows an issue is on the Supreme Court docket.[16] This is hardly surprising. It would put too great a burden on legislatures to expect them to take on, in addition to their normal legislative duties, the burden of intervening in every case where the meaning of statutes is unclear. Legislatures have courts and agencies to deal with such questions of interpretation, and don't need the courts pestering legislatures with certified questions every time the courts aren't entirely sure about the best interpretation. Taking up legislative time with such issues would be wasteful when the courts and agencies can accurately estimate the legislative preferences, and can divert the legislature from more important tasks, like enacting legislation to deal with problems the courts and agencies cannot solve for it through interpretations of old statutes. If the legislature thinks otherwise, it can always intervene already, without any certification process. A process of explicit certification would also delay litigation while the court waited for legislative action—a delay that would be fruitless in the typical case, where the legislature prefers to have the courts and agencies take the first stab at resolving the uncertainty.

In any event, whether we continue the current regime of implicit certification or adopt one of explicit certification, we still need default rules specifying what the statutory result will be if the current legislature chooses not to act, and in the interim before any legislative action. One thus still needs a theory for specifying those default rules. The theory here indicates that those default rules should maximize political satisfaction by tracking current preferences when those can reliably be ascertained.

Indeed, any choice between an enacting and current preferences default rule only matters in the marginal area where explicit action by the current legislative polity is unlikely or delayed. If the current legislative polity felt strongly enough about the conflict between its enactable preferences and past legislative preferences, it could always enact explicit legislation to that effect. However, sometimes this conflict is not strong enough to overcome legislative inertia and the costs of enacting legislation, and thus the default rule sticks permanently. Further, even if the current legislature would act, any legislation takes time, and in the meanwhile the default rule affects the outcome. In short, it takes a lack of explicit legislation by *both* the enacting and the current legislative polities to create the situation in which a current preference default rule matters.

This point reveals the error in the following sort of objection. That objection is that the enacting legislative polity would not prefer a current preferences default rule because, if it really did not like the interpretation of any past legislation during its time in office, it could always override it. It is certainly true that a legislature can always override any interpretation if it is willing to incur the requisite legislative costs. However, it is also true that the enacting legislative polity would realize that sometimes those legislative costs will exceed the benefits of correcting an undesirable result. It will also realize that, even when the benefits of statutory overrides exceed their costs, completing those overrides will take time, and meanwhile it will be stuck with an undesirable result. Further, the enacting legislative polity would realize that any default rule (such as an enactor preferences default rule) can govern in the future only to the extent that future legislative polities are likewise either insufficiently motivated to override it or delayed in doing so.

Thus, the real choice at each point in time is what default rule will govern in this marginal area where explicit legislation by *both* the enacting and current legislature is unlikely or delayed. Absent explicit legislation by either legislature, the unclear statute must nonetheless be interpreted somehow. The argument above shows that, in that marginal area, the enacting legislative polity would prefer to have its political preferences govern all unclear statutes during its time in governance, rather than have older preferences govern all unclear statutes during its time and its preferences govern the future interpretation of the subset of unclear statutes it enacted. Thus, in deciding in this marginal area, judges should use inferences about current preferences rather than equally reliable inferences about enactor preferences, However, in cases where both current and enactor preferences are highly uncertain, then Part III will show that the possibility of legislative correction may well suggest the advisability of a preference-eliciting default rule.

Limits on a Current Preferences Default Rule

My analysis thus indicates that a current preferences default rule would best satisfy the political preferences of the enacting legislative polity—and a *fortiori* those of the current legislative polity. But some important limitations on this conclusion must be stressed.

Current Preferences Should Not Alter Clear Statutory Meaning, Just the Interpretation of Unclear Statutory Language

Because a current preferences default rule does not rely on the claim that current legislative preferences are more important than those of the enacting legislative polity, it does not justify the position (taken by various prominent scholars) that current preferences should modify statutory meaning itself.[17] The proposition here rests on the much more supportable (and limiting) ground that—where statutory meaning is unclear—the enacting legislative polity itself would agree on a general default rule that maximizes the preference satisfaction of each legislative polity during its tenure in office. Like any default rule, this one only operates within the range of plausible meanings left by the original text.

Why not allow courts to change even unambiguous statutory meaning to conform to current political views? To begin with, the above rebuttals to the objections to a current preferences default rule depended, in large part, on the existence of statutory uncertainty to explain why the enacting polity did not have a special interest, or would not prefer greater durability, in the statutes it enacted. Likewise, when I respond (in Chapter 17) to the argument that reliance interests should bar a current preferences default rule, I will depend critically on the premise that there was no clear statutory meaning on which reasonable reliance could be made.

In addition, an unambiguous statutory meaning embodies the clearest indication of what was actually able to produce legislation. The current legislative polity has not in fact enacted a statutory provision on the relevant issue. It thus has not gone through the political process necessary to make its pronouncements authoritative—such as, in the United States, either winning a majority in two legislative chambers and presidential approval, or overcoming a presidential veto with a two-thirds vote in two chambers. Only the enacting legislative polity has, and thus if we ask what meaning to attach to the statute, we must ask what meaning to ascribe to its authoritative action.

The current legislative polity might want to change that meaning, but that proposition should be tested by having it actually do so through the same means that the enacting legislative polity used. Every political system has elaborate procedures for enacting statutes, in order to make sure that a considered choice was made that reflected prevailing political preferences. Sometimes these procedures seem inconvenient. But if these procedures have become too cumbersome, then they should be modified to allow a more nimble process, or the legislature should delegate ongoing lawmaking power to a more nimble entity. Action by the enacting legislature that completed the constitutionally required process cannot be reversed simply because a judge believes the current legislative polity would probably be able to complete the same process with a different result. Such a reversal would circumvent the constitutionally required procedure for enacting statutes, and allow the current legislative polity to use a *less* exacting procedure to undo what the earlier legislative polity did. Courts thus lack authority to deviate from clear statutory meaning in order to adopt mere estimates of current enactable preferences.

In contrast, using a current preferences default rule to resolve unclear statutory meaning does not circumvent legislative procedure, because the relevant uncertainty has been left by a duly enacted statute that covers the matter. If courts tried to resolve that statutory uncertainty by estimating the preferences of the enacting legislature, they would also (as Chapter 6 describes) be relying on some evidence extrinsic to the text that did not itself go through the enactment process. Referring to extrinsic evidence to estimate current legislative preferences thus cannot circumvent constitutional enactment procedure any more than can referring to such extrinsic evidence when estimating the enacting legislature's preferences.

Likewise, using extrinsic evidence to estimate current legislative preferences does not permit the current legislature to undo what the enacting legislature did through a *less* exacting procedure. After all, the alternative to estimating current preferences out of extrinsic evidence is, where no clear statutory text exists, estimating enactor preferences out of extrinsic evidence. Thus, relying on estimations of current legislative preferences at worst undoes estimations of enacting legislative preferences that were made using the same sort of procedure. The current legislature does not benefit from a less exacting procedure to make its views govern. To the contrary, as we shall see, courts tend to be *more* exacting about how reliable the evidence of enactable preferences has to be when applying a current preferences default rule than when estimating enactor preferences.

Even if we thought judges had legal authority to do so, deviating from statutory meaning is unlikely to actually increase the satisfaction of enactable preferences. After all, if we have an actual enactment with a clear provision on the relevant issue, then the enactable preferences of the enacting polity can by definition be ascertained with 100% accuracy. That is far more certainty than we could have for any contrary estimation of current enactable preferences, given that the current legislature has not enacted any clear statutory provision on the issue. Thus, such a case will necessarily fall into the category where enactor preferences can be estimated much more reliably than current preferences, which (as I indicated above) was a situation where a current preferences rule should not apply.

In short, extending the approach of estimating current enactable preferences to allow deviations from actual clear statutory meaning would introduce far more error, because judges would be substituting an uncertain estimate of current enactable preferences for certain knowledge of past enactable preferences. Thus, on simple grounds of relative accuracy, a considered definite choice by the enacting legislative polity should not be overturned simply because a current legislative polity probably would do so.

In contrast, where statutory meaning is unclear, using a current preferences default rule introduces no new form of error because the statutory uncertainty already forces judges to estimate what some legislative polity would have wanted. Judges' ability to accurately estimate how a legislative polity would have wanted to resolve unclear statutory language may indeed often be stronger for the current legislative polity than the enacting legislative polity. While the enacting legislative polity did enact a statute on the subject at hand, by definition it left no clear meaning on the particular issue in dispute. Moreover, any expressions of the current legislative polity's views are more easily interpretable because they are contemporaneous with the interpreter, and thus not thrown into doubt by changes in factual circumstances or linguistic conventions. In any event, courts tend to restrict themselves to relatively more reliable evidence of current preferences than of enactor preferences.

When statutory meaning is discernible, following it is also required by standard rule of law norms. As Lon Fuller observed, the rule of law requires that "in acting upon the citizen . . . a government will faithfully apply rules previously declared as those to be followed by the citizen and as being determinative of his rights and duties."[18] A defined statutory meaning constitutes such a declaration. While statutory ambiguities leave some matters to judicial interpretation, that is no excuse for expanding judges' interpretive power to cover all topics, including those resolved by an accepted statutory meaning. To the contrary, cabining judicial discretion at the point of legal application, when the identity of the parties benefited or hurt is known, is an important part of the rule of law.

In contrast, when the meaning of a duly enacted statute is unclear, then judges have no choice but to make some decision about what default rule to choose to resolve that unclarity. Such interpretation does not violate rule of law norms because there was no unambiguous statutory meaning that citizens could know to follow. To the contrary, the issue is by definition one that otherwise would be left to judicial judgment, and the default rule here is just a way of cabining that judgment.

Finally, where the enacting legislative polity has adopted a defined statutory meaning, it has made clear that it does want its political preferences regarding that meaning followed. In contrast, in deciding on the best statutory default rule, following the preferences of the current legislative polity (where they can reliably be determined) does not thwart the choice of the enacting legislative polity. Rather, it conforms to the default rule that the enacting legislative polity would itself choose.

Current Preferences Must Be Truly Enactable

The political preferences that are relied on to provide content to the current preference default rule must be the preferences of a set of political actors who could actually enact legislation. The courts should not use the leeway provided by a current preferences default rule as an excuse to favor the political preferences of one political party over the other, such as when one party controls the executive branch and the other the legislature, or each controls a different legislative chamber. In such a case, the political preferences of neither party alone suffice to enact legislation. Thus, neither party should be taken as an appropriate measure of current enactable preferences. Nor should courts impose majority views that, given actual voting and the political system, have not been translated into enactable preferences.

The enacting legislative polity would not want a default rule that tracked nonenactable political preferences, because that would not maximize the preference satisfaction of those political interests that could enact legislation. Legislative polities would not want to empower courts to take sides where political gridlock exists, rather than just serving as honest agents for the political forces that can command enough political agreement to enact statutes. That would just expand the influence of judicial preferences over political ones. Instead, legislative polities would want courts to rely on current enactable preferences. In cases where the two political parties are at loggerheads on the relevant issue—and either one can veto change by the other—the court must rely instead on the most recent indication it has of the political preferences that sufficed to enact legislation.

Even if the legislative polity did want courts to track nonenactable preferences, such an approach would be constitutionally problematic. For example, in the United States, the bicameralism and presentment clauses were meant to bar laws that could not secure sufficient approval under such a system. These clauses give a majority of states a veto over the majority of the population (where the states in the majority are less populated), give the majority of the population a veto over the majority of the states, and give the nationally elected executive a veto over legislators elected by district or state. Each political actor can thus insist that laws advance the interest of its constituency. Although we are within the realm of statutory interpretation, where some judicial judgment about the proper default rules is required, for judges to exercise that judgment to further political preferences that could not be enacted would undermine this constitutional structure. It would also create a divergence between the results when statutes have clear meaning, which do track enactable preferences, and the results when statutes are ambiguous, which would instead track some set of unenactable preferences that appeal to judges. There is no warrant for such a divergence.

My position on this point reflects another important difference from prior prominent scholars who have argued that contemporary values ought to be allowed to update old statutes. These scholars would have courts look to loose understandings about current public opinion or social norms, whether or not there is any evidence that those reflect the preferences most likely to be enactable by the current legislative polity.[19] Their approach thus requires the exercise of substantive judicial judgment about which of the unenactable current public opinions or values are meritorious enough to govern statutory interpretation. Indeed, these scholars would make statutory interpretation turn on a judicial view about which public opinions or majority preferences would be enactable, but for certain political realities that these scholars deem normatively undesirable, even when those political realities are constitutional.[20]

Such theories view judges more as partners than as agents, picking among current majority preferences to determine which reflect sound contemporary values that should govern statutory interpretation, based on the judges' own substantive judgments, even when those preferences are unenactable.[21] The theory here, by contrast, views judges interpreting statutes as agents for only those policy preferences that could actually secure enactment.

Further, these scholars would not make even this loose understanding of current public opinion binding on interpretive questions.[22] Professor Dworkin concludes that judges must also make their own normative judgment about whether the issue is an appropriate one for legislators to disagree with public opinion. He argues that judicial interpretation should be sensitive to "general public opinion" only when the judge "believes" the statutory issue does not "involve any question of principle" that merits deviation from public opinion. The substantive contestability of which issues involve such questions of principle is neatly illustrated by one of Dworkin's assertions: that no such principle is implicated by the preservation of a species that Dworkin does not consider valuable. In the end, the only limitation Dworkin puts on how far judges can deviate from majority opinion is that they should "not wholly ignore the public's opinion," because sometimes the judge's own view of "political fairness" will make public opinion normatively relevant. Dworkin's approach thus dissolves into a faith in substantive judicial judgment.

Likewise, Professor Eskridge argues that "statutory interpretations should often be counter- or nonmajoritarian."[23] In particular, statutory interpretation should in his view favor a minority group if it has been marginalized. But, as Professor Tribe showed long ago, judges cannot determine when a minority has too little political influence without making substantive judgments about the degree of political influence that minority ought to have.[24] Outside the limits of constitutional law, it is unclear what would authorize judges to impose their substantive judgments on a democratic political process.

Accordingly, even though these prominent scholars have suggested that judges should look to current political preferences, their approach actually has more in common with theories that advocate the exercise of substantive judicial judgment to resolve statutory ambiguity. They therefore differ sharply from my approach of adopting statutory default rules that maximize the satisfaction of those political preferences that are enactable. An approach limit ed to satisfying enactable preferences offers a more constraining methodology that is more limited in scope. It also rests on a more solid basis, because it is rooted in the authority of the legislature that enacted the relevant text.

Current Preferences Must Be Memorialized in Official Action

Especially where statutory precedent exists, a change in enactable political preferences can justify a change in interpretation only if the changed preferences are memorialized in some relatively well-defined official political action. It cannot be that every movement up or down in the polls, or changed reading of the political tea leaves, alters statutory interpretation. Such an unstable legal regime would fail to induce the behavioral reliance that is necessary to make interpretations effective enough to advance any political preferences. It might even violate rule of law norms by creating massive uncertainty about legal consequences and making notice and planning impossible.

Moreover, officially indicated changes in current preferences will be necessary to make sure those enactable preferences can reliably be ascertained. Legislative polities will want fairly high standards of reliability. They will recognize that judges are agents, and that giving judges open-ended interpretive power thus creates not only error costs (good faith errors in estimating legislative preferences) but also agency costs (interpretations that further judges' personal preferences in the guise of finding changes in legislative preferences). Because current preferences often cannot be estimated as accurately as the preferences of the enacting legislative polity, a current preferences default rule best reduces error if confined to cases where those current preferences can reliably be inferred from official action. Agency costs would also be increased if judges could alter interpretations with changing estimates of legislative preferences that were not grounded in any new official action by an agency or the legislature. Without an official action limitation, statutory precedent would be far less binding, and judges would be tempted to change interpretations as judicial personnel changed.

For all these reasons, statutory precedent should remain binding until any change in enactable political preferences has been memorialized in some official action. The most frequent sources of such official action are agency decisions interpreting the statute. As we shall see, however, there is also a complex set of exceptions for certain agency actions that seem unlikely to reflect current enactable preferences. Other times, the requisite official action is provided by recent statutes that, although they do not amend the relevant provision, do indicate where current enactable preferences lie. As we will see in the following chapters, this limitation on a current preferences default rule largely reflects actual judicial practice, which does not change interpretations to match current preferences unless there is some official action from which those current preferences can be inferred.

Legislature Can Opt Out, Within Limits

As with all default rules, a current preferences default rule is subject to opt out. That is what makes it a default rule rather than a mandatory rule. This provides another reason why courts should not modify explicit statutory meanings to conform to changes in legislative preferences, for adopting a defined statutory meaning is how legislative polities opt out of statutory default rules. Allowing judges to modify explicit statutory terms would thus take away the legislative power to opt out of a current preferences default rule.

True, sticking with an unambiguous statutory meaning will sometimes produce what even the enacting legislative polity would regard as an undesirable result. But by adopting explicit terms that opt out of the judicial process of filling and updating default rules, the enacting legislative polity clearly indicated that it viewed the error costs of following an inflexible explicit term as lower than the error costs of judicial adaptation. The enacting legislative polity effectively faced a choice between a rule and a standard, which required it to decide whether the inherent over- and underinclusion of a fixed rule is worse than the over- and underinclusion caused by erroneous application of a less precise standard.[25] This is a choice on which reasonable persons can differ, and adopt different conclusions for different areas, and it is a choice the enacting legislative polity is entitled to make. A default rule that (where statutory meaning is uncertain) changes to accommodate changing political preferences, in contrast, does not thwart a legislative polity's choice to opt out of judicially set default rules.

But my analysis also suggests limitations on such opt outs. A legislative polity can opt out by adopting defined statutory meanings, and normally by providing general interpretive rules. But plainly a legislative polity should not enact a general interpretive statute providing that its preferences govern both the interpretation of ambiguities in older statutes and the interpretation of its enacted statutes in the future. That is, a legislative polity should not simultaneously provide that a current preferences default rule governs past statutes, while an enactor preferences default rule governs its statutes when interpreted in the future. To do so would be to allow the legislative polity at one point in time to aggrandize its power relative to the power of past and future legislative polities. (Temporally speaking, a legislative polity need not be understood as lasting for only a two-year legislative session. Indeed, legislative polities will normally have little interest in aggrandizing one session over the next if the constellation of political forces in both are the same. A temporal legislative polity can rather be understood to last for as long as a distinctive political coalition lasts.)

A more problematic case is where a legislative polity enacts a general interpretive statute providing that—from now on—all statutory uncertainty should be interpreted to further the preferences of the enacting legislative polity. If applied both to older statutes interpreted during its time in office and to the statutes it enacted that are interpreted during the future, such a trade-off might seem unproblematic. But suppose such a change in interpretive rules were enacted toward the end of the legislative polity's reign. If so, that legislative polity would in effect have had the benefit of a current preferences default rule during its time in office, and then be imposing an enactor preferences default rule for the interpretation of its statutes in the future. Moreover, such a statute would also apply to future legislative polities that might have different views about the best default rule for statutes interpreted or enacted during their reigns. Courts would then have to decide between applying the current preferences default rule that seems likely to maximize the preferences of future legislative polities and using the enactor preferences default rule that was preferred by a past legislative polity that did not enact the future (or older) statutes being interpreted and does not represent current legislative preferences during the time of interpretation.

In both cases, the problem is that allowing a single legislature to adopt this general interpretive rule will enhance its political power at the expense of the political satisfaction of future legislatures. One might accordingly predict that such self-aggrandizing legislative opt-outs will be treated with hostility. After all, we need default rules for interpreting even statutes that offer interpretive codes. Given that such a statute would so strongly reflect the political interests of the enacting legislative polity over future legislative polities, it should be narrowly construed, for which we will see there is some precedent.

Even if clear, such a self-aggrandizing legislative opt-out probably violates the U.S. constitutional clauses vesting legislative power in each generation's legislature and interpretive power in the judiciary.[26] A legislature may not make its acts nonrepealable or bind future legislatures, nor even impose additional procedural requirements on the future legislature. An interpretive code that gives the enacting legislature the benefit of a current preferences default rule during its time in office, but deprives a future legislature of the benefit of that sort of default rule, effectively imposes on that future legislature greater procedural requirements to have its political will effectuated. It also impinges on judges' Article III power to interpret statutes on behalf of the polity.

True, not every congressional statute that restricts judicial discretion can violate the Constitution, because every statute that modifies the common law does so. To the contrary, such enactments of explicit statutory meaning normally constitute the best possible indication of the polity's enactable preferences. But it is an entirely different story to adopt interpretive statutes that further the interests of a particular legislative polity by restricting the judicial power of interpretation in ways that reduce the preference satisfaction of future polities. Article III should not be understood to preserve the maximum power for judges. But it might well make sense to understand Article III as assuring judges' independence in acting (within constitutional bounds) as an agent for legislative polities over time when interpreting statutes.

To be sure, if a legislative polity enacts an interpretive rule that favors itself over future polities, a future legislative polity could always repeal it. Some have thought this a dispositive answer.[27] But it is not, for several reasons. First, the issue may never reach the agenda of the future legislature, or the decisionmaking costs of adopting a new statute may outweigh the benefits. With all default rule issues, after all, judicial interpretation mainly matters, as explained above, only in that marginal area where legislative action is unlikely. Or the future legislature may be unable to form sufficient agreement on an alternative rule, or to overcome procedural obstacles like effective supermajority requirements. One thus cannot deduce, from the mere failure of the future polity to override the prior interpretive statute, that the statute corresponds with the future polity's enactable preferences.

Second, enactments take time, and in the meantime future legislative polities will have suffered a diminished influence that was effectively stolen by the legislative polity that enacted the interpretive rule. Such delays seem particularly likely if, as noted above, a temporal legislative polity is better understood as a legislature with a distinctive political coalition, for it will not always be clear when the political coalition has shifted. And during the transition to the new governing coalition, the old coalition favored by the interpretive rule may have enough political influence to block or delay change.

But the third problem is the most important. If and when the future legislative polity does get around to amending the interpretive rule, it would have little incentive to simply restore an evenhanded current preferences default rule. After all, the alternative legal regime we are considering is one where it would be permissible to instead enact one-sided interpretive statutes, which favor the legislatures that enacted them over legislatures at other times. Under such a regime, the future legislative polity would as soon as possible enact an interpretive statute that gave it a current preferences default rule during its remaining time in office, and tried to impose an enactor preferences default rule on legislative polities that are farther in the future. The legislative polity that is farther in the future would then be forced to do the same thing.

A regime that permitted such self-aggrandizing interpretive statutes would thus effectively give legislative polities a trans-temporal collective action problem. Given that legislative polities at other times could enact such self-aggrandizing interpretive statutes, each legislative polity individually has incentives to do the same when its time comes around. But the collective effect of all of them doing so is that each legislative polity would lose the benefit of its current preferences default rule in the period before it gets around to changing the interpretive rule, and gain an enactor preferences default rule in the future for only a similarly limited time. This would make each legislative polity worse off, given earlier analysis in this chapter, than it would be if instead the polities collectively agreed to refrain from enacting such self-aggrandizing interpretive rules, or were constitutionally prohibited from doing so. Curbing such legislative collective action problems is one important reason to have constitutional laws that put certain matters off limits as a matter of social contract.

Notice that a conclusion that such a self-aggrandizing interpretive statute would be unconstitutional does not mean a polity can never opt out of a current preferences default rule. Rather, it simply means that such an opt-out cannot be effectuated by one legislative polity through a statutory method biased toward itself. It should instead be done through a constitutional amendment, which can bind future legislative polities and modify the constitutional interpretive power of judges. Absent such an amendment, judges should wield their interpretive powers on behalf of the enactable political interests of all the polities over time. In any event, even if such a self-aggrandizing legislative opt-out were constitutionally permissible, it would remain ill advised, and thus outside the limits of this book's recommendations.

CHAPTER 4

Inferring Current Preferences from Recent Legislative Action

Suppose the 1950 legislature enacted a statute that is ambiguous about whether it means *A* or *B*. The current interpreting court thinks *A* is more likely to reflect 1950 enactable preferences. However, recent legislative action has consciously retained a past interpretation that chose *B*, or has otherwise made clear that *A* conflicts with current legislative policy. What do courts do in that situation? As we shall see, they tend to adopt interpretation *B*.

Such cases, which interpret an old statute based on subsequent legislative action, have long been criticized for failing to have any logical fit with an inquiry into the enacting legislature's meaning, intent, or preferences. This critique would indeed be compelling if we thought that it was the only legitimate inquiry. But these doctrines often make perfect sense if we understand them instead as current preferences default rules, for the recent legislative action means that interpretation *B* is more likely to reflect enactable preferences. Moreover, the theoretical limits on current preferences default rules can help explain the proper boundaries for these doctrines, and thus help explain what has otherwise often been criticized as the inconsistent application of these doctrines.

Subsequent Legislative Action Retaining an Otherwise Nonbinding Interpretation

When a higher court has interpreted a statute, lower courts are bound by that interpretation until the higher court changes its mind. When a court has itself interpreted the statutory provision, that precedent might be considered binding under *stare decisis*. But often courts face the question whether to resolve statutory uncertainty with interpretations by lower or coordinate courts that subsequent legislatures affirmatively decided to let stand.[1] Should courts follow those existing, otherwise nonbinding, interpretations because of such recent legislative action, even if those interpretations do not seem the best reading of the enacting legislature's preferences?

The mere fact of subsequent legislative *in*action in the face of a prevailing interpretation does not, under prevailing law, suffice to make the existing interpretation persuasive to a coordinate or higher court. But once the interpretation "has been 'fully brought to the attention of the public and the Congress,' and the latter has not sought to alter that interpretation although it has amended the statute in other respects," then the existing interpretation is presumptively correct.[2] More generally, the same follows if the legislature allows an interpretation to stand when it reenacts a statute, or enacts other statutes on the same subject. In short, recent legislative action that consciously lets an interpretation stand suffices, whereas mere legislative inaction would not.

This reliance on subsequent legislative action is hard to square with any claim that interpretation turns solely on inquiries into the enacting legislature's likely meaning or intent, because the actions of a subsequent legislature are irrelevant to such inquiries. Similarly, subsequent legislative action (at least when it comes significantly later in time) is irrelevant to estimating the political preferences of the enacting legislative polity, and thus cannot be explained under an enactor preferences default rule. Nor, in these cases, has the subsequent legislation enacted any amendment regarding the specific provision at hand, which would itself have the force of law or create a new statutory meaning. Instead, this line of cases can best be understood under a current preferences default rule, for the subsequent legislative action does provide a good indication of more current enactable preferences.

Consistent with this approach, courts are not willing to rely on the sort of subsequent legislative events that fail to provide any reliable means of ascertaining enactable preferences. Mere legislative inaction cannot offer such a reliable means, for inaction can result from lack of time or attention to the issue, or from an inability to gain the concurrence of some key committee, the other legislative house, or the executive branch. Neither inattention nor deadlock can indicate current enactable preferences with sufficient reliability to justify deviating from the likely preferences of the enacting legislature.

These sorts of objections to relying on subsequent legislative inaction also apply to some forms of affirmative legislative action. They apply to legislative action if, for example, the acting legislature was unaware of any prevailing interpretation, or believed (accurately or inaccurately) that no single interpretation prevailed. The objection would also still apply if the subsequent legislature was aware of a prevailing interpretation, but its legislative action focused on unrelated provisions of the statute. Consistent with this, courts in fact do not rely on subsequent legislative action to justify deviating from the preferences of the enacting legislature in cases meeting these descriptions.[3]

But the objection is unpersuasive where the subsequent legislature took the time to amend or reenact a statute, or to enact a statute covering the same area, without disturbing an existing interpretation in that area that had been brought to its attention. In those cases, the existing interpretation does become a fairly reliable indicator of the balance of political forces affecting how the more current legislature would want the default rule filled. The fact that the more current legislature took affirmative legislative action means that the other house and the executive concurred in the decision to let the interpretation stand, so that the preferences implied by that action are enactable. And these are the cases where judicial interpretation of old statutes in fact does rely on subsequent legislative action.

Sometimes, subsequent legislatures affirmatively rely on a particular statutory interpretation in enacting another statute. In such cases, even the justices who are most loath to draw inferences from subsequent legislative action agree that the relied-on assumption should be adopted.[4] The persuasive reason for this position is not, Chapter 17 will show, because mistaken reliance is generally a sensible ground for a default rule. It is, rather, because the reliance by the subsequent legislature provides a fairly reliable indication that more current political preferences favor the interpretation in question.

Other Legislative Action That Indicates
Current Enactable Preferences

What should a court do when subsequent statutes or legislative history do not retain or rely on a prevailing interpretation, but more generally indicate that the current legislative polity would resolve a matter differently from the enacting one? The U.S. Supreme Court has sometimes seemed inconsistent in its treatment of such subsequent legislative history or statutes. On the one hand, the Court has stressed that "the views of a subsequent Congress form a hazardous basis for inferring the intent of an earlier one."[5] On the other hand, the Court has held that "while the views of subsequent Congresses cannot override the unmistakable intent of the enacting one, such views are entitled to significant weight and particularly so when the precise intent of the enacting Congress is obscure."[6] In some cases, the Court has recited—as a "cardinal rule" no less—that "repeals by implication are not favored," thus indicating that Congress must be explicit when it repeals prior legislation.[7] In other cases, the Court has stated that "a specific policy embodied in a later federal statute should control our construction of the [earlier] statute, even though it ha[s] not been expressly amended."[8]

In short, the Supreme Court has sometimes been willing to be guided by the legislative history underlying subsequent legislation, even when such legislation has not repealed or modified the earlier statutory language that the Court is currently interpreting. This practice would be puzzling if these doctrines were just trying to implement some theory of statutory meaning. If the meaning of the statutory language were the touchstone, then it could not be altered by a subsequent nonrepealing enactment, and the views of subsequent legislators should be even less relevant. Such nonrepealing subsequent legislation and legislative history would also be irrelevant to any inquiry into the intent or preferences of the older legislature that enacted the relevant statutory language.

But none of this is puzzling if, instead, the interpreter is just applying a current preferences default rule because the statutory meaning is unclear. The views of the subsequent legislature are indeed a "hazardous basis" for inferring the meaning of an earlier legislature, but they are not being used for that purpose. They are, rather, being used to fill the default when the enacting legislative polity's meaning is "obscure." Current doctrine is thus consistent with my position: that indications of current enactable preferences provide a default rule that applies only when statutory meaning is unclear, and thus cannot alter statutory meaning itself.

Likewise, implied repeals are suspect when there is an enacted statutory meaning that has gone through the political process, but not when the prevailing interpretation just reflects a default rule that estimated enactable preferences in order to resolve unclear statutory meaning. The courts, accordingly, hold that the doctrine allowing statutory interpretation to be altered by subsequent legislation applies only when, at the time of enactment, the statute has "a range of plausible meanings." If that is the case, "subsequent acts can shape or focus those meanings," that is, they can provide a basis for selecting an interpretive option among the range of plausible statutory meanings.[9] In short, we have a doctrine against implied repeals of actual statutory meaning, not against implied repeals of the default rule interpretations that are used when meaning is unclear.

The fact that courts may, when statutory meaning is unclear, sometimes rely on subsequent legislative history does not mean that they can rely on legislative statements that were not memorialized in, or did not lead to, the enactment of actual legislation. Through enactments a legislature speaks in one voice, and manifests the political preferences that sufficed to secure the actual enactment of something. In other statements, legislatures speak through multiple voices, none of which may reliably indicate enactable preferences. Thus, the courts' use of subsequent legislative history is generally limited to cases where that history relates to the enactment of a subsequent statute in the same area, which reliably indicates the current political preferences most likely to be able to secure enactment. A new statute may be no more reliable an indicator of the earlier legislative polity's meaning, intent, or preferences than mere statements by current legislators would be. But a new statute is a more reliable indicator of current enactable preferences, and thus has greater influence on judicial interpretation of earlier statutes.

This analysis means that courts cannot be deemed internally inconsistent merely because they sometimes rely on subsequent statutes and legislative history when interpreting older statutory language and sometimes do not. Subsequent statutes and legislative history should, if nonrepealing, indeed be rejected when the original statutory meaning is clear. Moreover, even when the original meaning is unclear, subsequent legislative history should be rejected when it provides an unreliable indicator of current enactable legislative preferences on the issue at hand. But when it does provide a reliable indicator of current enactable preferences on the relevant issue, subsequent legislation (and the legislative history that underlies it) offers sufficient grounds for filling in the default rule.

Obscure or Ancient Enactor Preferences

As noted in Chapter 3, the more obscure or ancient the preferences of the enacting legislative polity, the less demanding one would expect courts to be about how reliable the indication of current preferences must be. For example, the 1983 Supreme Court decision in *Bob Jones* concluded that religious nonprofit universities that had racially discriminatory admissions standards were not "charitable" organizations entitled to tax exemption under an 1894 federal statute.[10] The Court conceded that the enacting legislature probably would have deemed such racist admissions standards unproblematic, given the prevalence of racial segregation in 1894. Thus, if the question were what interpretation would most likely reflect enactor preferences, the answer would be to grant the tax exemption.

By 1983, however, it was clear that granting such a charitable exemption fundamentally contradicted modern congressional race relations policy, even though the current Congress had not decided the precise question of this tax exemption. The Court could have reached this conclusion by relying simply on congressional acquiescence in an Internal Revenue Service (IRS) interpretation that Congress had repeatedly refused to alter even though it had otherwise amended the statute.[11] But the Court first made clear that the same conclusion would follow (even without any legislative acquiescence in a prevailing interpretation) because "[o]ver the past quarter of a century, every pronouncement of this Court and myriad Acts of Congress and Executive Orders attest a firm national policy to prohibit racial segregation and discrimination in public education." Further, when the Court later approved the IRS interpretation, the Court's basis was not that the IRS correctly divined what the 1894 Congress would have wanted, but rather that the IRS correctly estimated current legislative preferences.

> In 1970, when the IRS first issued the ruling challenged here, the position of all three branches of the Federal Government was unmistakably clear . . . Indeed, it would be anomalous for the Executive, Legislative, and Judicial Branches to reach conclusions that add up to a firm public policy on racial discrimination, and at the same time have the IRS blissfully ignore what all three branches of the Federal Government had declared.

The clear import was that both the courts and agencies should, in cases of uncertain statutory meaning, follow current political preferences that were reflected in the repeated enactment of actual laws.

A skeptic might wonder whether these enactments really reflected current enactable preferences in 1983. After all, the then-current Reagan administration had, through its Treasury Department, announced its intent to revoke the prevailing IRS interpretation, which barred tax exemptions to racially discriminatory schools.[12] However, the Reagan Treasury Department made plain that this revocation reflected its legal interpretation, not its political views. Indeed, the Reagan administration simultaneously introduced a bill before Congress that would by statute have denied any tax exemption to racially discriminatory schools. Democrats alleged that this bill was just a response to the political outcry about the administration's decision to rescind the IRS interpretation, but that is beside the point. What matters are not the private political preferences of political actors, but what their actions show about the state of current enactable preferences. If political actors who suffice to enact legislation would be unable to resist political pressure for a certain result, then that suffices to show that this result reflects an enactable political preference, regardless of the private preferences those political actors might have.

A skeptic might further worry: if current enactable preferences really supported a denial of tax exemption, then why didn't Congress enact this proposed bill? The answer seems plain. Because the issue was already before the United States Supreme Court, Congress figured it might as well wait and see whether the Court would resolve the problem for it. Bob Dole, the chairman of the relevant Senate committee, was quite explicit about this, adding: "I know we can't suggest that the Court go ahead and make that decision, but hopefully they read the papers."[13] This sort of legislative inertia is hardly unusual, and also explains why Congress had not bothered to enact any legislation codifying the IRS interpretation in the preceding twelve years, even though it did enact legislation denying a tax exemption to racially discriminatory social clubs.[14] Enacting anything requires the expenditure of time and political effort that will often not seem worthwhile (compared to other pursuits), especially when the enactment will not change the status quo. Congress's failure to enact a position thus fails to prove that, if it were necessary to address the issue, that position would not be enactable. Thus, the Court correctly inferred that the recent enactment denying a tax exemption to racially discriminatory social clubs did not mean the current Congress wanted a different rule for racially discriminatory schools. Instead, the recent enactment on social clubs most likely meant that, if an enactment were necessary, current enactable preferences would favor denying tax exemptions to racially discriminatory entities.

Naturally, any estimate of enactable preferences is necessarily less accurate than actually waiting to see what gets enacted. But the whole point of using a current preferences default rule is to minimize political dissatisfaction for issues too minor to provoke legislative action, or in the interim before the legislature acts, and to free the political process from the needless burden of making enactments it would probably make if time and political energy were not scarce. When what the legislative polity would enact is sufficiently uncertain, a preference-eliciting default rule may well be called for to provoke a legislative response, as Part III shows. But when official actions provide a sufficiently reliable estimate of current enactable preferences, then those should be followed. And the necessary threshold of reliability declines the more ancient any enactor preferences, as with the 1894 statute interpreted in *Bob Jones*.

Still, sometimes the indications of current preferences are quite general, whereas the enactor preferences were quite specific. In such cases, canons of construction provide that "[w]here there is no clear intention otherwise, a specific statute will not be controlled or nullified by a general one, regardless of the priority of enactment."[15] Under this canon, an old statute can trump a later one if the former is more specific. Thus, the Court has ruled that a general statute against employment discrimination should yield to an older statute that specifically allowed preferences for Native Americans. This holding might seem inconsistent with a policy of satisfying current enactable preferences. But it isn't. What the Court recognized is that often enactors adopt general principles without considering certain specific implications, and that enactable preferences on those specific implications can generally be ascertained more reliably by more specific legislation, even when the more specific statute is older. Indeed, in that case the Court relied on the confirming evidence that, after enacting the general anti-discrimination statute, the subsequent Congress enacted two new preferences for Native Americans, thus confirming that any general political views on discrimination did not indicate opposition to favoring Native Americans.

Conclusion and the Relevant Codes of Construction

Many judicial doctrines resolve unclear statutory meaning with the enactable preferences indicated by more recent legislative action, rather than by just examining the preferences of the legislature that enacted the statute being interpreted. These doctrines, I have argued, can best be explained as current preferences default rules, which maximize political satisfaction even for the enacting legislatures. We shall see more examples of judicial reliance on current enactable preferences when, in Chapter 12, we consider the cases in which judges overrule statutory precedent.

If one thought that these doctrines and current preferences default rules did not maximize political satisfaction, one would instead view these doctrines as imposed on unwilling legislatures by wayward courts. One would then expect to see legislatures enact codes of construction trying to overturn these doctrines. However, although each U.S. legislature has enacted a code of statutory construction, none has included a provision that tries to override these interpretive doctrines.

To the contrary, those codes of construction that do address these doctrines have embraced them. Two state legislatures have expressly directed that "[W]hen the words of a law are not explicit, the intention of the legislature may be ascertained by considering . . . legislative . . . interpretations of the statute." Similarly, another state legislature has provided that: "[t]he construction of a statute by the Legislature, as indicated by the language of later enactments, is entitled to consideration as an aid in the construction of the statute, but is not generally regarded as controlling." The fact that subsequent legislation is not "controlling" emphasizes that it provides only a default rule, not a ground for changing the actual meaning of the statutory language. Two state legislatures have also expressly adopted the default rule in favor of prevailing interpretations that the legislature elected not to alter when it enacted "subsequent laws on the same subject matter."[16]

To be sure, the content of current codes of construction cannot provide any ironclad proof that doctrines, like these, that track current enactable preferences do maximize political satisfaction. But these codes of construction are more consistent with the theory that these doctrines increase political satisfaction than with the theory that they thwart it.

CHAPTER 5

Inferring Current Preferences
from Agency Action

Suppose a court faces an unclear statute, no recent legislation that reliably indicates current enactable preferences on the issue, and a current agency interpretation of that statute. Should the court defer to the agency interpretation? The legal answer is normally yes under the *Chevron* doctrine, but sometimes no under *Mead* and other exceptions to *Chevron*. This is hard to explain if the relevant inquiry is about the enacting legislature's most likely meaning or intent. But it proves easy to explain if courts are, instead, applying default rules that track reliable indications of current enactable preferences, because decisions by current agencies normally provide such an indication, given the agencies' political accountability. Indeed, it turns out that this theory does a better job than prevailing theories of not only justifying the normal result under *Chevron* but also explaining the complex pattern of exceptions to it, which have so far seemed perplexing under prevailing theories. The exceptions all fit circumstances when, for one reason or another, the agency decision is less likely to be a reliable indicator of current enactable preferences.

Understanding the proper basis and limits of judicial deference to agency interpretations is vital for a simple reason: in the modern administrative state, most statutory interpretations are done by agencies. Thus, to understand the proper methods of agency interpretation, and judicial deference to them, is to understand most of the statutory interpretation that actually occurs.

Chevron as a Current Preferences Default Rule

Under *Chevron*, U.S. courts normally defer to agency interpretations of unclear statutes.[1] Deference to agencies was not new, but prior to *Chevron*, courts sometimes said they deferred to agencies on interpretive matters only when Congress had expressly delegated interpretive authority to the agency. *Chevron* made clear that courts were bound by a default rule that, unless Congress indicates otherwise, courts must defer to interpretations by the agency charged with administering the statute. One might wonder whether this judicial doctrine conflicts with legislative views about the best default rule. However, no legislature in the United States has rejected this interpretive rule, and it has been adopted in every code of construction to address the topic.[2]

If the objective were only to get the best interpretation of statutory meaning, this choice of a general default rule would be odd. Agencies may be very familiar with the statute in question, but they are not particularly skilled in legal interpretation, at least no more skilled than courts. Further, agencies might have certain biases (such as a bias in favor of expanding their power) that distort their interpretations. Courts thus seem better interpreters of statutory meaning.

But *Chevron* does make sense as a current preferences default rule, to cope with cases where statutory meaning is unclear. In the United States, agency heads have been nominated by the president and confirmed by the Senate, based largely on the acceptability of their policy views in a specific policy area. Executive interviews and Senate confirmation hearings pin down nominees on the issues likely to arise during what will be a relatively brief tenure. Consider the close questioning of John Ashcroft during his confirmation hearings, which produced commitments that help explain his later decision, as attorney general, to defend the legality of an affirmative action plan he had opposed as a senator.[3]

Agency heads are also supervised by the executive, and are subject to extensive committee oversight and budgetary review in the legislature. They are normally removable by the executive. Even in independent agencies, they serve limited terms, and thus depend on the executive and legislature for their reappointment. Agency heads also depend on the executive and legislature for cooperation on future initiatives, including any new legislation, executive action, or appointment of subordinates. The policy views that govern the actions of agency heads thus generally come about as close to being a barometer of current political preferences as we can get. (The personal political views of agency heads may be a different matter, but what matters here are the revealed political preferences that are implied by what they actually do.)

Agency decisions are particularly likely to reflect current political preferences when the agencies decide after current political forces had an opportunity to participate. Such participation not only helps political actors directly inform agencies about prevailing political preferences but also enables interested parties to trigger a "fire alarm," which alerts Congress when agencies are taking actions that might diverge from current political preferences.[4] As we will see, agency actions that do not afford such an opportunity for political participation in fact get denied *Chevron* deference. Agency decisions that receive *Chevron* deference are thus subject to a combination of political influences by the executive, the legislature, and outside political groups.[5] Such agency action generally provides the best available estimate of where current enactable preferences lie.

True, agency accountability to political oversight is not perfect. In part, this is because agency oversight probably gives the president and legislative oversight committees somewhat greater power, vis-à-vis other legislative participants, than they normally possess in securing enactments. Some deviation between agency action and current enactable preferences must thus be expected. But the deviation is not that great. After all, presidents and legislative oversight committees also have disproportionate influence over what is enactable because they have veto and gatekeeping powers. Further, studies show that oversight committee preferences are generally close to median congressional preferences, and that the committees that more accurately reflect congressional preferences are more likely to hold oversight hearings.[6] These studies also show that, to the extent committees deviate from median congressional preferences, their deviations tend to be in the opposite direction from the President's, a dialectic that models prove actually results in the optimal representation of median legislative preferences—better than if committees mirrored median legislative preferences.

In any event, the question is not whether agencies perfectly reflect current political preferences. The question is the overall comparative one: whether agency decisions generally reflect current enactable preferences better than would judicial estimates of those preferences. If so, then political satisfaction can be maximized by a general default rule of deferring to agency interpretations.

Focusing on the comparative question strengthens the case for deferring to agencies under a current preferences default rule. Compared to agency heads, judges were appointed a long time ago, with far less inquiry into their policy views. Any inquiries into the policy views of judges also confront the problem that (unlike agency heads) the relevant views would be limited neither to a specific policy area nor to a short period of time. This makes it harder for the legislature to foresee the relevant issues than when it is appointing an agency head. Judges are also politically insulated. They serve life terms, are not removable, and have salaries that cannot be lowered. They depend little on budgetary support, which anyway as a matter of practice is unaffected by their individual decisions. Perhaps more important, they are insulated by judicial norms and ethical canons from general contact with, and information flow from, political officials and groups. In contrast, the Administrative Procedure Act does not bar "ex parte contacts between agency personnel and outside persons in notice-and-comment rulemaking."[7] Judges can thus generally ascertain current political preferences only from a cold record of legislative action. Absent the sort of recent legislative action described in Chapter 4, such a record can be quite unrevealing about where current enactable preferences lie. Another advantage of deferring to agencies is that it provides a single source for the best estimate of current political preferences, rather than a multiplicity of possible conflicting sources.

The details may differ in other nations, but the general point likely remains valid. Being more accountable and informed by current political preferences than the judiciary, agency action is more likely to accurately reflect current enactable preferences than direct judicial estimates about what current political forces would enact. By following agency interpretations to resolve statutory ambiguity, courts thus follow a default rule that is best calculated to minimize current political dissatisfaction. Indeed, agency responsiveness to enactable preferences should even be stronger in parliamentary systems, where the agency does not enjoy the protection from legislative overrides that deadlock between the president and Congress sometimes provides.

The language of *Chevron* tracks this book's distinction between questions of meaning (on which there is no deference) and the policy choice of how to resolve uncertain meaning (on which there is deference). When courts can ascertain the meaning of a statute, *Chevron* provides that this meaning must be followed, notwithstanding contrary agency interpretations.[8] On the other hand,

> [w]hen a challenge to an agency construction of a statutory provision, fairly conceptualized, really centers on the wisdom of the agency's policy, rather than whether it is a reasonable choice within a gap left open by Congress,

the challenge must fail. In such a case, federal judges—who have no constituency—have a duty to respect legitimate policy choices made by those who do . . . While agencies are not directly accountable to the people, the Chief Executive is, and it is entirely appropriate for this political branch of the Government to make such policy choices—resolving the competing interests which Congress itself either inadvertently did not resolve, or intentionally left to be resolved by the agency charged with the administration of the statute in light of everyday realities.

This language justifies the *Chevron* default rule because of the rule's ability to track current political preferences by following the interpretations of agencies that were best positioned to ascertain where the current balance of political interests lay. The *Chevron* Court squarely considered the alternative default rule—that such matters should be left to judicial judgment—and rejected that rule as insufficiently responsive to current political preferences:

Judges are not experts in the field, and are not part of either political branch of the Government. Courts must, in some cases, reconcile competing political interests, but not on the basis of the judges' personal policy preferences. In contrast, an agency to which Congress has delegated policy-making responsibilities may, within the limits of that delegation, properly rely upon the incumbent administration's views of wise policy to inform its judgments . . . The responsibilities for assessing the wisdom of such policy choices and resolving the struggle between competing views of the public interest are not judicial ones: "Our Constitution vests such responsibilities in the political branches."

The *Chevron* Court also made clear that the proper default rule was not static, but should change over time. The Court chastised the appellate court for adopting "a static judicial definition" of the statutory term, "when it had decided that Congress itself had not commanded that definition," and rejected the argument that deference to agency interpretations should not apply where, as here, the agency had changed its interpretation over time.[9] Again, the distinction between ascertaining meaning and default rule analysis helps in understanding the point. Changing an interpretation over time does undermine the credibility of a judgment regarding statutory meaning, for it suggests the agency itself is inconsistent or uncertain about what that meaning is. But changing an interpretation does not undermine a default rule judgment about where current political preferences lie, for an accurate reading of those would change over time. Likewise, the rejection of static interpretations would be hard to understand if the default rule were intended to track the preferences of the enacting legislature, which should not vary over time, but fits well with a current preferences default rule.

Also consistent with this book's analysis, the Court rejected dynamic statutory interpretation (by agencies or courts) in cases where the enacting legislature's meaning was clear. It thus rejected the proposition, advanced by some scholars, that changing political preferences should change statutory meaning itself. Instead, this current preference default rule is limited, as is default rule analysis generally, to cases where statutory meaning is unclear.

Prior Theories of *Chevron*

Mine is not the first theory to explain *Chevron* deference. Some theories have focused on the proper source of law for the doctrine, other theories on its best normative justification. Each of the existing theories, however, in the end proves unsatisfactory and fails to explain the full pattern of which agency interpretations do and do not get judicial deference. Current preferences default rule analysis thus provides an improved way of justifying, and explaining the scope of, the *Chevron* doctrine.

1. Theories about the Source of Law

The current literature identifies three possible legal sources for the *Chevron* doctrine.[10] One possible source is constitutional separation of powers and anti-delegation norms. But *Chevron* does not cite any constitutional provision or rest on any constitutional argument. Further, if anything, *Chevron* enhances rather than deters the delegation of legislative responsibilities to agencies. Thus, few scholars are convinced that the source of law for *Chevron* is constitutional.

A second theory, to which most subscribe, is that when Congress enacts an ambiguous statute, and is silent about who it wants to resolve that ambiguity, it implicitly intends to delegate interpretive authority to the administering agency. The problem is that even adherents of this theory—including *Chevron*'s leading judicial champion, Justice Scalia—acknowledge that the evidence of such enacting congressional intent is "weak" and even "fictional."[11] At the time *Chevron* was decided, Congress had no reason to think that enacting an unclear statute delegated interpretation to agencies rather than courts, and Congress had never indicated any disapproval of the less deferential judicial interpretation that then prevailed. Moreover, *Chevron* itself acknowledged that statutory ambiguity might be created "inadvertently" because Congress "simply did not consider the question." Nor had Congress given any other affirmative indication of an intent to delegate interpretive decisions to agencies.

To the contrary, the most relevant statute Congress has enacted, the Administrative Procedure Act (APA), provides an opposite indication by stating that courts "shall decide all relevant questions of law [and] interpret constitutional and statutory provisions" when they review agency action.[12] Further, McNollgast's political analysis shows that enactment of the APA was motivated by a congressional desire to constrain agency discretion. It is thus dubious to conclude that Congress intended to give agencies discretion over the interpretation of unclear statutes.

If we instead view the issue as a current preferences default rule, we can make far more sense of *Chevron*'s implicit interpretation of the APA. What McNollgast's political analysis indicated, in more detail, was that the Democrat's that controlled the New Deal Congress enjoyed the benefits of agency discretion when they were in power and influencing the agencies. Then, when those Democrats saw their dominance about to end because of political shifts that favored Republicans, they tried to lock in their political gains by constraining agency discretion in the future. Further supporting this theory is another APA provision, which established the code of construction that future statutes should not be interpreted to modify the APA, unless they did so expressly.[13] The APA was thus a special case of the general situation described in Chapter 3, when a legislative polity enjoys the benefits of a current preferences default rule, then at the end of its reign tries to enact an interpretive rule adopting an enactor preferences default rule for future cases. My analysis there was that courts should treat such an opt-out with hostility because it would tend to reduce political satisfaction across legislatures over time. My conclusion there is thus consistent with the narrow reading given to the APA by the *Chevron* doctrine, and provides a normative justification for that otherwise anomalous reading.

Understanding *Chevron* as a default rule provides an alternative source of law, which avoids the weaknesses of the intended-delegation theory. Like that theory, my default rule approach rests on a view about what Congress wants. But it does not rely on any strained conclusion that the enacting Congress "intended" any delegation to agencies whenever Congress failed to eliminate all statutory ambiguities. Rather, my justification is that, where the enacting legislative polity has left no clear intent, its own preferences would be maximized by a current preferences default rule (for reasons explained in Chapter 3) and that *Chevron* is such a default rule. Nor is the APA a legal obstacle to this explanation, because the "relevant questions of law" that courts must resolve when they "interpret . . . statutory provisions" include deciding which default rule to choose when statutes are unclear. Thus, when courts choose *Chevron,* they *are* deciding the relevant "question of law" about how to interpret statutes; they are just deciding that question of law by using a default rule that defers to agency interpretations that are likely to reliably reflect current enactable preferences.

A third existing theory about the relevant source of law is that *Chevron* is a species of federal common law: that is, a canon of interpretation that just reflects judicial judgment. Thomas Merrill and Kristin Hickman critique this theory because it (1) does not match the language in court opinions that refers to implicit congressional desires, (2) cannot explain why *Chevron* is mandatory for courts to follow, (3) robs *Chevron* of its normative force, (4) does not explain how to prioritize the *Chevron* canon against other canons, and (5) fits poorly with the normal understanding that canons are used to ascertain statutory meaning.[14]

Understanding *Chevron* as a default rule avoids problems 1–4 with the federal common law theory. Like that theory, the default rule approach is judicially created. But because it is created based on a theory of what Congress would want if it thought about the general default rule issue, the default rule approach is consistent with passages in court opinions that refer to implicit congressional desires. The default rule theory also explains why *Chevron* is mandatory for courts to follow, and has such normative force: it conforms to the ultimate aim in statutory interpretation, which is maximizing the satisfaction of enactable preferences. Further, as noted in Chapters 1 and 2, one important advantage of default rule theory is that, unlike other theories, it does provide an objective to maximize, and an overarching structure for doing so, that prioritizes what otherwise seems like a mélange of conflicting canons.

On the other hand, my theory does fit poorly with the notion that statutory canons are exclusively about ascertaining statutory meaning, and thus cannot solve purported problem 5. However, this purported problem is not a real problem, because what the lack of fit reveals is that the mistake lies in the notion that canons only help ascertain meaning. Instead, as this book shows throughout, the canons can better be understood as default rules, which are calculated to maximize political satisfaction when statutory meaning is unclear. The lack of fit with the mistaken contrary notion is thus not problematic, but rather illuminating about the true nature of canons.

2. Normative Theories

Other theories focus less on explaining the source of law for *Chevron* than on establishing a good policy justification for it. One theory, developed well by Peter Strauss, is that *Chevron* deference furthers important interests of uniformity, in an administrative system where diverging lower court interpretations would otherwise be the norm, because the U.S. Supreme Court decides relatively few cases each year.[15] This is certainly an important virtue of deferring to agencies. It particularly helps ameliorate the degree of disuniformity that would otherwise result from the frequent agency practice of declining to follow one circuit's statutory interpretation in other circuits. This practice can create a lot of disuniformity when circuits diverge from agency interpretations and from other circuits. *Chevron* helps reduce this disuniformity by making all the circuit courts defer to one agency interpretation, at least when statutory language is unclear.

But the fit between uniformity and *Chevron* is not great. Uniformity does not explain why, as discussed later in this chapter, the Supreme Court denies *Chevron* deference to many sorts of agency interpretations that would confer the necessary uniformity, where the agency decision did not afford sufficiently reliable opportunities for political participation. Nor does uniformity explain why the Court itself defers to agency interpretations, or why there should be agency deference in state or foreign appellate systems that are less fractured. Uniformity also does not justify deference to agency decisions that are either formally or de facto appealable only to one intermediate appellate court (like the Federal Circuit or the D.C. Circuit), which can thus create national uniformity in the appellate system.[16] Nor can uniformity explain why the appellate courts do not also defer to agencies on the issues of whether a statute has a clear meaning and what that meaning is, issues on which an agency decision can also cure the disuniformity that might otherwise result from conflicting circuit decisions. Finally, if uniformity were the goal, then it could equally be advanced by the alternative default rule of interpreting all uncertain statutory language to mean that the statute has the most narrow regulatory effect possible. We need some other theory to explain why, among the uniformity-promoting default rules, the law instead chose the one that deferred to agencies. The structure of the doctrine thus reveals that, while greater national uniformity in the U.S. appellate system is an important benefit of *Chevron*, it is a subsidiary benefit rather than the driving force behind the doctrine.

This points to another advantage to a current preferences default rule approach. It frees *Chevron* from just being a parochial theory limited to the particular features of the United States. The alternative theories I have described above all depend, to varying degrees, on peculiarities of U.S. history, constitutional or statutory provisions, agency structure, appellate system, or practice of judicial common law. The alternative theories thus render *Chevron* a doctrine that is, to some degree, limited to a particular nation under particular legal circumstances. The analysis here, in contrast, provides a more general justification for judicial deference to statutory interpretations by politically-accountable agencies, a justification that would extend to legislation enacted elsewhere in the world or by political subunits of the United States. In particular, given the fact that many state legislatures have adopted (and none rejected) the *Chevron* rule, a satisfying theory for *Chevron* should not rest on peculiarities of the limited docket of the U.S. Supreme Court, and its inability to police circuit conflicts in the interpretation of U.S. statutes.

The leading alternative normative theory for *Chevron* is that agencies have greater policy expertise than courts. But the legal realists' hope that legal uncertainty could be resolved by objective policy expertise has long ago grown quaint. Although expertise can theoretically inform decisionmakers about the likely consequences of a given interpretation, it cannot resolve which statutory interpretation has the "best" policy implications. Such an ultimate resolution depends on political preferences about how to weigh those consequences. Both theory and experience have, to modern administrative law scholars, "sapped faith in the existence of an objective basis for social choice."[17] In practice, it is rare to find a field of social policy where there are not experts on opposing sides of an issue, each retained by a rival camp, undermining any claim to an objective expert resolution. This is true even for many scientific or empirical questions. Indeed, on probably most issues, the two main U.S. political parties are divided less by differing normative assessments than by contrary views (informed by rival expert academics and think tanks) about what empirical consequences will flow from certain policy choices. For example, rival empirical views seem to largely dominate policy debate on such contemporary issues as rent control, free trade agreements, global warming treaties, ballistic missile defense, the patients' bill of rights, Medicare reform, tax cuts, and the creation of individual Social Security accounts.

Finally, even if objective policy expertise could resolve the relevant issue, agencies may not decide based on that expertise. Agencies are, after all, subject to external political influences, or internal desires to expand their power or express their own ideological preferences, any of which might distort their expert judgment. Rather than reflecting objective expertise, "the exercise of agency discretion is inevitably seen as the essentially legislative process of adjusting the competing claims of various private interests affected by agency policy."[18] This is troubling under an expertise model. But under a current preferences default rule, the fact that the "required balancing of policies is an inherently discretionary, ultimately political procedure" does not undermine *Chevron* deference—it justifies it.

None of this means that agency expertise and uniformity are irrelevant. Agencies have substantive expertise that helps them resolve how any given political preferences should apply to particular facts. They are also better placed to coordinate, prioritize, or trade off conflicting regulatory preferences than are courts, which see only one statutory provision or fail to see how regulating one problem can worsen others.[19] But such factors are properly taken into account under the weaker deference doctrine of *Skidmore,* which explicitly depends on the degree of agency expertise, care, persuasiveness, consistency over time, and uniformity across the agency.[20] All these factors are logical features of a doctrine based on policy expertise, for one would expect judgments based on objective expertise to be made carefully and persuasively, and to be consistent over time and uniform across the agency, absent changed factual circumstances that should be evident from the record.

But these factors have little to do with the actual *Chevron* doctrine. While *Chevron* does refer to the fact that "[j]udges are not experts in the field," its analysis ultimately rests on the notion that agencies will rely on political determinations of wise policy and how best to trade off conflicting interests.[21] Unlike *Skidmore, Chevron* was untroubled by (indeed almost celebrated) the fact that the agency position changed over time with changing political preferences, rather than sticking to an objectively correct expert opinion. This willingness to defer to agency positions that changed over time has been repeatedly confirmed by subsequent cases. Unlike *Skidmore* deference, *Chevron* deference also does not depend on any showing of agency expertise, or on the care or persuasiveness of agency decisions. Instead, as shown in the next section, *Chevron* deference depends mainly on the opportunities for political participation in the relevant agency decision. Without such an opportunity, *Chevron* deference is denied, even if the agency decision is just as expert and uniform as decisions that get *Chevron* deference. These characteristics poorly fit a doctrine that tracks agency expertise or uniformity, but make sense if the doctrine instead tracks current political preferences.

The above analysis is limited to the issue of agency interpretations of unclear statutory language. A very different issue is raised when clear statutory language does expressly delegate to an agency the authority to interpret a statute, or exercise lawmaking power, without any political input. Agency action that proceeds without such political input would not satisfy the default rule provided by *Chevron,* but Congress has in these circumstances opted out of that default rule, perhaps because it finds the expertise model particularly attractive for that agency. This it has every right to do. Absent such an opt out, however, the *Chevron* doctrine is what provides the basis for judicial deference to agency interpretations of unclear statutory language.

Explaining *Chevron*'s Limits and the *Mead* Doctrine

The logic of a current preferences default rule also suggests limits on deference to agency interpretations. These limits help explain why current doctrine defers to some agency interpretations and not others—an inconsistency that has often baffled commentators under prevailing theories. Indeed, understanding *Chevron* as a current preferences default rule explains current doctrinal limits better than prior theories can.

One current limit is that courts do not defer to agency statutory interpretations that just reflect positions taken in litigation briefs, on the ground that they were not arrived at in the normal course of the agency's administration or exercise of rulemaking powers.[22] This doctrinal limit would not make much sense if agency expertise were the basis for deference, for an agency can provide just as much expertise and reasoned decisionmaking during litigation as outside of it. Nor does it fit well with a concern about uniformity, because a top-level agency decision to take a position in litigation could confer just as much uniformity as any other top-level agency decision.

But this distinction does make sense if the real ground for deferring to agency decisions is the likelihood that they reflect current political preferences. Unlike positions taken in litigation briefs, agency proceedings that allow regular opportunities for legislative oversight and political participation provide grounds for some reasonable confidence that the agency position reflects current political preferences. This is why the Supreme Court does defer when, in response to litigation, the agency promulgates a rule through notice-and-comment rulemaking.[23] Although such an agency decision also reflects a litigation position, in these cases the rulemaking process affords an opportunity for political input, and thus makes the agency decision a more reliable indicator of current preferences.

Similarly, the courts have never adopted the position, cleverly argued by Dan Kahan, that courts should give *Chevron* deference to Department of Justice interpretations of criminal law.[24] The Department of Justice is undoubtedly expert, and can render nationally uniform interpretations through enforcement manuals (or other means) in advance of undertaking any litigation. Such decisions thus need not fall within the rule against deferring to agency interpretations taken during litigation. Deference to Department of Justice interpretations of criminal law would, accordingly, seem required by *Chevron* if uniformity or expertise were its true basis.

If *Chevron* is a current preferences default rule, in contrast, the lack of deference to the Department of Justice on criminal law makes perfect sense. Far from rendering itself accountable to prevailing political preferences, the Department of Justice proudly takes great pains to insulate itself from political interference, especially with respect to criminal prosecutions. There is, accordingly, no reason to think that Department of Justice interpretations bear any relation to current political preferences. Thus, they do not fall within a current preferences default rule, which explains why they do not in fact get *Chevron* deference, even though the uniformity and expertise rationales would suggest otherwise.[25]

More generally, the U.S. Supreme Court has recently made clear that it will not grant *Chevron* deference to agency interpretations contained in agency letter rulings, opinion letters, policy statements, manuals, and enforcement guidelines.[26] Again, from an expertise or uniformity perspective, this is puzzling, because such agency statements might well reflect an expert judgment applied uniformly throughout the agency. However, these sorts of agency statements can be made without the sort of notice to (and participation by) interested parties that is likely to trigger more serious legislative oversight and executive involvement. They thus do not ordinarily provide a sufficiently reliable assurance that the agency decision reflects prevailing political preferences.

In *Mead*, the Supreme Court arrived at a different formulation to summarize the various exceptions to *Chevron* deference, stating that to get such deference, agency action must have the "force of law."[27] But there is a rather poor fit between this formulation and the actual doctrinal results. *Mead* held that agency action qualifies for deference if it involves notice-and-comment rulemaking, formal adjudication, or "other" cases where agencies speak with the force of law, and cited only one example (the *Nationsbank* case discussed below) of this residual "other" category. This seems hard to square with the ordinary understanding, ably championed by Merrill and Hickman, that actions have the "force of law" if, of their own force, they can command behavior or impose penalties.[28] As Merrill and Hickman themselves argue, their formalistic force-of-law notion would extend deference to many forms of agency rulemaking that are undertaken without notice and comment, and deny deference to formal agency adjudications that are not self-executing. Yet the Court shows no sign of extending or denying deference along these lines.

Rather than focusing on whether the agency action has coercive legal force, the Supreme Court continues to define the rulemaking that has the requisite "force of law" as "notice-and-comment rulemaking" and the adjudication that has the force of law as "formal" adjudication.[29] Further, in justifying its holding, which denied deference, *Mead* stressed the lack of any broad-based notice-and-comment opportunity, rather than any alleged lack of coercive force. Likewise, *Christensen* denied deference based in part on the proposition that an agency guideline that is not subject to "public notice and comment" is entitled only to "some deference." The Court has also repeatedly deferred to interpretations that were rendered through formal agency adjudications, even when they were not self-executing.[30]

Understanding *Chevron* as a current preferences default rule can make sense of these apparent anomalies. While different forms of rulemaking have equally coercive effects on third parties, unless rulemaking is conducted after an opportunity for notice and comment, it cannot provide a reasonable assurance that the agency surveyed the current political preferences before acting. The notice-and-comment process also alerts congressional members and the president's political advisors that an issue is coming up that they may be interested in influencing, or at least alerts private parties who then alert these political officials.

Likewise, formal adjudications require hearings that give the immediately affected parties an opportunity to be heard, and generally permit third parties to participate as well.[31] True, at least one case cut back on the prior doctrine requiring agencies to allow intervention by third parties.[32] But in practice, formal adjudications provide affected parties with opportunities to make their political views known, either directly or by alerting supportive members of the political branches. Thus, although some formal adjudications do not have coercive force, they do satisfy the conditions for a current preferences default rule, and thus merit *Chevron* deference.

Ordinary notions of when agency action has the coercive "force of law" are also hard to square with the actual result in *Mead*, which denied deference to a Customs ruling letter that imposed a duty before certain goods could be imported, even though by statute and regulation that ruling was "binding" on all Customs Service personnel.[33] The letter ruling thus had the concrete coercive effect of restricting importers' freedom to import the goods without paying a duty. Indeed, the effect was equivalent to a court injunction, which no one would deny has the coercive "force of law" under ordinary understandings.

The fact that the agency reserved the right to change its rulings in the future, although noted by the *Mead* Court, does not reduce the coercive force of law of those rulings until they are changed, any more than a trial court injunction could be said to lack the force of law just because the trial or appellate court might modify that injunction in the future. Moreover, *Chevron* itself stressed the importance of allowing agencies the flexibility to change their interpretations over time, and thus mandated deference even though the agency at issue had changed its interpretation in the past and might do so again in the future. As the Court has stated, "change is not invalidating, because the whole point of *Chevron* is to leave the discretion provided by the ambiguities of a statute with the implementing agency."[34] An agency interpretation thus clearly need not be regarded as binding future agency action in order to merit *Chevron* deference.

The denial of deference in *Mead* instead rested on an entirely different notion of what the "force of law" meant. That notion requires that the agency position (1) be articulated as a general rule, which is uniformly applied by the agency to a defined class of persons, and (2) be based on a serious solicitation of input, such as through notice-and-comment rulemaking, by the members of the affected class. In addition to the lack of any notice-and-comment period in the actual case, the *Mead* Court stressed that the agency rendered 10–15,000 letter rulings a year, through forty-six separate branch offices. Further, agency regulations provided that third parties would not receive notice of any change in letter rulings, and should not rely on them or "assume that the principles of that ruling will be applied in connection with any [other] transaction."[35] Such agency decisions, although having an individualized coercive effect on the recipients of the letter rulings, could not be said to have the force of a generally applicable rule of law for a class of parties. Instead, *Mead* indicated that to have the "force of law" that merits *Chevron* deference, the agency action must "bespeak the legislative type of activity that would naturally bind more than the parties to the ruling." The Court did not mean to require formal rulemaking, because it recognized that principles articulated in agency adjudication could suffice. But the Court did mean to exclude individualized arbitrations that bound only the parties to them, and failed to create any general rule applicable in other cases.

This distinction—between individualized determinations and rulemaking for a general class of persons—may not make much sense if we focus on the coercive effect of the decision, but is entirely understandable if we instead understand this doctrine as a current preferences default rule. Individualized determinations cannot be said to reflect the current enactable preferences of any general set of interested parties. One-shot individualized interpretations are also unlikely to provoke any legislative oversight. They thus do not suffice to justify judicial application of a current preferences default rule, especially since adopting that default rule would create an interpretation that would be binding on the general class of affected persons.

Mead thus offers an interesting lesson about uniformity. The fact that an agency position creates national uniformity is not, as noted above, a sufficient condition for *Chevron* deference. *Mead* itself noted as much when it said that, even when an agency ruling was precedent for other agency decisions, as with interpretive rules, that did not suffice to confer *Chevron* deference.[36] But *Mead* indicates that agency uniformity is probably a necessary condition for judicial deference. This makes sense if the *Chevron-Mead* doctrine reflects a current preferences default rule. Agency uniformity may not reflect prevailing political preferences, and thus should not suffice for deference. But uniformity is a necessary condition for *Chevron* deference because, if the agency position is not uniform across the nation, it cannot be considered an accurate manifestation of enactable national preferences. Indeed, a ruling by one of forty-six agency interpreters, which is not binding in other cases, has serious uniformity *dis*advantages compared to interpretations by an appellate system, especially an agency that (as in *Mead*) was subject to appeals through a nationwide Court of International Trade to a single Federal Circuit.

Justice Scalia disagreed with *Mead* in a vehement dissent, taking the position that an authoritative (and thus uniform) agency position had been taken, because the agency head signed the brief defending the interpretation in court.[37] But the Court has never accepted the position that litigation briefs suffice, and seeing *Chevron* as a current preferences default rule helps us understand why. Part of the explanation, as noted above, is that positions taken in litigation briefs are less likely to reflect a solicitation of political views. But *Mead* illustrates a further point. If the Court had deferred to the interpretation, then in the future any one of the forty-six branch office interpretations would have had to be considered binding in court, if the agency head later proved willing to defend it. Under this alternative rule, an agency head who generally committed himself to a strategy of defending interpretations by his forty-six branch offices could, accordingly, create a system of agency interpretations that were binding, even though there was no reasonable assurance that they reflected current political preferences. The *Chevron-Mead* doctrine instead effectively requires that the agency provide the assurance that its interpretations reflect prevailing national preferences *before* it imposes those interpretations on others.

Understanding *Chevron* as a current preferences default rule also helps provide some content to its residual "other" category of decisions that were deemed by *Mead* to have the requisite "force of law" to merit deference. The only example the *Mead* Court cited for this "other" category was a "deliberative conclusion" by the comptroller of the currency in the *Nationsbank* case.[38] This decision had two noteworthy differences from *Mead*. First, it was a top-level decision by the head of the agency, under a system whereby the Office of the Comptroller of the Currency itself decided whether bank applications to expand their activities were legally "permissible." Second, the agency head's decision reflected his "deliberative conclusions" about what banks could legally do, which was formally manifested in his decision to grant the bank application, and was not taken during litigation. This case thus did not raise the same concerns as in *Mead* about disuniform agency interpretations that failed to reflect national enactable preferences. Similarly, two other cases, which Justice Scalia's dissent argued were inconsistent with *Mead*, did involve opinion letters or guidelines. But those two other cases were not one-shot opinion letters, which might reflect agency disuniformity or a failure to test the interpretation against prevailing political preferences. Instead, those two cases involved multiple opinion letters and guidelines, which clearly reflected a uniform national position by politically accountable agencies, and were thus amenable to legislative oversight.[39]

One could try to rationalize all these distinctions by referring to an implicit congressional intent. The *Mead* Court itself referred to claims about what Congress "would expect" or "meant" when Congress created the sort of agency power that does not satisfy the Court's "force of law" test.[40] But efforts to explain *Chevron* by reference to enacting legislative intent are generally strained. And they were especially strained in *Mead* itself, where the most direct indicator of legislative intent was a statutory provision that cut in the opposite direction, specifying that the agency decisions must be "presumed to be correct" on judicial review. Moreover, as Justice Scalia pointed out, if *Chevron* were truly based on an implicit congressional intent to delegate authority to the agency by enacting the relevant statute, then it would seem that the mere conferral of rulemaking authority to resolve statutory ambiguity should suffice, and deference should be granted even if the agency chose to resolve statutory uncertainties through some other method.[41]

Understanding *Chevron* as a current preferences default rule provides a better explanation. By referring to what Congress "meant" or "expected," the Court is really referring to what general default rule the enacting Congress would want, not what the enacting Congress intended for this statute in particular. And the reason the doctrine depends not just on how much power the agency was granted, but also on how the agency exercises its power, is that only certain methods of exercise provide the reasonable assurance that the agency action reflects current governmental preferences.

Also consistent with current preferences default rule theory is the Court's otherwise puzzling distinction between interpretive and legislative rules. An interpretive rule binds agency personnel, but not the regulated community. Unlike legislative rules, "interpretive rules . . . enjoy no *Chevron* status as a class."[42] As a matter of legislative intent, this distinction makes little sense. If the enacting Congress intended to delegate any authority to agencies, it would be authority over the agencies' own personnel. Less deference, if any, seems merited when the agency tries to exert authority over third parties. To the extent one can read any intent from congressional statutes, they affirmatively cut against the prevailing distinction. The "housekeeping statute" of 1789 provides: "The head of an Executive department or military department may prescribe regulations for the government of his department, [and] the conduct of its employees."[43] This is an express and very general authority for agencies to adopt interpretive rules binding agency personnel. In contrast, both the APA and relevant case law deny agencies any general authority to issue legislative rules that bind third parties, unless such authority has been expressly provided in other specific statutes.[44] Thus, any implied legislative intent would support a doctrine of super-*Chevron* deference for interpretive rules, rather than the actual doctrine of lesser deference.

Under a current preferences default rule, in contrast, the distinction does make sense because interpretive rules do not require any notice-and-comment process, whereas legislative rules do.[45] Thus, while legislative rules are promulgated after the sort of political participation that provides some assurance that they track current political preferences, interpretive rules need not be. On the other hand, some agencies (like the Treasury Department) make it a practice to use notice-and-comment procedures when adopting interpretive regulations. If notice and comment is provided, such interpretive regulations do fit within a current preferences default rule and merit *Chevron* deference. This probably explains the tradition of great deference to IRS interpretations. It also explains why the *Mead* Court did not say interpretive rules never get *Chevron* deference, but only that they do not automatically get it "as a class."[46]

A current preferences default rule also better explains why *Chevron* deference is granted even when a statute makes agency decisions that are subject to a *de novo* trial in court.[47] Under the legislative intent model, this result has seemed odd because the enacting Congress signaled, if anything, a desire for nondeferential judicial review. The only explanation, within an intent-based model, has been that the presumption that the legislature intends courts to defer to agencies is extremely difficult to rebut, which is hard to justify because the basis for that presumption is acknowledged to be weak and even fictional. As a current preferences default rule, in contrast, the result follows naturally. *De novo* review of the facts involves the exercise of a traditional adjudicative function, which does not require accurately ascertaining prevailing political preferences. Such *de novo* fact review is thus not at all in tension with the court deferring on how the agency resolves statutory uncertainties, because the latter is justified under a current preferences default rule by the agency's advantage in estimating current enactable preferences.

Finally, a sometimes underappreciated limit is that *Chevron* deference only applies to agency interpretations that reflect a "reasonable policy choice."[48] This, the Court took pains to point out, does not mean a choice that is reasonable according to a judge's personal policy preferences, but rather a reasonable accommodation of competing political interests. This doctrinal limit does mean, however, that to merit *Chevron* deference the agency decision must be based on its policy or political judgment, not on its disagreement with the courts about either (1) how to ascertain statutory meaning or (2) what default rule should be used when meaning is unclear. The courts defer to agencies because the policy views of agencies are more in tune with prevailing political preferences, not because agencies are better at legal interpretation than courts. If the agency by its own account is not reflecting current political preferences, then its decisions do not merit deference under a current preferences default rule.

Bob Jones is illustrative.[49] Although the then-current Treasury Department interpreted the statute to allow tax exemptions for racially discriminatory schools, it made no claim that its interpretation reflected sound policy or current political preferences on whether racially discriminatory schools should get tax exemptions. To the contrary, the agency supported a new statute to expressly deny such tax exemptions. The Treasury interpretation was instead based on its view about statutory meaning, and its premise that enactor preferences, rather than current preferences, should resolve any statutory ambiguity. The Court not only failed to defer to this agency interpretation, but gave no indication it even considered deferring to it. If *Chevron* were really based on an implicit legislative intent to delegate to the agency the authority to resolve unclear statutory language, this is hard to understand because, if such a delegated power existed, the Treasury Department was exercising it.

Understanding *Chevron* instead as a current preferences default rule, in contrast, readily explains why the Supreme Court would ignore a Treasury position that made no pretense of reflecting current political preferences. The courts are not looking to agencies for expertise in how best to conduct legal interpretation of administrative statutes, but rather for their expertise in determining where current political preferences lie, to resolve ambiguities left by legal interpretation. Thus, courts should not, and do not, give *Chevron* deference to agency interpretations that admittedly do not match current enactable policy preferences.

This requirement that the agency make a "reasonable policy choice" given competing political interests also suggests that courts should deny deference if, even though the agency does not openly admit it, the agency interpretation plainly conflicts with current enactable policy preferences. This is obviously an exception that must be construed narrowly, lest it swallow the rule. If courts in every case made their own assessment of where current enactable preferences lie, and rejected every agency interpretation that conflicted with that assessment, there would be no effective deference. Nor would such a general exception advance political satisfaction, because the entire premise of *Chevron* is that agencies generally know better than courts where current enactable preferences lie. However, there is a definable set of extraordinary cases where a court can determine with confidence that the agency interpretation conflicts with current enactable preferences. But before reaching those cases, we need to confront an issue I have so far deferred: what should courts do when the political views of the executive and the legislature conflict?

Conflicts between the Executive and the Legislature

The affirmative argument I have laid out for *Chevron* deference depends on agencies being fairly accurate barometers of current enactable preferences, or at least more accurate than judicial estimates would be. Although the phrase "legislative preferences" is often used as a shorthand for enactable preferences, in systems like the United States' the set of preferences that are actually enactable is strongly influenced not just by legislators but also by the executive, who has the powers to veto legislation and put issues on the public agenda. Each is in turn influenced by outside political forces, which lobby, organize, contribute, and otherwise constrain the actions of both legislators and executives. In such a system, agencies must be responsive to executive, legislative, and general political influences for their actions to be likely to minimize the dissatisfaction of enactable political preferences in a way that merits *Chevron* deference.

Academic critique of *Chevron* has tended to presume that agencies respond to presidential preferences but not congressional ones, and that *Chevron* thus alters the original constitutional balance of power by shifting power from Congress to the president where their preferences conflict.[50] Where the premises of this argument hold, this is a powerful critique. But the premises are not generally applicable, for two reasons.

First, most agency decisions that get *Chevron* deference do not involve dramatic conflicts between the executive and legislative branches. The real world is notably less exciting. Most agency decisions involve issues too minor to interest the legislature, or for which there is no clear indication where legislative preferences lie. This does not mean such cases are unimportant. The entire point of all preference-estimating statutory default rules is, after all, to resolve the interstitial gaps or ambiguities where legislative action is unlikely. Indeed, it is precisely in such cases that the default rule matters most, because that is when the default sticks and becomes enduring law.

In this typical set of cases, where there is no other clear indicator of legislative preferences, an agency decision that is responsive to presidential preferences may be the best available indicator of where enactable preferences would lie if the issue ever came to a vote. The president is, after all, responsive to the same electorate as Congress as a whole, and while the different electoral rules for registering that electorate's preferences in presidential and congressional elections will lead to many differences, a shared overall electorate should also lead to broad areas of likely agreement. Thus, absent any contrary indicator of legislative preferences, tracking presidential preferences is likely to minimize political dissatisfaction.

Second, and more important, the premise of agency–executive equivalence that underlies this critique is contradicted by an extensive literature, summarized above, showing that agencies in fact are subject not only to presidential influence, but also to various forms of influence by Congress and outside political groups. Indeed, the fact that agencies are typically influenced by a combination of executive and legislative accountability helps explain not only *Chevron* but also *Chadha* and *Bowsher.* Those who hold the contrary premise, that the agencies receiving *Chevron* deference reflect only executive preferences, have concluded that the statutes in these cases, which attempted to give Congress a unilateral legislative veto over agency regulations, and to delegate administrative powers to a legislative agency run by Congress itself, were both proper efforts to restore the original constitutional balance.[51] Under their premise, *Chadha* was thus wrong to invalidate the legislative veto, and *Bowsher* was wrong to invalidate delegations to a legislative agency. However, because agencies in fact are responsive to *both* the executive and legislative branches, what would alter the proper balance would be legislative vetoes and delegations to legislative agencies, each of which try to make agencies responsive only to the legislative branch. That would have effectively circumvented the president's constitutional veto power, explaining why *Chadha* and *Bowsher* were both correctly decided.

To be sure, the academic critique that *Chevron* is based solely on accountability to the president finds support in some language of *Chevron* itself, which justified its deference rule with references to agencies' accountability to the president, rather than to the political branches as a whole.[52] But if so understood, these statements reflected a very superficial understanding about the relationship between agencies and the president. Not only did the above forms of de facto influence from Congress and outside political interests clearly exist, but at the time the president was understood to lack legal authority to direct how agencies should exercise discretionary authority delegated to those agencies by legislation.[53]

Any implication to the contrary in *Chevron* was just dicta, about a topic the Court did not directly consider, because that case did not involve any clear clash between the president and Congress. Although the new agency interpretation considered in *Chevron* did come in response to a change of administration, the Court stressed that the interpretation the agency was abandoning had not reflected any prior understanding about current enactable policy preferences, but was rather a mechanical response to a lower court decision.[54] Indeed, if *Chevron* were based on accountability to presidential views, then independent agencies should get less deference than executive agencies that are subject to the president's removal power.[55] In fact, *Chevron* draws no such distinction.

Moreover, the various doctrinal limits detailed above mean that *Chevron* deference cannot, in fact, be triggered by mere agency responsiveness to executive preferences. If such responsiveness sufficed, then none of the *Chevron* limits should apply, because all agency decisions potentially have the requisite accountability to the executive. Instead, the doctrines that limit *Chevron* require broader indicia that the agency was accurately informed about current political preferences outside the executive branch before it took action. The analysis here suggests a further limit on *Chevron* deference: the agency action cannot just reflect executive views that plainly conflict with the legislature's.

This last limit was not always clear. In the 1991 decision in *Rust v. Sullivan,* the Court (perhaps overly influenced by the loose language in *Chevron* that mentioned accountability only to the president) deferred to an agency interpretation that did seem to clearly side with the president over a Congress that had expressed a contrary view.[56] However, the issue came to a head in the Clinton administration because, as former Clinton policy advisor (and now dean) Elena Kagan has shown, the Clinton administration aggressively expanded presidential authority over agencies.[57] President Clinton began appropriating agency action and assuming the power to direct it. Further, "Clinton's use of directive authority over the executive branch agencies accelerated dramatically when the Democrats lost control of Congress." Such a sustained shift would, if my current preferences default rule theory is right, naturally make the court less willing to give *Chevron* deference. If agency action can largely be directed by the president, then it is more likely to reflect only presidential preferences. Such agency action is more likely to take positions that create sharp conflicts with Congress. More important, such agency action is less likely to reflect current enactable preferences, because the president's views reflect only one piece of the political puzzle that is necessary to create enactments. Agency action that just takes one side in a heated political disagreement between the executive and legislative branch should, under my theory, thus be denied *Chevron* deference.

This is precisely what has happened. Two cases dramatize the shift in the application of *Chevron* that took place in reaction to the Clinton expansion of presidential authority over agencies. One case involved the most prominent example of presidentially led agency action given by Kagan: Clinton's announcement that, as executive, he would restrict the marketing of cigarettes through Food and Drug Administration (FDA) regulations.[58] This presidential announcement came before any FDA rule had actually been adopted, and indeed before any notice-and-comment period had begun, but nonetheless stated the regulatory principles the president said "will" be adopted "by executive authority," and the FDA later adopted precisely those principles. Further, the president announced that he was "authorizing" the FDA regulations, thus presupposing an answer to the contested question of statutory interpretation over whether the FDA's statutory authority to regulate drugs extended to cigarettes.

This statutory issue ultimately was resolved in *Brown & Williamson*, where the Supreme Court rejected the FDA's interpretation that cigarettes were a "drug" or "device" within the meaning of the Food, Drug, and Cosmetic Act.[59] The Court did not claim that this agency interpretation conflicted with the plain meaning of the statute. Instead, the Court relied mainly on a series of subsequent statutes that retained or relied on the FDA's lack of authority to regulate tobacco. Those subsequent statutes opted instead for a more limited regulatory strategy of requiring warnings, limiting advertising, and banning sales to minors. The Court also noted that the agency itself had just recently altered its longstanding interpretation that the Act did not give it authority to regulate cigarettes. But the Court took pains to stress that its "conclusion does not rely on the fact that the FDA's assertion of jurisdiction represents a sharp break with its prior interpretation," recognizing that this would conflict with *Chevron*. Rather, the important point to the Court was that several intervening

Congresses had effectively incorporated the agency's prior interpretation into a broad political compromise leading to several subsequent statutes.

The Court's objection, then, was not so much that the FDA was changing its interpretation as that in doing so it was deviating from the most recent official indications of enactable political preferences. The Court was well aware that the FDA's changed interpretation was vigorously championed by President Clinton and vociferously opposed by then-current Republican majority in Congress. It was also aware that, given this deadlock, "Congress could not muster the votes necessary either to grant or deny the FDA the relevant authority."[60] Sustaining the FDA interpretation would thus amount to allowing the agency (and presidency) to dictate the resolution of a political fight between two factions, neither of which was sufficiently powerful to enact legislation on its own. The Court rejected Justice Breyer's dissenting position that political accountability to the president should suffice when such a political deadlock exists. Instead, the Court in effect relied on the most recent indications it had about what could sufficiently satisfy political preferences to enact legislation: the preferences of intervening Congresses reflected in subsequent legislation. Had the current Congress instead supported the FDA's changed interpretation, the case would likely have come out the other way.

The Court explained its non-application of *Chevron* under what has become known as the "extraordinary case" exception.

> Deference under *Chevron* to an agency's construction of a statute that it administers is premised on the theory that a statute's ambiguity constitutes an implicit delegation from Congress to the agency to fill in the statutory gaps. In extraordinary cases, however, there may be reason to hesitate before concluding that Congress has intended such an implicit delegation.[61]

The issue is: what made the case extraordinary? Sheer importance cannot explain the exception, for *Chevron* itself involved an extraordinarily important environmental policy that affected all industrial manufacturing.[62] Moreover, creating an exception for important issues is inconsistent with *Chevron*'s premise that agencies generally provide better statutory interpretations than courts. If that premise is right, then the importance of the issue would make deference even more vital. After all, why would anyone want to move to a less accurate system of interpretation the more important the issue?

Some have viewed the extraordinary case exception as adopting the claim that courts should not defer to agencies' interpretations about the scope of their own jurisdiction, because agencies have a conflict of interest on that issue.[63] The problem with this claim is that *every* statutory interpretation implicates the scope of agency jurisdiction, by defining what comes within the statutes over which the agency has uncontested jurisdiction.[64] A "scope of jurisdiction" exception thus does not helpfully distinguish a set of cases that differ from the other cases where deference *is* given. Moreover, if the evidence otherwise indicated that an agency decision reflected current enactable preferences, a default rule of deference would still maximize political satisfaction, regardless of whether we can characterize the decision as jurisdictional.

What the *Brown & Williamson* Court stressed, to support its conclusion that the agency interpretation was "extraordinary," was not only that the issue was important enough for Congress to have preferences, but also that the agency action conflicted with the political views reflected in a series of congressional actions subsequent to the initial enactment.[65] That is, the case manifested precisely the two factors that the analysis above suggested would undermine *Chevron* deference: (1) political salience, and (2) a clear conflict with legislative evidence of what was enactable. Thus, one way to provide more concrete content to the vague "extraordinary case" exception would be to conclude that cases are "extraordinary" if they involve a split on a politically salient issue between the president and Congress, which makes it clear that the agency position does not reflect political preferences that are enactable.

The census case was the second one in the Clinton administration that raised the question whether *Chevron* deference applies to agencies that take sides in an executive–legislative dispute.[66] In that case, the question was whether the census statute could be interpreted to allow statistical sampling in apportioning congressional seats. The statute, in various amended versions, had been interpreted to prohibit statistical sampling from 1790 until 1994, when the Census Bureau changed its interpretation. The majority agreed the matter was not settled by the plain language of the statute. Nonetheless, the agency waived any claim to *Chevron* deference in light of its changed position.

This waiver might seem odd because *Chevron* expressly approves of changes in agency interpretation. But the agency no doubt recognized its tenuous political position, given that the change reflected its decision to side with President Clinton, on a decision where his position was strongly opposed by the then-current Republican majority in Congress.[67] Thus, any choice of default rule could not be overturned by the political process: the Republican Congress would block any statute that authorized statistical sampling, and the Democratic president, coupled with a veto-sustaining congressional minority, would block any statute that took such authority away. Deferring to the agency on the default rule would thus give it the power to take sides in this political stalemate. The agency did not claim such power, perhaps understanding the implicit limits on *Chevron*, and the Court instead resolved the matter with its assessment of the political preferences that had actually sufficed to enact prior versions of the statute.[68]

The resolution of the census case is consistent with the point that, when statutory meaning is unclear, and there is no reliable basis for determining current or recent enactable preferences, the proper tack is to rely on the best estimate of the preferences of the enacting legislative polity. That will generally be the case when the current political branches are at loggerheads on some issue. Tracking current enactable preferences is not the same as deferring to presidential administrations; nor is it an invitation to pretend that a sufficient political consensus exists when it plainly does not.

Similar agency interpretations under the George W. Bush administration have received similar treatment when other evidence indicated they were unlikely to be enactable in Congress. For example, *Gonzales v. Oregon* involved the Controlled Substances Act, which delegates to the attorney general the power to define which drugs are controlled substances criminalized by that Act and which can be given by medical prescription. After Oregon legalized physician-assisted suicide, the attorney general adopted an interpretive rule, which provided that using a controlled substance to assist suicide was not a "legitimate medical purpose" and thus violated the Act. The Court conceded that this term was ambiguous, but nonetheless denied *Chevron* deference.[69] The Court reasoned that the rule did not fall within the scope of the authority delegated to the attorney general. However, given the sweeping authority the statute gave him, which included the authority not only to define what was a controlled substance but also to determine when using a controlled substance violated the "public interest," that conclusion seemed contrary to the ordinary sort of deferential reading that *Chevron* provides.[70]

More explanatory is what the Court stressed at the outset: Congress had tried to enact a bill authorizing the attorney general to criminalize the use of drugs used in physician-assisted suicide, but "it failed to pass."[71] This made it clear that his rule was not currently enactable. Further, the Court emphasized that the attorney general had not consulted "anyone outside his Department" before issuing his rule, thus depriving his rule of the sort of exposure to outside political influence that normally provides some assurance that agency decisions are likely to reflect current enactable preferences. This formed the backdrop for the Court's ultimate conclusion, citing *Brown & Williamson*, that this issue was too politically contentious to fall within *Chevron* deference.[72]

A somewhat different illustration of this phenomenon was raised in *Hamdan*. There, the administration strenuously argued that the Supreme Court should defer to the administration's interpretation of various statutes covering the adjudication rights of Guantanamo detainees.[73] The Supreme Court declined to defer to the president's interpretation. One explanation for this decision, offered by Professor Katyal, is that the asserted interpretation was offered by the president, rather than by an agency, and that *Chevron* deference only applies to agencies. But the limit to agency interpretations actually underscores the point that *Chevron* deference cannot really be based on accountability to the president alone. After all, who could represent the views of the president better than the president himself?

If accountability to the president were the basis for deference, then extra deference should be given to his own interpretations, rather than less deference than is given to agencies who may diverge from presidential views. But that is not the law. *Chevron* deference is given only to agency interpretations, which makes sense under my theory because agencies are generally accountable to *both* the president and Congress. Here, the problem was that many of the relevant agencies shared a view, common in Congress, that the relevant statutes should not be interpreted to allow detainees to be excluded from their own trials or in violation of the Geneva Convention. As a result, there was no reliable basis for concluding that the president's contrary interpretation was likely to be enactable. The Court alluded to these sorts of concerns when it stressed that, even in times of war, the president had to act jointly with Congress to change statutes about the conduct of military trials.[74]

In short, when faced with unclear statutory language, courts defer to agency interpretations that have, as usual, been influenced by a combination of presidential, legislative, and outside political input. Courts do not defer to the president himself, who reflects only one piece of the political puzzle necessary to create an enactable political preference, nor to an agency that simply sides with the president over Congress. This limit on *Chevron* is (like the others) hard to explain if *Chevron* were really based on the conclusion that the enacting Congress intended to delegate interpretive authority to the agency, because the agency would be exercising delegated authority whether or not it conformed to this limit. Nor does it make sense if *Chevron* is based on agency expertise, uniformity, or accountability to the president alone. But it does make sense if *Chevron* is a default rule that estimates current enactable preferences.

A current preferences default rule more generally suggests that courts should deny deference to any agency interpretation that Congress voted to override, in a bill that was vetoed by the president. Nor would the unenacted congressional bill be entitled to deference. Instead, neither would reflect a currently enactable preference. Accordingly, the court must turn to the most recent legislative action that indicated enactable preferences (as in *Brown & Williamson* and the census case) or, absent any reliable evidence from such recent legislative action, to a preference-eliciting default rule (as we shall see happened in *Hamdan*).

Distinguishing Stephenson

We can contrast the above conclusions with some recent work by my brilliant colleague, Matthew Stephenson, on deference to agency interpretations. One of his pieces analyzes when the legislature would prefer interpretation to be done by agencies, rather than courts. He concludes that the goal of satisfying legislative preferences does not clearly favor agencies over courts, despite the political insulation of the latter.[75] However, this conclusion is based on a combination of two mistaken premises. First, like other rational choice scholarship, he mistakenly asks only the statute-specific question: namely, what interpretive rule would the enacting legislature want for the statutes it enacts. This premise, not surprisingly, leads him to the conclusion that legislators fear agency political accountability to future legislatures. But the premise mistakenly ignores the fact that any legislature would also be acutely interested in the interpretation of all the previous statutes being interpreted while it is in office, rather than being fixated only on future interpretations of the subset of statutes they themselves enacted. Second, he assumes that the preferences underlying statutory delegations to agency are purely legislative (excluding presidential preferences), but that agencies mainly follow presidential preferences. These premises thus, again not surprisingly, lead him to the conclusion that legislatures fear agencies' political accountability to the president. But these premises mistakenly ignore the fact that any statutes giving agencies interpretive authority have to be enacted with presidential involvement, and that agencies are also heavily influenced by legislatures and lose *Chevron* deference when they take the president's side over the legislature.

Professor Stephenson's analysis thus excludes what, to my mind, is the main thing that matters: the extent to which interpretations deviate from enactable preferences. But, to be fair, he does not purport to offer normative conclusions, or to cover all the factors that bear on legislative preferences.[76] Rather, he aims simply to analyze one subset of preferences the enacting legislature might have, those regarding consistency and risk diversification, and he does so with great nuance and sophistication. But having focused solely on these second-order enactor preferences, and failed to consider the possibility that the enacting legislature would prefer a current preferences default rule, his analysis cannot really explain or justify the full landscape of *Chevron* and its exceptions.

A second piece instead focuses on what deference doctrine judges would prefer. He assumes that judges have two conflicting goals that they trade off—textual plausibility and agency policy achievement—the latter of which gets more weight the more formality the agency uses.[77] This theory comes closer to fitting the doctrine, for formality does (as we saw above) bear on whether an agency decision is likely to reflect current enactable preferences. However, the latter is what ultimately matters. *Brown & Williamson* refused to defer to an agency decision that was as formal as they come, because it clearly deviated from current enactable preferences. *Nationsbank* deferred to an informal agency decision, because it was likely to reflect current enactable preferences. The later decision in *Barnhart* again confirmed that formalities were not required for deference.[78] The doctrine also does not allow greater degrees of textual implausibility the more formal the agency decision. The courts do not defer at all if they deem the text clear. If the text is unclear, then any agency decision, no matter where it is located within the zone of textual plausibility, gets total *Chevron* deference if it is a reliable indicator of current enactable preferences. Once such deference is earned, increased levels of formality gain an agency nothing.

Nor, if we understand it as a current preferences default rule, is there any good reason for *Chevron* deference to have levels that vary continuously with the degree of formality. If the agency decision is made in circumstances that make it a better reflection of current enactable preferences than judicial estimates could provide, then complete deference is warranted, because it will increase political satisfaction, no matter what the formality level. Stephenson's conclusion is simply the logical result of his contrary assumption that, even when statutory language is unclear, judges care about some factor other than having agencies achieve the policies that best indicate current enactable preferences. Under my assumption that the latter becomes the judicial objective when statutes are unclear, there is no need for any trade-off, at least not when the agency is acting in ways that make its views better indicators of current enactable preferences than judicial decisionmaking. Stephenson's theory does, however, significantly illuminate hard look review and *Skidmore* deference, which do seem to have varying deference levels, depending on the level of agency formality or demonstrated expertise.

Another important recent piece by Stephenson argues that some degree of agency insulation from political actors will actually lead to results that advance the satisfaction of democratic preferences, if the relevant political actors exhibit some variance from democratic preferences, with the optimal agency insulation lower the lower the political variance and the higher the agency divergence from democratic preferences. (There are various reasons, discussed in the note, to wonder whether the other assumptions necessary for this conclusion hold, but let me put those aside here.) If one agrees with me that both the President and Congress influence agencies and that the relevant democratic preferences are enactable preferences, then the political variance will be small, and thus his model indicates that the optimal degree of agency insulation should also be small. Still, there will be some variance because the political actors who influence agencies are not identical to those who can enact legislation. In any event, the Stephenson result is consistent with my analysis. His conclusion that some degree of agency discretion advances the relevant democratic preferences reinforces the basic case for *Chevron* deference to agencies. His conclusion that agency discretion should be less the more the agency varies from the relevant preferences likewise reinforces my conclusion that the exceptions to *Chevron* deference do and should apply in cases when it is less likely that agency action reflects enactable preferences.[79]

Conclusions and Implications

Chevron does not require deference to all agency action, but limits that deference in many ways. The courts defer on how agencies resolve uncertain statutory meaning, not on whether that meaning is unclear, nor on whether the default rule for resolving unclear cases should look to enacting or current preferences. The courts defer to agency interpretations that are arrived at after general political input, not to agency interpretations that are insulated from such outside input. And the courts refuse to follow agency interpretations that contravene current enactable preferences by fashioning a false political consensus out of what is in fact obvious political gridlock. Because the *Chevron* doctrine merely states a default rule that applies when statutory language is unclear, the same limits would not apply if clear statutory language expressly delegated interpretive authority to the agency. But outside of cases involving such a clear statutory delegation to agencies, these exceptions set very substantial limits on judicial deference to agency interpretation.

This pattern of exceptions does not fit prior theories of *Chevron*, but does fit my theory that *Chevron* is instead a current preferences default rule. This pattern of exceptions to *Chevron* deference is also hard to square with a more cynical theory, which is that judges defer to agencies in order to save themselves the time and effort of analyzing tedious regulatory issues.[80] If courts wished to minimize their decisionmaking costs, they would be better off deferring to all agency decisions rather than frequently making exceptions.

None of this means that agency deference rests on any unrealistic view that, where the exceptions do not apply, agencies perfectly reflect enactable preferences. Enactable preferences may be highly uncertain, and agencies may often fail to reflect them. To justify *Chevron* as a current preferences default rule, it need only be the case that, within *Chevron*'s limits, agencies are more likely to reflect enactable preferences than judicial judgment would. If judicial judgment is 55% likely to reflect an enactable preference, and agency decisions are 60% likely to do so, then a general policy of following agency decisions will still maximize the satisfaction of enactable preferences. But where judges have special reason to know the agency action has 0% odds of reflecting an enactable preference, the court should not defer. More generally, the nuanced doctrines that set the limits on *Chevron* can properly be understood as excluding those cases where there is little reason to think the agency has any comparative advantage in reflecting enactable preferences.

One might wonder why, if agencies are generally better at estimating current preferences than judges, legislatures do not simply create an Agency of Statutory Interpretation to decide all interpretive issues. The answer is that, as detailed above, an important part of the judicial role is to deny deference when the agency is unlikely to reflect current enactable preferences. This includes cases where the agency (1) does not provide sufficient opportunities for political influence; (2) furthers its own theories about how to interpret meaning, rather than reflecting current enactable preferences; or (3) takes sides on an issue about which the political branches are deadlocked in a way that means there is no current enactable preference. Thus, while agencies are better at estimating current enactable preferences than judges, an independent judiciary remains vital to make sure agencies are confined to that role.

This analysis also provides guidance for how agency officials should interpret statutory language, in those cases where they enjoy no express statutory delegation of lawmaking authority. It indicates that, where the statutory language is unclear, agency officials should try to track their best estimate of current enactable preferences. Otherwise, agency decisions would not serve the function that merits judicial deference under *Chevron*. Agency officials thus should not resolve unclear statutory language by trying to track the preferences of the enacting legislative polity, lest they get the same back-of-the-hand treatment from the courts that the Treasury Department got in *Bob Jones*. Nor should agencies just try to implement the views of the president, even when they know those views could never get enacted because they conflict with what could get through the legislature. If they do, agencies will get the same lack of deference that the FDA received when it tried to regulate cigarettes as a drug or device.

Instead, agencies should track current enactable preferences as best they can. In doing so, agencies cannot limit themselves to inferring current enactable preferences from official action, for the agencies themselves are supposed to provide the official action on which judges can rely. Agencies should rather consider the full set of formal and informal evidence about where current enactable preferences lie. Indeed, if agencies fail to expose themselves to broad-based political input, they are unlikely to receive judicial deference to their views. Thus, unlike judges, agencies should not be confined to estimating current enactable preferences from official action.

PART II

Enactor Preferences Default Rules

CHAPTER 6

From Legislative Intent to Probabilistic Estimates of Enactable Preferences

Using Legislative History to Estimate Preferences Rather Than Ascertain Meaning

Suppose we have neither clear statutory language nor any reliable basis for inferring current enactable preferences from official actions, be they agency decisions or recent related legislation. Then, courts must turn to making their best estimate of the enactable preferences of the original polity that wrote the statutory language. What default rules should courts adopt about how to estimate such enactor preferences?

In discussing this issue, we risk treading on theories of statutory meaning, and embroiling ourselves in the voluminous debate about whether legislative history helps to accurately ascertain statutory meaning. Let me avoid this thicket by simply saying the following. Whether or not one invites legislative history into the initial inquiry as to a statute's meaning, there is a separate question: should legislative history be used to resolve cases when, after employing her favorite methods of ascertaining meaning, the interpreter is left genuinely uncertain as to the statute's meaning? The latter is the question I wish to address. I thus am not considering whether legislative history should be used to ascertain what the statute actually meant, or what the legislature intended. I am rather considering whether, where our inquiry into meaning is inconclusive, legislative history should be used to make frankly probabilistic estimates about which statutory interpretations are most likely to reflect enactable political preferences.

My answer is that it should. Legislative history may not alter statutory meaning under certain theories, which stress that what the legislature enacts is the statutory text, not the legislative history. But legislative history certainly helps to estimate the general political preferences that motivated the enacting legislative polity. And those estimates of political preferences are all we have, where statutory meaning and current preferences are unclear, to determine which interpretation will maximize expected political satisfaction.

The enacting legislative polity itself would want a default rule whereby courts examine legislative history to resolve such unclear statutory meaning, because such an examination would increase the extent to which its political preferences are satisfied by statutory interpretation. We can test this proposition by inquiring about what legislatures have actually provided in the codes of construction they have adopted about how to interpret their statutes.

It has long been the actual practice of most judges to inquire into legislative history. If this common practice increased political dissatisfaction, then one would expect legislatures to try to outlaw it when they enact codes of statutory construction. In fact, although Congress and all state legislatures have enacted a code of construction, none has outlawed reliance on legislative history.

To the contrary, the ten state legislatures to enact statutes that explicitly consider the issue all expressly authorize courts to look at legislative history.[1] Further, thirty other state legislatures have effectively done the same by directing judges to consider the legislative "intent," "object," or "purpose."[2] Given that ascertaining legislative intents, objects, and purposes has, under prevailing methods, long involved judicial inquiry into legislative history, these statutes seem to authorize such inquiry implicitly.

All told, then, forty of the fifty state legislatures have enacted statutes that explicitly or implicitly authorize judicial inquiry into legislative history and intent. Coupled with the fact that no legislature has enacted a statute directing courts to generally ignore legislative history, this helps confirm the conclusion that it maximizes political satisfaction to adopt the general default rule that, where the statutory meaning is unclear, courts should examine legislative history in order to estimate the enacting legislature's preferences.

It might justifiably be doubted that any theory could explain the pattern of uses of legislative history by the courts, which often seems highly inconsistent from case to case. But the distinction between ascertaining meaning and default rules may explain some of the seeming inconsistency. A judge might ignore legislative history in one case, because she considers it irrelevant to understanding a statutory meaning that can independently be established. The same judge might then use legislative history in the next case, because meaning is unclear and the history helps in estimating enactable preferences. It can thus be entirely consistent for a judge to reject legislative history in some cases but not others.

Other judges may have no general aversion to using legislative history to figure out statutory meaning. However, in one case a judge might decline to look at post-enactment legislative history, because he considers that irrelevant to statutory meaning. The same judge might then consistently consider such post-enactment legislative history in the next case, because statutory meaning is unclear and he finds the post-enactment history relevant to estimating enactable preferences. Post-enactment legislative history can either (1) help ascertain what current enactable preferences to infer from recent legislative action, or (2) be sufficiently close in time to the original enactment to help estimate the preferences of the enacting legislative polity. Thus, it can be consistent for judges to sometimes use post-enactment legislative history and other times reject its use.

The phrase "legislative history" is sometimes read too literally to include only statements or actions by legislators. But in a system like that of the United States, which gives executives the power to veto legislation, one must consider executive views because they strongly influence which preferences are actually enactable. Default rule analysis also suggests that, where justified by unclear statutory meaning, inquiry into likely enactable preferences should be broader than legislative or executive deliberations about the particular ambiguity at issue. The inquiry should include any legislative history that helps estimate the general enactable preferences of the legislative polity, whether or not that legislative history involves specific answers to the specific question of meaning.

The inquiry should also include consideration of other provisions enacted in the same statute, from which enactable preferences might be inferred, as judges generally do under the rubric of considering "statutory purpose." Indeed, because such statutory text was enacted at the same time, it provides the best body of evidence for inferring which political preferences were actually enactable. The inquiry should also—and in actual legal practice does—even include general information about the events that provoked the enactment, or about which political forces were most influential during the particular historical period.[3]

A recent case shows that even highly textualist justices look at the latter sort of evidence, when it bears on enactable preferences. That case concerned the Solomon Amendment, which denied federal funding to universities that did not give military recruiters "access to students . . . that is at least equal . . . to the access . . . provided to any other employer."[4] Various law professors made the clever argument that law schools did not deny equal access when they barred military recruiters, because those schools also barred any other employer who discriminated against homosexuals. Thus, the law schools treated the military like any other employer, barring both if they discriminated and neither if they did not. The Court rejected this reading, interpreting the statute to require that military recruiters get not just equal treatment but most-favored-employer treatment: access as good as the best access provided to any employer, including a nondiscriminatory one. The text, however, hardly dictated the Court's reading; standing alone, it seemed, if anything, to cut in favor of the law professors. What really drove the Court's reading was that this text had been enacted to override a prior district court opinion, which had interpreted an earlier version of the statute to require law schools to give military recruiters an equal right to enter the campus, but not equal access once they were there. This indicated that enactable preferences clearly favored giving the military a broader right of access than the district court did, not the even lower right of access that the law professors' reading provided. The real issue was thus whether those enactable preferences were constitutional, which the Court went on to address.

The implications are even broader: the inquiry should include legislative history regarding entirely different statutes. Such debates about other statutes can provide information bearing on what sorts of preferences were then enactable, which can be relevant to determining how the same legislative polity would have wanted to resolve ambiguity in the statute at issue. Even more revealing would be the pattern of statutes actually enacted before or after the statute in question, which indicates the political preferences that could actually command legislative action. Legislative history about widespread political forces, and about actual legislative action on other provisions or statutes, is in fact likely to be a more accurate indicator of enactable preferences than other forms of legislative history, such as statements by individual legislators or committees. Again, this broader set of materials is often used in actual statutory interpretation.[5]

The analysis here also provides an alternative basis for the statutory canon that, where statutory meaning and legislative preferences are uncertain, statutes should be interpreted to be consistent with other enactments on the same subject.[6] Once again, this canon is popular with legislatures. Every legislature to enact a code of construction on the issue has agreed that its statutes should be interpreted to be consistent with other statutes on the same subject, whether those other statutes were enacted before or after the statute in question.[7]

Redescribing many uses of legislative history as a means of making probabilistic estimates of enactable preferences, rather than as a means of ascertaining statutory meaning or legislative intent, helps put to rest three objections that are commonly made to the use of legislative history. Addressing those objections, in turn, helps to determine how best to estimate enactable preferences.

Objection 1: There Is No Legislative Intent

Max Radin long ago argued that it made no sense to speak of a common legislative intent or purpose, because legislative action was the product of combined action by multiple actors, each with different motives. More recently, scholars have argued that legislative preferences often cycle, so that one cannot accurately speak of what a legislature intended or would have wanted. Rather, legislative desires are often intransitive, which means that what a legislature chooses may depend solely on how its agenda is structured.[8]

These may well be valid objections to a theory that interpreters can determine with certainty one common legislative intent or purpose, which would establish a fixed statutory meaning. Radin himself assumed the need for great certainty, demanding evidence that "several hundred [legislators] each will have exactly the same determinate situations in mind" and that "the litigated issue, will not only be within the minds of all these [legislators], but will be certain to be selected by all of them."[9] But statutory default rules need not depend on any such proposition. Instead, the only proposition I will be relying on is that interpreters can make some probabilistic assessment of relative enactability, for the various interpretive options that are plausible readings of the statutory language.

Suppose, for example, a court concludes that there are two plausible interpretations, and that the relative probabilities that the legislature would have enacted the interpretations (given a choice between the two) are 60% for the first and 40% for the second. The court need not be under any illusion that the first interpretation was in the minds of all the enacting legislators, was dictated by some general purpose that was in their minds, or reflected a common legislative intent or purpose in any other sense. The court need merely have estimated that, if the legislature had addressed the issue, the first interpretation is more likely to have been what it would have enacted than the second. Assuming that these probabilistic estimates are more accurate than random guesses, choosing the first interpretation would still minimize the dissatisfaction of enactable preferences. Thus, the enacting legislature would want courts to choose a default rule that tracked judges' best estimate of enactable legislative preferences, even if those estimates do not reflect a common legislative "intent" in any meaningful way.

One might object that the cycling problem means that judges may not be able to meaningfully assess (or even order) the odds of various interpretations being enacted, because the legislature would cycle among them. But this objection overstates the cycling problem. True, Kenneth Arrow mathematically proved that it was impossible to define a method of aggregating preferences that both satisfied certain rationality principles and *guaranteed* it would always avoid cycling. However, this proof does not mean that cycling always occurs. Indeed, on plausible assumptions, the odds that majority preferences will not cycle on any given policy choice are 94–99%. If voting behavior is probabilistic rather than known with certainty, then collective choice theory itself shows that majority voting is even more likely to avoid cycling problems. Further, a great body of theoretical work has shown how, even when majority preferences are cyclical, a political equilibrium is commonly produced by legislative structures. Those structures include the need to get committee approval, consent from multiple legislative houses, and either executive approval or a legislative supermajority to override an executive veto. Finally, the empirical literature has proven that, as theory and common observation suggest, legislative cycling is not actually common.[10]

True, the legislative structures that avoid cycling may sometimes mean that the legislative results depend on how the agenda is ordered, but courts can take that into account. In particular, the cycling literature indicates that what the legislature enacts can turn heavily on the political preferences of whichever elected officials have agenda-setting power, such as committee chairs, legislative sponsors, and legislative leaders.[11] The political preferences of these agenda setters are thus very likely to influence where enactable preferences lie. Even without any cycling issues, committee reports offer strong evidence about enactable preferences, especially in any legislative system that effectively requires committee consent to enact legislation within that committee's jurisdiction. The fact that such a gatekeeping committee rejected a particular option is especially telling. It indicates that either the committee does not prefer that option or it has determined that it must signal opposition to that option to procure enactment. Either way, the rejected option would not reflect enactable preferences if the committee had an effective veto on new legislation. Consistent with the above analysis, interpreting courts treat committee reports and sponsor statements as especially persuasive legislative history.[12]

More generally, influential modelers like McNollgast have concluded that, when one takes into account the actual existence of agenda and veto powers, one can arrive at determinate conclusions about whose political preferences determined what was enactable. In their model, they assume that legislation requires the consent of multiple actors (committees, house majorities, the president) who have political preferences that lie in a policy spectrum on one side of the status quo.[13] For any legislation that occurs, the preferences of the actor who can last propose a law (which the others can only accept or veto) will govern, *if* those preferences are closer to the status quo than the veto point of any other actor. If not, the political preferences that govern will be those of the actor with the veto point closest to the status quo.[14] The legislative result thus depends only on where each actor's political preferences lie in relation to the status quo, and on which actor can make the last offer under legislative procedures. For example, if the legislative procedure does not allow amendments, then the committee is the last offeror and has more influence. If the legislative procedure does allow amendments, then the house majority (perhaps represented by its majority leader or caucus) is the last offeror.

There are problems with this model. In particular, it effectively assumes that the last offeror can grab all the joint gains from agreement for itself. Thus, in this model, Congress can get the president to sign a statute only marginally better than one he would regard as worse than the status quo. It seems more reasonable to assume that a president would probably veto such a statute, not only in order to get a better deal on that particular statute but also to prevent Congress from persisting in such one-sided deals on future statutes. More generally, given that all the legislative participants are repeat players, they are likely to veto such one-sided deals, in order to induce offers that give them a larger share of the joint gains in the future. Thus, the McNollgast model seems to overstate the certainty with which courts could determine whose political preferences were enactable. But, coupled with some common sense about bargaining dynamics, it does provide helpful guidance for at least making estimates about enactable preferences.

One might still object that this approach allows the result to be distorted by the veto or agenda-setting power of certain legislators, who are not representative of the entire legislature. But under an approach that maximizes the satisfaction of enactable preferences, as explained in Chapter 2, the court's role is not to determine what the legislative polity would have enacted if it had a different legislative process than it actually has. That legislative process, whatever its flaws, is apparently desirable enough to justify compelled obedience to enactments whose meanings are clear. Statutory default rules just aim, where the legislative polity left unclear instructions, to minimize the dissatisfaction of whatever preferences are enactable under the regime that actually exists.

Further, the very literature that suggests great agenda-setting power over legislative decisions also indicates that some agenda-setting is necessary to avoid legislative cycling. It thus hardly makes sense to ask what the legislature would have done without anyone setting the agenda. That question has no answer. Nor can one realistically speak of the legislative process being "distorted" by agenda-setting power when it is inevitable that any process would necessarily have to have someone set the agenda.

Others have objected to inquiries into legislative purpose on the grounds that statutes may reflect a bargain or trade-off, or may choose a rule over a standard. Either of those statutory choices could be upset by using generalizations about statutory purposes to extend the statute beyond the limits of the statutory bargain, or to convert a statutory rule into a judicial standard.[15] These are valid objections to loose-minded purposivism, but not to examining legislative history or estimating legislative preferences. To the contrary, examining legislative history will often reveal the limits of the bargain, or a preference for a rule, either of which are proper bases for estimating legislative preferences. However, there is no reason to assume that legislatures *always* prefer the most narrow bargain or most bright-line rule.

In short, an enactor preferences default rule calls for estimating the probabilities of enactable preferences, not for claiming a common legislative intent or unrestricted purpose that would have commanded consent regardless of the actual legislative procedure used or trade-offs made. Although these estimates may sometimes be uncertain, as long as they are more accurate than random guesses they should improve the satisfaction of enactable preferences.

To be sure, judges may often be unable to reliably estimate the preferences of the enacting polity. But that does not mean that the default rule approach should be abandoned. Rather, when courts cannot make reliable estimations of either current nor enactor preferences, then they should (as Part III shows) employ a preference-eliciting default rule to obtain an accurate answer to the question about where enactable preferences lie. And when that approach is also unavailable, they should (as Part IV discusses) apply a supplemental default rule that is based on deference to political subunits or judicially developed views.

The same rebuttal applies, only more broadly, for those who have a more thoroughgoing skepticism about any judicial ability to estimate enactable preferences. Judge Easterbrook, for example, has written that the effects of agenda manipulation and logrolling on legislative outcomes are so extensive that "judicial predictions of how the legislature would have decided issues it did not in fact decide are bound to be little more than wild guesses."[16] This strikes me as somewhat extreme, in part because the interpreting judge need not guess what precisely the legislature would have done, but need only select which among some limited set of interpretive options the legislature is more likely to have chosen. But even if one shared Easterbrook's bleak assessment, it would not mean that default rules to maximize political satisfaction have no place. It would merely mean that one should favor more extensive application of current-preferences, preference-eliciting, or supplemental default rules.

Objection 2: Legislative History Is Inaccurate

Another argument against using legislative history is that, even if a coherent legislative intent existed, the legislative history would not accurately reveal it. Commentators from Max Radin to Justice Scalia have argued that statements by legislators or legislative committees offer a very inaccurate picture of legislative intent.[17] They stress that legislators or committees may make statements strategically, to lull opponents or mislead interpreters, even if the speakers do not believe their own statements. Further, even if the legislative statements accurately reflect the speakers' own preferences, we cannot assume that other legislators read those statements or shared those preferences.

Others have disputed this claim of great inaccuracy in legislative statements, or (perhaps more to the point) denied that it is less accurate than the alternative methods of resolving statutory ambiguities.[18] They note, for example, that studies indicate legislators are more likely to read committee reports than statutory text. Moreover, the alternative to relying on legislative history to resolve textual ambiguities is relying on dictionaries, treatises, and case law—and legislators are even less likely to have read those. Some scholars also argue that committee chairs and floor managers act as agents for the legislative majority, and are subject to removal or reputational sanctions if they are inaccurate.

I do not propose to resolve this longstanding debate here. Rather, I wish to stress how these problems can be minimized if the question is, instead, whether to use a general default rule of inquiring into all forms of legislative history that bear on enactable preferences. The essential problems with relying on statements by legislators and committees are that they may either be insincere or fail to reflect the views of other legislative participants. But an enactor preferences default rule would, as noted, generally focus on evidence that is objectively verifiable and harder to fake or hide. It would focus on the inferences that can be drawn from other provisions in the same statute, other actual legislative enactments, or widespread political clout. If legislator and committee statements are unreliable, that would not at all contradict a default rule of estimating enactable preferences, but would instead counsel for limiting such a default rule to using the more reliable sources.

As for statements by legislators and committees, a default rule approach could help in two ways. First, courts could adopt default rules about which forms of legislative statements to rely on, and how much reliance to give them, that are more firmly linked to determining which political views are actually enactable. For example, legislative statements provided by those who opposed a bill (and were thus not part of the coalition necessary for enactment) cannot determine which political preferences were actually enactable. Likewise, while sponsor and committee statements are invaluable when accepted by other legislators, they are likely to be at the extreme end of enthusiasm for the statute. They thus should not be regarded as controlling when rejected by the median legislators, whose agreement was necessary for enactment.

Second, to deal with the residual uncertainty created by concerns about the possible inaccuracy of any legislative statements that make it through these screening rules, let us divide the issue into two possible cases: (1) the case where the legislative statements accurately reflect enactable preferences, and (2) the case where they do not.

If the legislative statements accurately reflect enactable preferences, then there is plainly a strong preference-estimating argument for courts relying on legislative statements. Accurate evidence about enactable preferences should increase the extent to which judicial preferences accurately ascertain those preferences. (I defer until Chapter 18 the argument that judges might inaccurately use even accurate legislative history, made most powerfully by Adrian Vermeule, because it raises more general questions about whether judges will misapply any complex method of interpretation.) The enacting legislative polity would thus want courts to use such accurate legislative statements, as actual legislatures have indicated in their codes of construction.

If the legislative statements inaccurately reflect enactable preferences, then there is a strong preference-*eliciting* argument for relying on them in statutory interpretation. Knowing that their statements will guide interpretation, legislators will be encouraged to make more accurate statements about their own preferences. Or they will accurately state what they are willing to accept on the particular issue to procure an enactment they otherwise favor; such statements may not reflect their own personal preferences on the particular issue, but do reflect the enactable preferences we seek to find. Having judges use legislative statements also encourages other legislators to contradict a legislator who makes an assertion about the legislature's political preferences that does not match their own. Those who do not voice such objections will suffer the penalty of having those adverse statements guide interpretation.

Thus, a default rule of relying on legislative history will encourage both sides to state their disagreement with whatever their colleagues are saying, so that any interpretive problem is out in the open. This not only will make the final set of legislative statements a more accurate reflection of overall enactable preferences, but also will reduce inaccuracy by alerting the legislature about issues it may want to resolve explicitly. Thus, even if many legislative statements are inaccurate, the legislative polity should generally prefer a default rule of relying on them, because such a rule will produce an increase in the satisfaction of its political preferences overall.

A default rule of examining legislative history also usefully elicits legislative-wide reactions to improve the accuracy of its legislative history. Suppose the current forms of legislative history that the legislature generates are inaccurate. Then, a default rule of relying on such legislative history will increase the legislature's political dissatisfaction with statutory interpretations. This will give a legislature incentives to take steps to improve the accuracy of its legislative history. For example, it might publish committee markups, identify the bill sponsor on the record, state whether certain articulated views represent a consensus among the enacting coalition, and require that committee members sign the committee reports to make sure they reflect the full committee's views.[19] Judges could move that process along by, for example, recognizing that committee reports that are signed only by the chair may not signal majority support even at the committee level, and thus are far less determinative of what is enactable.

The above analysis also suggests limits on the reliance on legislative history. Some legislative statements might not be disseminated widely enough to alert others to respond, or might come too late in the legislative process to allow time for contradiction. This is generally not a problem for the sort of committee reports and sponsor statements that are normally treated as most persuasive by courts. But it is a serious problem for statements made in final House-Senate conference reports about statutes, which are then enacted with little or no opportunity for debate. Even worse problems are presented by reports or statements in one legislative chamber that are delivered too late to be considered by the other chamber, or by statements inserted in the *Congressional Record* that were never actually uttered in Congress.

A willingness to refer to legislative history need not dictate a blind willingness to accept anything that can go under that label. Instead, an interpreter should properly be skeptical of any legislative statements that were offered under circumstances that did not permit others to contradict them. This is clearest if those last-minute statements are likely inaccurate. But even if they are likely to be accurate, courts might reasonably ignore them, effectively using a form of preference-eliciting default rule that encourages legislators either to make such statements earlier in the process (and thus allow more time for contradiction) or to put the point into explicit statutory language. Such a default rule would likely produce both more preference satisfaction and better deliberation. Consistent with the above, courts often reject legislative history that is placed on the congressional record but that other legislators did not have an opportunity to correct before enactment.[20]

This provides us with a framework for assessing the current controversy about presidential signing statements. Although George W. Bush's particular use of them has created controversy, in fact presidential signing statements have repeatedly been used by prior presidents of both parties.[21] Most of the current controversy has been about President Bush issuing signing statements that declare that he will not enforce particular provisions, no matter how clear their language, because he views them as unconstitutional incursions on presidential authority. Those statements really raise questions of constitutional interpretation, rather than statutory interpretation. They thus should not bind courts, who remain the final arbiter on questions of constitutional interpretation, just as legislative history stating Congress's views about constitutional validity does not bind the courts. Other presidential signing statements take the related tack of narrowly interpreting statutory text to avoid alleged constitutional doubts. These raise the issue, considered in Chapter 14, of the extent to which that canon should govern at all. But whatever the answer to that question, such signing statements should not bind courts, who must decide whether the alleged constitutional doubts really exist. Although not binding on courts, the above sort of signing statements do serve an important function: they indicate how the president plans to enforce the statute in the meantime, pending a judicial decision on whether the statute is constitutionally invalid or doubtful.

What is of present interest are presidential signing statements that interpret the statutory text on nonconstitutional grounds. Common slogans like "legislative intent" or "legislative preferences" sometimes mislead commentators into thinking that court consideration of such issues should exclude all presidential statements, because the president is not part of the legislature.[22] This view is misguided. The president is a vital part of the legislative process because his veto power can strongly influence what is actually enactable. There is thus no reason to categorically exclude presidential statements regarding the preferences or interpretations that led him to approve a bill, rather than veto it. Such an exclusion would be no more justifiable than excluding the views of thirty-four senators (the number necessary to sustain a veto) when they state the preferences or interpretations that led them to vote for a bill, rather than against it. Nor is there any persuasive reason to insist that the president must veto all unclear bills, rather than express his preferences or interpretations regarding them. Such an insistence would be no more justifiable than saying each legislator must vote against any unclear bill, rather than express her own preference or interpretation in legislative history.

What makes presidential signing statements problematic is not that the president is trying to influence statutory interpretation, but the *timing* of these statements. Because they are "signing" statements, they are necessarily made after the bill has already passed Congress, when it is too late for legislators to rebut any interpretation that does not reflect enactable views. The point is thus not that presidential statements should be treated differently from legislative statements, but rather than they should be treated the *same:* excluding both when they come too late for rebuttal. Thus, the doctrine excluding untimely legislative statements should be extended to presidential signing statements based on the latter's timing, not on their inherent illegitimacy or irrelevance. Such an exclusion would not make presidential signing statements irrelevant. They would remain important clarifications about how the president intends to enforce the statute pending any judicial interpretation. But they would be excluded from influencing the ultimate interpretation of the statute.

Nor would excluding presidential signing statements from consideration in statutory interpretation amount to a categorical exclusion of all presidential statements of interpretation. Rather, it would amount to a preference-eliciting default rule, requiring a president who wants to influence statutory interpretation with his statements to put those statements on the record while the bill is still pending in Congress, and while others have an opportunity to offer contrary views. True, the president does not actually sit in the legislature. But the president can always have his legislative allies put his interpretive views on the *Congressional Record*. If the president does not have enough legislative support to do even that, then he does not have the one-third support he needs to sustain a veto, which would make his views irrelevant to determining what preferences are enactable.

The available caselaw, while scant, is consistent with the above analysis. Courts generally accord no or little weight to presidential signing statements when interpreting statutes.[23] Most recently, the Supreme Court in *Hamdan,* without discussion, excluded a presidential signing statement from its analysis of legislative history, notwithstanding the fact that this omission was pointed out by a dissent.[24] Although one appellate court has relied on a presidential signing statement to interpret a statute, it indicated it was generally doubtful about the relevance of such statements, but was willing to rely on the statement in that case because the president had articulated the same views during the process of negotiating the legislation.[25] This fits the above analysis of when we should, and should not, apply a preference-eliciting default rule to the reliance on presidential signing statements.

A different approach would be appropriate when the presidential signing statement interprets text that Congress inserted at the last moment, perhaps in the conference committee, without allowing adequate opportunity for contrary interpretive views to be offered. In such a case, a preference-eliciting default rule of ignoring presidential signing statements when interpreting the statute would have no benefit, because the president could not have articulated his views any earlier. The prospect of unrebutted presidential interpretation should thus probably be a cost Congress must bear, for enacting text without allowing any opportunity for offering contrary interpretive views.

Finally, an important implication follows from the premise that the whole preference-estimating approach of examining legislative history just reflects a default rule. That premise means the legislature can always opt out of this default rule, if the legislature determines that legislative history on balance will decrease the accuracy with which its preferences are estimated. In actual practice, as we have seen, those legislatures that have considered the question have done precisely the opposite. This strongly suggests that legislatures themselves do not believe that judicial reliance on legislative history generally reduces the satisfaction of legislative preferences.

But even if this is a generally sensible default rule, it might not be advisable for particular forms of legislative history or particular statutes. Thus, legislatures can tailor opt-outs for particular statutes, or forms of legislative history, and have done so at least once.[26] The availability of this rarely used fail-safe procedure does not undermine, but rather confirms, the wisdom of the general rule, because it means legislatures can deviate from the general rule when particular circumstances merit it.

Objection 3: Using Legislative History Is Unconstitutional

The objection might remain that, whether or not using legislative history improves political satisfaction, its use is unconstitutional. One standard textualist argument is that courts should not rely on legislative history, because that history has not satisfied the constitutional requirements for enacting statutes, which in the United States requires bicameral adoption by both legislative houses and presentment to the president for signing or veto.[27] Courts should instead rely only on the statutory text that did comply with these constitutional requirements. This claim can be generalized beyond the U.S. Constitution, for its logic posits that, if the relevant constitution specifies a particular procedure for enacting statutes, then that specification bars courts from relying on sources that have not gone through that same procedure. Thus, if valid, this claim would extend to statutory interpretation under all systems of constitutional government.

But the claim is not valid. The main reason is that it is not really possible for any interpreter to rely solely on text. Although we often experience our interpretation of texts as not requiring any resort to extrinsic evidence, the truth is that it always does. No interpretation of words can rely solely on the squiggles on the page. Even if we reference nothing else, we are relying on what our parents and teachers (or general experience and education) told us about how to decode the meaning of written squiggles. That outside education and experience, which produces our understanding of how to best interpret squiggles and words, never satisfied bicameralism and presentment. Indeed, even the purest of textualists rely on more concrete forms of extrinsic aids to interpret words, such as dictionaries, treatises, caselaw, and agency interpretations, and none of those have satisfied bicameralism and presentment either.[28] It thus seems plain that the bicameralism and presentment clauses cannot, by themselves, exclude reliance on all outside information that (because it was not part of the enacted text) never satisfied bicameralism and presentment.

Moreover, for a textualist argument, this one has surprisingly little support in the constitutional text. In the U.S. Constitution at least, the bicameralism and presentment clauses do not discuss how statutes shall be interpreted. The only constitutional clause that comes close to doing so is Article III, which simply states that courts have the "judicial Power," and tells us nothing about how judges are supposed to conduct statutory interpretation. If we take a consistent textualist approach, we cannot examine the legislative history of the U.S. Constitution itself to resolve its own textual ambiguity, because the constitutional history never went through the ratification process and is not part of the constitutional text. If we do examine the legislative history of the Constitution, then we are instead logically conceding that texts should be interpreted according to legislative history that did not satisfy the process for becoming text, which is contrary to the very point this textualist argument tries to establish.

Even if we put aside this problem with the position's internal logic, the legislative history of the U.S. Constitution does not support prohibiting the use of nontextualist sources in statutory interpretation. To the contrary, many have cited evidence that the original understanding of "judicial Power" included various English equitable doctrines, which gave judges discretion to modify statutory terms to better serve the statutory purpose.[29] This notion was part of the English law background relevant to the framers' understanding of what "the judicial Power" meant, was expressly cited in the ratification debates, and was applied by American state and federal courts shortly after ratification.

Professor Manning skillfully argues (from a combination of structure and history) that the U.S. Constitution changed this English doctrine.[30] But we need not take sides in this dispute, for even Manning does not claim that the Constitution prohibits judicial resort to nontextual sources when the text by itself is unclear. Rather, Manning argues only that the Constitution requires courts to be faithful interpretive agents. This conclusion is fully consistent with my claim, because I show how such a honest agent view leads to the default rules in this book. Indeed, if accepted, Manning's conclusion makes this book's default rules constitutionally compulsory.

Suppose one instead disagrees with Manning's conclusion that the Constitution rejects these doctrines of equitable interpretation. That still would not justify rejecting statutory default rules that maximize political satisfaction. These equitable doctrines did not purport to authorize courts to interpret statutes in whatever way judges found best. Rather, they directed courts "to suppose that the law-maker is present, and that you have asked him the question you want to know touching the equity, then you must give yourself such an answer as you imagine he would have done, if he had been present."[31] This approach is precisely what a preference-estimating default rule requires. Nor would it matter if the U.S. Constitution incorporated equitable doctrines that did give courts a common law power to interpret statutes in whatever way the judge finds best. It would remain the case that the courts should choose to exercise that power to resolve statutory ambiguities in ways that maximize political satisfaction.

The more serious question with extrinsic evidence is not whether to rely on it, but what *types* of extrinsic evidence we should use. Here we confront a more clever argument against the use of legislative history, which was offered by Justice Scalia and well developed by Professor Manning. They point out that legislative committees are agencies controlled by Congress. Thus, they argue, relying on committee statements as authoritative interpretations is an unlawful *self*-delegation of administrative powers to an agency controlled by Congress, which violates constitutional separation of powers principles.[32]

Even if this constitutional theory were valid, it is consistent with the approach I am here advocating. Professor Manning himself concedes that this anti-self-delegation principle does not bar courts from examining legislative history that takes the form of other actual legislative acts or failures to act—like the adoption or rejection of amendments, or the enactment of, or failure to enact other statutes.[33] Nor does it provide any bar to relying on other provisions in the same statute, general political forces, or agency interpretations. As for statements by legislative committees and sponsors, Manning claims only that it would violate the self-delegation ban for courts to treat such statements as "authoritative."[34] This is consistent with an enactor preferences default rule, which treats legislative statements as merely one piece of evidence that is relevant for inferring which political preferences were enactable. Indeed, under my approach, a major advantage that committee and sponsor statements have, compared to other sources of extrinsic evidence (like dictionaries, treatises, and case law), is that they are more likely to alert the other legislators necessary for the enactment, who can then object when those statements do not accurately reflect their views. This opportunity for objection can be meaningful only if the committee or sponsor statements are *not* treated as irrebuttable. Thus, my approach is fully consistent with Professor Manning's conclusion that such legislative statements should not be given authoritative weight.

The truth is that judges do not rely on committee and sponsor statements because they have any inherent authority. Judges rely on them only because (and to the extent that) other legislators rely on them to explain the import of the bills on which they are voting. Ignoring committee and sponsors' statements would be unfortunate because, especially when other legislators acquiesce in them, they constitute the best evidence of what political preferences were actually enactable.

Professor Manning himself ultimately argues that judicial interpretations that do not use legislative history are desirable precisely because they are more likely to deviate from legislative preferences, which thus provide a structural incentive for Congress to clarify more in the statutory text.[35] This argument implicitly concedes that legislative history does help accurately estimate legislative preferences, but invokes a preference-eliciting argument for thwarting legislative preferences to provoke legislative clarification. Although Part III shows that a preference-eliciting default rule is sometimes desirable, the conditions when this is true are limited. When those conditions do not hold, imposing a preference-eliciting default rule systematically increases political dissatisfaction. Moreover, without those limiting conditions, the principle of judicial encouragement of legislative clarification through statutory text lacks any logical stopping point. Rather, it would generally require that courts adopt the worst interpretations they can imagine, because an undesirable interpretation is always more likely to elicit clarifying text than a more desirable interpretation.

Even in terms of preventing self-delegation, Manning's argument has the internal problem that legislatures usually also delegate the drafting of statutory text to committees and sponsors. Indeed, other legislators review the text even less closely than they review the committee reports and sponsor statements. Thus, the logic of his position indicates that it would also violate his principle of self-delegation for courts to treat the text as authoritative. Professor Manning would doubtless reject such a crazy conclusion, but it suggests an underlying root problem with his theory. Delegation is an inherently forward-looking concept. It thus cannot be implicated by reliance on preceding legislative history or text. Such reliance instead involves at most ratification, or incorporation by reference, of those past statements or text, which is clearly legitimate.[36]

The Canons on Avoiding Invalidity and Favoring Severability

As the above suggests, inquiries into enactor preferences are normally highly tailored, requiring an inquiry into the preferences of those particular enactors, rather than of enactors in general. Statutory default rules are thus typically about how to conduct that inquiry, rather than about particular results. But there are a few enactor preference default rules that generally seem to dictate similar results for all legislation.

Consider the canon against interpreting statutes to create constitutional invalidity. Any enacting legislative polity would normally want such a default rule. The reason is that, in order to maximize the satisfaction of the political preferences that led to the enactment, it usually would want to preserve as much of its statute as possible. Likewise, it would generally want a canon of severability, in order to preserve as much of any partially invalidated statute as can be preserved, without undermining the preferences that produced enactment. Consistent with this analysis, all fifty state legislatures have provisions providing for the severability of invalidated provisions, and every legislature that has enacted a statute on the subject has directed courts to construe statutes to avoid constitutional invalidity. The Supreme Court has also adopted both canons for the interpretation of federal statutes. The legislature can always opt out of these canons, by saying that it wants a statute to have effect only if it is given a broad interpretation, or only if all its provisions are valid. Absent such an opt-out, however, these canons generally provide the default rule.[37]

Further, these canons are just presumptions, and can be overturned where there is evidence that they would not advance the preferences of the particular enactors. This was highlighted in the recent decision in *Booker*. The Court there held that the federal sentencing guidelines, which required that judges impose certain sentences given certain judicial findings, violated the Sixth Amendment because those findings were not made by a jury. The Court stressed that the canon on severability dictates neither simply retaining any portions of the statute that are not invalidated, nor retaining those portions that would be grammatically coherent.[38] Instead, it requires an inquiry into what, given the invalidation of some provisions, the legislature would have wanted to retain. Here, there were two choices: (1) changing the provisions which specified that the findings would be made by judges rather than by jurors, or (2) invalidating the provisions that gave those findings a mandatory effect on sentencing. The Court concluded that Congress would have preferred invalidation of the entire statute to the first option, and would prefer the second option to total invalidation, based on a complex inquiry into the policy preferences that animated the guidelines. Thus, the canons on invalidity and severability remain firmly subordinate to the overarching goal of satisfying legislative preferences.

CHAPTER 7

Moderation, Unforseen Circumstances, and a Theory of Meaning

The Rule of Moderation

Where a statute has only two plausible interpretations, applying a preference-estimating approach is relatively easy: courts should choose whichever interpretation has the higher probability of matching enactable preferences. Its relative probability of being enactable will, by definition, exceed 50%.[1] But what should courts do when a statute has more than two plausible interpretations, no single one of which is more than 50% likely to match enactable preferences? Suppose, for example, the court's best estimate of the relative odds of what would have been enactable is 40% for interpretive option 1, 30% for option 2, and 30% for option 3.[2] Should the court just go with option 1, on the ground that its odds of matching enactable preferences are higher than the others'?

A similar theoretical problem has been raised, but never satisfactorily resolved, for contract or corporate default rules.[3] But under the general framework of this book, the abstract answer seems clear. The goal of an honest interpretive agent is to maximize the extent to which interpretations satisfy the preferences of the text-making authority. An interpreting court should accordingly choose the interpretive option that minimizes the expected preference dissatisfaction of the parties that created the legally binding text. This is true whether that text is a contract, charter, or statute. In the case of statutory interpretation, the court should choose the option that minimizes the expected dissatisfaction of enactable preferences.

Perhaps surprisingly, this is *not* the same as choosing the option that has the highest odds of accurately reflecting enactable preferences. A diagram might help. Suppose unclear statutory language leaves us with three plausible interpretive options that can be plotted on a single line, where the distance between options indicates the extent to which the preferences of a enacting government desiring one option would be dissatisfied with the other option. Let's call the options Narrow, Moderate, and Broad, with each separated by 10 units of preference dissatisfaction. In other words, if the enacting polity would have preferred the moderate option, it suffers 10 units of dissatisfaction from either the narrow or broad options. If the enacting polity would have preferred one of the extremes, it suffers 10 units from the moderate option and 20 units from the opposite extreme.

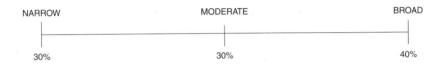

Suppose further that, while a court cannot be sure which option best fits enactable preferences, its best estimate is that the broad option is 40% likely to match enactable preferences, with the other options each 30% likely.[4] Choosing the broad option is more likely to fully satisfy enactable preferences, but overall will produce more expected preference dissatisfaction than the moderate option. If the court chooses the broad option, the expected preference dissatisfaction will be $(.4)(0) + (.3)(20) + (.3)(10) = 9$. But if the court chooses the moderate option, the expected preference dissatisfaction will be only $(.3)(10) + (.3)(0) + (.4)(10) = 7$. The court should thus choose the moderate option, even though it is less likely to match enactable preferences than the broad option.

This proposition can be generalized to any case where a statute has three plausible interpretations, which can each be conceptualized as points along a one-dimensional policy line, so that the further the point is away from the enactors' ideal point, the more dissatisfied they are. As I prove elsewhere, courts can always minimize expected political dissatisfaction by choosing the moderate interpretive option, as long as neither of the extreme options is 50% or more likely to reflect enactable preferences.[5] This analysis is equally applicable to contracts and charters.

For example, suppose the broad option is 49.9% likely to match enactable preferences, and the narrow option is 26.1% likely to do so, leaving the moderate option 24% likely to do so. Then, choosing the moderate option will still minimize the expected dissatisfaction of enactable preferences. This is true even though, in this example, the moderate option is the one least likely to reflect enactable preferences.

I should emphasize that I am not saying that judges, when deciding cases, should try to measure units of expected political dissatisfaction. I am rather using this example to show why, when no one interpretation is more than 50% likely to reflect enactable preferences, adopting the moderate interpretation will naturally lead to less political dissatisfaction, even if a more extreme option is more likely to reflect enactable preferences. The units of dissatisfaction drop out of the analysis and need never be measured by judges.

Relatedly, my claim is not that this default rule of moderation maximizes utility, a goal that is normatively controversial and that may or may not be maximized by the enactment process. My claim is rather that this rule of moderation will maximize the satisfaction of those preferences that are enactable. If it were thought desirable for statutes to maximize utility, then the enactment process should be designed to do so, and then interpretations that tracked enactable preferences would maximize utility. Otherwise, they would not.

The interesting result is that when, among the plausible interpretive options, no one option is more likely than not to be what the legislature would have enacted had it made a choice, a court trying to minimize expected political dissatisfaction should choose a moderate interpretive option, even though extreme options are more likely to match enactable preferences. This proposition goes beyond the point, considered above, that in estimating what political preferences are enactable, the court should focus on the marginal legislators whose agreement was necessary to enact the legislation. That point is true, and the views of that marginal legislator should be followed when a court can determine, with greater than 50% odds, that his preferences would have governed. But suppose that, after going through this thought process, the court determines that no single interpretive option is more than 50% likely to reflect enactable preferences. Then, even if the court predicts that the marginal legislator would be more likely to pick an option that, among the available interpretations, is more extreme, the court should nonetheless choose a more moderate option.

Of course, courts will rarely have these sorts of precise percentages in mind. However, one can employ the same insight in the form of a cautionary axiom. The axiom would simply provide that, where multiple interpretive options seem plausible, courts are justified in favoring moderate options when interpreting what the legislature would have wanted. One often sees just such a tendency in statutory interpretation cases, in part because the need to get a majority of multi-member appellate panels naturally encour-. ages it.

Indeed, this proposition provides one justification for the whole appellate structure of using multi-judge panels. It further explains why courts follow the moderate position when they are fractured, even when it reflects the position that garnered the fewest votes. For example, *Bakke* involved a challenge by a white applicant to a medical school program that reserved 16% of admissions for minorities. Four justices concluded that Title VI permitted affirmative action programs to use racial quotas to remedy minority under-representation. Another four justices concluded that Title VI prohibited any program that excluded a white applicant because of his race. Justice Powell concluded that Title VI barred strict racial quotas, but did not bar affirmative action programs that considered race as a plus factor. Although Justice Powell's position only commanded one of nine votes on the Supreme Court, it was the moderate position on affirmative action, and thus became the interpretation that governed.[6]

The more interpretive options there are, the more judicial panel members one would want to have, because a greater number of members increases the likelihood that the median judicial vote reflects the moderate political view. This provides another justification for why the U.S. Supreme Court, which addresses issues where the legal materials have most divided the lower courts, sits in panels of nine, rather than panels of three like the lower appellate courts. Other nations similarly use more judges the higher the court, and the more ambiguous the legal materials.

Updating for Changed Circumstances

Although an enactor preferences default rule tracks the static political preferences of the enactors, static preferences need not dictate a static default rule. The reason is that the same enactable preferences may dictate a different result when applied to changed factual circumstances.

Consider the following example from corporate law. Even if one assumes a static preference for the most efficient default rule, it is well accepted that the corporate default rules used for closely held corporations often do and should differ from those used for publicly held corporations.[7] But if this is correct, it follows that the proper corporate default rules will often change as the corporation grows from closely held to publicly held. Thus, if one asked which default rule a corporation's original shareholders would have preferred at the time of incorporation, the answer would not simply be the default rule that is best for closely held corporations. Such a static default rule would, when the corporation grows, produce inefficient results, the prospect of which would in turn depress the original share price. Instead, the original shareholders would prefer a default rule that starts out as the rule best suited to closely held corporations, but changes as the corporation grows to the rule best suited to publicly held corporations. Such a changing default rule will maximize the original share price, which in part impounds the likely future price if the corporation goes public.

Take the corporate opportunities doctrine. Few corporate charters define which business opportunities are corporate opportunities, and thus unavailable to corporate fiduciaries. We thus need some default rule. Suppose the following standard analysis is correct. Because fiduciaries in closely held corporations often have outside business interests in the same line of business as the corporation, every business opportunity that lies within a close corporation's line of business should not be considered a corporate opportunity, or else the rule would discourage skilled persons from participating in close corporations. But in a publicly held corporation, whose officers generally work full-time for it, it makes more sense to define everything within its line of business as a corporate opportunity. If this analysis is true, then the appropriate default rule on corporate opportunities changes as the corporation grows from closely held to publicly held. And the original shareholders would prefer a default rule that adjusts over time to reflect this. This appears to be implicitly accepted by corporate law, which does in fact vary the corporate opportunities doctrine for closely held and publicly held corporations.[8]

This is not to say that the courts would be justified in changing an explicit charter provision on corporate opportunities. If the corporate founders wished to opt out of judicially set default rules, by providing an explicit provision, their preference for that explicit term would be thwarted by judicial modification. If the corporate founders prefer default rules that change with changing circumstances, they are free to leave gaps or ambiguities. But where they have enacted an explicit term, it must be given effect until the charter itself is amended. In some applications, giving effect to explicit terms will no doubt turn out to be unwise and undesirable to the corporate founders. By opting out of judicial default rules, however, the founders have indicated that, in their view, the costs of having an inflexible explicit term are lower than the costs of judicial error in filling and updating a default rule. The corporate founders are entitled to trade off the greater flexibility of judicially updated default rules against the greater accuracy from tailoring a fixed rule themselves.

The above sort of rationale for—and limits on—dynamic default rules in corporate law will also often be true for those who enact legislative statutes. Pursuing the enactors' preferences may well call for a default rule that responds to changes in technology, society, the economy, and surrounding legal framework. Courts are then justified, where the statute is unclear, in updating the default rule along with those changed circumstances, because doing so maximizes the political satisfaction of the enacting polity. Enacting legislative polities may always opt out of this dynamic default rule. But unless they opt out, they should be understood to have accepted judicial updating of the default rules that are used to resolve unclear statutory meaning.

Consider, for example, the following question of interpretation, and how the answer to it evolved over time. Norris-LaGuardia Act §4 prohibits federal courts from enjoining strikes arising out of labor disputes. Taft-Hartley Act §301 later gave federal courts jurisdiction to adjudicate actions for breach of collective bargaining agreements. In a case where the collective bargaining agreement itself prohibited strikes (because it favored binding arbitration of any labor dispute), does the Taft-Hartley Act §301 implicitly repeal Norris-LaGuardia Act §4's prohibition on injunctions?

In 1962, the U.S. Supreme Court held that the answer was "no," relying in part on legislative history that indicated the Taft-Hartley Congress had preferred that such injunctive actions "be left to the usual processes of law," namely, state law actions for breach of contract.[9] Thus, the 1962 Court concluded that, although Congress wanted to add a federal court action to the state court claims, this did not mean that Congress also wanted the federal court action to include the sorts of claims for injunctive relief that were available in state court.

In 1976, however, the Supreme Court in *Boys Market* overruled its 1962 decision. It agreed with the 1962 case that the congressional preference underlying the Taft-Hartley Act was to supplement, rather than replace, state court actions.[10] However, unlike in 1962, unions could in 1976 remove state court actions to federal court. Adhering to the statutory precedent in the light of these changed circumstances would thus have the effect of restricting the preexisting state court jurisdiction, which had allowed those courts to enter injunctions requiring compliance with no-strike provisions. That would thwart the enactor's legislative preference. Because of these changed circumstances, the Court concluded that overruling its 1962 interpretation would better reflect the preferences of the enacting Congress.[11] In short, both the 1962 and 1976 interpretations were justified because they satisfied enactor preferences. But the interpretations differed from each other because, given different factual circumstances, different interpretations satisfied that static set of enactor preferences.

This provides a more solid (but more limited) ground for a proposal by many notable scholars that courts should update statutory meaning and even overrule "outdated" statutes to adjust for changed circumstances.[12] Many of these proposals would consider changed political preferences a change in circumstances that justifies a different interpretation. In contrast, I sharply distinguish the argument for allowing updated interpretation when changes in factual circumstances indicate that enactor preferences would favor a new interpretation, which is all this section argues, from the claim that courts should update interpretations when current preferences differ from enactor preferences. The latter claim requires a different and more complicated sort of justification (as Part I discussed) and proves valid only in a more narrow set of circumstances, where official action provides some reliable indication that those new preferences are actually enactable.

In addition, these prior proposals would generally allow changed circumstances to authorize judges to update even a statute whose original meaning was clear. In contrast, my claim is that a dynamic default rule is appropriate only when statutory meaning is unclear enough to require resort to a default rule. If the statute is taken to have a fixed meaning, then the legislative polity that enacted that meaning has effectively opted out of any default rule, including dynamic default rules. The inflexibility costs of adopting such a fixed meaning would surely be significant when factual circumstances change. But it would be entirely rational for an enacting legislative polity to conclude that (for some issues or statutes) such inflexibility costs would be outweighed by the judicial errors that would result if courts were freely permitted to update statutory meanings to adjust for changed circumstances. As honest interpretive agents, courts cannot decline to follow such a legislative opt-out, and thus are not free to deviate from any fixed meaning they find in the statute.

But while bound by the meaning of what was actually enacted, courts need not be bound by inquiries into what the enactors most likely thought the statutory language meant. Asking that question (in cases where meaning is unclear) is likely to produce a meaning restricted to expectations that were constrained by the factual circumstances that existed at the time of enactment. And a meaning fixed by those circumstances will likely thwart the enactors' preferences when circumstances change.

Again, corporate law offers a fruitful analogy. Suppose a news reporter asked a founding shareholder in a closely held corporation what specific fiduciary duties he meant to imply by the provisions creating the corporate office of treasurer. That shareholder would likely provide whatever specifics make the most sense for a closely held corporation, including allowing a freedom to pursue other business opportunities within the same line of business. But if the shareholder has not specified this as a fixed meaning in the charter, he should not be understood to have opted out of the normal default rule that fiduciary duties change as the corporation grows. To do so would thwart his likely interest in having the most efficient duties attach to the office of treasurer, without any indication that he meant that result.

In the field of statutory interpretation, the point is nicely illustrated by the female juror cases. Before women had the right to vote, many state statutes provided that jurors had to be "electors." How should courts have interpreted these statutes in the period that was before equal protection caselaw guaranteed women equal rights in jury service, but after the Nineteenth Amendment gave women the right to vote? Some courts reasoned that the enacting legislature most likely thought "electors" meant "men," because only men could vote at the time of enactment, so that the right interpretation was that only men could serve as jurors.[13] Other courts concluded that "elector" was a generic reference to whoever was eligible to vote, and thus the interpretation should be updated to include women as jurors once they became eligible to vote.[14]

The former courts, in my view, made the mistake of asking what the enactors most likely meant, which produced an answer that reflected expectations constrained by now-obsolete circumstances. There is no reason to think that, if the possibility that women would become eligible to vote had been considered, enactable preferences would have dictated their exclusion from juries. In fact, we can be pretty darn sure that no legislature interested in self-preservation would want to offend the majority of its electorate by deeming them unqualified to serve on juries, and that such a preference would thus not have been enactable had the circumstance been foreseen. In any event, the most reasonable reading is that the enactor preferences were simply to have its jury pool coincide with the persons eligible to vote, rather than to fix the former even though the latter changed over time. Nothing in the use of the terminology "electors" suggested a desire to opt-out of the default rule, which updates unclear statutory meaning to better advance enactor preferences when the factual circumstances have changed.

The above analysis provides my own theory for the proper dividing line between (1) inquiries into statutory meaning and (2) default rule inquiries into enactable preferences. Although the inquiries share similarities, in my analysis the line is crossed when the enacting legislative polity indicates a desire to opt out of any process of judicial gap-filling or updating. Such an indication should be understood to bear on statutory meaning, and not just on preferences. But, like the shareholder in the close corporation or the legislatures in the female juror cases, the enactor may leave no indicia that it meant to opt out of normal default rules. If so, then the relevant evidence should be taken to establish not a fixed meaning, but rather the most likely political preferences, out of which to form a default rule that will operate on changed circumstances.

In short, my preferred approach would build a theory of meaning out of indications the legislature wanted to opt-out of default rules, rather than try to define the scope of default rules based on an independent theory of when meaning was absent. The next section offers one way to ascertain when the legislature signaled a desire for such an opt-out. But I hasten to add that the remainder of the analysis in this book stands whether or not one accepts this definition of how best to ascertain statutory meaning. Even if one has an entirely different theory of how best to ascertain statutory meaning, one needs a set of default rules that resolve cases where meaning is unclear, and this book would provide the proper set of default rules.

Uncontemplated Circumstances and the Absurdity Doctrine

The above distinction also helps us address a difficult set of cases, where applying the "literal" meaning of a statute to uncontemplated circumstances would conflict with any plausible understanding of enactable preferences. These are not cases of changed circumstances. The problem is not that a change in general conditions indicates a change in interpretation is necessary to satisfy static preferences. Rather, the problem here is that there are certain unusual circumstances—which could have been equally prevalent at the time of enactment—that the legislature nonetheless did not contemplate when it adopted statutory language that, if read literally, would thwart its clear preferences in those circumstances.

In such cases, courts often invoke the absurdity doctrine, which provides that statutes should be interpreted to avoid absurd results.[15] Thus, the Supreme Court has stated that, even though the literal meaning of statute was to the contrary: (1) a statute that punished residents who "drew blood in the streets" did not prohibit a surgeon from drawing blood in a medical emergency; (2) a statute that prohibited breaking out of prison did not apply if the prison was on fire; and (3) a statute that prohibited interfering with U.S. mail carriers did not apply when officers arrested a mailman for murder.[16] Further, even strong textualists concede that (1) a statute that unqualifiedly condemns taking another's life should not be read literally when the person taking another's life is a policeman stopping a terrorist or assassin from killing others, and (2) an unqualified statute of limitations should not be read literally if the defendant has fraudulently concealed his wrongdoing.[17]

Textualists defend many of these cases on the theory that the legislature acts with the understanding that there exist background rules of interpretation, like the last two.[18] But this argument cannot explain many of these oddball cases, which involve absurdities of first impression that do not fit within any existing background rule. Nor can any set of background rules hope to capture all the possible absurdities that might arise in the future. Another weakness to this argument is that none of these absurdity rulings rests on any evidence that the enacting legislature actually knew about these background interpretive rules. In any event, this justification just begs the question of which background interpretive rules the courts should choose. Indeed, this doctrinal defense would suggest that courts are free to deviate from literal statutory meaning with *any* interpretive rule they want, as long as courts publicize it sufficiently and make it generally applicable to all statutes.

If we instead understand the absurdity doctrine (and these background rules) as enactor preferences default rules, then we can provide a more persuasive justification and limitation. These doctrines are appropriate default rules only because courts can be confident that, if the enactors did think about these uncontemplated cases, they would prefer to create an exception rather than apply the language literally. Consistent with this understanding, a statutory interpretation is considered "absurd" not only when it violates common sense but also when it conflicts with the statute's purpose.[19] In the former set of absurdity cases, common sense indicates that *any* legislative polity would prefer to exclude the uncontemplated case. Thus, exclusion furthers enactable preferences even though the enactors left no specific indication on the topic. The absurdity is "so monstrous, that all mankind would, without hesitation, unite in rejecting the application."[20] In the latter set of cases, the rejected interpretation instead conflicts with the general statutory purpose that is inferred from the other provisions of the relevant statute. This does not indicate the sort of absurdity that any legislature would reject, but rather a conflict with the clear enactable preferences of the particular enacting legislature, which it would be absurd to attribute to that legislature.

In either set of cases, the justification for rejecting an absurd interpretation is not that such an interpretation would conflict with judicial preferences or some independent policy standard. An "absurd" interpretation should thus not be understood to mean an interpretation that the judge believes reflects a highly unwise policy. It is rather an unusual statutory result that the court is confident either (a) no legislative polity (within the range of plausible political preferences in that jurisdiction) would ever want, or (b) the actual enacting legislative polity would clearly not want, given its other statutory language.

One might object that these cases deviate from the statutory meaning, and thus go beyond use of a default rule. But this is true only if we deem the "literal" meaning to be the same as the statutory meaning, and even textualists agree that the two are not at all the same thing, because much of linguistic meaning comes from context.[21] Typically in these cases, the statute used general language that literally covers all contingencies, but did not specifically advert to the particular contingency at issue, which was sufficiently marginal that it was not likely to be what the legislature was contemplating at the time. If the statutory language *did* advert to the particular contingency, and specified the same result, then it could not be rejected as absurd. For example, suppose a statute said "it is illegal to interfere with U.S. mail carriers, even when officers are trying to arrest them for murder." Then the prohibition would apply, notwithstanding the fact that (without that specific clause) the absurdity doctrine held otherwise. But when a statute simply makes it "illegal to interfere with U.S. mail carriers," we cannot conclude with any confidence that the legislature really meant to bar arresting carriers on murder charges.

A complete specification of meaning would require a statute that identified the statutory result for every possible contingency. But requiring such a comprehensive set of contingency-outcome pairs is unrealistic. Thus, legislatures must proceed by promulgating statutes with general language, whose application to the most common set of contingencies they have presumably contemplated and addressed with statutory language or explicit exceptions. But it would be unrealistic to conclude that whenever a legislature uses such general language without excluding *all* the uncontemplated absurd applications that might literally fall within its scope, the legislature meant to include those applications. The meaning in such cases seems unclear, the product of the unfeasibility of identifying every possible application of general language in advance, and thus requires a default rule for resolution.

One might press this notion even further. For contract interpretation, Professor Shavell has shown that the preferences of contracting parties will be maximized if judges interpret contracts as written only in the rare (perhaps nonexistent) case where the contract has specifically anticipated the precise contingency at issue in all its possible detail.[22] Otherwise, courts should deviate from the text whenever doing so would, given the contingency that did arise, maximize the expected payoff of the subgroup of persons who would write that contractual language. Under this view, one might conclude that statutes likewise should have no fixed meaning that binds judges, other than in the rare (maybe nonexistent) case where the statute has explicitly anticipated the precise contingency at issue in detail. Instead, the words of a statute would generally be taken to indicate only the most likely enactor preferences, and all statutory interpretation would involve only the default rule question of what statutory result would maximize enactable preferences. The statutory text would be constraining only in the sense that it provides the most persuasive evidence of the preferences the enactors most likely had. Default rules would dominate statutory interpretation.

This possible extension of Shavell's theory has a certain rough congruence with the second set of absurdity cases, which allow courts to deviate from any literal statutory meaning that conflicts with the statutory purpose indicated by the rest of the statutory text. This is quite similar to maximizing the expected payoff of the enactors who would write that text. Because it relies solely on text, one could even say such a theory is consistent with textualism. It would just be thoroughly textualist, rather than isolatedly literalist.

However, the conclusion that such an interpretive methodology would maximize the interests of the enactors depends heavily on an implicit assumption: that judges would act as perfectly accurate, honest agents for those enactors. Enactors may not share that assumption. Instead, enactors may reasonably conclude that judicial decisions estimating their preferences are likely to contain many errors, with those errors perhaps being biased by agency costs if courts have any interest in furthering their own ideological views. This can be true even if those estimates are just based on other enacted text. Enactors might further conclude that such judicial errors would likely outweigh any errors that would result from the inflexible application of literal statutory language to the broad range of unspecified contingencies. In such cases, enactors will want to opt-out of an interpretive methodology that permits deviations from their literal meaning whenever a judge thinks another meaning might be more likely to advance enactable preferences.

Any manifestation of such a legislative desire to opt-out of a default rule would itself indicate a fixed statutory meaning, under the theory of meaning I sketched out above. When, though, should we understand legislatures to have indicated a desire for such an opt-out? It would be unrealistic to say that legislatures never intend to opt out unless they specify each and every possible contingency, for such complete specification is unfeasible, and perhaps impossible, depending on how much detail one requires to specify a contingency. Nor would it be sensible to say that legislatures can opt out only by saying magic words, such as "we really want this provision interpreted literally,"[23] for that would require legislatures that wanted an opt out to bear an onerous tax. That tax would be making a costly commitment to unwanted results even in the range of cases the legislature could not reasonably contemplate.

Instead, legislatures should be understood to opt out of a preference-estimating default rule whenever (1) they use precise language, rather than open-ended language like "reasonable" or "unfair" that effectively delegates the process of developing standards to courts or agencies, and (2) the contingency in question was either within the set of contingencies they actually contemplated, or common enough at the time that we can assume it was within their normal range of contemplation when they enacted the statute. Although it would be unrealistic to expect legislatures to specify all such contingencies in their statutes, their use of precise statutory language can be understood as a shorthand that defines the outcome for all contingencies within this reasonably contemplated set. If that outcome conflicted with enactable preferences for any such reasonably contemplated contingency, the legislature presumably would have written an exception to its precise language.

We can add one more sort of situation where the absurdity doctrine makes sense. Sometimes the evidence suggests a scrivener's error in drafting, so that precise statutory language produces a result absurdly contrary to apparent enactor purposes even in the normal range of cases one would contemplate.[24] In *Cernauskas,* for example, a statute giving municipalities the power to alter public streets and alleys included a clause that, read literally, repealed all other Arkansas statutes. Because such a repeal covered all regulated experiences, one could hardly say it did not cover matters within the normal range of contemplation. But the court quite reasonably concluded that the legislature had merely made a drafting error: neglecting to add language limiting the repealer clause to prior statutes that were inconsistent with the new statute.

Under my framework, we should understand cases deemed to constitute scrivener's error as situations where the statutory language does indicate a legislative opt out, but there is reason to doubt the accuracy of that language, and thus reason to doubt the accuracy of the apparent opt out. Absent such an obvious error in drafting, the application of the absurdity doctrine to otherwise clear precise statutory language should be limited to contingencies that were not reasonably contemplated and where a literal meaning would produce a result contrary to likely enactable preferences. (The same sort of limitations should apply to allegedly absurd interpretations of contracts or corporate charters.)

One might still object that, although in theory a canon against absurd interpretations would advance political satisfaction, in practice judges would (even with the above limitations) abuse the discretion conferred by that canon in ways that thwart legislative preferences. But if this were so, one would expect to see legislatures opting out of the default rule specified by the absurdity doctrine. In fact, every legislature within the United States has enacted a code of construction that leaves the well-known canon against absurd interpretations undisturbed. Further, those legislatures that have considered the matter have all expressly adopted the canon against absurd interpretations.[25] No legislature directs courts to follow the plain meaning of a statute even when it leads to absurd results. This evidence tends to confirm the claim that this canon reflects a general default rule that maximizes political satisfaction.

Even if one disagrees with my theory of when statutes have a fixed meaning, the above analysis still matters. Such disagreement would simply limit the analysis to whatever set of statutes one believes have a sufficiently unclear meaning to justify use of default rules. Whatever that set of unclear statutes is, the default rules used to interpret them should try to maximize enactable preferences, and that will entail rejecting statutory interpretations that would be absurd, in the sense of conflicting with any legislature's preferences or with the preferences reflected in the rest of the statute.

PART III

Preference-Eliciting Default Rules

CHAPTER **8**

Eliciting Legislative Preferences

The Conundrum about Canons

Many canons of statutory construction cannot plausibly be justified as best reflecting what the enacting or current legislature would most likely prefer. The rule of lenity, for example, favors criminal defendants, a group that seems to be the favorite target of every political campaign. Other canons, such as the linguistic canons, are paired with counter-canons, both of which cannot reflect general estimates of legislative preferences because they cut in opposite directions.

Why, then, do courts so often employ canons of statutory construction that seem to have nothing to do with likely legislative preferences and often seem inconsistent with each other? The common intuition is that they do so to further judicial preferences or values. This conflicts with ordinary understanding of judicial neutrality, but might seem consistent with the traditional legal position that, where statutory meaning is unclear, judges must exercise their own substantive judgment. It might also seem consistent with the more skeptical assumption in the political science literature (discussed in Chapter 15) that judges choose whichever interpretations come closest to their own ideological viewpoints, or at least so choose among the set of interpretations that would not provoke legislative override.

As detailed in Part I, such a position or assumption sits uneasily in a democracy, or with any conception of the judicial role as being honest interpretive agents. Moreover, this position and assumption run against the reality that many of these canons do not reflect wise policy or sensible values, or are applied too inconsistently to advance any coherent set of judicial preferences or values. The traditional legal position raises the additional problem that many of these canons are supposed to be linguistic aids and tools for ascertaining statutory meaning, making it illegitimate to use them to deviate from legislative preferences. And the political science assumption conflicts with the fact that (as we shall see below) judges often apply canons known to be more likely to provoke legislative overrides, and indeed frequently invite such overrides, which runs contrary to their supposed ideological interest.

The solution lies in understanding that many canons reflect preference-eliciting default rules. These default rules are not designed to choose the interpretations that have the highest odds of embodying enactable preferences. Instead, they are designed to choose the interpretations that are most likely to elicit legislative reactions, which will produce a statutory result that embodies enactable preferences more accurately than any judicial estimate could. That legislative reaction might be ex ante, through more precise legislative drafting to avoid the prospect of the default rule. Or it might be ex post, through subsequent legislative override of the interpretation imposed by the default rule. This preference-eliciting approach can increase political satisfaction, as long as there is no reliable basis for estimating enactable preferences, if choosing one of the possible interpretations is more likely to make it clear just where enactable preferences lie.

The justification for preference-eliciting canons thus need not rest in their correspondence to either likely legislative preferences or sound policy. The justification—and necessary predicate—is rather that the default result is more likely to be corrected by the legislature because it burdens some politically powerful group with ready access to the legislative agenda. Where this is true, and both statutory meaning and enactable preferences are unclear, a preference-eliciting default rule can increase political satisfaction. Even though the preference-eliciting default rule does not itself reflect the most likely estimate of legislative preferences, the statutory results it produces will maximize the accurate measurement of political preferences.[1] The goal remains maximizing political satisfaction, but rather than being confined to considering satisfaction with the immediate interpretations, the goal includes satisfaction with the full array of statutory results, including those elicited by interpretations.

As subsequent chapters will show, this preference-eliciting analysis explains and justifies many common canons of statutory construction better than existing interpretive theories. A theme throughout will be that what is commonly bemoaned as the inconsistent application of statutory canons can often be explained by preference-eliciting analysis. That is, the reason that use of the canons looks inconsistent is often that the baseline for measuring consistency is assumed to be conformance to legislative preferences or to some substantive policy. But once it is recognized that these canons often serve a preference-eliciting function, then the seeming inconsistency often goes away, for the pattern of canon use can frequently be explained by whether or not the conditions for using a preference-eliciting default rule are met. This improved understanding of the reasons underlying these canons, and the justifiable grounds for their seemingly inconsistent application, should render them more determinate, and thus more constraining of judges. But before we get into these canons, we first need a better understanding of preference-eliciting theory.

The General Theory of Preference-Eliciting Canons

A statutory default rule that provokes a legislative reaction can increase expected legislative satisfaction in two basic ways. It can eliminate uncertainty about which of the plausible interpretive options best matches enactable preferences. Or it can elicit a more nuanced or precise statute that satisfies enactable preferences more exactly than any plausible interpretation could. Sometimes it does a bit of both. But one can intellectually separate the two phenomena.

Suppose a statute has two plausible meanings: option A is 60% likely to reflect enactable preferences, and option B is 40% likely to do so. Suppose also that, if option A turned out not to conform to enactable preferences, the odds are 0% that the legislature would correct it. In contrast, if option B did not match enactable preferences, the odds are 100% that the legislature would correct it. If the court chooses option A, then the expected political satisfaction will be 60%, because in the 40% of cases where this interpretation did not match enactable preferences, the legislature would not correct it. However, if the court chooses option B, then the expected political satisfaction will be 100%, because in the 40% of cases where the default rule does turn out to match enactable preferences, the legislature will leave it in place, whereas in the 60% of cases where the default rule does not match enactable preferences, the legislature will replace it with option A. Choosing preference-eliciting option B will thus ultimately increase the expected satisfaction of enactable preferences, even though option B itself is less likely to reflect enactable preferences than A.

Other times the benefit from eliciting a legislative reaction is not eliminating uncertainty about whether the legislature prefers options *A* or *B*, but producing a more nuanced or precise result (call it option *C*) that reflects enactable preferences more accurately than could any plausible interpretation of statutory meaning. This can occur in at least three possible ways. First, more explicit phrasing can offer a more precise statutory resolution that both is unavailable as a plausible legal interpretation and reflects enactable preferences more accurately than judicial estimates of what the legislature would have done. Second, inserting the explicit terms in bills can help alert opposing groups to become involved, thus producing legislation that calibrates and trades off the relevant political interests more precisely than courts could. The latter can be analogized to the correct "pricing" of contract and corporate terms, with the price here exacted in political capital or compromise. The same will be true under a deliberation model, for greater explicitness should produce more focused deliberation and include more of the affected parties. Third, when a legislature responds to a preference-eliciting default rule by enacting more explicit legislation, it helpfully updates the statute to take account of any changes in circumstances or political preferences, which maximizes political satisfaction, for reasons explained in Parts I–II.

The existence of preference-eliciting default rules means that an ex post statutory override does not prove that the judicial interpretation was mistaken, as is often supposed.[2] To the contrary, such statutory overrides mean that the preference-eliciting default rule achieved its purpose: forcing explicit decisionmaking by the political process. Indeed, it is the very fact that it is more likely to provoke legislative correction that makes a preference-eliciting default rule preferable to a default rule that is more likely to reflect legislative preferences. Absent legislative correction, for example, there would be no reason to choose option *B* over *A* in the above hypothetical. However, a successful preference-eliciting default rule need not always provoke an ex post legislative override. More typically, the correction will come ex ante in the original legislative drafting, and be largely unobservable. Other times, as in the 40% of cases for option *B* above, the explicit ex post legislative decision may, after consideration, be not to change the preference-eliciting default rule.

Although preference-eliciting default rules thus do have an important role, they also have important conditions and limits, which are best to lay out at the outset. In particular, preference-eliciting theory must be distinguished from another claim: the claim that courts should always interpret statutes in whatever way is most likely to elicit or require legislative action

why wouldn't the plain-meaning doctrine have a similar effect?

to resolve statutory unclarity. That alternative claim would argue for the misguided position that courts should always adopt the most numbskulled interpretation they can think of. If the goal is maximizing political satisfaction, a preference-eliciting default rule should instead be used, for reasons explained in the next sections, to choose only among plausible interpretive options, and only when three conditions are met: (1) estimated enactable preferences are unclear, (2) significant differential odds of legislative correction exist, and (3) any interim costs from lowering immediate expected political satisfaction are acceptable.

Condition 1: Uncertainty about Enactable Preferences

Any preference-eliciting interpretation must be within the range of plausible statutory meanings. This follows from the fact that our topic is limited to default rules, but is worth emphasizing, lest the theory here be confused with the claim that courts should always interpret statutes in whatever way legislatures like least. No default rule theory, including preference-eliciting theory, can justify adopting an interpretation that has been rejected by the clear meaning of a statute that has been enacted through whatever process the society deems authoritative. Any meaning enacted by statute opts out of the default rule. Nor does preference-eliciting theory justify adopting interpretations that parties were entitled to assume lay outside the range of possible statute meanings.

Moreover, even if it lies within the range of plausible statutory meanings, a preference-eliciting default rule should not be chosen unless the interpreting court is uncertain which meaning within that range the legislative polity would prefer. For example, suppose statutory meaning seems unclear, yet one of the two plausible meanings would clearly match legislative preferences. Then, a preference-eliciting default rule should not be imposed, because the point of preference-eliciting default rules is to procure explicit legislation that avoids inaccurate judicial guesses about legislative preferences. There is no reason to endure the interim costs of incorrect results, if the court can avoid any inaccuracy because it already knows what the legislature would want. In the hypothetical noted above, if the court were 100% sure that the legislature would want option A, then there would be no point in adopting option B because, while B would ultimately result in the same 100% preference satisfaction, it would (in the interim before override) produce clear preference dissatisfaction. Further, because option A is

100% likely to match legislative preferences, there is no prospect that option *B* will induce the legislature to enact a more nuanced option *C* that matches enactable preferences more precisely.

In many cases, though, there will be great uncertainty about what will turn out to be enactable by the legislature. In part, this is because information is limited, and the inferences we can draw from current official action or the enactor's legislative history may be uncertain. Even if courts have excellent information about the preferences of each individual legislator, the way the legislature aggregates its preferences will turn heavily on the vagaries of how its agenda is ordered. This does not mean some estimation of probabilities is impossible, but it does create uncertainty. In addition, a court might believe the legislature is more likely to prefer option *A* to *B,* but be uncertain whether it would instead prefer some nuanced option *C,* which is unavailable as an interpretive option and whose precise contours the court cannot meaningfully estimate. The more uncertainty one believes such problems create, the more attractive preference-eliciting default rules will be.

The uncertainty necessary to merit a preference-eliciting default rule does not exist when it is clear, as a matter of statutory meaning or legislative preferences, that what the legislature wanted to do is delegate the issue to be resolved by agencies or courts according to their own judgment. Perhaps some constitutional doctrine of nondelegation might be invoked in some such cases, though that seems unlikely, given that doctrine's lack of bite. In any event, preference-eliciting default rules would provide no warrant for rejecting such a delegation, for their aim is to maximize the satisfaction of legislative preferences, and one such legislative preference may well be to delegate the matter to be decided by others deemed more fit to decide the matter.

This is another important way in which statutory default rules differ from contractual and corporate default rules. In the contractual or corporate context, courts may impose preference-eliciting default rules in order to prevent parties from shifting the costs of resolving textual gaps onto a publicly subsidized judicial system.[3] Such concerns about cost-shifting have no applicability to statutes, because the public subsidizes the legislatures who leave the gaps as well as the courts or agencies who might fill them. Thus, absent a nondelegation constraint imposed by the Constitution, the legislature has the authority to decide which publicly-subsidized method it believes is more effective.

Condition 2: Significant Differential
Odds of Legislative Correction

It does not make sense to use a preference-eliciting default rule if one believes it will stick, unmodified, even when it does not match prevailing political preferences. Preference-eliciting default rules only make sense when one believes they might elicit legislative correction, either in the initial drafting or after the interpretation.

Where the statutory issue is foreseeable at the time of enactment, the knowledge that a preference-eliciting default rule exists can induce the legislature to enact more explicit language in the original statute. This eliminates the ambiguity ex ante, thus providing a more precise resolution of what was enactable before the statute is ever applied to anyone. But many legislative corrections can only come ex post, after the statute is interpreted. Gaps or ambiguities in statutory meaning often arise from unanticipated applications, or unforeseen changes in circumstances, which are unlikely to be amenable to ex ante clarification in drafting because the legislature (by definition) was unaware of them. In such cases, preference-eliciting rules can still be salutary because they elicit ex post correction through statutory overrides.

If the enacting legislators understood that the statutory language was unclear but nonetheless enacted the statute without resolving that unclarity, this may sometimes signal an intentional delegation of lawmaking power to the courts, not an occasion for a default rule aimed at eliciting more precise preferences ex ante. But the fact that the legislature intentionally left unclear statutory language undisturbed does not, standing alone, suffice to infer an intention to delegate to courts the power to make substantive policy. The legislature may, instead, have been willing to leave the unclarity precisely because it was confident the courts would apply statutory default rules that try to maximize the satisfaction of political preferences. Or perhaps the legislature saw the issue, but did not think it was as unclear as the courts later did, and thus did not realize it was worth the cost of ex ante clarification.[4] Or maybe the legislature thought that leaving the unclarity unresolved would make the statute inapplicable to the issue, rather than delegating to courts the power to exercise common lawmaking powers.[5] Thus, intentional statutory unclarity can itself have an unclear significance, whose ex ante clarification can be encouraged by a preference-eliciting default rule.

A preference-eliciting default rule can usefully encourage ex ante clarification even when the legislators themselves were unaware of the unclarity. This is because that unclarity may be known or foreseeable to a political group, which is in a position to either draft or correct the drafting of legislation. If so, a preference-eliciting default rule that cuts against such a group can have the requisite ex ante effect by encouraging the group to raise the issue with the legislature and have it resolved. In essence, applying a preference-eliciting default rule helps the legislature strike an informed bargain with the group, by encouraging the group to reveal information to the legislature.

Even if ex ante clarification fails, ex post legislative reaction remains possible. One might mistakenly dismiss this possibility of ex post legislative reaction, given the old bromide that legislatures rarely know about, let alone correct, statutory interpretations. But a remarkable study by Professor Eskridge has shown that, in fact, congressional staffers routinely monitor Supreme Court statutory decisions, that Congress holds legislative hearings on nearly 50% of these interpretations, and that at least 6–8% are legislatively overridden.[6] This 6–8% statistic is alone significant. Further, it understates the general incidence of legislative overrides because it excludes cases where Congress either did not explicitly say that it was seeking to override an interpretation or only partially codified an interpretation and thus implicitly rejected the rest.[7]

More important, the percentage of all statutory interpretations that are legislatively overridden greatly understates the effectiveness of preference-eliciting default rules, for several important reasons. First, if one wants to measure ex post legislative responsiveness, the right measure is not the likelihood of statutory override for all interpretations, but rather the likelihood for the subset of interpretations that conflict with enactable preferences. The percentage of all interpretations that are overridden should be relatively low if, as I have shown above, the Court normally employs preference-estimating default rules that track, where reliably ascertainable, the enactable preferences of the current legislature. For example, if only 10% of Supreme Court interpretations conflict with current enactable preferences, then the above 6–8% statistic for overrides of all interpretations translates into a 60–80% rate of override for interpretations that conflict with enactable preferences.

Second, the odds of legislative override are far higher for the selected areas where preference-eliciting canons are most merited and actually used. Suppose, to continue the last example, the percentage of conflicting interpretations that are overridden is 60–80%. This statistic will include overrides not only of preference-eliciting default rules but also of interpretations that tracked a statutory meaning that conflicted with enactable preferences, that mistakenly estimated current preferences, or that relied on enactor preferences that turned out to conflict with current preferences. Because the preference-eliciting default rules were deliberately chosen for their special propensity to provoke legislative reactions, the percentage of over-rides for conflicting interpretations that reflected preference-eliciting default rules should be higher than the 60–80% average; maybe 80–90%. Given that the argument here is not that preference-eliciting default rules should always be used, but only that they should be used in selected circumstances, the more relevant statistic is this higher percentage of overrides for the sub-set of conflicting interpretations that used preference-eliciting default rules.

One would also expect legislative overrides to be even more plentiful in parliamentary systems, which need not secure approval by separate cham-bers (and committees) and the executive. This would suggest preference-eliciting default rules should be even more attractive in those jurisdictions.

Third, what matters is not the probability of legislative override itself, but of serious legislative reconsideration. In my example above, with interpre-tive options A and B, in 40% of the cases the legislature does not override interpretation B, the preference-eliciting default rule. Such confirmation of a preference-eliciting default rule should happen less than 50% of the time, because (by hypothesis) that rule does not reflect the most likely estimate of legislative preferences, but it will happen often, and when it occurs it pro-vides an important benefit. Unless the preference-eliciting default rule is chosen in those cases, interpretation A will not be reconsidered, and thus the legislature will not enact option B in this 40% of cases when it matches its preferences. Indeed, I will show in Chapter 12 that, absent some other re-liable evidence of change in legislative conditions, if the legislature fails to override a preference-eliciting interpretation after legislative reconsidera-tion, that failure itself means that the non-overridden interpretation is now the interpretation most likely to reflect enactable preferences.

The last point means that the odds of actual override may matter less than the statistic that Congress holds hearings on 50% of all Supreme Court in-terpretations. Presumably, the percentage of hearings is even higher for the subset of interpretations that conflict with enactable preferences, and higher still for the further subset of preference-eliciting interpretations that were chosen for their propensity to provoke legislative reaction. Provoking ex post legislative reconsideration through such hearings can achieve the benefits of a preference-eliciting default rule, even when it does not provoke a legislative override.

Fourth, preference-eliciting default rules do not exist solely to provoke ex post legislative reconsideration. They also have the important benefit of provoking ex ante clarification in legislative drafting, and those will not show up in statistics about ex post overrides. Thus, any benefits from ex post correction must be multiplied by all the cases where the preference-eliciting default rule elicits an ex ante clarification, which means the ambiguity and dispute never reaches any court. Unfortunately, data are not available on the extent to which an interpretive rule has in fact increased ex ante resolution of statutory ambiguities, because that occurs in the murky world of legislative drafting. It may be that for every case actually applying a preference-eliciting default rule (because the ex ante clarification failed to occur), there are nine where the default rule successfully induced an ex ante clarification. If so, then even a preference-eliciting default rule that provoked ex post legislative reconsideration only 20% of the time would actually be 92% successful at provoking legislative consideration of all kinds.

Given a lack of data on the extent to which ex ante clarifications are induced by preference-eliciting default rules, this book relies on a more limited assumption: that if a group has a differential ability to procure ex post legislative correction of interpretations that disfavor it, then that group probably also has a differential ability to procure ex ante clarification when it can foresee the ambiguous issue. Thus, the following chapters will recount mainly examples of ex post legislative corrections, using them as a proxy for a differential likelihood of both ex ante and ex post correction. This should help determine when to adopt a preference-eliciting default rule, and which group it should disfavor. But the fact that mainly ex post examples will be cited should not be allowed to obscure the fact that much (and probably most) of the benefit from preference-eliciting default rules will come in the form of ex ante legislative clarification.

Fifth, what matters is not so much the absolute odds of correction but the extent to which those odds are higher if the preference-eliciting default rule is chosen. If whichever side loses the interpretive issue is equally capable of procuring legislative correction, then there is not much call for employing a preference-eliciting default rule that disfavors one side. The court might as well apply the best estimate it can make of likely legislative preferences, confident that any error is equally subject to correction by the losing group, and that in the interim the court will have maximized expected political satisfaction. Instead, a crucial premise for adopting a preference-eliciting default rule is that, among the interpretations that turn out to inaccurately estimate legislative preferences, some are more likely to elicit a legislative reaction than others.

More generally, it can be shown that (leaving aside interim costs) whether it maximizes political satisfaction to choose the preference-eliciting interpretation, rather than the one that reflects the best estimate of enactable preferences, turns on a comparison of (1) how great an advantage the eliciting option has in provoking legislative correction to (2) how certain it is that the other option will better match enactable preferences. As I have proven elsewhere,[8] even if preference-estimating option A is more likely to match legislative preferences, preference-eliciting option B will maximize political satisfaction if:

$$P_{Astick} / P_{Bstick} > P_A / P_B.$$

In the formula, P_A is the relative probability that A matches legislative preferences, P_B is the relative probability that B matches, P_{Astick} is the conditional probability that the legislature would fail (either ex ante or ex post) to correct default choice A *if* option A does *not* accurately reflect legislative preferences, and P_{Bstick} is the conditional probability that the legislature would fail to correct default choice B if option B does not accurately reflect legislative preferences. (This formula ignores any interim costs under the assumption that the legislative clarification occurs either ex ante, and thus inflicts no interim costs, or so quickly ex post that interim costs are trivial.) Thus, what matters is not so much the absolute odds of correction but a comparison of the ratio of the odds of provoking correction to the ratio of the odds of correctly estimating enactable preferences.

To return to the prior illustration, assume that the relative probability that A matches enactable preferences is 60% and the probability that B matches is 40%. Then $P_A / P_B = 1.5$, and the inequality tells us that option B should be chosen not only in the extreme case, where the odds that A would stick uncorrected are 100% and that B would stick uncorrected are 0%, but in any case where the ratio of the odds of being uncorrectable (P_{Astick} / P_{Bstick}) is greater than 1.5. Note that $P_{Astick} + P_{Bstick}$ need not equal 1. For example, even if the legislature is relatively vigorous about correcting all mistaken interpretations or default rules either ex ante or ex post, option B should still be chosen if the probability that A would stick uncorrected were 5% and the probability that B would stick uncorrected were only 1%.

If the legislature is unlikely to correct any interpretive choice, either ex ante or ex post, then a preference-eliciting default rule generally will not make sense. Suppose, for example, that the likelihood that option B would stick, uncorrected, even when it does not match legislative preferences, is 50% or greater (i.e., legislative correction is unlikely). Then the maximum that P_{Astick} / P_{Bstick} can equal is 2, and P_A should be chosen as long as $P_A > 2(1 - P_A)$, or $P_A > 2/3$. Thus, where the court is at least 67% confident that the legislature would prefer option A, it never makes sense to instead adopt a preference-eliciting default rule B that is less than 50% likely to provoke a legislative correction.

However, great uncertainty about which interpretive option the legislature would prefer can justify a preference-eliciting default rule *even when legislative correction is highly unlikely.* In the last example, if the odds that option A matches legislative preferences are 66% or less, then option B should be chosen, even though legislative correction is unlikely. To take the extreme case, suppose a court is completely uncertain about whether the legislature would prefer option A over option B, assigning the same odds to either. Then, a court should choose preference-eliciting option B whenever $P_{Astick} > P_{Bstick}$, that is, whenever option A is more likely to stick uncorrected than option B. Thus, where a court is completely uncertain about whether a legislature would prefer option A or B, a preference-eliciting default rule makes sense as long as the legislature is to *any* extent more likely to correct B than A. Even if the odds that B will stick uncorrected are 99%, and the odds that A will stick uncorrected are 100%, option B should be chosen when the court has no reason to think the legislature might prefer option A over B.

More generally, when there is great uncertainty about which interpretation a legislature would prefer, it only takes a slight advantage in provoking legislative correction to make a preference-eliciting default rule desirable, even when the overall odds of legislative correction are very small. Thus, whether any differential odds of correction are sufficiently significant turns on how uncertain enactable preferences are.

Why should we expect differential odds of correction at all? The usual reason is that political forces on one side of the interpretive issue have greater ability to command time on the legislative agenda, raise issues, and/or influence statutory drafting. Empirical evidence confirms that this does create political asymmetries in different groups' ability to command time on the legislative agenda.[9] Or it might be because, as other empirical studies have indicated, politically influential groups have greater ability to block legislative change than to enact it.[10] One reason for such an asymmetry is that legislative committees generally have greater power to block than enact legislation, and politically influential groups often have greater influence over the committees than the general legislature.

Whatever the cause, preference-eliciting analysis provides a reason for favoring the politically powerless that has nothing to do with whether their claims are attractive on policy grounds or correspond to prevailing political wishes. The point of favoring the politically powerless (in resolving a statutory ambiguity) is not that their interests are more meritorious. The point is that favoring them will produce a precise legislative appraisal of the weight the political process wishes to give those interests.

The argument for preference-eliciting default rules thus differs entirely from Professor Macey's influential argument, which is that courts should adopt public-regarding interpretations to force interest groups to be explicit if they want to further private-regarding purposes.[11] Although Macey in a sense takes an information-forcing approach, the difference is that, in his approach, the burden of clarification is placed on parties pursuing the substantive results he disfavors, mainly those that are not "public-regarding," measured by such controversial criteria as whether or not they constitute a derogation from the common law.[12] One problem with Macey's approach is that it presupposes just what is in doubt—that we know which interpretations are public-regarding—and leaves that question to judicial judgment. Further, some of the groups who are most influential in the legislature, and should thus be burdened by a preference-eliciting default rule if our aim is to maximize political satisfaction, may well be the most "public-regarding" under ordinary conceptions. For example, we shall see in the next chapter that the rule of lenity can be explained as a preference-eliciting default rule that burdens public prosecutors, whose crime-fighting purposes would seem public-regarding under most conceptions.

We should also distinguish the point here from the argument recently made by Professor Katyal to explain the result in the Guantanamo detainees case: that where the views of the president and Congress are in conflict about a statutory ambiguity, a penalty default rule should side with Congress, because the president could veto any effort to override an interpretation that favored him.[13] The problem with this argument is that it is equally true that

Congress could decline to approve any override of an interpretation that favored Congress. In cases of presidential-congressional conflict, the mere availability of a presidential veto cannot show there are *differential* odds of override, any more than the need for congressional approval can.

However, although Katyal's version fails, there is a preference-eliciting default rule that can explain the result in the Guantanamo detainees case— the default rule the Supreme Court actually cited: the canon that statutes should be interpreted to preserve *habeas* rights.[14] The set of prisoners who generally benefit from *habeas* rights have little ability to command the legislative agenda, and the particular set of terrorist suspects at issue in this case have even less political clout. Had the Court interpreted the statute to make adjudication rights too narrow (compared to what was enactable), the terrorist suspects clearly could not have secured enactment of a statutory override. An interpretation denying adjudication rights thus would have stuck. In contrast, those favoring the war on terror clearly had far more political ability to secure an enactment overriding any interpretation that granted adjudication rights that were too broad (compared to what was enactable). This is precisely what happened. Within months after the Supreme Court decision, the president and Congress agreed to largely override it in the Military Commissions Act of 2006. This new statute gave adjudication rights to detainees that were more narrow than the interpretation adopted by the Court, but broader than the detainees would have had under the interpretation the Court rejected. In short, the Supreme Court decision did not lead to a pro-detainee result, but rather provoked a legislative reaction that made clear just how anti-detainee current enactable preferences were. (Whether those enactable preferences will turn out to be constitutionally permissible is another question.)

Preference-eliciting default rules may not be the most narrow construction of a statute. The groups that are most influential in the legislature sometimes benefit from broad constructions and sometimes benefit from narrow constructions. It may thus be a broad construction that burdens the more politically influential group. Indeed, that was the case in the Guantanamo detainees case itself, where the narrow interpretation denying judicial jurisdiction was rejected.

Rather, in order for a preference-eliciting approach to be helpful, the issue must involve a persistent one-sided political demand for legislation. When there are politically influential groups on both sides of a statutory issue, a preference-eliciting default rule generally does not make sense. Not only are such cases unlikely to exhibit much *differential* odds of legislative correction, but cases of conflicted demand for legislation are the least likely to produce legislative action in general, and quick legislative overrides in particular.[15]

Whether the requisite one-sided political demand exists should not vary with the political vagaries of the moment, such as whether Democrats or Republicans are in power. Nor should it turn on fine-tuned assessments of the ebbs and flows of relative power among various groups within different Congresses. If there is significant conflicted demand for legislation, then no matter who is in office, Republicans or Democrats, and no matter which side of the conflict each favors, significant differential odds of legislative correction are unlikely, and a court thus should not employ a preference-eliciting default rule.

Condition 3: Acceptable Interim Cost

Where ex ante clarification does not seem likely, such as when the relevant issue was not foreseeable at the time of enactment, the advisability of a preference-eliciting default rule may well depend on how much expected harm it will cause before the ex post legislative override can happen. Even for ex post correction, the interim costs will be small if the interim is short. The two most exhaustive empirical studies indicate that half or more of statutory overrides occur within two years of a statutory decision.[16] The interim costs may also be small if there is little difference in the odds that either interpretation will satisfy enactable preferences in that interim.

Another factor influencing the degree of interim costs is how amenable the statutory result is to correction after the fact. For example, a statutory result that mistakenly creates property rights is harder to correct, given the takings clause, than one that denies property rights. Likewise, a statutory result that endangers a species is harder to correct than one that preserves the species in the interim. Large uncorrectable interim costs will sometimes call for a default rule that is the best estimate of legislative preferences, even though it will not procure the more explicit legislative decision that a preference-eliciting default rule would have.

Conclusion

In short, a statutory preference-eliciting default rule is merited only when statutory meaning is unclear and (1) courts are sufficiently uncertain what the legislature would have preferred; (2) the preference-eliciting default rule is more likely to provoke legislative correction (ex ante or ex post) than the default rule that better matches likely legislative preferences; and (3) either any correction could generally be expected ex ante, or any ex post interim costs (from not choosing the interpretation the legislature would more likely prefer) are not unduly large or uncorrectable. When these conditions are not met, the preference-eliciting default rule should not be employed. These are not "on/off" conditions, but rather involve implicit trade-offs. The less certain legislative preferences are, the smaller the advantage in provoking legislative correction need be to justify applying a preference-eliciting default rule. The more certain legislative preferences, the greater the advantage in legislative correction must be. And so forth.

But this does not mean that the choice whether to apply a preference-eliciting default rule should be left to the vagaries of an open-ended, case-by-case balancing test. Although sometimes that is the best approach, better results often follow from using rules that, although not directly correlated to the underlying norms of social desirability, have a greater precision that renders them less over- and underinclusive in actual application than open-ended standards.[17] Judges would, for example, probably have a hard time determining relative political influence in particular cases, and thus would achieve more accurate results overall by instead using rules that are based on whether the case fits a category where differential political advantage is likely. Further, in the choice between a rule and a standard, one often needs to consider other factors, like the ability of legal clarity to increase the likelihood of behavioral compliance, decrease the costs of ascertaining the law, and provide fair warning. These factors further argue in favor of preference-eliciting default rules based on certain categories of cases rather than case-by-case measurements of relative political influence, which is largely the approach the courts have actually taken. But even under a rule-based approach, the factors identified above are crucial for deciding how best to define both the rules and their exceptions.

One might wonder whether a more straightforward approach would not simply be to have courts elicit legislative reactions by certifying cases to the legislature when the court finds statutory meaning and likely legislative preferences unclear. But, as noted in Chapter 3, the U.S. Supreme Court already implicitly certifies statutory issues to Congress by putting them on the Supreme Court docket, adding a process of explicit certification would delay cases, and any certification does not eliminate the need to have some default rule specifying the statutory result if Congress fails to act. The analysis here indicates there are two further problems with the alternative of such a certification process. First, certification would not have the helpful feature of eliciting ex ante clarification in the original statute. Second, without the actual imposition of a preference-eliciting default rule that disfavors the more politically powerful groups, certification is less likely to trigger any ex post legislative action.

By now, some more concrete illustrations are no doubt overdue. What actual doctrines could be said to serve as preference-eliciting default rules? The next chapter begins to address this question.

CHAPTER 9

Canons Favoring the Politically Powerless

If the legal goal were solely to maximize the likelihood that the interpretations being made satisfied enactable preferences, it would not make much sense to employ canons that favored the politically powerless. Legislative preferences are more likely to be furthered by favoring politically powerful forces, which most influence where enactable preferences lie. But in fact many statutory canons favor the politically powerless. This includes the rule of lenity, which favors criminal defendants, the presumptions against antitrust and tax exemptions, many applications of the constitutional doubts canon, and the canon favoring Indian tribes. While inexplicable as current or enactor preference default rules, these canons can (where those preferences are uncertain) be explained as preference-eliciting default rules. The reason is that applying these canons is likely to elicit legislative reactions that more precisely indicate which preferences are enactable. The following discussion considers each in turn.

The Rule of Lenity as a Preference-Eliciting Default Rule

The rule of lenity provides that "ambiguity concerning the ambit of criminal statutes should be resolved in favor of lenity."[1] Thus, where criminal statutes are ambiguous, the effective default rule is to select the interpretation that provides the lowest possible penalty for the allegedly criminal act. This canon hardly seems to track the most likely legislative intent or preference. Most legislative polities are hostile to criminal defendants. If there is any serious politician running on a "soft on crime" platform, it has escaped my attention. True, here we are talking about conduct that is ambiguously criminal.

But conduct that can reasonably be considered criminal is hardly politically popular, and certainly most criminal defendants are not. In part, this is because the persons who become criminal defendants are selected by prosecutors, who themselves are politically accountable or appointed. Indeed, if one had to choose one extreme or the other, one might conclude that, in ambiguous cases, the legislature would likely prefer a "rule of severity," which chose the greater punishment for the criminal defendant.

Even if legislatures were not prone to lean against criminal defendants, a canon that always chose the narrow end of the range of possible meanings would systematically thwart legislative preferences, compared to a canon that chose a moderate interpretation or whichever interpretation most likely reflects legislative preferences for that particular statute. In other words, rejecting a rule of severity could mean a rule of moderation or preference estimation rather than a rule of lenity. This alternative default rule would seem particularly attractive, because statutory ambiguities are often hard to anticipate or unavoidable given limited information and changed circumstances. As Professor Kahan has persuasively argued, legislatures would likely prefer to have judges resolve such ambiguities, rather than systematically leave important social problems unregulated whenever the inevitable uncertainties arose.[2]

But preference-eliciting analysis provides a ready justification for this counterintuitive canon. By providing the most lenient reading in unclear cases, the rule of lenity forces legislatures to define just how anti-criminal they wish to be, and how far to go with the interest in punishing crime when it runs up against other societal interests. If instead courts broadly (or even neutrally) interpreted criminal statutes in cases of unclarity, this would often produce an overly broad interpretation that would likely stick, because there is no effective lobby for narrowing criminal statutes. In contrast, an overly narrow interpretation is far more likely to be corrected by statutory interpretation, because prosecutors and other members of anti-criminal lobbying groups are heavily involved in legislative drafting and can more readily get on the legislative agenda to procure any needed overrides.

Empirical evidence about ex post correction supports this supposition. Statutory interpretations in criminal law are more likely to be legislatively overturned than any other type of statutory interpretation.[3] But the ability to secure legislative overrides is markedly one-sided. Criminal prosecutors have the best record of getting Congress to overturn adverse statutory interpretations, whereas criminal defendants have one of the worst.[4] This differential influence over legislative overrides is probably also true ex ante, in the initial drafting of legislation.

True, this differential record, standing alone, could be explained a consequence of the rule of lenity, rather than a justification for it. Criminals might have little success in the legislature because they already had all ambiguities read in their favor, whereas prosecutors did not and are thus seeking legislation that is more likely to reflect legislative preferences. But in terms of organization and ability to testify before legislatures, criminal defendants are clearly far behind. In part this is because no one wants to identify himself as likely enough to become indicted that he has an interest in the issue. Consistent with this analysis, the legislative success rate for criminal defendants is statistically far lower than the rate for other actors seeking to overcome other adverse statutory presumptions.[5]

To illustrate the phenomenon, consider *Keeler v. Superior Court*, which presented the question whether a murder statute that prohibited the "killing of a human being" covered the intentional killing of a viable fetus that the mother wished to carry to term.[6] The case involved a divorced man who, angry that his ex-wife was pregnant by another man, carried out a plan to "stomp it out" of her by kneeing her abdomen and fracturing the fetus's skull. The statutory text was ambiguous: as a legal term, "human being" did not clearly cover or exclude a viable fetus that the mother intended to carry to term. The legislative history provided no real indication of enactable preferences on this specific issue.[7] However, there was no doubt that the defendant's conduct was undesirable, horrifically so. If one asked which result the legislature was most likely to prefer—imposing a sentence for murder or letting the defendant get off on mere assault charges—the former seems more likely. Nonetheless, citing the rule of lenity, the California Supreme Court interpreted the murder statute to exclude the defendant's actions.

Although not a plausible reading of the most likely legislative preference, the *Keeler* decision can readily be explained as a preference-eliciting default rule. The case was decided in 1970, before *Roe v. Wade*. Thus, while a court could be fairly confident that the legislature would prefer to cover Keeler's conduct, it would be quite unsure how to define the offense of killing fetuses in such a way that would not raise a large risk of deviating from then-current enactable preferences on abortion. If instead the court applied the rule of lenity, it was readily predictable that, because prosecutors have ready access to the legislative agenda, and because there was consensus that what the defendant did was egregiously wrong, the legislature would react. This is precisely what happened. Within months, the California legislature adopted an amendment overriding the decision. This statute made it "murder" to kill a fetus, but carefully defined exceptions for abortions to save the mother's life or with her consent, with the latter nonetheless remaining punishable as a lesser offense.[8] This amendment provided a more precise assessment of 1970 enactable preferences on the boundaries between murder and abortion than courts could have ascertained or fashioned as a legal interpretation. Consider what likely would have happened if the court had instead ruled that the defendant's conduct constituted murder. The better result would have obtained in the *Keeler* case itself. But in 1970, it was doubtful that proabortion political forces could have gotten on the legislative agenda to exclude abortion from the definition of murder, especially because abortion was a crime at the time (other than in cases to save the mother), albeit one punished less severely than murder.

The phenomenon that applications of the rule of lenity often provoke legislative correction has deep historical roots. Way back in 1765, *Blackstone's Commentaries* cited two cases for the rule of lenity. In both cases, he noted that the rule of lenity decision provoked legislative override. In one case it "procured a new act for that purpose in the following year," and in the other case "the next sessions, it was found necessary to make another statute."[9] In neither case does Blackstone seem to treat the legislative override as a ground for criticizing the court's statutory interpretation. Rather, although Blackstone never explicitly says so, the desired effect seems to have been provoking a more precise definition of what the legislature wanted criminalized.

The pattern continues into modern times: decisions invoking the rule of lenity often provoke legislative overrides.[10] This does not mean the courts should use the rule of lenity willy-nilly in all cases. As noted in Chapter 8, preference-eliciting default rules should be employed only after preference-estimating default rules fail. This limit is consistent with judicial pronouncements about the rule of lenity.[11] They have stressed: "we have always reserved lenity for those situations in which a reasonable doubt persists about a statute's intended scope even after resort to 'the language and structure, legislative history, and motivating policies' of the statute." This clearly confirms that this canon comes later in priority than preference-estimating rules. "The rule comes into operation at the end of the process of construing what Congress has expressed, not at the beginning as an overriding consideration of being lenient to wrongdoers." This confirms that the canon does not rest on any judicial preference for favoring criminal defendants, but is subordinated to the goal of ascertaining legislative preferences. Indeed, "[t]he rule of lenity applies only if, 'after seizing everything from which aid can be derived,' we can make 'no more than a guess as to what Congress intended.'" Application of this canon thus requires relatively high uncertainty about enactable preferences, confirming the other main condition for a preference-eliciting default rule.

The Weakness of Alternative Justifications for the Rule of Lenity

There are alternative, more traditional, justifications for the rule of lenity. But, for reasons explained next, their persuasiveness is dubious. Moreover, even if these alternative justifications were persuasive, they would extend at most to crimes that are *mala prohibita* (wrong because prohibited) and would exclude crimes that are *mala in se* (wrong in themselves), such as the acts of the *Keeler* defendant. However, the distinction between *mala prohibita* and *mala in se* offenses not only fails to fit the doctrine, but turns out to be the opposite of how the doctrine is applied. Preference-eliciting theory better fits the pattern of cases, and provides a stronger justification that helps illuminate the doctrine.

Alternative 1: Legislative Supremacy

One alternative traditional theory, based on separation of powers and legislative supremacy, is that legislatures, not courts, should define criminal law violations.[12] But this is a dubious argument for the rule of lenity. To interpret an ambiguous statute in line with the judge's best reading of what the legislature preferred is not the equivalent of creating a common law crime. The legislature has created the statute that effectively authorizes the judge to resolve the ambiguity, just as contracting parties create the contracts that authorize judges to resolve ambiguities in contractual text. No reasonable person thinks that, because contract law resolves contractual ambiguities, judges can just create contractual duties on their own initiative. Likewise, judicial resolution of statutory ambiguities does not tread on the legislative role, but rather executes the legislative instructions as best judges can.

Even if allowing courts to interpret ambiguities in criminal statutes were viewed as a delegation to courts to fashion the details of criminal law, it is hardly clear why an antidelegation doctrine makes sense here, when it has been abandoned elsewhere in law.[13] Indeed, even as to crime definition, the antidelegation doctrine does not bar Congress from delegating to agencies the power to create rules whose violation then constitutes a crime.[14] If agencies can define crimes out of whole cloth, it is hard to see why judges cannot do so while exercising their traditional interpretive role, within the bounds of plausible statutory meanings.

If anything, legislative supremacy cuts the other way, because the rule of lenity causes courts to systematically interpret criminal statutes more narrowly than the legislature likely would have wanted. This is true even if one assumes that legislative preferences are probably at some middle point in the ambiguity spectrum, rather than at the pro-prosecution extreme. Unless later overridden by more explicit statutes, rule of lenity interpretations will produce greater frustration of legislative preferences regarding criminal law compared to a rule of adopting the best estimate of what the legislature likely would have wanted. The rule of lenity thus cannot be justified as required by legislative supremacy. If the lenient interpretation sticks, it probably accomplishes precisely the opposite: thwarting legislative preferences. Certainly, the lenient interpretation is highly likely to conflict with legislative preferences when the crime is *malum in se.*

Alternative 2: Legislative Under-Representation

Another alternative theory concedes that the rule of lenity thwarts legislative preferences, but applauds this, favoring the rule of lenity precisely because it embodies a substantive view that is contrary to likely legislative preferences. One version of this theory argues that the liberty interest of criminal defendants requires that all doubts be resolved in their favor.[15] This theory necessitates a substantive judgment that, when the statutory language is ambiguous, the liberty interest of criminal defendants is stronger than the interest of their victims in vindication or of society in deterrence and incapacitation. Another version argues that judges should lean in favor of criminal defendants because they are "under-represented" in the legislative process.[16] Though this version sounds like a process claim, in the end it rests on the same substantive judgment. If the legislature gives "appropriate" substantive weight to the liberty interest of criminal defendants, then they would not be "under-represented" but appropriately represented, and there would be no reason to resolve doubts about the extent of their liberty interest against likely legislative preferences.

Whichever version we stress, positions resting on such independent substantive views are hard to justify generally, and even harder to justify for this specific canon. The general problem is the political illegitimacy of imposing substantive judicial views that are designed to thwart the best estimate of political preferences. To state that criminal defendants (or their liberty interests) are "under-represented" in the political process requires some normative baseline of the appropriate degree to which they (or their interests) should be represented, which in turn is indistinguishable from a normative view of the punishment in question.[17] Whatever the defects of the political process, there is little reason to think the judicial process is generally better at making such normative judgments, and even less reason to think it has been given authority to make them, absent some pertinent constitutional provision.

The specific problems are even more devastating. Because the canon applies only when legislative preferences are highly uncertain, it cannot effectively combat under-representation of criminal defendants or their liberty interests. Moreover, the ambiguously criminal conduct that is exempted by the rule of lenity is generally undesirable, and often heinous, like the conduct in *Keeler*. Such conduct would presumably be condemned by any political or deliberative process—no matter how ideally everyone's interests were represented. Even if courts are justified in using the rule of lenity to exempt conduct whose undesirability is questionable, how can they possibly be justified in using it to exempt conduct whose undesirability is plain? In short, like the prior rationale, this under-representation theory cannot explain why the rule of lenity is applied not just to *mala prohibita* cases but to *mala in se* cases as well.

Alternative 3: Advance Specificity

A final alternative rationale has traditionally been advance specificity. Ambiguous criminal statutes should be construed narrowly, the theory is, because otherwise criminal defendants would lack fair warning that their conduct is criminal, and suffer arbitrary or discriminatory enforcement.[18] Ehrlich and Posner offer the related argument that, without advance specificity, criminal sanctions would excessively deter desirable activity in the ambiguous zone.[19] Advance specificity provides the requisite notice, constraints on enforcement, and minimization of uncertainty risks.

In fact, there is probably much more undesirable activity than desirable activity in the zone of ambiguity surrounding any criminal statute. This reality suggests that Ehrlich and Posner's concerns about ambiguity overdeterring desirable activity are probably less weighty than concerns that clarity might create loopholes, which would underdeter undesirable activity.[20] This reality also means that providing fair advance warning, and restraining enforcement discretion, can be purchased only at the cost of helping wrongdoers circumvent the law by searching for ambiguities they can exploit.

But suppose Ehrlich and Posner's contrary empirical assumption were correct. Or suppose the cost of encouraging additional bad behavior were considered worth bearing if necessary to vindicate the principles of fair warning and limited enforcement discretion. Even so, these arguments for advance specificity would not explain the rule of lenity, for the following reasons.

To begin with, if advance specificity were really the problem, courts could just apply any non-narrow interpretation prospectively. This could be accomplished by, for example, holding that the non-narrow interpretation is correct for future cases, but violates due process under the void-for-vagueness doctrine as applied retroactively. Advance specificity arguments provide no reason to also narrow the statute prospectively, which requires the legislature to correct the narrow interpretation for future cases. Any non-narrow interpretation adopted prospectively by the courts would itself have to be sufficiently definite to provide advance notice, constrain enforcement discretion, and minimize risk aversion. But whether it does so is a matter resolved not by the rule of lenity but by the void-for-vagueness doctrine, which clearly—and correctly—provides that a (prospectively applied) judicial interpretation that itself is not vague cures any vagueness or fair-warning problem in the original statute.[21]

As for the risk of arbitrary and discriminatory enforcement, that risk would seem to be equally curbed by the prospect of nonarbitrary and nondiscriminatory judicial interpretation. Prosecutors who are tempted to enforce statutes in an arbitrary or discriminatory manner will be deterred if they anticipate regular and evenhanded judicial interpretations, and juries with similar temptations will be constrained by jury instructions that provide the requisite specificity. Thus, even as applied to retroactive interpretations, concerns about unbridled enforcement discretion justify statutory interpretations that eliminate ambiguity, but not statutory interpretations that always lean in favor of criminal defendants.[22]

Nor does the rule of lenity really provide much notice to criminal defendants. They rarely read the criminal code before acting, and thus advance specificity in the statutory code cannot normally provide them with notice, nor lessen their risk aversion. Moreover, the rule of lenity does not apply if the statutory ambiguity can be resolved by resort to legislative history, contemporaneous practice, prior caselaw, and legal or historical dictionaries, and prospective criminal defendants are even less likely to read and understand those specialized legal materials.[23] Indeed, as noted above, the rule of lenity only applies if legislative preferences are highly uncertain, which means it is often denied when some lesser amount of uncertainty existed even after assessment of all those legal materials. This would hardly be a sensible condition if the goal were to assure clear advance notice to defendants.

In any event, one wonders why any of the justifications for advance specificity apply when, as in *Keeler,* the conduct is *malum in se.* Where conduct is clearly wrongful, notice of the obvious seems unnecessary. Everyone knows to avoid such conduct already. Nor would cases of clearly wrongful conduct raise any concerns about deterring desirable activity, or any need to curb enforcement discretion. Like the other rationales, then, the advance specificity argument is especially weak whenever persons are engaged in conduct that is *malum in se.*

Explaining the General Pattern of Rule of Lenity Cases

In addition to better explaining the rule of lenity generally, preference-eliciting theory helps explain something about its application that is inexplicable under the traditional theories. These traditional theories indicate that the rule of lenity should be strongest in *mala prohibita* cases and weakest in *mala in se* cases, which has led many scholars to suggest that its application should be limited to the former. But the actual doctrine does not draw this distinction. Indeed, the pattern of application is precisely the reverse. The rule of lenity is applied more consistently to *mala in se* offenses than *mala prohibita* ones.

Regulatory crimes like antitrust and securities violations are often defined with enormous ambiguity. Yet the rule of lenity is rarely applied to them. In antitrust, for example, the Supreme Court has held that defendants can be criminally liable for violating the rule of reason, which is notoriously ambiguous. In doing so, the Court had no trouble rejecting a rule of lenity argument.[24]

Similarly, securities law has for decades allowed prosecutions for insider trading based on very ambiguous statutory language. Perhaps most striking, for one decade defendants were routinely convicted for trading on "misappropriated" information, even though the law was so ambiguous that the only applicable Supreme Court ruling had split, four to four, on whether the securities statute covered misappropriation.[25] At the end of the decade, the Supreme Court interpreted the statute to cover misappropriation, totally ignoring a dissent objection that the rule of lenity should have precluded the result.[26]

Why is this? The above antitrust and securities crimes are *mala prohibita* rather than *mala in se:* scholarship is split on whether either is even wrongful, let alone inherently criminal.[27] They thus involve the strongest case for applying the rule of lenity under traditional rationales. So these traditional rationales cannot provide the explanation for why, in practice, they are the sorts of cases in which the rule of lenity is least likely to be applied.

But preference-eliciting analysis can. Recall that the preference-eliciting premise for applying the rule of lenity was a differential likelihood of override. That is, the premise is that those seeking a broader construction would be very likely obtain legislative correction to avoid an excessively narrow interpretation, whereas those seeking a narrower construction would be very unlikely to obtain legislative correction to avoid an excessively broad interpretation. When business regulation is at issue, such a premise would be misplaced. Businesses often have enough political influence to get involved in legislative drafting or have their issues placed on the legislative agenda, or to block prosecutors from securing legislative overrides to correct narrow constructions of business regulations (or resolve initial ambiguities), especially regulations that impose criminal sanctions.[28] As Chapter 8 shows, unless businesses and prosecutors have different odds of procuring a statutory override, a preference-eliciting default rule cannot be justified. Indeed, situations where organized business interests are arrayed against prosecutors generally reflect conflicted political demand, which are the sort of situations least likely to lead to legislative action or correction in either direction.[29]

Because in these cases prosecutors are less able to get legislatures to correct any ambiguity or unduly narrow construction, it makes less sense to adopt a default rule that automatically construes statutes against prosecutors, which might leave society stuck with a likely bad statutory result. Instead, courts should adopt the interpretation they think best estimates legislative preferences, because any decision the court makes will likely remain uncorrected. Or the court should do so because errors in either direction are equally likely to be corrected by the legislature, so there is no reason to bias interpretation in either direction. That appears to be what the Supreme Court has largely done by generally declining to apply the rule of lenity to business crimes.

Opting Out of the Rule of Lenity and Other Preference-Eliciting Default Rules

Another explanation for why the rule of lenity is not used in the areas of antitrust, securities, and federal fraud is that statutory ambiguity in these areas reflects not unintended unclarity, but intentional delegation. Many view antitrust, securities, and federal fraud law as areas where Congress has intentionally delegated to federal courts the power to devise and revise rules of conduct in common law fashion. If so, these are areas where Congress understood the ambiguity and clearly indicated that it wanted courts to resolve it, not to return the matter to Congress.

This Congress has every right to do. For under the theory here put forth, the rule of lenity is merely a default rule and (like all default rules) should operate only if the relevant actor does not opt out of it. The legislature would have executed such an opt out if it indicated that it wanted courts to exercise judicial judgment, rather than narrow the statute and return it to the legislature. Such delegation also likely means that the criteria for the preference-eliciting default rule are not met, because the legislature normally delegates matters it is unlikely to reconsider. On either ground, the situation is unlike *Keeler* or other cases of unintended ambiguities in criminal statutes, where there is no reason to think the legislature intended to delegate the issue to courts.[30]

Should a legislature be able to opt out of the rule of lenity, not only for particular statutes, but for criminal statutes generally? Most state legislatures have arguably tried to do just that, by enacting statutes that direct courts to give a "fair," not narrow, construction of criminal statutes. This was true in *Keeler* itself, where California had the typical statute, which provided as follows.

> The rule of the common law, that penal statutes are to be strictly construed, has no application to this Code. All its provisions are to be construed according to the fair import of their terms, with a view to effect its objects and to promote justice.[31]

But, as *Keeler* suggests, these statutes have not caused courts to abandon the rule of lenity.

In part, this is because what these statutes arguably meant to overturn was something far broader than the rule of lenity: a rule of strict construction that would narrowly interpret any statute whose text was less than crystal clear, even if the ambiguity seemed strained or resolvable through extra-textual sources. This strict construction doctrine was based on substantive opposition to what courts considered legislatures' excessive willingness to use capital punishment.[32] The rule of lenity, in contrast, does not come into play unless a genuine certainty exists about both statutory meaning and legislative preferences, and (properly understood) aims to produce an ultimate set of statutory results that maximize the satisfaction of legislative preferences.

But suppose we do read such a statute as intending to overturn the rule of lenity itself? Even then, the judicial resistance that has occurred is understandable. The problem is that the legislature enacting such a statute would be opting out of the default rule not only on behalf of itself, and for a particular statute intended to delegate power to courts, but also on behalf of future legislatures, and for any statute with unintended unclarity where legislative preferences were uncertain. These are factors that raise problems for any effort to opt out of a preference-eliciting default rule.

Even if we put aside the effect on future legislatures and polities, the problem remains that, given one-sided political access to the legislative agenda, politically favored groups will (without a preference-eliciting default rule) enjoy statutory results that on average exceed their actual political influence and ability to enact favorable legislation. This is because, without a preference-eliciting default rule, when a court resolves ambiguous statutory meaning and uncertain legislative preferences, it will err equally for and against the politically advantaged, but the errors that go for them will remain uncorrected. Statutory results will thus on average be skewed in their favor, in ways that deviate from actual enactable preferences. Opting out of a preference-eliciting default rule would thus allow the legislature to interfere with the interest of the legislative polity in having the statutory results that most precisely correspond to its preferences.

These effects grow even more serious when one considers their implications for future legislative polities. They mean future courts would face a choice between (1) applying the preference-eliciting default rule they thought was best calculated to produce maximum satisfaction of enactable preferences and (2) using the default rule preferred by a past legislature that neither enacted the future statute being interpreted nor represents current legislative preferences. To instruct courts not only about what the legislature means for its own statutory language, but also how courts should interpret future legislatures' statutes, would thus interfere with the prerogatives of future legislatures, and the satisfaction of their political preferences.

A future legislature could, to be sure, enact legislation to amend the rule of interpretation to restore the preference-eliciting default rule. But the very nature of the one-sided political demand at issue should block that issue from reaching the legislative agenda. Further, the future legislature may never have thought about the matter, may not believe that the benefits to itself outweigh the decisionmaking costs, may be unable to form sufficient agreement on an alternative rule, or may be unable to overcome procedural obstacles or effective supermajority requirements.

None of this necessarily dictates a black-and-white choice that the rule of lenity, and preference-eliciting default rules generally, either are legislatively immutable or not. Interpretive statutes may quite helpfully modify various canons without undermining their preference-eliciting function, and the analysis here would offer no reason to question such legislative opt-outs. Further, before reaching any constitutional issues, the interpretive statute must itself be interpreted, and we need default rules for doing that as well. Because any legislative opt-out of a preference-eliciting default rule would predictably reflect the same sort of one-sided political demand that justifies that rule, the default rule for interpreting the opt-out naturally should also be the preference-eliciting one of interpreting the opt-out narrowly. That appears to be what we have seen in actual practice, as the courts have not outright invalidated legislative efforts to opt out of the rule of lenity, but have universally given them a narrow reading.

Where a legislature does clearly enact an interpretive statute that aims to undermine the preference-eliciting function of a statutory canon like the rule of lenity, however, that type of opt-out arguably violates (for reasons noted in Chapter 3) whatever constitutional clauses in the particular jurisdiction vest legislative authority in each generation's legislature and interpretive authority in the courts. This is not to say that an opt-out of this sort cannot be done. But given the fact that such an opt-out may interfere with the political satisfaction of multiple legislatures, and given the constitutional power of judges to interpret statutes to advance the enactable interests of the polity, it may not be proper for such an opt-out to be done through legislation by one legislature. It arguably requires a constitutional amendment that can not only alter the judicial function, but bind future legislatures and polities. Even if a single legislature were not constitutionally prohibited from adopting such an opt-out, the theory here would certainly indicate that such an opt-out is inadvisable, and thus recommend against it.

The Presumptions against Antitrust and Tax Exemptions—And the General Issue of Interest Group Influence

Antitrust law features powerful presumptions against interpreting any federal statute to create an antitrust exemption, and for narrowly construing any exemption that is created. Likewise, state legislation must clearly authorize any state regulatory action to immunize that action from federal antitrust invalidation. In tax law, statutes are construed not to provide a tax exemption in ambiguous cases.[33] These default rules do not seem to reflect what a legislature would most likely prefer. Usually, in such situations, the legislature was trying to favor supporting constituencies or interest groups with regulatory protections or tax breaks. However, we can understand these canons as preference-eliciting default rules.

After all, the constituencies and interest groups that can obtain antitrust and tax exemptions are more likely than others to have enough influence, whether over initial legislative drafting or future legislative agendas, to make that exemption explicit. A preference-eliciting default rule that burdens them is thus more likely to result in more explicit legislation, which makes sure they would be able to get their exemption through Congress, and that better defines the precise extent of that exemption. This is confirmed by evidence that such groups procure statutory overrides at statistically high rates.[34]

A default rule that broadly interpreted antitrust or tax exemptions would, in contrast, put the burden of securing legislative correction on consumers and other taxpayers, who are too numerous and diffusely interested in the question to organize effectively. Such a statutory result is thus unlikely to be corrected even though the prevailing political preferences would, if put to the test, either not enact the exemption or would narrow its scope.

One might think that the choice of default rule does not matter because the interest groups will win no matter what default rule is chosen. But the empirical literature indicates that interest groups are more effective in blocking government action than in securing it.[35] In securing the actual enactment of a statute, interest groups must offer some minimal satisfaction to their less well-organized (but often more numerous) opponents, but in blocking enactment they often need not offer any.

We might generalize these two canons into a more general preference-eliciting default rule. Namely, where statutory meaning is unclear, estimated legislative preferences are uncertain, and a political group has a significant advantage in commanding the legislative agenda compared to those favored by an alternative interpretation, then the interpretation disfavoring that political group should be chosen.

In contrast, when a tax ambiguity does not concern whether a particular set of taxpayers is entitled to a special exemption, but rather concerns the general scope of tax liability for all taxpayers, the default rule is the opposite one: interpreting the statute to favor the taxpayer.[36] This, too, is justified on preference-eliciting grounds. Here, the affected taxpayers are a large diffusely interested group, which is less able to command the legislative agenda than the IRS, an entity that is normally closely involved in annual tax legislation.[37] Like other agencies, the IRS can also, through proper regulation, establish a reliable current preferences default rule under the *Chevron* doctrine. Thus, this canon favoring taxpayers on matters of general tax liability is limited to cases where what is ambiguous is not only the statute but any applicable regulation.[38] But where no clear regulation exists, it makes sense (as with the rule of lenity) to elicit an official government action, which provides a more precise measure of enactable preferences.

As I will discuss in Chapter 16, many prominent scholars have made seemingly related proposals that courts should adopt an anti-interest-group default rule: narrowly interpreting all legislation that benefits concentrated interests over diffuse interests. However, their proposals differ sharply from mine in several ways. First, they are based on the contrary premise that special interest legislation is normatively undesirable, and that judges should narrow it when they can. Second, because of this contrary premise, these prior proposals do not apply to all politically-influential groups, but rather require distinguishing between those that statutory interpretation should disfavor (because they are special interest groups) and those it should not (because they are public interest groups).

I reject the premise of these proposals because, as I demonstrate in chapter 16, interest group theory does not justify normatively disfavoring interest groups, nor does it suggest that the litigation process would be less susceptible to their influence. Thus, my preference-eliciting theory does not require distinguishing between special interest and public interest groups. Rather, my preference-eliciting logic applies to *any* political group—special interest or public interest—with disproportionate influence over the legislative agenda. Special interest groups seeking antitrust and tax exemptions are one such group. But so are public interest groups, like prosecutors and anti-crime groups, whose influence justifies the rule of lenity, or the IRS, whose ability to set the agenda (especially for its own regulations) justifies the canon favoring taxpayers on general issues of tax liability.

Third, because prior proposals to interpret statutes against special interest groups are based on normative condemnation of those groups, they advocate any plausible statutory construction against them, even when such constructions conflict with a reliable estimation of legislative preference. Fourth, these proposals are designed to shift lawmaking power to judges for those interpretations that the political process *cannot* overturn quickly, precisely because judges are supposed to offer a normatively superior method of lawmaking.

In contrast, I thus carefully restrict application of the correct preference-eliciting default rule to cases where (a) there is genuine uncertainty about estimated legislative preferences, and (b) the legislature is likely to correct the statutory result dictated by the default rule. The point is not to disfavor politically-influential groups, but to test just how powerful the interest groups are (and get more explicit instructions of what the political process wants) by requiring their power to be exercised and weighed against other interests. Nor is the point to shift power from legislatures to judges less susceptible to interest group influence, but to the contrary to get the legislatures to act explicitly because they can more precisely weigh that influence.

In short, the aim of preference-eliciting default rules that disfavor politically powerful groups is not to curtail those group's influence, but to accurately measure the degree of that influence. Preference-eliciting theory thus does not rest on any normative claim that certain political groups are "over-represented." It rests rather on the notion that their influence over the legislative agenda justifies putting the default burden against them to procure legislative correction. The same adverse default rule applies to any group—special interest or public interest—that enjoys similar advantages in legislative access.

Applications of the Constitutional Doubts Canon That Favor the Politically Powerless

The canon against interpretations raising constitutional doubts has long had an attraction that seems to exceed the strength of its justifications. The canon cannot really be justified on constitutional grounds, because it only has bite when the statute is not constitutionally invalid. Nor (as Chapter 14 shows) could categorical application of the canon be justified as reflecting likely legislative preferences. But in some applications, the canon has been employed to favor groups that have had a systematic disadvantage in securing access to the legislative agenda. These applications can be justified as a preference-eliciting default rule.

For example, two recent cases have concerned whether aliens who were deportable or inadmissible could be detained indefinitely when the Immigration and Naturalization Service was unable to find a nation willing to take them.[39] The statute provided that aliens "may be detained beyond the [ordinary ninety-day] removal period" if they are inadmissible, a risk to the community, or deportable for crimes or national security reasons. In the first case the Supreme Court concluded that although the statute set no time limit, reading the statute to allow indefinite detention of deportable aliens should be rejected in order to avoid serious constitutional questions. Instead, the Court interpreted the statute to allow such detentions only as long as reasonably necessary to secure removal to another nation, presumptively less than six months, with no detention authorized once such removal was not reasonably foreseeable. Suppose it would be constitutional to indefinitely detain persons who have neither a legal right to be in the country nor any other country willing to take them. Even so, given that statutory meaning and legislative preferences were unclear, these rulings can be justified on preference-eliciting grounds because aliens have little political influence.[40] Thus, an interpretation favorable to aliens was more likely to be reconsidered legislatively.

In fact, less than four months after the first decision, Congress enacted a statute that partially overrode it, allowing the indefinite detention of aliens who were deportable but unable to find a nation that would take them, if they were terrorists or presented a national security threat. This statutory override thus partially adopted the interpretation the Court rejected, but overrode it only for the most dangerous criminal aliens. In the second case the Court then held that the interpretation banning indefinite detentions applied not only to deportable aliens but to aliens who were never admissible in the first place. Interestingly, the decision did so even though it seemed to assume that detaining inadmissible aliens would raise no constitutional doubts. This interpretation is hard to explain if the only goal were avoiding constitutional doubts, for such doubts could easily have been avoided by interpreting the statute differently for deportable and inadmissible aliens. But this interpretation makes sense if the real underlying reason for it was its preference-eliciting function, for both types of aliens are equally lacking in relative political clout. Consistent with this interpretation, the second decision proudly noted that Congress had partially overriden the first case, and openly invited Congress to do the same in reaction to this case, an invitation that has so far produced bills in both Houses.[41]

Another recent case concerned whether a statute should be interpreted to preclude *habeas corpus* review of a decision to deport a resident alien. The Court rejected that interpretation, citing the canon against interpretations raising constitutional doubts, as well as a more specific canon requiring a clear statement to repeal *habeas* review.[42] Even if the limit on *habeas* review of deportations would not have been unconstitutional, such a decision can again be justified on preference-eliciting grounds, given the relative inability of aliens to get access to the legislative agenda. Consistent with those grounds, this decision provoked a congressional statute that ended *habeas* review by district courts of deportation decisions but made them reviewable by appellate courts. Understanding this case as evidencing a preference-eliciting default rule is also consistent with another canon, which construes unclear statutory language in favor of aliens in deportation cases.[43]

More generally, many constitutional laws can be understood as intended to protect discrete and insular minorities who have little access to the legislative agenda.[44] The notion that being a discrete and insular minority entitles a group to normative protection from legislation has been criticized by noted scholars like Professor Tribe, because often such a minority deserves to be treated badly, such as with the class of people who are professional burglars.[45] But when the canon against constitutional doubts is used to protect such groups, it serves an important preference-eliciting function, without necessarily offering these groups any absolute normative protection from this type of legislation. This can be true for racial or religious minorities who are politically disadvantaged, or for other marginalized political groups. Even if legislation that burdens them is not unconstitutional, using the canon against constitutional doubts to interpret ambiguous legislation not to burden them, where legislative preferences are unclear, usefully results in more precise legislation. This is also even true for groups that are less normatively attractive, like burglars. Indeed, burglars are protected by the rule of lenity, for precisely the same preference-eliciting reasons.

This does not mean that all discrete and insular minorities merit a preference-eliciting rule. As Professor Ackerman has pointed out, being discrete and insular might sometimes confer an advantage in political organization, as with interest groups.[46] Others may not have an advantage, but do have enough influence that issues affecting them are better characterized as reflecting conflicted political demand. What matters, then, is whether the particular group suffers the sort of political disadvantage that creates a differential likelihood of legislative correction.

The above analysis also does not mean that all applications of the constitutional doubts canon can be justified in preference-eliciting terms. To begin with, a necessary predicate is uncertainty about legislative preferences. Further, even when legislative preferences are uncertain, a preference-eliciting default rule would be inappropriate (even though constitutional difficulties exist) where the issue is marked by conflicted political demand. For example, abortion rights certainly raise constitutional difficulties, but legislation on that topic is characterized by highly conflicted demand between pro-life and pro-choice forces. Consistent with this analysis, the Court declined to apply the constitutional doubts canon to a statute it felt was best interpreted to forbid government funding of programs that gave abortion advice.[47] Other applications of the canon (we will see in Chapter 14) can be justified only as supplemental default rules used in cases where legislative preferences cannot be reliably estimated or elicited.

The Canon Favoring Indian Tribes

Another canon, which has no roots in constitutional law but provides similar protection to a discrete and insular minority, is the canon that ambiguous statutes and treaties should be construed to favor Indian tribes.[48] This canon goes back to 1832, when congressional policy was not exactly pro-Indian. The canon seems unlikely to generally reflect congressional preferences, which even in modern times would presumably prefer a more neutral interpretive stance. Nor was the canon ever justified as reflecting congressional preferences. Instead, the justification given was that "doubtful expressions, instead of being resolved in favor of the United States, are to be resolved in favor of a weak and defenseless people, who are wards of the nation, and dependent wholly upon its protection and good faith."[49] This justification seems to directly acknowledge the lack of political influence Indian tribes and their allies have historically had.

This analysis does not mean that Indian tribes are entitled to be normatively favored if Congress has reached a considered judgment to adopt a constitutionally valid statute that burdens them. The usual condition that statutory meaning and legislative preferences are unclear must be met to apply this preference-eliciting default rule. "The canon of construction regarding the resolution of ambiguities in favor of Indians . . . does not permit reliance on ambiguities that do not exist; nor does it permit disregard of the clearly expressed intent of Congress."[50] The rationale is not that Indian tribes should always be favored—there are, after all, competing interests in all these cases. It is rather that, because Indian tribes are unlikely to be able to reverse a statute interpreted to burden them, adopting the opposite interpretation is more likely to lead to legislation that makes clear the precise extent to which Congress wanted statutory results that impose such burdens.

Conclusion

Preference-eliciting analysis explains many canons that disfavor the politically powerful: from the rule of lenity to the presumption against antitrust and tax exemptions; from the canon favoring Indian tribes to applications of the canon of avoidance to narrow statutes that burden politically powerless groups. The groups disfavored by these default rules may be public interest or special interest groups. The point is not that the disfavored groups normatively deserve to be disfavored. The point is rather that disfavoring them (where legislative meaning and preferences are uncertain) leads to legislative responses that more precisely identify the extent of their political influence.

CHAPTER 10

Linguistic Canons of
Statutory Construction

There are also many linguistic canons of construction whose application can often be explained as a preference-eliciting default rule. Here we must come to grips with Karl Llewellyn, who famously claimed that every canon lies in conflict with a counter-canon, and that courts pick and choose among canons in ways that seem arbitrary under the formal logic of the canons. In fact, the conflict was overstated, because many of Llewellyn's counter-canons merely defined the grounds for rebutting a presumption established by the canon, or defined limits to the scope of that canon.[1] There is nothing inconsistent about adopting a presumption about legislative meaning that is rebuttable by clear evidence of a contrary legislative meaning. Nonetheless, other canons do seem to be in formal conflict, and courts sometimes apply a canon in one case and then ignore it in others. What, for example, is one to make of a judge who sometimes applies the canon that a statute that lists some applications excludes unlisted ones, and other times applies the canon that a statute that lists certain applications includes analogous unlisted applications that further the same statutory purpose?

Preference-eliciting analysis provides a possible explanation. Applying each linguistic canon sometimes reflects a sensible preference-eliciting default rule. Other times, the conditions for applying such a rule do not exist, and therefore a preference-estimating rule (generally reflected in the counter-canon) should be applied.

Accordingly, neither the fact that a given canon is not always applied, nor that it has a counter-canon, offers reasonable grounds for criticism. What such varying applications mean, rather, is that the canons and counter-canons must be supplemented with a better theory of when they should be applied. Llewellyn was in fact trying to offer such a theory, which he called "situation-sense," but it was hopelessly vague.[2] Preference-eliciting analysis, I propose, provides a better theory for guiding canon application. The seemingly uneven application of canons is often not a mark of arbitrariness, but of selectively applying the canons and counter-canons in those case where they are most appropriate.

Does Listing Applications Exclude Unlisted Applications or Include Them by Analogy?

One of the more famous (and frequently employed) linguistic canons of construction is *expressio unius est exclusio alterius,* or "the expression of one thing excludes others."[3] Under this canon, statutory language that lists certain statutory applications excludes the possibility that the statute covers unlisted applications. For example, if a statute lists certain conditions under which an insured loses its right to collect insurance, that excludes other conditions under which an insured might lose its right to collect insurance.

As a theory of statutory meaning, this exclusion canon rests on the assumption that, if the legislature meant to include the unlisted applications, it would have listed them with the ones it did list. But this assumption seems a dubious basis for ascertaining statutory meaning or legislative preferences. Statutory language that lists certain applications may indicate a legislative desire to identify examples and inclusions, rather than limitations and exclusions. Alternatively, failing to list the application at issue may reflect simple error or inadvertence, a failure to focus on details or foresee the issue, or changed circumstances that create new applications of the same statutory concept. Omissions can also be intentional without signaling any intent to exclude the omitted applications. Omissions might instead reflect an unwillingness to incur the legislative costs of drafting for every conceivable contingency and getting agreement on such resolutions, or perhaps even an affirmative legislative desire to sidestep the issue of the statute's precise meaning and delegate it to the courts.

For all these reasons, the exclusion canon will often inaccurately reflect legislative meaning or preferences. Moreover, the canon seems to lie in formal conflict with a counter-canon. That counter-canon provides that listing certain applications may indicate a statutory purpose that should be extended by analogy to include unlisted applications that advance the same purpose.[4] Without any guiding principles, the exclusion canon and inclusion counter-canon seem to leave the court free to do whatever it wants in any given case, by just selecting the canon that produces the result it favors.

By seeing the exclusion canon as a preference-eliciting default rule, one can make more sense of it and its ostensibly uneven application. Where statutory meaning is unclear, and the conditions for a preference-eliciting approach hold, the exclusion canon helps elicit a more precise reading of enactable preferences. If the political forces that can or could have explicitly included the unlisted application have influence over the legislative agenda or drafting, and their opponents do not, then it makes sense for judges to exclude the application. Such exclusion is justifiable even if the court thinks the legislature most likely would have voted for the excluded application, because exclusion forces the legislature to explicitly make that choice and remove all doubt. Such explicit legislative choices will reflect enactable preferences more accurately than judicial guesses about what those choices would have been. They will also make sure that other affected parties have an opportunity to weigh in and deliberate on the matter.

But sometimes the conditions for a preference-eliciting default rule do not hold. Legislative correction (during drafting or after the interpretation) may be unlikely for the type of statute at hand, or unnecessary because the court feels highly confident about legislative preferences. Or it may be that either side affected by the choice of meaning can equally correct any default rule, so that there is no reason to apply a preference-eliciting default rule that burdens one of the affected sides.

Where the conditions do not support a preference-eliciting default rule, a preference-estimating default rule makes more sense. And that is what the counter-canon provides. It asks whether, given the statutory purpose (i.e., estimated preferences) evidenced by the listed applications, those preferences would be furthered by including the unlisted one or not. Such an inquiry is more likely to produce interpretations that further enactable preferences than the exclusion canon, which makes a blanket (often incorrect) assessment that legislatures always prefer to exclude all unlisted possibilities.

Thus, a court is not being inconsistent if it applies the exclusion canon in cases that satisfy the conditions for a preference-eliciting default rule, but applies the opposing inclusion canon in other cases that should be resolved by a preference-estimating default rule. If one examines the cases Llewellyn cites for this proposition, it turns out they fit this pattern.

The case Llewellyn cites for the exclusion canon held that a statute, which gave an annexing municipality a share of a partially annexed municipality's "real property," excluded any possibility that the annexing municipality was entitled to a share of the annexed municipality's personal property.[5] Because annexing municipalities are highly influential in legislatures, one would expect this result to be reconsidered if it did not reflect legislative preferences. And in fact the legislature overrode it four months later with a statutory amendment, which entitled the annexing municipality to a share of the partially annexed municipality's "personal property" as well.

Now, if it had been applying a preference-estimating default rule, the court could well have guessed that the legislature would probably prefer such a sharing of personal property. The reason is that the original statute provided for the division of liabilities.[6] It thus would have been odd to have a regime that divided the liabilities of a partially annexed municipality, but not its assets. Such a regime would create an incentive for municipalities to borrow money to fend off partial annexation. But the matter was in some doubt. More important, it would have been hard to anticipate the precise manner of division the legislature would prefer, for the division of personal property could not be limited to the division of property "in the territory annexed" (as was real property under the statute) because personal property is movable and often intangible. Further, because municipalities that are the object of successful annexation votes are (almost by definition) politically weak, it was unlikely that a court decision about whether and how to divide their personal property would have been revisited had it been in error.

By instead using a preference-eliciting default rule that put the burden of securing explicit legislative action on annexing municipalities, the court provoked the creation of a statute that eliminated any doubt about legislative preferences. The override statute also provided an explicit resolution of precisely how the legislature wanted to deal with the complexities raised by the movable and intangible nature of personal property. Thus, here application of the canon admirably served a preference-eliciting purpose.

In the case Llewellyn cites for the opposing inclusion canon, the court held that a congressional statute that constituted the Philippine government did not, by listing the appointments the governor general had power to make, exclude other appointments from his executive power.[7] Here, a preference-eliciting default rule of excluding the other appointments from the governor general's power seemed unlikely to provoke congressional correction, for the statute in question was the Organic Act, which filled a role similar to a state constitution and whose structural provisions were never amended.[8] Indeed, the Supreme Court expressly noted that Congress had taken no action in the eleven years since the Philippine executive had been deprived of this appointment authority. This inaction was rejected as inadequate evidence of legislative acquiescence, but it also meant the Court knew it could not rely on Congress to revisit a Supreme Court decision, if it approved the exclusion of this appointment power as a preference-eliciting default rule. Thus this was a more appropriate case for the preference-estimating default rule reflected in the opposing canon.

Closely related is another canon that the Supreme Court has often employed in recent cases, which provides that "a negative inference may be drawn from the exclusion of language from one statutory provision that is included in other provisions of the same statute."[9] In *Hamdan,* the Supreme Court faced three jurisdiction-stripping provisions, two that said they applied to pending cases and a third that was silent on that issue. The Court inferred from the first two that Congress did not mean the last one to apply to pending cases. As an estimate of enactable preferences, this conclusion seemed dubious, especially since Supreme Court precedent provided that, unless they said otherwise, jurisdiction-stripping provisions did apply to pending cases. Moreover, although the *Hamdan* Court acted as if it was simply obligated to apply this canon, in fact it has declined to apply it in other cases. In *Ours Garage,* for example, the Court confronted a statute with a preemption clause that had numerous provisions that included both states or its political subdivisions, but one exception that listed only states.[10] The Court declined to apply the canon, and thus did not draw the negative inference that Congress did not mean the last exception to apply to political subdivisions of a state.

This inconsistent application is hard to explain linguistically, but does make sense in terms of preference-eliciting analysis. In *Hamdan,* the canon was applied because (as Chapter 8 discussed) that case met the conditions for a preference-eliciting default rule, given the combination of unclear language and a differential likelihood of override. Favoring the Guantanamo detainees in fact had the desired effect of triggering a legislative reaction that, while hardly favorable to them, was somewhat less harsh to them than the contrary interpretation would have been. In *Ours Garage,* in contrast, it seemed unlikely that the odds of override were that differential, for the case pitted motor carriers (a fairly strong interest group) against municipalities (which are also quite influential in Congress). Further, there were reliable grounds to estimate enactable preferences, because the statute aimed to preempt *economic* regulation of motor carrier prices and services. This enactable preference would not be thwarted by interpreting the relevant exception, which was for *safety* regulation, to allow regulation by municipalties as well as states. Nor did the enactable preference suggest any congressional desire to interfere with how a state allocated regulatory authority between itself and subdivisions.

Certainly, I am not claiming that every case to cite one of these canons fits this pattern. Even an effort to derive some looser statistical correlation faces problems. These canons are often used as makeweight, to support conclusions otherwise merited on independent grounds. Other courts use them formalistically or incorrectly, reaching random or unjustifiable conclusions. But preference-eliciting reasoning does offer a theory to explain many results, including those Llewellyn himself focused on as inconsistent, and can help produce more consistent future results if applied in good faith by the courts.

Does Specific Statutory Language Limit General Language to Applications of the Same Kind or Not?

Another canon is designed to deal with situations where the statutory language that lists specific statutory applications is accompanied not by silence, but by words of generalization. This canon is *ejusdem generis* (of the same kind), and it provides that statutory language identifying specific applications limits more general language to applications of the same kind.[11] One illustrative case involved a statute that defined a "hotel" to "include inn, rooming house, and eating house, or any structure where rooms or board are furnished." The canon meant that this statute was interpreted to exclude hospitals—even though they were within the last general language because they are literally "structure[s] where room or board are furnished"—on the ground that hospitals are not the same kind of structure as the hotels and rooming houses that were mentioned in the more specific language.

This generality-limiting canon is, if anything, more dubious than the exclusion canon, from the point of view of ascertaining meaning or estimating likely legislative preferences. A legislature that adds general language on top of specific applications might well mean or desire to add something broader than the meaning already conveyed by those specific applications. After all, one would normally add a word like "such" before "other" if one meant to confine the more general language to similar applications. Moreover, all the arguments that applied to the exclusion canon apply here as well, for this canon also seeks to infer an exclusion—here from generality rather than from silence. Indeed, the addition of general language following specific applications might well reflect an affirmative legislative strategy for coping with problems of inadvertence, unforeseeability, and change, or for defining areas of clear legislative agreement without resolving other areas of possible disagreements about statutory meaning.

Not surprisingly, this canon also has its counter-canon, which provides that the more general words can indicate a statutory purpose to broaden the scope of the statute beyond the specific applications.[12] Again, Llewellyn's challenge is that, without guiding principles, this canon and counter-canon allow the court to do whatever it feels like.

However, the generality-limiting canon can make sense as a preference-eliciting default rule. Using general words after more specific language often creates ambiguity about statutory meaning, which requires some default rule. Where the conditions for a preference-eliciting default rule hold, the canon usefully forces the legislature to be explicit about just how far it wants to take any generalization from the specifically resolved statutory applications. The burdened political group can, if the narrow reading of the general language does not meet prevailing political preferences, obtain legislative correction to broaden it, or to at least include the application in question. But if the conditions for a preference-eliciting default rule are not met, then any statutory interpretation that is out of line with prevailing political preferences is unlikely to be revisited. Instead it will likely stick, and thus the court must do its best to determine how the legislature would have wanted the general language interpreted in the case at hand.

Again, if one examines the cases that Llewellyn cites as indicating opposing canons, they support this preference-eliciting analysis. For the generality-limiting canon, he cites the case noted above that excludes hospitals from the language "any structure where rooms or board are furnished," because that language follows more specific references to hotel-like structures. The effect was to deny hospitals a lien available to hotels.[13] As one might expect, the hospital lobby did not have great difficulty getting on the legislative agenda, and this decision promptly provoked a legislative reaction creating a hospital lien within a year. Further, the provoked legislation distinguished hospital liens from hotel liens, creating a lien on damage recoveries rather than on belongings, and provided statutory detail about precisely how the lien could be enforced. Such nuance would have been difficult for any court to provide through statutory interpretation of the general language in the original statute.

In contrast, the cases Llewellyn cites for the counter-canon involved situations where preference-eliciting seemed unlikely, so preference-estimating was more in order. One case concerned a federal statute, which exempted transactions approved by Interstate Commerce Commission (ICC) order "from the operation of the antitrust laws . . . and of all other restraints or prohibitions by or imposed under authority of law, State or Federal."[14] The Supreme Court rejected the generality-limiting canon's implication, which was that the general language exempted the railroad only from statutes similar in kind to antitrust laws, and held that it also exempted the railroad from state regulations that inefficiently required the railroad to keep duplicative offices in that state. The Court seemed right that rejecting the canon better fit the legislative preference for lowering transportation costs. Nor was application of the canon likely to further preference-eliciting purposes, because it is difficult to get on the congressional agenda to protect a large diffuse group (railroad consumers) by eliminating inefficient regulation that benefits a concentrated local group. At best one might get concentrated groups on both sides, and that sort of conflicted political demand fails to meet the conditions for a preference-eliciting default rule.

The other case cited for the opposing canon concerned a state statute that taxed "kerosene," defining it to include various heating, lighting, and motor oils, or any substance that met certain scientific tests.[15] The defendant, a seller of a paint solvent that met the scientific test, argued that the statute should be restricted to oils similar in kind to heating, lighting, and motor oils. The court rejected application of the generality-limiting canon. Here, a preference-eliciting default rule was not warranted, because it is seldom easy to get on the legislative agenda to add a new tax on a concentrated group like paint solvent dealers. Thus, the court could have little confidence that the legislature would have reconsidered any tax exclusion of paint solvent dealers.

Plain Meaning or Legislative Purpose and History?

Canons providing that judges cannot go beyond the text and its plain meaning are often set against counter-canons, which provide that judges can go beyond the text if the statutory purpose indicates the contrary or if the literal language would produce an absurd result.[16] This brings us close to a dispute about statutory meaning; but suppose for a moment that (after applying whatever combination of text, purpose, or legislative history you prefer) you find the resulting meaning unclear, and thus need to reach the question of what default rule to employ.

As Part II showed, a preference-estimating default rule is likely to look to legislative purpose or history or absurdities because, even if they do not indicate statutory meaning, they are highly relevant to the underlying political preferences. Where the purpose, history, or absurdity is clear, then the court knows which preferences are enactable, and there is little cause to apply a preference-eliciting default rule. But where they are unclear, then a court might well be uncertain about legislative preferences, and thus have good grounds to use a preference-eliciting default rule that relies only on the plain meaning of the text. Such a plain meaning rule makes sense if the group harmed by such an interpretation has disproportionate legislative influence, so that it could have put the issue in the text of the original statute, or can easily command the legislative agenda to put it in the text in a statutory override. But absent such conditions, a preference-eliciting default rule makes little sense, and the court might as well rely on all indicia (inside or outside the text) that indicate what the legislature likely would have wanted and make the best estimate it can.

Here, the cases cited by Llewellyn are consistent with this thesis but not as illuminating as one might like. One case Llewellyn cited for the plain meaning rule did not actually involve any claim that the statute in question had a plain meaning.[17] The other case he cited employed the plain meaning canon to refuse to add, to the statutory text, any judicial rules for coordinating separate statutes that respectively authorized: (1) judgment lien suits against debtors (who then died), and (2) executor suits to settle the estate.[18] That decision did in fact provoke a legislative correction within a couple of years, which provided better guidance about how to coordinate such suits. This decision was thus probably justifiable on preference-eliciting grounds, given that usually creditors are more concentrated and thus better organized politically than debtors, and thus could have been expected to be more likely to command the legislative agenda to clear up the confusion. But the opinion leaves unclear both the facts on this score and the relative interests of creditors and debtors in this issue.

Of greater interest are two of the most famous cases for the opposing canons—the snail darter case and the case of the murdering heir—which Ronald Dworkin juxtaposed in a famous argument against the plain meaning canon.[19] Dworkin persuasively shows that these cases are irreconcilable on interpretive grounds. But they can be both explained and strongly justified by the analysis above about when preference-eliciting and preference-estimating default rules should apply.

The snail darter case applied the plain meaning canon to interpret the Endangered Species Act, which prohibited carrying out federal projects that "jeopardize[d] the continued existence of [an] endangered species" or "result[ed] in the destruction or modification of habitat of such species."[20] As a $100 million dam was nearing completion, it was discovered that the dam would do precisely that to the snail darter, an endangered species. The question, in Dworkin's words, was whether this Act required halting "a vast, almost finished federal power project to save a small and ecologically uninteresting fish." The Supreme Court held that it did. This result certainly did not indicate the Court's view of sound policy, for it explicitly disavowed any claim that it thought it was wise to sacrifice $100 million to save this species. Nor did it reflect likely political preferences, for legislative appropriations committees had repeatedly considered the dam's impact on the snail darter, each time concluding that the project should proceed anyway and obtaining congressional approval of appropriation acts that provided an overall budget for the relevant agency that included the funds it planned to use to complete the dam. But the Court held that its decision was warranted by the plain meaning rule, which prevented the Court from creating an exception for relatively unimportant species that were holding up enormous, nearly completed projects.

Such compunctions about plain meaning did not seem to trouble the court in the case of the murdering heir. There the statute provided that a properly executed will transferred the deceased's property to the named beneficiaries.[21] The question was whether this statute governed even when the named beneficiary had murdered the deceased to prevent him from revoking the will. The court conceded that, "if literally construed," the statute dictated giving the murderer the property, for it contained no exception for murdering heirs. But the court declined to follow the plain meaning rule, and instead applied the counter-canon that a literal interpretation would not be followed if contrary to the lawmakers' intention. Here there was no direct evidence of a contrary intention, but the court was confident that "it never could have been their intention" to allow murderers to inherit from their victims, and that "[i]f such a case had been present to their minds . . . it cannot be doubted that they would have provided for it" by excluding murderers from the statute.

To Dworkin, the murdering heir case is a Herculean triumph, the snail darter case a formalistic mistake. Both cases featured plain language that seemed to dictate a bad result, for which the statute provided no exception.

But in neither case was there any indication that the legislature had thought about the bad result and desired it. The snail darter case seems, if anything, a stronger case for excluding the bad result based on likely legislative preferences, given the concrete evidence that Congress continued to make appropriations despite the dam's known impact on the snail darter. But Dworkin is right only if we assume that the court's role is solely to determine which interpretation best fits the likely political convictions or preferences of the legislature. Consider how the cases look when one instead takes into account preference-eliciting analysis.

In the snail darter case, the Supreme Court could have tried to create a preference-estimating exception to the Endangered Species Act, but there would have been various problems with this approach. To begin with, the alternative interpretive option actually being offered was that the Endangered Species Act did not apply to projects that were more than half completed when the Act became effective.[22] But that interpretation would have exempted mostly done projects that threatened *any* species, which was clearly contrary to the enactable preferences of Congress, as the Court explained at great length. Indeed, it is striking that the fourteen-page discussion reaching this conclusion was *based almost entirely on legislative history,* suggesting the opinion was driven by something other than a belief that the Court could not go beyond the statutory text.

The more persuasive basis for making a preference-estimating exception was that it was not worth losing $100 million to save *this* species, because it was unimportant. But this interpretive option raised two problems as well. The smaller problem is that, while this exception seemed likely to be enactable given the appropriations decisions, this was far from certain. After all, the appropriations committees were not the whole Congress. All Congress had done was approve lump-sum budgets for the agency, without any evidence that Congress was aware of any implications for the Endangered Species Act, and under a procedural rule that specifically provided that no appropriations bill would change existing law.[23] The Court further noted that it was unsure that any such exception could have gotten past the relevant committees that would have considered any amendment to the Endangered Species Act. And while Dworkin seems convinced that the snail darter was "ecologically uninteresting," all endangered species must be ecologically interesting to some extent. One man's snail darter might be another man's snow leopard.

But this smaller problem pales before the bigger one: what exactly would a judicially created exception have looked like? The Court could hardly have interpreted the Endangered Species Act to mean that federal projects cannot jeopardize an endangered species, "except the snail darter." It would instead have had to interpret the words of the Act to define some general parameters, which would determine when the ecological interest in preserving a species should be deemed outweighed by the cost sacrificed if a project were abandoned. There seems to be no way for the Court to have defined such an exception without embroiling the courts in open-ended trade-offs between project and species importance, trade-offs that the courts lack the budgetary, scientific, and political expertise to make, as the Court stressed.[24] And any defined exception would have erred, to some extent, in identifying the precise balance of prevailing political preferences on such trade-offs.

The case was thus an appropriate one for a preference-eliciting default rule, if the Court could be confident that application of the plain meaning canon would prompt legislative consideration to correct the decision. Here that seemed likely because powerful legislators strongly favored the project. Just to be sure, the Court majority and dissent both effectively called on Congress to override by statute the Court's own ruling.[25] They were not disappointed. Congress immediately did just that, creating both a general exception through a statute authorizing an agency to make exemptions to the Act, and overturning the result in the snail darter case in particular. Thus, the Court's use of a preference-eliciting default rule not only removed all doubt that proceeding with the project satisfied enactable preferences, but provoked more explicit legislation creating a detailed mechanism for a politically accountable agency to make future exceptions.

Another reason to adopt such a default rule lies in its relative correctability. The Court's interpretation allowed Congress to override the particular result and complete the project. Had the Court instead chosen to allow the project to proceed but been mistaken about legislative preferences, it would have left Congress unable to overturn the particular result—for, once extinct, the snail darter could not have been resurrected. Thus, in the event that either interpretation turned out not to match legislative preferences, the interim costs would be much lower for the Court's plain meaning interpretation than for the contrary interpretation.

The case of the murdering heir was entirely different. Presumably, any decision allowing the murderer to inherit would also have prompted a quick legislative override. But why bother to provoke override? Allowing a murderer to inherit from the one he murdered is absurd, and the court could be 100% sure no legislature would want that result. The court applied precisely such a standard in concluding that the legislature "never" would have intended that result, and that "it cannot be doubted" the legislature would provide the exception if presented with the question.[26]

Nor did the court have any great difficulty defining the exception the legislature would have created, because that merely required a holding that murderers cannot inherit from their victims.[27] This was not an issue presenting serious social trade-offs, for which the precise balance of political powers was relevant. In short, while the anti-murder lobby was doubtless influential enough to override any failure to create an exception, there was no earthly reason to stomach the wrong result in the interim. Other potential murders might even have been encouraged by any interim reward of inheritance before the corrective legislation could be enacted.

Finally, if the court had interpreted the statute to allow the murderer to inherit, the legislature could never correct the wrong result in the case at hand. Once the murderer took the property, any legislation stripping him of that property would be an unconstitutional taking of property and ex post facto punishment. Nor could any murders encouraged in the interim before override ever be undone. The interim costs of an interpretation mistakenly favoring murdering inheritors would thus be high. Accordingly, this was a poor case for any preference-eliciting function that the plain meaning rule might provide, and it is not surprising that the court instead went with a preference-estimating default rule.

In addition to this case analysis, more systematic empirical evidence helps support the thesis that the plain meaning canon often serves a preference-eliciting function. What the empirical evidence shows is that statutory interpretations that rely on the plain meaning canon are the most likely to be overriden by Congress, more than three times as likely as interpretations that rely on legislative history or statutory purpose.[28] This suggests that the plain meaning canon serves a preference-eliciting function more often than do other forms of statutory interpretation.

However, it is also true that most plain meaning decisions are not overridden by Congress. Even when such decisions are preference-eliciting, this may merely mean that the canon successfully produced ex ante precision or ex post confirmation of the less likely preference. Other times, the lack of override may simply mean that the usage was not preference-eliciting. The canon may have been used to correctly derive statutory meaning. It might also have been invoked as a makeweight for interpretations that were justifiable on other grounds, or invoked formalistically and arbitrarily. The raw numbers do not distinguish among these possibilities, and thus the proposition that the plain meaning canon often serves preference-eliciting functions cannot be established by statistics alone. It must rest on careful analysis of actual cases, like those discussed above.

While not all uses of the plain meaning canon reflect preference-eliciting default rules, many do, and preference-eliciting default rules can explain some of the most perplexing—and seemingly inconsistent—applications of the canon. Preference-eliciting analysis seems particularly applicable to those plain meaning decisions that openly invite legislative override.[29] If the preference-eliciting logic that underlies these applications of the canon is understood, that should produce more consistent statutory interpretations in the future.

Variations among Jurisdictions

Not all legislatures are equally responsive and likely to override statutory interpretations. If my preference-eliciting analysis is correct, one would thus expect applications of preference-eliciting canons to vary with the responsiveness of the legislature in question. Some evidence is consistent with this prediction, but much more empirical work remains to be done.

Compared to the U.S. Congress, the British Parliament is a highly responsive legislature, because parliamentary enactments require the action of only one legislative body. Further, Parliament is not subject to executive veto, is normally dominated by one party, and is marked by party discipline in voting. Conflicts between legislative institutions are thus less likely to block legislative action. The committee system is also more centralized under the prime minister, and thus conflicts between particular committees and the legislature as a whole are less likely to block legislative action. Given these lower obstacles to legislative override, and the argument above that many applications of the plain meaning canon reflect a preference-eliciting default rule, one would expect British courts to be more willing to apply the plain meaning canon than U.S. courts.

And historically they have been. It was not until 1993 that the British courts announced that, for the first time, they would begin considering parliamentary debates when resolving textual ambiguities.[30] This shift toward allowing some inquiry into legislative history might reflect the fact that, as society gets more populous and complex, limited legislative time becomes scarcer, so that even parliamentary systems become less responsive to judicial interpretations that conflict with political preferences.

In contrast, the U.S. Supreme Court went through its shift on the topic in 1892, the date of its first important use of legislative history.[31] This difference between Great Britain and the United States suggests that the less responsive the legislative structure, the earlier the historical point at which society becomes too complex to have the sort of general legislative responsiveness that justifies a preference-eliciting default rule against using legislative history. Indeed, even after their recent shift, the British courts remain more likely to rely on plain meaning than their American counterparts, as one would expect, given the fact that their legislative structure remains more responsive.[32]

This is not to suggest that these structural factors alone determine the use of legislative history. Intellectual forces and changes in personnel play a role too, as exemplified by the effect Justice Scalia has had on the U.S. Supreme Court. But whether intellectual movements and leaders find willing listeners depends, at least in part, on whether circumstances render those listeners receptive. So it is hardly surprising that different levels of legislative responsiveness produce different levels of receptivity to plain meaning arguments.

Courts at different appellate levels also predictably differ in the likelihood they will provoke a legislative reaction. The Supreme Court is far more likely to provoke congressional overrides than lower courts.[33] One might thus expect that lower courts would use preference-eliciting canons less often. To be sure, even if it does not lead to legislative override, a lower appellate court might sometimes be tempted to employ a preference-eliciting default rule to provoke a Supreme Court decision that will lead to override. However, the odds of certiorari are small enough that this seems an unlikely strategy, except perhaps in cases where a clear and important circuit conflict is created.

Conclusion and the Problematic Nature of the Distinction between Substantive and Linguistic Canons

Perhaps nowhere have judges been more accused of incoherence, and of manipulating canons to further their own views, than in the use of linguistic canons of construction. Ever since Llewellyn first argued that for every such canon there is a counter-canon, scholars have condemned their haphazard application. But the seeming incoherence can often be reconciled by preference-eliciting analysis. The relevant canons are generally applied when the appropriate conditions exist for a preference-eliciting default rule, and when those conditions do not exist, a counter-canon embodying a preference-estimating default rule is instead used. Different political structures and circumstances in different jurisdictions also help explain, to at least some extent, the variation we see among courts in the use of canons with a preference-eliciting function.

One implication of this chapter is to cast doubt on a distinction that current scholarship on statutory interpretation routinely draws: the distinction between linguistic canons (which are supposed to help interpret the probable meaning of text) and substantive canons (which are supposed to further some substantive policy that judges have found persuasive). This standard distinction often will not track the underlying difference in default rule approach. Linguistic or textual canons may sometimes be applied to arrive at the best interpretation of meaning or best estimate of legislative preferences. But often they intentionally deviate from the most likely meaning or preferences in order to elicit a more precise understanding of enactable preferences. Likewise, substantive canons may sometimes deviate from likely legislative preferences, as with the rule of lenity noted above. But even when this is so, this need not mean those canons are furthering a substantive policy favored by judges, rather than trying to elicit legislative reactions that will produce more ultimate satisfaction of political preferences. Further, often substantive canons do reflect likely legislative preferences.

CHAPTER 11

Interpretations That May Create International Conflict

Suppose a U.S. statute has two reasonable interpretations, one that makes it applicable to extraterritorial conduct in a way that might create conflicts with the interests of other nations, and another interpretation that does not. Suppose also that the judge's best estimate is that current or enactor preferences lean in favor of the extraterritorial interpretation, but are uncertain. If so, then we have a strong case for a preference-eliciting default rule that interprets the U.S. statute narrowly. Domestic interests are probably more able than foreign ones to gain access to the legislative agenda to override any interpretation that conflicts with enactable preferences. This creates a significant differential likelihood of override, which justifies adopting the narrow interpretation unless it has excessive interim costs. But where enactable preferences are reasonably clear, or interim costs are high, then such a preference-eliciting approach should not be used.

This analysis helps to explain two canons of statutory construction. Both have their basis in a more general canon, which provides that an unclear statute should be interpreted not to conflict with international law.[1] Given the content of international law, this general canon implies two, more specific, canons. The first is the exterritorial-conduct canon, which provides that unclear statutes should be construed not to govern exterritorial conduct, unless it was reasonably foreseeable that the conduct would have direct, substantial effects within the United States.[2] The second is the comity canon, which provides that, even when they do apply extraterritorially, unclear statutes should be interpreted to be inapplicable in cases where the interests of other nations clearly outweigh U.S. interests.[3]

204

The Extraterritorial-Conduct Canon. This canon was applied in *Aramco,* which addressed the question whether Title VII applied to discrimination, in Saudi Arabia, by an American corporation against an American citizen.[4] The Court found the statutory language "ambiguous," and thus applied the canon to interpret the statute to be inapplicable to such extraterritorial conduct.

Some critics have argued that the result in this case failed to advance likely legislative preferences, which should have been ascertained by balancing the relevant national interests at issue. Other critics have argued that the canon generally fails to advance likely legislative preferences, because of the strong congressional interest in protecting U.S. citizens while they are abroad. Both of these critiques essentially assume that preference-estimating analysis would have been more appropriate.[5]

But suppose we instead understand the canon as a preference-eliciting default rule. Then the *Aramco* decision makes considerably more sense, because any extraterritorial interpretation would have raised tricky issues that the Court feared might create "unintended clashes between our laws and those of other nations which could result in international discord."[6] The Court expressly pointed to one such issue: an interpretation covering discrimination in foreign workplaces against American citizens would apply not just to American employers operating abroad, but to foreign employers as well. This would raise "difficult issues of international law by imposing this country's employment-discrimination regime upon foreign corporations operating in foreign commerce." Moreover, if the *Aramco* situation should be governed by U.S. rather than Saudi law when the conduct occurred in Saudi Arabia, parallelism would suggest that Title VII should be inapplicable to discrimination by a foreign employer against a foreign employee in the United States itself.

Any interpretation the *Aramco* Court could make might thus fail to capture the nuances of just what Congress would want. However, the Court could obtain more explicit legislative guidance by provoking a legislative reaction with a preference-eliciting default rule, such as the extraterritorial-conduct canon. This is precisely what happened. Congress promptly overrode *Aramco* less than nine months later.[7] Its amendment neither made the statute applicable to all extraterritorial conduct, nor made application turn on case-by-case balancing of interests. Instead, the amendment limited extraterritorial application to discrimination in foreign workplaces by American employers against American citizens. It excluded discrimination in foreign workplaces by foreign employers against American citizens, as well as by American employers against foreign nationals. Congress also provided that the statute did not apply to extraterritorial conduct that was required by foreign law, and added provisions specifying how to treat foreign firms controlled by American firms. In short, the preference-eliciting default rule provoked Congress into providing just the sort of nuanced specificity and limitations that the Court would have had difficulty divining. The Court had good reason to expect this result because, when courts had previously used the same canon to deny extraterritorial application of the Age Discrimination in Employment Act, Congress had quickly overridden that result.[8]

A preference-eliciting default rule also makes more general sense when considering the application of statutes to extraterritorial conduct that does not have substantial, foreseeable effects within the United States. First, such cases usually satisfy the condition of uncertain enactable preferences, because it is normally difficult to determine what legislatures would want regarding the extraterritorial application of their statutes to such cases. Courts could certainly weigh the relevant national interests to arrive at reasonable guesses, but the general political preferences will typically be unclear, because legislatures rarely think about the extraterritorial application of their statutes. The details of how legislatures would like to resolve conflicts will be even less clear, for such decisions involve not just the usual complications in estimating legislative policy preferences, but open-ended political judgments about how far to push the legislative policy when it conflicts with foreign governmental policy. A national legislature's willingness to inflict extraterritorial effects that annoy foreign governments does not turn only on a neutral balancing of interests. It turns as well on a *realpolitik* assessment of that nation's bargaining power in the international arena, as well as on the importance the nation places on this matter among others at issue in international affairs. One must also weigh the likelihood that affected nations will respond with blocking statutes, or with their own efforts to impose extraterritorial regulation on the first nation. Courts will thus often guess wrong about what the legislature would have wanted to do about the extraterritoriality issue in such cases.

Second, cases of extraterritorial conduct that harm domestic interests that are operating abroad will generally exhibit a differential likelihood of override. If the national government wants a ruling of nonextraterritorial application reversed, it can likely do so, because it has the best access to the legislative agenda. Indeed, the U.S. government has the best statistical record

of any entity in securing legislative override of adverse statutory interpretations, and frequently does secure legislative overrides of cases that apply the
canon against extraterritorial application.[9] Moreover, such cases generally
pit domestic interests against foreign interests, and the legislature is usually
far more responsive to the former. Foreign interests will generally exercise
influence by exerting pressure on the executive branch, which is better
placed than the judiciary to decide how strongly to weigh those foreign interests.

To be sure, one might reasonably argue, as Professor Goldsmith has, that
interpreting statutes to have broad extraterritorial application might be even
more likely to elicit legislative reactions, by creating the sort of international
discord that requires some response.[10] I doubt he is right in his empirical
premise that such interpretations would be more likely to provoke legislative reactions, because the predominant influence of domestic interests
means that such a rule would put the burden of legislative correction on foreign actors that are less able to command the legislative agenda. But the
larger problem is that this alternative would not meet the third condition for
a preference-eliciting default rule. It would impose excessive interim costs,
in the form of unnecessary international conflict in many cases. Congress
will generally not want a broad extraterritorial application that creates such
international conflict, but may take awhile to get around to narrowing the
statute to avoid it. Thus, even if both extremes were equally likely to provoke legislative reactions, the canon against extraterritorial application would
typically be more desirable, given interim costs.[11]

The Comity Canon. Suppose now that we have extraterritorial conduct that
does have substantial foreseeable effects within the United States. This is
typically the case for many forms of market conduct, such as a foreign conspiracy to fix prices that adversely affects prices within the United States.
Even though such a case does involve extraterritorial conduct, we can reasonably assume that Congress would not have wanted to completely immunize foreign conduct with such substantial foreseeable U.S. effects. Such
immunity would create a massive loophole, for it would not only leave U.S.
markets vulnerable to foreign cartels but also mean that any domestic firm
that wanted to fix prices could simply take a trip abroad in order to enter
into a price-fixing conspiracy. This is thus one interpretive option we can
confidently conclude conflicts with likely enactable preferences. In any
event, it would have interim costs that would be too high to make it accept-

able as a preference-eliciting default rule. The courts thus, not surprisingly, hold that the canon against extraterritorial conduct does not immunize foreign conduct with such substantial foreseeable U.S. effects.[12]

However, the fact that a statute is interpreted to apply to such extraterritorial conduct does not mean that it must apply to it in the same way. Instead, the courts apply the comity canon against interpretations that interfere with foreign interests that are clearly greater. Sometimes this canon is applied in a case-by-case way, by weighing the U.S. and foreign interests.[13] But it can be applied more categorically as well. For example, *Empagran* addressed the question whether, when an international price-fixing conspiracy allegedly had both substantial foreseeable U.S. effects and independent separate effects in foreign nations, the U.S. antitrust statute applied to claims against the latter effects. The Supreme Court ruled that it did not, applying the comity canon to interpret the statute to never apply to such independent foreign effects.[14]

Depending on how it is applied, we can understand application of such a comity canon as either a preference-estimating or preference-eliciting default rule. Under the preference-estimating version, courts would examine both U.S. and foreign interests, but would base decisions entirely on whether, given the likely backlash to the United States from harming foreign interests, U.S. interests would really be advanced in the long run by the broad interpretation. This would reflect the best estimate of congressional preferences, because Congress presumably aims to maximize U.S. interests, not aggregate world interests. Under the preference-eliciting version, courts would weigh foreign interests equally, or perhaps even more strongly, in order to elicit from Congress a more precise indication of just how far it wants to go in impeding those foreign interests in order to advance U.S. interests.

It is certainly unsettling that the comity canon is so open-ended that it is difficult to be sure about something as basic as what the canon is trying to maximize. Various methods might reduce this uncertainty. First, greater clarity would be provided if courts using the comity canon made clear whether they give foreign interests weight only to the extent that they bear on ultimate U.S. interests (the estimating approach) or give foreign interests greater weight (the eliciting approach). The fact that the Foreign Relations Restatement limits the comity canon to cases where the foreign interest is "clearly" greater suggests that it leans more toward the first approach.[15] But a clearer articulation of what the canon seeks to maximize, and how it does so, would reduce its uncertainty.

Second, given the uncertainty about how to weigh U.S. interests against foreign interests, courts might reasonably adopt a rule of always following whatever the U.S. government advises about comity issues, in any case where the United States participates as a party or amicus. After all, the U.S. government seems much better placed to assess such open-ended trade-offs. Some courts have adopted precisely such a rule.[16] One might go further, and say the courts should elicit such government views by asking for briefing in any such cases.

Third, one might in such cases instead adopt a *treaty*-eliciting approach, by concluding that comity issues never bar extraterritorial applications, unless the relevant statute would require conduct prohibited by foreign law. Some decisions interpreting antitrust statutes in both the United States and the European Community (EC) have this flavor.[17] Such an approach is likely to create international policy conflicts (as these U.S. and EC decisions did) in a way that might be more likely to provoke an international agreement, compared to more narrow decisions that avoid such conflict at the cost of creating international underregulation. Assuming that this is true, and that the interim costs of such conflict would not be excessive, then this approach could serve a useful preference-eliciting function if the following two additional conditions were met.

1. The relevant issue must be one that can be resolved effectively only by international agreement, because each nation has perverse incentives to externalize costs onto other nations, so that all the nations have a collective action problem that requires resolution by a collective agreement. If so, estimating or eliciting the preferences of the legislature from one nation would not help, because each nation individually has incentives to adopt statutes that externalize costs. Nor could a court solve the problem by interpreting unclear statutory language to adopt whatever the court predicts would have been produced by international agreement. The reason is that these collective action problems mean that other nations would still have incentives to allow conduct that externalizes its harm onto nations other than themselves. What needs to be provoked is an international agreement that can bind multiple nations.

2. An international forum must exist that makes it likely that an international agreement will be struck. Trade negotiations seemed like they might constitute such a forum for an international antitrust agreement, and indeed were once on the agenda for the Doha round of World Trade Organization (WTO) trade negotiations.[18]

Although in theory such a treaty-eliciting approach can make sense, I am no longer convinced (as I once was) that these conditions apply to antitrust. The claim that the first condition was satisfied depended on the argument that international markets created collective action problems for antitrust regulation, by giving each nation incentives to underregulate exporters and overregulate importers.[19] But although each nation does exempt exporters, this does not create problems, because the nations that import their goods can regulate their conduct. Nor do importing nations have an incentive to overregulate because under the consumer welfare standard applied by both the United States and the European Community, no nation would want to condemn any conduct that created efficiencies that resulted in lower consumer prices. The only thing nations really need to cooperate on is collecting evidence and enforcing each other's judgments, and it is on such issues (rather than on substantive rules) that we have actually seen international cooperation.[20]

The claim that the second condition was satisfied by WTO negotiations likewise seems mistaken, or at least premature. In 2004, the Doha negotiations on international antitrust rules collapsed, even on rules limited to the relatively uncontroversial issue of hardcore cartels.[21] While this does not mean that the WTO cannot form a sensible forum for such international negotiations, it suggests that the likelihood of provoking some international agreement is not currently high enough to merit a treaty-eliciting default rule. But that might change in the future, given the growing internationalization of our world.

CHAPTER 12

Explaining Seeming Inconsistencies in Statutory *Stare Decisis*

The Difficulty of Explaining the Doctrine under Current Theory

The blackletter rule is that judicial precedents that interpret statutes have especially strong *stare decisis* effect. Indeed, such statutory precedent is often said to enjoy a doctrine of "super-strong" *stare decisis*.[1] This doctrine has been strongly criticized on two grounds. First, the doctrine is inconsistently applied: the courts often adhere to statutory precedents, but also often overturn them. To many, this suggests that the courts ignore the doctrine whenever they find it inconvenient. Second, scholars have roundly criticized the principal rationale for the doctrine—that legislatures can always override any statutory precedent they do not like[2]—on the ground that legislatures rarely review statutory interpretations.

Given the underlying rationale, this doctrine may seem to be the quintessential preference-eliciting default rule. But while the critique of this rationale is overblown, the doctrine cannot in fact be justified on this basis. The critique is overblown because, as noted in Chapter 8, in fact Congress routinely monitors Supreme Court statutory interpretations, holds actual hearings on 50% of them, and overrides 6–8%, with the percentage of overrides presumably higher for that subset of interpretations that conflicts with enactable congressional preferences. Nonetheless, it remains dubious to think that legislative override is always likely when the legislature is displeased. More important, Chapter 8 shows that a preference-eliciting default rule is justified only when the likelihood of legislative correction *differs* for the two sides affected by an interpretive issue, and it is even more dubious to think that statutory precedent always burdens the side of a dispute that has preferential access to the legislative agenda.

Thus, given the limited conditions that justify a preference-eliciting default rule, across-the-board application of a doctrine of super-strong *stare decisis* for statutory precedent seems misguided. Instead, to make sense of the doctrine, and its pattern of application, we must consider the various bases for reaching the initial statutory interpretation and what they indicate about when adhering to that precedent is likely to maximize political satisfaction.

Why Courts Should Stick to Statutory Precedent Absent Evidence of a Change in Legislative Conditions

Consider first the case where there is no evidence that legislative conditions have changed since the statutory precedent was decided. In other words, assume that we have a case where (leaving aside the lack of legislative override itself) any estimates would remain unchanged, both of enactable preferences and of the likelihood that, if incorrect, a statutory interpretation would be overturned. If so, then even though statutory *stare decisis* is not itself generally a good preference-eliciting default rule, it can be shown that the absence of any legislative override (however unlikely it was) provides a strong reason to stick to that precedent, and thus indirectly supports the presumption of statutory *stare decisis* doctrine. This is true even when that precedent reflects a default rule designed to maximize political satisfaction, rather than a conclusion that the statute has a fixed meaning.

This conclusion hardly seems surprising when the precedent initially reflected the best estimate of enactable preferences. After all, absent any independent change in legislative conditions, the lack of a legislative override can only increase the confidence of any initial estimate that the precedent reflects enactable preferences. But this conclusion may seem counterintuitive when the precedent itself was meant to be preference-eliciting. When a statutory precedent reflected the imposition of a preference-eliciting default rule, why wouldn't any case where the precedent failed to elicit a legislative override mean that judges should abandon the default rule, because it failed in its mission?

Part of the answer is that preference-eliciting default rules also aim to elicit ex ante clarification. This goal could not be achieved if courts were willing to abandon a preference-eliciting default rule every time the legislature failed to override it. To the contrary, such a judicial practice of abandonment, if sufficiently quick, would give politically influential groups incentives not to spend any effort on securing legislative clarifications, because an easier judicial override would be forthcoming. It could even give them incentives to affirmatively block legislative action that might lead to clarifying compromises, which would be less advantageous to them than a judicial override. This would thwart one of the objectives Chapter 8 explained preference-eliciting default rules can have: encouraging legislative clarifications that reflect nuanced enactable preferences better than could any of the interpretive options available to courts.

Sticking to a preference-eliciting default rule also generally makes sense even if (as with unforeseeable ambiguities) no ex ante clarification seems plausible, so that the only purpose for imposing the default rule would be to provoke ex post correction. Part of the reason is the same as for the ex ante case: if rapid judicial correction were in the offing, then politically influential groups would have incentives to avoid, or even block, efforts at achieving ex post legislative overrides that are more costly to secure or may entail more damaging compromises.

But we can go further. Assuming no other change in legislative conditions, it always turns out to be desirable to stick to the preference-eliciting default rule, even if the judiciary has a practice of waiting long enough, after the initial statutory precedent, that politically influential groups would prefer to seek quick ex post legislative correction. The reason is that one reason to impose a preference-eliciting default rule is precisely to test an uncertain, probabilistic estimate about which interpretive option is more enactable. For example, one reason for choosing interpretive option *B* in my initial illustration in Chapter 8 was that it would stick in the 40% of cases where *B* reflected actual legislative preferences. That advantage would be lost if option *B* were judicially reversed because the legislature failed to overturn it. More generally, any legislative failure to override a preference-eliciting default rule signals that the court was probably incorrect to presume that its initial interpretation did not reflect likely legislative preferences.

Indeed, one can prove that, if the legislature has failed to correct a statutory precedent that met the conditions for a preference-eliciting default rule, that precedent will now reflect the best available estimate of legislative preferences, even though it did not seem so at the time the precedent was handed down. This proof will require some inquiry into the mathematics of conditional probabilities. Call option *B* the statutory precedent that reflects a preference-eliciting default rule. Then, using the same notation described in Chapter 8, we can describe the decision tree as follows. In the left branches of the decision tree, P_B and P_A reflect the relative probabilities that (between the two interpretive options) B and A correctly reflect enactable legislative preferences. The right branches then reflect the conditional probabilities that legislative override will occur if option B is right or wrong.

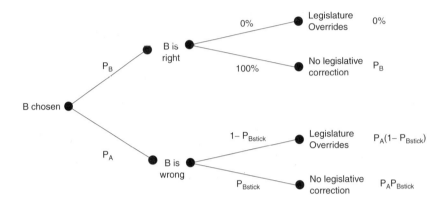

If option B correctly reflects enactable preferences, then the odds of legislative override are 0%, and the odds that there will be no legislative correction are 100%.[3] If B does not correctly reflect enactable preferences, then the probability that B will stick uncorrected is P_{Bstick}, and the odds that B will be overridden are $1 - P_{Bstick}$. The odds at the far right are then derived from multiplying the probabilities in the decision tree that are necessary to get to that point.

The key point is that the fact that there was no legislative correction provides valuable information, which can alter initial estimates of whether B accurately reflects legislative preferences. It means we can exclude the far right probabilities of legislative override and focus solely on the two cases involving no legislative correction. The decision tree reveals that, in the set of cases without any legislative correction, the probability is P_B that this reflects a case where B actually does accurately reflect legislative preferences, and $P_A P_{Bstick}$ that this reflects a case where B does not. Thus, even if it did not initially seem the option most likely to match legislative preferences, B will now be the option most likely to match legislative preferences if $P_B >$ $P_A P_{Bstick}$. But we know from the fact that option B was initially chosen as the default rule that (absent some intervening change in circumstances) $P_B >$ $P_A P_{Bstick} / P_{Astick}$. Because P_{Astick} cannot be greater than 1, this means that P_B

must be greater than $P_A P_{Bstick}$ and that B has now become the option most likely to match legislative preferences.

This is a rather striking conclusion: *whenever* a preference-eliciting default rule is used and fails to elicit a legislative correction, then (absent some change in legislative conditions) it *now* represents the best preference-*estimating* default rule, even though it was initially chosen despite its *lack* of correspondence to likely legislative preferences. Furthermore, because a preference-estimating default rule must also satisfy the same inequality to be chosen, the same goes for precedents that reflect preference estimation as well. But that is not too surprising, because those precedents initially reflected the best estimate of enactable preferences, and absent a change in legislative conditions, there is no reason to think that conclusion would have been changed by a legislative failure to override that result.

Importantly, this conclusion holds true even if we assume, as the critique of strong statutory *stare decisis* doctrine does, that legislative correction is infrequent and that legislative inaction does not affirmatively indicate enactable preferences.[4] Nothing in the above analysis depended on the propositions that legislative correction happens frequently, or that inaction affirmatively indicates enactable preferences. It suffices that legislative correction occurs sometimes and that legislative inaction provides a statistical signal. This helps explain why statutory *stare decisis* remains a strong presumptive doctrine, and why courts and commentators continue to intuitively rely on the possibility of legislative override, despite its infrequency and lack of affirmative significance.

This is not to say that overruling statutory precedent is never justifiable unless legislative conditions have changed. Changed circumstances may mean that the precedent embodies an interpretation that no longer advances an unchanged estimate of legislative preferences. If so, then overruling the statutory interpretation will maximize political satisfaction, as Chapter 7 pointed out, which is what courts do. Alternatively, perhaps the unchanging legislative preference was, as Chapter 2 mentioned, to delegate the matter to the courts for ongoing development in a common law fashion, as with the antitrust rule of reason. Such a delegation implies that the legislative preference is to have judges correct decisions that proved mistaken, not stick with them. Where such a legislative preference for delegation exists, it would be thwarted if courts did not feel free to overturn their own statutory precedent. But absent such situations, a strong presumption of statutory *stare decisis* is justified, unless legislative conditions have changed.

Why Precedent Based on Statutory Default Rules Should Be Overruled When Legislative Conditions Have Changed

Now take the case where legislative conditions have changed. Such a change might come in two forms. First, estimations may have changed about the enactable preferences the legislature holds. Second, estimations may have changed about the likelihood that the legislature would correct an interpretation that fails to reflect enactable preferences.

Changes in Enactable Preferences

Suppose initial precedent reflected a preference-estimating default rule, and courts now have reliable evidence, based on new official action, that current enactable preferences have changed. Or suppose the precedent reflected a preference-eliciting default rule chosen because there was no reliable basis for estimating preferences, but this new official action does provide reliable evidence that enactable preferences differ from the precedent. Then it would maximize political satisfaction to override that statutory precedent, and we would thus expect to see courts deviate from the presumptive rule of super-strong *stare decisis*.

Consistent with this analysis, the recent Supreme Court decision in *Brand X Internet Services* holds that, as long as the prior judicial interpretation did not rest on the claim that the statutory meaning was clear, an agency is not only free to deviate from that statutory precedent but also entitled to *Chevron* deference when it does deviate from it.[5] That is, when statutory meaning is unclear enough to apply a default rule, then that default rule should change with changing agency interpretations that provide the best indication of how enactable preferences are changing over time. The Court reasoned that agencies were better equipped than courts to make policy choices about how to interpret ambiguous statutes, and thus should not be bound by the way judges resolved ambiguities in old statutes. The Court also worried that the alternative would unduly ossify statutory law, by preventing agencies from updating prior judicial interpretations of ambiguous statutes.

Likewise, as Professor Eskridge has persuasively shown, courts tend to stick with statutory precedent when it conforms with current legislative preferences, but not when it conflicts.[6] Court decisions sticking to statutory precedent often rely expressly on indications that the current legislature favors the precedent, whereas court decisions overruling statutory precedent frequently rely expressly on indications that the current legislature disfavors that interpretation.

To be sure, often court decisions about whether to overrule statutory precedent make no express statement about current enactable preferences. Even then, an implicit effort to conform to current enactable preferences can be inferred from an interesting fact: judicial decisions overruling statutory precedent are the *least* likely to be legislatively overridden. Indeed, an astonishingly low 0% of Supreme Court cases overruling statutory precedent were overridden by Congress from 1967–1990. This is far below the 6–8% rate at which Congress generally overrides statutory interpretations by the Supreme Court.[7]

The Court's willingness to override statutory precedent is particularly high when it concludes that the precedent based its initial estimate of enactable preferences on incorrect analysis or information. In *Boys Market* the Court overruled precedent, partly because that precedent interpreted the statute to conform to the preferences of the enacting legislature, rather than to current congressional preferences. In *Monell,* the Court overruled precedent on the grounds that the prior precedent had ignored legislative history that would have led to a different conclusion about the preferences of the enacting legislature. It then overruled the precedent on the basis of inferences about then-current congressional preferences, which were drawn from recent legislative action.[8]

Other the other hand, when there is affirmative evidence that current enactable preferences favor a precedent, it should not be overruled, even though the court has come to the conclusion that the precedent conflicts with likely enactor preferences. A prominent example was the *Patterson* case. There the Supreme Court admitted to some uncertainty about whether a precedent interpreting "§1981 as prohibiting racial discrimination in the making and enforcement of private contracts is right or wrong as an *original* matter."[9] Without resolving whether the precedent matched enactor preferences, the Court held it should not overturn the precedent because *recent* enactments indicated that current congressional preferences embodied a "deep commitment to the eradication of discrimination" consistent with that precedent.

Where current enactable preferences either affirmatively agree or disagree with statutory precedent, applying a current preferences default rule is relatively clear. But what about when the current legislature is split or has simply failed to act? In Chapter 4, I noted that mere legislative inaction is generally an insufficient basis for concluding that legislative preferences have changed. Thus, such inaction does not justify following an otherwise nonbinding interpretation that seems to conflict with enactor preferences. But where there is statutory precedent by the same court that otherwise would be binding as a matter of *stare decisis,* the matter is different. Then legislative inaction can be relevant, because it indicates the *absence* of any demonstrable change in enactable legislative preferences that might justify overruling the initial statutory precedent. In short, while legislative inaction cannot affirmatively establish current enactable preferences, it can sometimes *rebut* a claim that current enactable preferences have changed in ways that require overruling statutory precedent.

This seems the best explanation for the Supreme Court's much-maligned 1972 decision in *Flood v. Kuhn,* which declined to overrule statutory precedent that for five decades had held that the business of baseball was not "commerce" subject to antitrust scrutiny.[10] "Commerce" is not a self-defining term, but the precedent announcing this interpretation in 1922 probably accurately reflected legislative preferences about whether the antitrust laws should apply to baseball. The main argument for overruling this interpretation in 1972 was that because baseball had developed into a big business and other sports had judicially been denied any antitrust exemption, the then-current 1972 legislature would prefer to abandon the baseball antitrust exemption. The *Flood* Court rejected this argument on the ground that Congress had repeatedly rejected bills that would eliminate the baseball antitrust exemption. The only statute Congress had enacted expanded this exemption to allow other sports to collectively bargain about television rates, and expressly stated that it did not intend to otherwise change any existing antitrust exemption or nonexemption for any sport. Likewise, the only other bills to get out of committee (one passed by each legislative chamber at different times) would have expanded the baseball exemption by extending it to other sports.[11]

The standard critique is that such failures to act need not indicate congressional approval of the baseball exemption—they may merely mean that Congress was too busy or divided to take any action.[12] But this critique misses the point. The Court was not relying on legislative inaction to support an interpretation that was initially flawed. The Court was invoking this legislative inaction to rebut the argument that changed political preferences meant it should now abandon otherwise binding precedent, which did seem to accurately reflect enactor preferences. For such a rebuttal, it sufficed that there were no indications that enactable preferences had changed and that, to the extent current political preferences could be ascertained, they cut against changing the interpretation. Given the absence of any reliable evidence that enactable preferences had changed, the absence of legislative action to overturn the precedent made its retention the decision most likely to maximize political satisfaction. Indeed, the analysis above proves that this conclusion would hold even if we thought the 1922 precedent reflected a preference-eliciting default rule, designed to get Congress to explain precisely to what extent it wanted antitrust to apply to baseball.

Changes in the Likelihood of Legislative Correction

New information about the likelihood of legislative correction might justify abandoning a preference-eliciting default rule that was based on incorrect information about that likelihood. Further, such information might sometimes be provided by the *way* in which a legislature fails to respond to precedent, even though the mere fact of legislative inaction does not itself justify overruling statutory precedent.

To illustrate, suppose the initial statutory precedent that chose preference-eliciting option B reflected an estimate that B was 40% likely to reflect legislative preferences and A was 60% likely, but B when wrong was 50% likely to stick uncorrected, whereas A when wrong was 90% likely to stick uncorrected. Then the initial decision to choose option B would correctly maximize political satisfaction because $0.4 > (0.6)(0.5) / 0.9 = 0.333$. Now suppose that the legislature not only failed to override option B, but failed to even examine the question or introduce a bill about it. While one cannot entirely discount the possibility that the legislature did not want to waste its time on what would ultimately be a losing issue, such evidence would tend to reduce any initial estimate about the relative ability of opponents of option B to command attention on the legislative agenda, which would increase the court's estimate of P_{Bstick}. Suppose, given this new information, the court concluded that the likelihood that B would (when wrong) stick uncorrected was actually 80%. Then it would no longer make sense to stick with precedent B, even if there were no other evidence to suggest a change in the odds that it accurately reflected legislative preferences. Option B would no longer be a desirable preference-eliciting default rule because $0.4 < (0.6)(0.8) / 0.9 = 0.5333$, meaning that option B no longer would be predicted to have sufficiently desirable ex ante or ex post consequences on legislative correction to infer that option *B* maximizes ultimate political satisfaction. Nor would the absence of legislative override allow one to infer that option *B* now reflected a good preference-estimating default rule, because $0.4 < (0.6)(0.8) = 0.48$. Similarly, a court might reassess the desirability of a preference-eliciting precedent if that precedent was mainly meant to elicit a third nuanced option, and intervening events have persuaded the court that it misestimated the odds that the precedent would do so.

Given the considerations noted above, the courts would have to be careful not to change the precedent too quickly, because doing so would give political opponents of option *B* an affirmative incentive to refrain from asking for any legislative inquiry. But if a sufficiently long time has passed, then the fact that this group has had to live with an adverse interpretation for that long a period should provide them with sufficient incentives to seek ex post legislative correction. We would thus expect to see that courts sometimes abandon a longstanding precedent that was initially preference-eliciting when it has failed to elicit any legislative interest at all. To do so means admitting that the court initially misestimated the likelihood of such legislative correction. But such errors are inevitable, for no analysis is perfect, and predicting legislative responsiveness under preference-eliciting analysis is certainly no exception. Thus, the harm from errors can be reduced if courts are willing to abandon the preference-eliciting default rule judiciously when it has proven misbegotten.

Preference-eliciting analysis thus predicts that courts may sometimes abandon a longstanding precedent that, given a changed estimate of the likelihood of legislative correction, no longer seems sufficiently preference-eliciting. Sometimes courts might instead adopt a different preference-eliciting default rule that is more likely to provoke legislative action. Other times, courts might instead deviate from the precedent to adopt a preference-estimating default rule.[13]

Likewise, intervening events may also persuade a court that it misestimated the interim costs of using a preference-eliciting default rule. Again, a court must be careful, because the mere fact that a preference-eliciting default rule has stuck for a long time may instead mean that it turned out to reflect legislative preferences more accurately than the alternative interpretation. But the nature of the intervening events might persuade the court that the legislature takes much longer to get around to these issues than the court previously thought, that having the wrong interpretation in the meantime is more harmful, or that the costs of legislative override are higher.

If so, that may be a reason to overrule a statutory precedent that reflected the imposition of a preference-eliciting default rule.

The last few paragraphs have an interesting implication. Namely, when statutory precedent reflects a preference-eliciting default rule, the fact that the precedent is of long standing may support, rather than undermine, the argument for overruling it. Even for precedent that reflects a preference-estimating default rule, the longer the passage of time, the more likely it is that legislative preferences have changed. Thus, to some extent, the age of the statutory precedent correlates positively with the odds that it should be overruled, no matter what sort of default rule it reflects. But in the preference-estimating case, the age of the precedent is not an affirmative reason for overruling it. In the case of a preference-eliciting precedent, in contrast, the length of time the precedent has stood may well be an affirmative reason for overruling it, when combined with other factors indicating that the initial court misestimated either the likelihood of legislative correction or the level of interim costs.

General Implications

The possibility that legislative conditions have changed explains why the presumption of statutory *stare decisis,* while strong, is not conclusive. Instead, it will often be the case that a court properly chooses to abandon statutory precedent. Consistent with the above analysis, the supposedly super-strong rule of *stare decisis* for statutory precedent is in fact often honored in the breach. In the period 1961–1991, the Supreme Court overruled no less than ninety statutory precedents under this supposed super-strong rule.[14]

Although some of these cases of judicial overrule likely involved decisions to abandon a failed preference-eliciting default rule, the analysis above also indicates that a preference-eliciting precedent should not be abandoned when the lack of legislative override reflects a deliberate legislative decision, rather than a failure to consider the question. This is because one important objective of preference-eliciting default rules is to resolve uncertainty about which interpretation the legislature prefers. To achieve this objective, the default rule must be allowed to stick when legislative reconsideration indicates that, despite initial appearances, it actually is the option more likely to satisfy enactable preferences. In these cases, the statutory precedent reflects a successful preference-eliciting default rule, not an unsuccessful one. Consistent with this prediction, the Court does not overrule statutory precedent when the legislature has affirmatively let that precedent stand after reconsidering it.[15]

Conclusion

Statutory *stare decisis* has been a favorite target of academic critique. Academics have generally found the underlying rationale that the legislature could override statutes implausible, given the unlikelihood of legislative overrides. They have also decried apparent inconsistencies in judicial willingness to follow statutory *stare decisis* or pay attention to subsequent legislative inaction.

But default rule analysis supports a strong presumption of statutory *stare decisis* when legislative conditions have not changed, even though the odds of legislative override are negligible. Where legislative conditions have not changed, it turns out that the doctrine of strong statutory *stare decisis* can be justified as the best preference-estimating default rule. This is true even though the precedent reflected a preference-eliciting default rule that failed to provoke any legislative correction, and even if legislative correction were generally unlikely.

Further, default rule analysis indicates that critiques of inconsistency cannot justifiably be founded merely on the facts that either (1) the statutory *stare decisis* is sometimes applied and sometimes is not or (2) subsequent legislative inaction is sometimes deemed relevant and sometimes not. Whether statutory *stare decisis* should govern depends on many other factors. It depends on whether the precedent reflected a clear statutory meaning (which can't be overruled by changing estimates of legislative conditions) or a default rule (which can be). For precedent reflecting a default rule, it depends on whether legislative conditions have changed in a way that changes estimates of either enactable preferences or the odds of legislative correction. It depends on whether factual circumstances have changed in a way that indicates unchanging legislative preferences would support a changed interpretation. It also depends on whether the statute reflects a delegation to courts to develop the statute in a common law fashion, which requires the discretion to overrule precedent.

Finally, subsequent legislative inaction generally should not be (and is not) used to justify deviating from statutory precedent that conformed to legislative preferences, but properly should be (and is) used to rebut an argument that enactable preferences have changed in ways that justify such a deviation. Further, while legislative inaction does not itself justify abandoning a preference-eliciting default rule, it can when the way in which the legislature failed to act indicates a lack of willingness to consider the issue, which alters the court's estimate of the odds of legislative correction of wayward precedent.

To be sure, many decisions on whether to retain or overrule statutory precedent are in fact unjustifiable, or are based on arbitrary or ideological factors. But at least some of the apparent inconsistency in applying the special statutory *stare decisis* doctrine seems explicable by reference to default rule analysis. To this extent, the extensive complaints about the inconsistent application of statutory *stare decisis* are overblown, as are complaints that the doctrine lacks a strong affirmative rationale.

PART IV

Supplemental Default Rules

CHAPTER 13

Tracking the Preferences of Political Subunits

What should an interpreter do in the residual case where he can neither ascertain statutory meaning nor reliably estimate enactable preferences, and the conditions for a preference-eliciting default rule are not met? For example, in a case where the interpreter really has no idea whether the current or enacting legislature would prefer one interpretation or the other, a preference-eliciting default rule will still not make sense if there is also no reason to think one interpretation is more likely to provoke legislative correction than the other. What should the interpreter do then?

One tempting answer is that the interpreter should just make the best guesstimate she can, on the ground that unless the interpreter's guesses are actually worse than random, making some guess about enactable preferences will tend to lead to somewhat greater political satisfaction than the alternative. And that might well be the answer if there were just one government and one interpreting court. But in fact there are often subordinate political units and courts. As we shall see, their existence helps explain certain default rules we in fact see. Because these default rules apply only when a preference-estimating default rule provides no answer and a preference-eliciting default rule is inappropriate, I will call these supplemental default rules. They are the default rules that apply (by default) when the other default rules don't.

Interpretations Incorporating State Law into Federal Statutes

In a federal system, often courts face an uncertain statutory meaning on which federal political preferences are utterly unclear. For example, what should courts do when a federal statute fails to specify any statute of limitations? One could imagine the courts assuming that Congress meant the cause of action to be unlimited in time, but that has not been the standard interpretive practice. Instead, courts have assumed the gap was inadvertent, and that Congress would want some statute of limitations. But what period, among the infinite possibilities, should federal judges choose? Before Congress finally specified a default rule of four years for post-1990 statutes, the normal practice of federal judges was not to make the choice themselves, but rather to incorporate, by reference, whatever limitations period had been chosen by states for similar causes of action.[1]

If the issue were ascertaining statutory meaning, incorporating state limitations periods would seem somewhat dubious. Why would courts assume Congress meant the same limitations period as states, when Congress was enacting a federal cause of action that, by definition, was designed to provide a remedy additional to state remedies, and thus must implicitly deem those inadequate? The truth is that, on this issue, courts have no grounds to assume anything about congressional meaning or intent. This default rule thus does not seem to reflect likely congressional preferences for any particular limitations period. Nor does it appear to be well-calculated to elicit a congressional reaction.

We can, however, explain this rule as a supplemental preference-estimating default rule. The courts could be confident that national political preferences would support *some* limitations period. Unfortunately, they had no indication about what period those national preferences would favor. Further, the choice of any particular time period would reflect an open-ended political judgment about how to weigh conflicting interests, for which some reading of prevailing political preferences was vital.

Given a lack of reliable information about the enacting or current Congress's preferences, the default rule best calculated to minimize political dissatisfaction is to track local democratic choice. This default rule improves the political satisfaction of each state polity, without any expense to the national polity because national preferences are unknown. To be sure, the political preferences being followed in these cases do not really provide an accurate indicator of the enactable preferences of the national legislature. But because those enactable preferences are unclear, the next best means of satisfying political preferences is to track the clear preferences of political subunits. These are more likely to comport with political preferences than having judges exercise their own judgment about what the best limitations period would be.

More generally, federal courts often define ambiguous terms in federal statutes (like "real property" or "children") by incorporating state law on the topic.[2] This practice seems to be in considerable tension with another general default rule articulated by federal courts, which provides that Congress does not intend to make federal statutes dependent on state law. The current doctrine provides no satisfactory way of reconciling this apparent conflict.

In contrast, the theory here provides a way of reconciling these diverging doctrinal strands. The general default rule against making federal statutes dependent on state law captures the fact that a federal statute should ordinarily be read to estimate or elicit federal legislative preferences, rather than to incorporate state law. On the other hand, when no congressional preference can be reliably estimated or elicited, then incorporating state law is the best courts can do in trying to maximize political satisfaction. The apparent conflict just reflects the priority that estimating and eliciting default rules have over supplemental ones.

Canons Protecting State Law or Autonomy

A similar argument can be made about the plethora of canons that protect state interests. Consider the pro-state canon that is most frequently applied: the canon adopting a presumption against interpreting federal statutes to preempt state law. This canon would be hard to justify as a preference-estimating default rule, because reliable estimates of enactable federal preferences will often indicate a desire to preempt. Moreover, in applying this canon, the Court has stressed that "'[t]he purpose of Congress is the ultimate touchstone' in every pre-emption case."[3] Thus, it is clear that where a reliable estimate of enactable federal preferences exist, they govern. In other words, preference-estimating default rules have priority over the anti-preemption canon.

Nor are preemption issues ordinarily suitable for a preference-eliciting default rule. To be sure, Professor Hills has forcefully argued that the anti-preemption canon serves a preference-eliciting function because pro-preemption business groups have strong political influence in Congress. But Professor Goldsmith has argued with equal force that courts should instead adopt a pro-preemption presumption because states have such strong political influence in Congress. The problem is that both of them are right. Thus, we would predict that legislative efforts to override decisions that either deny or grant preemption will evidence the sort of conflicted political demand that makes legislative correction unlikely in either direction.[4]

Consistent with this prediction, a recent empirical study shows that congressional overrides are extremely unlikely. Of 127 Supreme Court preemption decisions between 1983–2003 (half of which went each way), Congress overrode only two and part of a third. Moreover, in the rare cases when they occur, congressional overrides are as likely to go in one direction as the other. In the three overrides, one reduced preemption, another increased preemption, and the third reduced preemption but in a way that benefitted the business interests that are normally pro-preemption. This empirical evidence confirms what theory suggests: that preemption cases are not likely to have sufficient differential odds of legislative correction that could justify a preference-eliciting default rule.[5]

Instead, the anti-preemption canon can best be explained as a supplemental default rule, to deal with cases where federal enactable preferences can be neither reliably estimated nor elicited. In such cases, the default rule might as well favor state law, because that at least provides some reliable indication of regional political preferences. And tracking political preferences is generally likely to maximize political satisfaction in cases where federal political preferences cannot be ascertained.

Given that this canon is really only a supplemental default rule, one would not expect to see a strong pattern in the outcomes of preemption cases. Most will be resolved by estimated federal preferences. Because explicit federal statutory provisions have strongly trended towards preemption, most cases where federal preferences can be estimated are likely to similarly trend toward preemption. It is only in the residual cases where no federal enactable preferences can be estimated that courts would turn to the supplemental default rule against preemption. Overall outcomes in cases where preemption issues are raised thus seem theoretically as likely to grant preemption as to deny them. This is precisely what we see. The empirical study noted above found that of the 127 preemption decisions, 59 preempted the state law, 59 denied preemption, and 9 were mixed decisions that partly granted and partly denied preemption.[6]

This pattern is consistent with the conclusion that the anti-preemption canon is just a supplemental default rule, to be applied only *after* efforts to estimate current or enactor federal preferences have failed. Understanding the supplemental role of the anti-preemption canon thus helps rebut the standard critique, which is that preemption doctrine is incoherent because the Supreme Court does not consistently apply the anti-preemption canon.[7] Because of its supplemental role, consistent application of the canon would neither be expected nor justified. Instead, it should be applied only when all other default rules fail, and when application is likely to satisfy state political preferences.

Four other pieces of empirical evidence are likewise consistent with this supplemental theory for the anti-preemption canon. First, as Professor Sharkey has shown, preemption rulings tend to favor preemption positions that were taken by federal agencies, at least in the products liabilitiy cases she examined.[8] This is consistent with my theory that a current preferences default rule of deferring to agencies (along the lines of Chapter 5) has first priority.

Second, an impressive empirical study by Professors Greve and Klick finds that the Supreme Court preemption rate is higher (62.5%) for state common law and lower (47.9%) for state statutes.[9] This difference in rates makes sense if the purpose of the canon is, where federal preferences are unclear, to further state political preferences because those preferences will be embodied best in state statutes. In contrast, common law decisions by state judges may be no more likely to advance political satisfaction than decisions by federal judges.

Third, Professors Issacharoff and Sharkey have shown than courts are more likely to preempt a state law if the relevant state is inflicting externalities on other states.[10] This makes sense because, in such a case, one can no longer say that the absence of ascertainable national enactable preferences means that a default rule of deferring to state law is likely to maximize political satisfaction. Insteady, applying the default rule in such a case would increase the political satisfaction of one state at the expense of others. Such externalities mean we have exceeded the justification for the supplemental default rule against preemption, and thus we would not expect to see it applied.

Fourth, Professors Greve and Klick also found that the preemption rate is higher (63%) when the state government is a not party to the suit and lower (40%) when it is. This is consistent with my supplemental default rule theory because the willingness of the state government to involve itself in a case sends a stronger signal that preemption would thwart state political preferences. Further, the likelihood of preemption drops down to 31% if many states file amicus briefs supporting the state party.[11] Again, this is consistent with the supplemental theory because such support by many states both increases the signal about regional political preferences and also tends to negate any concern about externalities on other states.

Similar to the anti-preemption canon, other pro-state canons provide that when federal intent is not clear, federal statutes should be interpreted so that they do not regulate states, impose conditions on federal grants to states, or waive state sovereign immunity.[12] These canons effectively protect state autonomy, as opposed to protecting specific state laws.

One might be tempted to deem the canons that protect state autonomy to be preference-eliciting default rules because, in many prominent cases, decisions using these canons were overriden quickly by Congress.[13] But normally these pro-state canons cannot be justified on preference-eliciting grounds because they favor a set of parties, the states, that has unusually strong, not weak, access to the congressional agenda to get statutes overridden.[14] Given the logic of preference-eliciting default rules, this evidence would, if anything, justify an anti-state default rule.

A more promising explanation is to see the canons protecting state autonomy as supplemental default rules. One might reframe these canons as raising the following question. What should an interpreting court do when national political preferences are unclear, but some state action, which one party seeks to limit, does provide a reliable indication of regional political preferences? If national preferences are truly unknown, then tracking state political preferences seems best calculated to maximize political satisfaction, for the reasons noted above.

This supplemental theory probably does not explain the full extent of the clear statement rules protecting state autonomy. Those rules are sometimes applied with such ferocity that courts decline to follow not just guesstimates of federal intent, but fairly reliable indications of federal preferences that were not made crystal clear in the federal statute. One time the Court applied its pro-federalism canons in a way that required Congress to enact a statute three times in order to make plain its intent to abrogate state immunity.[15] More generally, these canons are often applied notwithstanding an agency interpretation that would otherwise merit *Chevron* deference as the best indicator of current enactable preferences.[16]

These sorts of cases go well beyond a default rule approach that is designed to maximize political satisfaction. They instead embrace a substantive protection of federalism values against political preferences, by increasing the legislative costs of infringing on those federalism values. Such an aggressive approach must be justified not on interpretive grounds but on a substantive constitutional theory, the most promising theory being that federalism is an underenforced constitutional norm, because the Supreme

Court has so far been unable to develop intelligible rules to provide content to the Tenth Amendment.

But the above analysis indicates that a canon favoring the autonomy of political subunits need not depend on the persuasiveness of this constitutional argument, nor even on the particularities of the U.S. Constitution. Default rule analysis would, for example, also support a presumption that unclear state legislative action does not preempt or abridge local municipal action. Such a presumption is in fact consistent with the home rule doctrine of local government law, though that doctrine is generally based on state constitutional provisions.

Likewise, this book's default rule analysis would justify a presumption that unclear laws of the European Community do not preempt or limit contrary action by European nations. This would support European application of the "principle of subsidiarity" to statutory interpretation. The analysis here would also indicate that, where a European statute is ambiguous, and the preferences of the European Community cannot reliably be estimated or elicited, then courts should, where possible, incorporate the law of European nation-states into the European statute. This would serve the same supplemental default rule function of tracking the preferences of subordinate political subunits that is served when U.S. law incorporates state law on similar questions.

Conclusion

When a court cannot meaningfully estimate or elicit the preferences of the relevant government, political satisfaction can often be maximized by tracking the political preferences of a *subordinate* government. This explains many canons that interpret ambiguous federal statutes to incorporate state law, avoid preempting state law, or protect state autonomy. However, some applications of the latter seem explicable only as means of enforcing otherwise underenforced constitutional norms of federalism.

CHAPTER **14**

Tracking High Court Preferences

The Supplemental Role for Substantive Judicial Policymaking

What should the judiciary do when it has no reliable basis for estimating the preferences of either the legislature or any political subunit, and a preference-eliciting default rule is inappropriate? In such cases, the premise that underlies most of the current debate on statutory interpretation finally seems to hold: unable to track or elicit any legislative preferences, the only thing the judiciary can do is exercise its own judgment about which rule would be most desirable. This is not because it is desirable for the judiciary to ignore legislative preferences. It is, rather, because what the legislature would have wanted the judiciary to do in such cases is to choose the option that makes the most policy sense, and in such cases the only source the judiciary has to rely on is its own judgment, informed by briefing on what the best legislative policy would be.

In applying its own judgment, however, the judiciary should exclude those policy preferences it is confident could not get enacted in the current political process. There remains the worrisome concern under democratic theory that the judiciary will be imposing policy preferences that, while not clearly rejected by the political process, have not procured clear assent either. But one should not exaggerate the worries. We are after all talking of the judiciary making a choice only when a statute is enacted through a legislative process that leaves (1) an ambiguous range of statutory meaning, (2) no reliable estimate of current or past legislative preferences for resolving that ambiguity, (3) no indication of the political preferences of political subunits, and (4) little possibility of eliciting an indication of legislative preferences. The range of choice is small, and implicitly authorized by the legislative process itself. Choice by the judiciary is

234

unavoidable in such cases because any choice within that range, even choosing the most narrow option, would remain a choice that requires justification.

Moreover, if (within this limited range) each judge applies her political preferences, the judiciary collectively is likely to come close to the aggregate political preferences of the old political processes that appointed them. This may not be ideal, but given a situation that does not permit any more precise accounting of legislative preferences, correspondence to the preferences of the appointing political process is the best the judiciary can do.

The Need to Reduce Variance in Regimes with Multiple Courts

That might be the end of the story if only one court existed. But most interpretive regimes have multiple courts that are subordinate (through some chain of appeals) to a high court. Even if the average statutory result in each interpreting court comes out fine, the variance among them means that many specific statutory results will reflect the idiosyncratic judgment or policy views of the individual judge, who happens to have been assigned the particular statutory interpretation case.

The judiciary as a whole, as an honest interpretive agent, would want to reduce this variance through some set of substantive default rules. Even if greater variance does not increase the magnitude of judicial error in estimating enactable preferences, it increases legal uncertainty and the costs of ascertaining what the law says. Both of those effects would undermine planning by individuals in society. They also undermine the statute's effectiveness at influencing behavior for two reasons. First, uncertainty about what a court will do reduces the effective difference in sanctions between compliance and noncompliance. Second, a higher cost of ascertaining the law will deter some individuals from investigating the law enough to know whether their conduct is likely to comply or not.

Moreover, the highest court in the jurisdiction will have its own incentives to control discretionary choices by lower courts. This will lead the high court to want to adopt general substantive default rules to guide the lower courts in cases where legislative preferences are unknown. Default rules adopted by high courts not only will reduce variance in the interpretive decisions of lower courts, but also will produce results that correspond better to the preferences of the appointing political process, because the political views of high court justices are far more likely to be considered seriously during their nomination and confirmation.

We can thus understand many canons of construction not as reflections of likely legislative preferences, but as the means by which high courts constrain lower courts and limit variance when legislative preferences are unknown. This understanding also provides strong limits on the use of such canons. These canons are appropriate but, absent constitutional compulsion, their use should be limited to cases where legislative preferences really do not lend themselves to reasonable estimation or elicitation.

Interpret Consistent with Common Law

The canon that statutes should be interpreted to be consistent with common law has been greatly maligned as thwarting legislative preferences in order to further judicial policy views. This critique is entirely valid when, as happens too often, the canon is used to adopt statutory constructions that are more narrow than would be indicated by an estimate of legislative preferences. Thus, it is not surprising that all but one of the state legislatures that have considered the question have explicitly rejected the canon that narrowly construes statutes that are in derogation of the common law.[1]

But when statutory meaning is unclear, and legislative preferences are unknown and difficult to elicit, the canon makes a great deal of sense as a supplemental default rule. The point missed by prior commentators is that, in such cases, the canon helps constrain wayward lower courts. If each judge instead resolved such cases on the basis of what struck him as wise policy, the results would be highly variable and less within the control of the high court. What the common law provides is an articulated body of law, common to all the courts in the jurisdiction, that presumably reflects the judiciary's own considered judgment of wise policy. For common law is by definition judge-made law in those areas where statutes have not provided any answer, and thus policy arguments are made freely in reaching common law conclusions. Further, such common law decisions are made in a hierarchical appellate system and thus ultimately reflect supervision by the highest court in the jurisdiction, whose members' political views are the most likely to have been considered by the political branches during the appointment process.

To serve this function well, this canon must be limited to the sorts of cases that justify this sort of judicial discretion. Consistent with this theory, application of the canon has actually been more limited than its phrasing might suggest. In particular, the canon has not been applied to ambiguities created by "remedial" statutes, that is, to statutes that try to cure a substantive problem with common law doctrine or provide a remedy for a legal wrong that was previously left unremedied.[2] In such cases, the courts may not know what legislative preferences are, but they know what they are not. What such a legislature was against was the prior application of judge-made common law or remedial decisions. It thus makes sense for courts to desist from application of the canon in such cases, because courts remain bound by the general goal of maximizing political satisfaction.

Illustrating this supplemental approach is the code of construction adopted by New York, the one state legislature to expressly retain the canon that narrowly construes statutes in derogation of the common law.[3] Although it retains this canon, the New York code does so only after first stressing, repeatedly and at length, that the "primary" consideration in statutory construction is furthering legislative purposes.[4] The implication seems plain that the legislature regards this canon as only a supplemental default rule, to be employed when the primary default rule of estimating legislative preferences has failed. Also consistent with the above analysis, the New York legislature has cabined this supplemental canon by providing that remedial statutes must be liberally construed.[5] The various state statutes that have rejected the canon against interpretations in derogation of the common law are probably best read as rejecting a primary role for this canon, which could trump estimates of legislative preferences, rather than rejecting a supplemental role when no such estimate can be divined.

Interpret to Avoid Constitutional Difficulties

While the canon advising courts to interpret statutes to avoid actual invalidity can be explained as a preference-estimating default rule, as Chapter 6 explained, the same is not true for the canon advising courts to interpret statutes to avoid constitutional questions or difficulties.[6] The problem is that the latter canon has no bite in cases of actual constitutional invalidity, because the first default rule already governs those cases. Thus, the latter canon only changes the result when it is used to reject an interpretation that reflects the best estimate of the legislative polity's preferences even though that interpretation is not, in fact, constitutionally invalid. Such a canon cannot be justified on constitutional grounds. Nor is it likely to reflect the preferences of any legislative polity that prefers to maximize the satisfaction of its political preferences. Consistent with this analysis, no state legislature directs courts to avoid constitutional doubts that do not result in actual invalidity.

To be sure, in those cases where the interpretation raising constitutional difficulties burdens a politically powerless group, the canon can, as Chapter 9 showed, be explained as a preference-eliciting default rule. However, there is no general reason to think that all interpretations that raise constitutional difficulties would burden groups that are relatively powerless in gaining access to the legislative agenda. Thus, preference-eliciting analysis cannot explain a more general application of the canon.

However, if a court cannot otherwise estimate or elicit legislative preferences, then the canon of avoiding constitutional difficulties makes a great deal of sense as a supplemental default rule. In many cases, "constitutional difficulties" refer to cases where some interpretations of the statute would conflict with deeply held national principles, even though it is unclear that those principles are embodied in binding constitutional doctrine. Absent any contrary indication about legislative preferences, it makes general sense to assume the political branches would prefer to resolve their statutory ambiguities with something consistent with fundamental national principles.

Moreover, to the extent that general constitutional principles are elaborated in U.S. Supreme Court decisions, this canon plays a similar role to that of the canon construing ambiguous statutes to conform to the common law. It affords the Supreme Court a way to guide lower courts to adopt more uniform interpretations. Because the Court regularly promulgates constitutional decisions, an interpretive rule to avoid constitutional difficulties (when all else fails) is a way of reducing lower court variance and bringing lower court decisions closer into line with Supreme Court views. Because the U.S. Supreme Court does not itself render common law decisions, one would expect it to invoke this canon somewhat more often than state courts, which can instead invoke the canon against deviations from common law to reduce and police lower court variance.

At least one line of cases is consistent with this limitation, suggesting that the canon against constitutional doubts should be applied only when legislative preferences are unclear.[7] These cases effectively relegate the canon to a supplemental role once the preference-estimating inquiry has failed. The recent case about the Solomon Amendment implicitly fell into this category. As Chapter 6 noted, the statutory language was, by itself, unclear about whether it required that military recruiters get equal treatment or access as good as the most-favored employer. Nor could one deny that constitutional doubts were raised, given that the Court took eight pages of detailed analysis to dispel them.[8] Thus, if the canon against constitutional doubts took priority whenever the statutory text was unclear, it would have dictated a ruling in favor of the law schools. Instead, the Court resolved the question of statutory interpretation on the basis of enactor preferences, and then turned to the issue of whether, so interpreted, the statute was constitutionally invalid.

Still, one should not oversell this explanation. Courts often invoke this canon even when they do have a fairly reliable contrary indication about enactable preferences, such as an agency interpretation that would otherwise merit *Chevron* deference.[9] And often courts invoke this canon when they seem to have little doubt that the objectionable interpretations would be unconstitutional. In such cases, the main purpose of the canon may well be to avoid, if possible, an open constitutional conflict with the legislative branch.[10] Such a prudential application of the canon aims not at maximizing legislative preference satisfaction, but at preserving the court's political capital to enforce constitutional judgments.

If so, though, the canon should be restricted to cases where the statute would (if the issue were reached) actually be deemed unconstitutional. Otherwise the canon would be creating additional court–legislature conflict, thus undermining the supposed purpose. In other words, if the prudential theory were really pursued, the constitutional doubts canon would merely offer a means of *phrasing* a constitutional holding in a less confrontational way, but would add no difference in substantive result to the constitutional invalidity canon.

An alternative theory is that the constitutional doubts canon aims to force legislative deliberation to make up for underenforced constitutional norms, such as the nondelegation doctrine.[11] This theory has some force. But if pursued, then the canon should be confined to cases where the relevant constitutional norms are in fact underenforced, and would not justify applying the canon indiscriminately to all constitutional doubts.

In any event, under either explanation, the justification for applying the constitutional doubts canon so broadly must rest on substantive constitutional principles beyond the scope of this book, rather than on any effort to interpret statutes or satisfy political preferences. To the extent that substantive constitutional principles do not justify application of the canon, it should be applied only when the court feels it cannot meaningfully estimate or elicit legislative preferences.

Conclusion

Where all means of estimating or elicting political preferences at any level have failed, the judiciary must resolve the statutory ambiguity with the default rule that (within the politically plausible range) the judiciary deems best. But this does not mean that every judge must be left to her own devices. Instead, canons of construction in such cases serve mainly to limit judicial variance, by requiring judges to follow common law or constitutional principles. Limiting such variance is desirable because it minimizes uncertainty, even if it does not reduce the magnitude of likely judicial error in estimating enactable preferences. It also brings interpretations into closer line with the views of high court judges, which are more likely than those of lower court judges to reflect the preferences of the appointing political process. However, some applications of the canon of avoiding constitutional doubts are sufficiently aggressive that they can be explained only either as prudential ways of phrasing holdings of actual constitutional invalidity, or as a means of enforcing a constitutional norm that would otherwise go underenforced because of the lack of definable limits.

PART V

Objections

CHAPTER 15

The Fit with Prior Political Science Models and Empirical Data

The conclusions here diverge sharply from those in most political science models. This might seem troubling to those (like me) who have been impressed by the rigor and ingenuity of these models, which have made such important contributions to how we think about statutory interpretation. It thus may help to explain the source of the divergence. As is often the case, differences in conclusions are traceable to differences in assumptions. Part of the reason for the difference in assumptions is that, unlike most prior models, part of my goal is normative: to describe what statutory interpretation ought to look like. In contrast, these other models generally try to provide only an account of what actually happens. But, as I shall also show, my assumptions also turn out to be more consistent with the available empirical evidence. Thus, my theory ultimately provides a better descriptive account as well. This is true not only for rational choice models of how judges interact with other political actors, but also for attitudinal models that assume judges further their own ideologies without considering other political actors. I address each in turn.

The Difference in Assumptions from Prior Rational Choice Models

This book differs, in various ways, from prior rational choice scholarship that models interactions between judges and other political actors in statutory interpretation. The prior scholarship ignores any distinction between ascertaining statutory meaning and choosing default rules. It also generally assumes that: (1) courts can make any interpretive choice in an infinite policy continuum; (2) courts make whatever choice furthers judicial views; (3) the preferences of every political actor are perfectly knowable; and (4) judges aim to avoid any interpretations that would trigger ex post statutory overrides, which turn solely on how far interpretations deviate from political preferences. Given these assumptions, these models conclude that statutory interpretations will just involve judges choosing whichever policy option is closest to judicial preferences, as long as it lies within the set of policy options that would not trigger an ex post statutory override. My assumptions differ on each score and thus, not surprisingly, lead to different conclusions.

1. Constrained versus Unconstrained Interpretive Options

To begin with, prior rational choice models generally ignore any possible limits created by interpretive methods, and instead assume judges always have discretion to reach whatever statutory interpretation they want.[1] That is, they leap from an observation that does seem true—that judges often have discretion to choose among interpretive options—to the conclusion that interpretive choice not only exists in every case, but is so unconstrained that judges choose among an infinite set of policy options, rather than being restricted by legal methodology to a limited set of plausible options.

This leap is unjustified, and contrary to my own observations about actual cases of statutory interpretation. Standard legal methodology dictates the interpretation on many issues, especially those so uncontroversial that they never give rise to adjudicated cases or appeals. Even when standard methodology does not dictate a single answer, it generally narrows the interpretive options to a handful, rather than leaving judges free to choose any policy option they wish. To be sure, this leaves judges with the considerable power to choose among the interpretive options, but their choice of options is not infinite, and any accurate theory of statutory interpretation needs to incorporate that fact.

2. Maximizing Judicial versus Political Satisfaction

Prior rational choice models virtually all assume that, in exercising whatever discretion they have, courts just try to maximize the satisfaction of judicial views to the extent that they can without being overridden.[2] I, in contrast, assume that courts adopt default rules that maximize the satisfaction of enactable political preferences. I do so in part because, as I have argued, this is what courts should do, and what legislatures should require through codes of construction or otherwise if courts failed to do it. Thus, I am normatively interested in modeling what it would look like to have default rules that maximized that goal. But I also do so because the current pattern of actual doctrinal results generally fits a political satisfaction model. To be sure, "generally" does not mean "always." Judges to some extent do deviate from these default rules, and the reasons for such deviation range from different views about the right methodology to mistakes, ignorance, ideology, or self-interest. But, by and large, these default rules do a surprisingly good job of predicting most doctrinal results.

One might wonder how this book's statutory default rules could possibly constrain judges, especially because many of the default doctrines are not that rule-like, but rather offer guidance whose content will be determined by context. However, a doctrine need not be 100% determinate to have a meaningful effect on judicial outcomes. True, clever and dedicated subverters of these default rules can, if inclined, manipulate them to reach whatever result they personally prefer in most cases. So it is with any legal doctrine, or with any instruction a principal gives to any agent. But it is hard to see why the political process would want to appoint the kind of judicial agents who intentionally misuse their interpretive powers in order to pursue their own political views or judgments.

To the contrary, the political process would want to commit itself to a strategy of refusing to appoint—and, where feasible, reversing the statutory decisions of—judges who just tried to further their own political views or judgments. After all, legislative commitment to such a strategy would maximize the expected influence of those in the political process. Some mistaken judicial appointments will no doubt slip through the screening process. However, over the entire range of judges and cases, identifying the correct default rules should increase the extent to which statutory results accurately reflect enactable political preferences.

If the judiciary deviates sufficiently from maximizing political satisfaction, the legislature has many other mechanisms to induce it to do so. The legislature can try to reestablish the supremacy of democratic choice by enacting codes of construction, which would specify the statutory default rules that maximize political satisfaction. Further, the political branches can and do influence the judiciary by holding hearings, making public statements, threatening impeachment, limiting jurisdiction, cutting budgets, withholding pay raises, denying promotions, expanding courts, and resisting implementation of judicial orders.[3] Any and all of these political methods might be employed if a judiciary insisted on maximizing its own preferences, rather than those of the political branches. State judges who face elections and recalls should be even more reluctant to deviate from political preferences.

For purposes of my descriptive thesis, it does not matter why judges' doctrinal results generally maximize political satisfaction. Perhaps it is because judges feel constrained by external forces like doctrine, gratitude to those who appointed them, prospects of promotion or reelection, fear of legislative reactions, or other factors. Or perhaps it is because judges have some internal motivation, or sense of duty, that causes them to behave like honest agents. Either way, all that matters is that the model that results from this assumption turns out to explain the general pattern of doctrinal results.

A few rational choice models entertain the alternative assumption that judges try to act as honest agents for the enacting legislature. Normally they leap to the conclusion that this assumption would mean judges should interpret the statute to match enactor preferences when they conflict with current preferences.[4] In an ingenious twist, Ferejohn and Weingast argue that, while this is what a naive textualist would do, a more politically sophisticated honest agent for the enacting legislature would realize that an interpretation that matches the preferences of the enacting legislature might provoke a statutory override by the current legislature. They then conclude that an honest interpretive agent who seeks to maximize the satisfaction of enactor preferences should, first, ascertain the range of interpretations that would not get overriden by the current legislature, and then choose the option within that range that comes closest to the enacting legislature's preferences.[5]

Like conventional rational choice scholars, Ferejohn and Weingast are led to a conclusion that differs from mine because they share another assumption with other rational choice models, an assumption so taken for granted that it is just left implicit. That assumption is that the only legislative preferences to further are those reflected in the statutes enacted by that legislature, and that thus enactor preferences are maximized by achieving future statutory results that come as close as possible to them. If one instead asks which *general* default rule the enacting legislative polity would prefer for both old and new statutes, the inquiry produces instead the conclusion I described in Chapter 3. The enacting legislative polity itself would want a default rule that tracks current enactable preferences (where reliably ascertainable) because it cares more about present influence over all statutes than about future influence over a subset of statutes. Thus, in my analysis, unlike the Ferejohn and Weingast model and other prior models, an honest interpretive agent for the enacting legislature would choose a current preferences default rule.

3. *Perfect versus Probabilistic Knowledge of Political Preferences*

Sully

Prior rational choice models assume that executive and legislative preferences are perfectly known.[6] This assumption seems entirely unrealistic. Perfect knowledge is rare in life, especially when trying to ascertain the preferences of collective bodies. It seems especially unrealistic that judges would have perfect knowledge about executive and legislative preferences, given that judges are largely insulated from many sources of political knowledge.

In contrast, I assume that judges are generally uncertain about executive or legislative preferences. Indeed, it is precisely judicial uncertainty about those preferences that best explains many interpretive canons, for those canons provide indirect means to estimate or elicit those uncertain preferences. If courts perfectly knew executive and legislative preferences, then courts would not need a *Chevron* doctrine of deferring to agencies to help judges estimate current political preferences. Likewise, if political preferences were perfectly knowable, then preference-eliciting default rules would never be justifiable. It is only the fact that political preferences are uncertain that justifies using preference-eliciting rules at all. In short, if the assumption of perfectly known legislative preferences were true, most statutory canons and default rules would be unnecessary.

The prior models on *Chevron* deference also wrongly assume that agencies only reflect executive preferences.[7] In fact, as Chapter 5 noted, agencies are also strongly influenced by legislative preferences. Further, these prior models wrongly assume that *Chevron* deference applies when the agency position sides with the executive in a conflict with plain legislative preferences. Indeed, because these prior models ignore the possibility that courts use agency action to gain information about current enactable preferences, these models assume that agency action only matters when it poses such a conflict. In fact, as Chapter 5 showed, courts do not apply *Chevron* deference in cases that pose such a conflict between known executive and legislative preferences. Thus, *Chevron* deference in fact matters only when the agency decision does *not* pose such a conflict, but to the contrary helps the court ascertain current enactable preferences.

Prior rational choice models of statutory interpretation also tend to focus on a particular legislative structure—normally the division among presidential, House, and Senate authority in the U.S. system, and sometimes even the particular legislative committee structure.[8] My aim here is instead to develop an interpretive theory for general application across different legislative structures, including parliamentary ones that do not involve a similar separation of legislative powers.

4. Avoiding Ex Post Legislative Overrides versus Eliciting Legislative Reactions When That Maximizes Political Satisfaction

Prior rational choice models also virtually all make various assumptions about legislative reactions to statutory opinions that are contrary to mine. First, these models generally assume that judges try to further their own preferences as much as they can without being legislatively overturned, so that any statutory overrides mean the judges made a mistake.[9] In contrast, in my analysis, courts often should and do try to elicit statutory overrides. Such overrides do not reflect a mistake, but rather a successful effort both to obtain ex post legislative instructions in the face of uncertainty about legislative preferences and to encourage the provision of ex ante legislative clarity in similar future cases.

Second, prior models also assume that legislative reactions to statutory interpretations turn only on the existence of legislative preference dissatisfaction and (in the more sophisticated models) the degree of dissatisfaction compared to the costs of making a fresh enactment.[10] They thus exclude, by their assumptions, the possibility of differential odds of legislative correction. In reality, whether and how the legislature reacts to a statutory interpretation turns not just on benefits and costs equally applicable to all political groups, but also on asymmetries in the abilities of political forces to command time on the legislative agenda. Therefore, in Part III, this book assumed this political asymmetry exists on some set of issues. If this asymmetry never existed, a preference-eliciting default rule would never be warranted.

Finally, almost all prior rational choice models implicitly assume that any legislative reaction comes only ex post, after the statutory interpretation, rather than ex ante in the initial promulgation of statutes. Generally they do so simply by modeling only the ex post reactions, without considering whether ex ante legislative reactions might alter the extent and nature of statutory ambiguities created. In contrast, I assume that there are both ex ante and ex post legislative reactions to any default rule of statutory interpretation.

Exceptions. There are two exceptions to the above description of current rational choice scholarship, each of which modifies some (but not all) of these standard rational choice assumptions. They thus require a more detailed response to explain the differences from my model.

One is an ingenious article by Spiller and Tiller that drops the assumption that judges choose among an infinite policy space and always aim to avoid being overridden, but otherwise tracks all the standard assumptions.[11] Indeed, they adopt an even more extreme assumption that courts not only perfectly know the preferences of each political actor, but also know precisely what will result from bargaining between them to override any given statutory interpretation. This leads them to conclude that judges, when constrained to choose between two interpretive options, will not choose the one that is closer to judicial preferences if judges know both (1) that the preferred option cannot be legislatively overridden, and (2) that the other interpretation will be overridden in a way that achieves a final result that corresponds even better to judicial preferences. Those judicial preferences are assumed to include preferences not just about "policy," but about the best "rules" of statutory construction. These preferences mean that judges will apply what they regard as the best rule, even when it leads to a policy outcome they disfavor, because they expect the legislature to override the bad policy outcome and leave them with their optimal result: the best combination of judicial rule and policy outcome.

While this is an intriguing advance over prior models, my assumptions are decidedly different. Spiller and Tiller's extreme assumption that judges can, with perfect accuracy, predict the result of any future legislative bargaining seems implausible and inconsistent with their own bargaining model.[12] Nor, if judges could make such predictions, would it be legitimate for judges to deliberately choose an interpretation that did not fit legislative preferences because the judges knew the final outcome would correspond better to their own personal preferences. The Spiller-Tiller model is instead driven by the rational choice premise that anything judges do must be advancing their personal preferences, which causes their model to conflate all views about the best canons of construction into judicial preferences. This excludes from the outset the possibility that courts choose those canons that maximize political satisfaction. Indeed, it leads Spiller and Tiller to the odd conclusion that the judges who are behaving "strategically" are those who follow the best rule of statutory construction, even when it leads to policy outcomes they disfavor, whereas the "nonstrategic" judges allow their policy views to overcome their views about the best legal rule.[13] This amounts to trying to jam the round peg of judicial views about legal theory into the square hole of the assumption that judges maximize the satisfaction of personal preferences.

More important, the Spiller-Tiller assumption that judges have preferences for certain rules of statutory construction renders their analysis tautological, because they provide no theory of what generates judicial preferences for those particular statutory default rules. The task of my project is precisely to explain why judges should adopt statutory default rules that maximize political satisfaction—which also explains what default rules legislatures should impose if judges fail to do so. On this last point, Spiller and Tiller mistakenly make the crucial explicit assumption that legislatures can override policy outcomes, but cannot override rules of statutory construction.[14] Had they understood that in fact legislatures can (and do) adopt codes of statutory construction, they might have realized that this can constrain judges to adopt statutory default rules that tend to maximize political satisfaction. (Their model also implicitly ignores a vast array of other means by which legislatures could influence a judiciary that tried to favor judicial preferences over legislative preferences.) In any event, the empirical evidence—including the evidence Spiller and Tiller themselves present—is more consistent with my model than theirs, as discussed in the next section.

The second exception is an article by Schwartz, Spiller, and Urbiztondo that adopts all the standard rational choice assumptions, except that it assumes incomplete knowledge and admits the possibility of ex ante legislative clarification. But these authors make many other dubious assumptions in their article that lead them to conclusions vastly different from mine. They assume that more specific legislative language increases, rather than decreases, the flexibility of courts to interpret statutes however they want, and that the only purpose of ex ante statutory specificity or legislative history is thus to signal a willingness to legislatively override the judiciary ex post.[15] This assumption effectively eliminates the possibility that ex ante specification can be a benefit of a statutory default rule. Indeed, this assumption makes it unclear why even an ex post override would have any influence on the court, because a court could ignore the specificity in any statutory override, too. It also leads these authors to the odd conclusion that the legislature is less likely to be specific ex ante when the costs of ex post override are high, which seems precisely contrary to reality. Further, their analysis and model implicitly assume that no interim costs result ex post from having the wrong rule, which effectively underestimates both the costs of ex post override and the benefits of ex ante specification.

Finally, the above assumptions, combined with these authors' assumption that courts just try to maximize judicial preferences, leads them to the conclusion that legislatures will want to send the judiciary false signals, whose inaccuracy they apparently assume judges cannot gauge.[16] I, in contrast, assume that courts are in a cooperative agency relationship with legislatures, and try to adopt default rules that best estimate or elicit legislative preferences. Given these contrary assumptions, including the exclusion of the possibility of differential correction odds, it is not surprising that this article failed to consider the possibility of preference-estimating or preference-eliciting default rules.

The Empirical Evidence

As I will explain below, my theory predicts doctrinal results that fit the empirical evidence better than prior rational choice models do, and thus provides a better theory even as a purely descriptive matter. However, it is worth pausing first to note that, even if this were not true, these prior models would fail to provide an adequate *legal* theory. The reason is that, as Chapter 1 noted, a legal theory must be limited to the set of theories that *both* fit legal doctrine and offer normatively attractive guidance for resolving future cases. Even if the rational choice model assumption that judges just maximize their own preferences were more descriptively accurate, such a corrosive assumption could not offer normatively acceptable guidance for future cases. This makes these models a poor choice for a legal theory to undergird current interpretation doctrine. They cannot offer that combination of descriptive accuracy and normative acceptability necessary to provide a viable legal theory. Because my primary goal is to provide a legal theory of statutory interpretation, this point suffices to establish my primary point.

But I am also pressing the purely descriptive claim. For that claim, we can test the different conclusions reached by this book and prior rational choice models against two sorts of empirical evidence: the legal doctrine and the statistical data. In terms of doctrine, Parts I–IV have provided a detailed analysis of how my theories fit the existing doctrines on statutory interpretation, and have explained what otherwise seem like anomalies in those doctrines. All the doctrines and canons can be explained as reflecting either current preferences, enactor preferences, preference-eliciting, or supplemental default rules, with the choice among them depending on which the conditions indicate would best maximize political satisfaction. The same doctrines and canons, and their pattern of application, do not fit the alternative assumption that judges just try to further their own preferences as far as they can rather than trying to maximize political satisfaction. Thus, the prior rational choice models fail as a descriptive matter to fit the existing legal doctrine.

Still, one might argue that, even if the doctrine and leading cases are more consistent with my theory, statistical data of how judges act is more consistent with the prior rational actor models. It turns out this argument fails factually, but even if were factually accurate, it would not alter my primary descriptive theory, for that theory is about the fit of my theory with legal doctrine, not with judicial behavior. Any statistical showing that judges regularly deviate from that doctrine would thus not alter the descriptive accuracy of my theory in explaining current doctrine. It would merely provide a basis for condemning a lot of judicial behavior for deviating from current doctrine and leading cases.

In any event, it turns out my theory also better explains the statistical data on actual judicial behavior. *First,* prior rational choice models rely on statistical evidence that statutory interpretations are affected by changing congressional preferences, and that 70% of conference discussions in nonconstitutional cases refer to the preferences or likely reactions of current legislatures or other governmental actors.[17] Their inference is that judges track current political preferences to avoid overrides. But this statistical evidence is at least equally consistent with this book's theory that judges employ a current preferences default rule. Indeed, this statistical evidence fits my theory far better. Why? Because the rational choice assumption that judges just want to maximize their own preferences cannot persuasively explain why a fear of legislative override would cause judges to avoid any result that might trigger such an override. The reasons are several.

1. Statutory overrides take time. Thus, if judges were just maximizing their own preferences, they would be motivated, to some extent, by the desire to have their favored result hold in the interim before any statutory override occurs.
2. If the rational choice model assumptions were accurate, then judges could respond to any statutory override by interpreting the override

to fit judicial preferences too.[18] In contrast, if (as my theory predicts) courts follow statutory meaning and legislative preferences when they can, and provoke statutory overrides only to elicit legislative preferences when they cannot estimate them, that explains why courts do not simply evade statutory overrides with fresh misinterpretations.

3. In most areas, legislative override is far less likely than legislative nonresponse. Thus, judges normally could best satisfy their personal preferences by directly interpreting statutes to match those preferences. Nor would pursuing that direct approach harm a personal preference–maximizing judge by much in the minority of cases where override did occur, because the alternative would be an interpretation that (to avoid override) also deviated from judicial preferences. The only gain (in this minority of cases) would be that this deviation from judicial preferences might be somewhat smaller than the deviation that the predicted override would create. This small gain is unlikely to offset the loss from issuing interpretations that deviate from judicial preferences in most cases, especially given the difficulty of predicting just what an override would produce. A personal preference–maximizing judge would thus have little strategic reason not to simply interpret statutes in ways that furthered judicial preferences, rather than following current legislative preferences.

Second, other statistical data refutes the premise in rational choice models that courts pay attention to current preferences only to the extent necessary to avoid legislative override. Given their assumption that courts have perfect knowledge of legislative preferences, these models would predict that judicial interpretations are never overridden.[19] Instead, as Part III detailed, they are overridden with surprising frequency. Unlike the prior rational choice models, my theory can explain these overrides in many ways. Most directly, when legislative preferences are uncertain and a differential likelihood of legislative correction exists, my theory predicts that courts trying to maximize political satisfaction should and do affirmatively try to elicit legislative reactions. Consistent with this, cases where such a preference-eliciting default rule is appropriate are most likely to trigger legislative overrides. In addition, my theory predicts that overrides will occur when courts are tracking a clear statutory meaning that conflicts with current preferences, when judges use rules (like *Chevron*) that can estimate current preferences only imperfectly (and thus sometimes deviate from them), or when judges lack any recent official action to infer current preferences and thus use enactor preferences default rules instead.

One might try to salvage the prior rational choice models by modifying them to assume that courts try to maximize their own ideological preference satisfaction (or that of the enacting legislature) by coming close to the line that triggers override, but have imperfect knowledge and sometimes step over the line by mistake.[20] But even if we adopt this charitable modification, these rational choice models are still inconsistent with the empirical data in various ways.

1. If this modified model were correct, one would expect that, when the political views of judges and Congress coincide, the judges will not have to come even close to the line and are thus less likely to trigger override. But, in fact, conflicts between the ideological views of the court majority and Congress do not increase the likelihood of even congressional interest in considering overrides, let alone the likelihood of successful overrides.[21] This evidence is inconsistent with prior rational choice models.

    In contrast, this book's model is consistent with this evidence that greater political differences between courts and legislatures does not increase the likelihood of legislative overrides. The reason is that, under this book's model, judges are not just satisfying their own preferences. Instead, judges are following statutory meaning where ascertainable (which may sometimes provoke overrides because legislative views have changed), estimating political preferences (which may provoke overrides when current preferences cannot reliably be estimated or the reliable estimate proves mistaken), or trying to elicit a legislative reaction (where meaning and preferences are unclear and a differential likelihood of legislative correction exists). In all these cases, the likelihood of override would not be expected to vary with political differences between the judges and the legislature. Because courts using the right default rules are not basing decisions on their own political views, where those judicial views are located in relation to legislative views should not affect interpretations and thus should not affect overrides.

2. The rational choice models posit that judges are at least trying to interpret statutes in ways that would be favored by a sufficient legisla-

tive faction to block override. Thus, these models should predict that, when judges err, the resulting statutory overrides would be partisan and controversial. This prediction is inconsistent with the empirical data. One study shows that statutory overrides decrease during times of divided government and increase when the president and Congress agree.[22] Another study shows that only 26% of statutory overrides are on party-line votes, and "many (perhaps most) responsive statutes are not highly controversial."[23]

The theory of this book is, in contrast, entirely consistent with the existence of bipartisan and noncontroversial statutory overrides. Sometimes courts are trying to elicit such nonpartisan overrides. Sometimes the overrides occur as an inevitable result of following clear meaning or default rules that cannot always capture current preferences. But because courts applying the right default rules are not trying to press their own views in partisan ways, one would not expect overrides to be partisan.

Alternatively, some rational actor models would predict that statutory overrides would always be led by interest groups. This is especially true if, as some have argued, judicial interpretations leaned against interest groups or reflected judicial preferences for advancing their conception of the public interest. Instead, only 44% of statutory overrides seem to involve the sort of concentrated benefits and diffuse costs that are taken to define interest group legislation.[24] The theory offered here can explain why courts choose not only statutory interpretations that trigger overrides by interest groups, but also those that trigger the other 56% of statutory overrides by public interest groups.

3. If statutory overrides resulted from judges mistakenly overreaching, one would think courts would avoid using canons of construction that predictably are more likely to trigger overrides. But as we saw in Part III, judges routinely employ canons—such as the rule of lenity, the rule favoring narrow constructions of antitrust or tax legislation, or the plain meaning rule—even though they are statistically more likely to trigger overrides. And judges continue to do so even after this tendency has been pointed out to them. In one famous case, the Court used the plain meaning canon to decide a case despite a dissent pointing out that six past uses of the plain meaning canon had led to statutory overrides.[25] Congress then overrode that case within a few months. It seems very difficult to ascribe such practices to judicial mistakes.

Indeed, one study found that 10% of Supreme Court statutory interpretations expressly invite congressional override—with 7% having invitations categorized as strong.[26] Such invitations appeared in the opinions of all the justices. And opinions that invited congressional override were in fact twice as likely to be overridden. This evidence is hard to square with the assumption that judges are trying to minimize the odds of override when they interpret statutes.

To be sure, not all invitations to override reflect preference-eliciting default rules. When the Court's interpretation has been dictated by the statute's clear meaning, it may also want to call for override to make clear to Congress that its holding does not mean any policy agreement with the conclusion. Hausegger and Baum present statistical evidence that such invitations are four times as likely to occur when the interpretation conflicts with the ideological view of the majority coalition, but, interestingly, not when they conflict with the views of the majority opinion writer.[27] This study provides strong evidence that the justices feel constrained by the law.

The Hausegger and Baum study also shows that invitations to override are twice as likely to occur when (1) the case involves a legal area in which most cases involve circuit conflicts, or (2) amicus briefs indicate a lot of political opposition to the Court's ruling.[28] These two variables both correlate to the advisability of a preference-eliciting default rule. The existence of a circuit conflict suggests uncertainty about statutory meaning and preference estimation, which would satisfy one of the conditions for applying a preference-eliciting default rule. The opposition by amicus briefs suggests a greater likelihood that a group exists that can command the legislative agenda to secure override, which would satisfy another condition. As Hausegger and Baum point out, 97% of statutory overrides go in the opposite political direction to that of the interpretation. Thus, the fact that invitations are more often issued when the interpretation conflicts with that of the majority coalition may (at least partly) reflect cases where the majority expected an override (because they realized that Congress shared their general political views) but were uncertain about the specifics and thus used a preference-eliciting default rule. Unfortunately, Hausegger and Baum do not measure the parallel political views of Congress, so their study does not allow one to test that possibility.

A study that does measure congressional political views comes from Spiller and Tiller. As they note, the greater the political divergence between the House and Senate, the more difficult it should be for them to override judicial interpretations. If judges were just adopting interpretations that reflected their own views, one would thus expect to see statutory overrides decline in frequency as the political divergence between the House and Senate increased. Instead, what the data show is an inverted U curve—statutory overrides are infrequent when House–Senate political divergence is low, overrides increase when divergence is moderate, but overrides go back down when divergence is high.[29]

Spiller and Tiller think this inverted U curve confirms their own thesis that judges maximize their own preferences, but do so by strategically taking into account the predicted outcome of statutory override. But this conclusion rests on their mistaken premise that, when the House and Senate are not divergent, strategic judges who are maximizing their own preferences would never adopt an interpretation they know will be overridden. They reason that judges would not do so because such an interpretation cannot influence the final outcome.[30] But this reasoning is mistaken. If judges were just maximizing their own preferences, then the fact that they cannot influence the final outcome means they should focus *solely* on the *interim* outcome before any override happens. And that is an outcome they can totally determine by choosing the interpretation that best matches judicial preferences. Thus, if Spiller and Tiller's assumptions were true, one would not expect an inverted U curve. Instead, one would expect lower political divergence should always increase the frequency of statutory overrides.

In contrast, the inverted U curve fits the model offered in this book very well. Where political divergence between legislative chambers is low, courts are likely to have less uncertainty about enactable preferences. Thus, one would expect courts to use preference-estimating default rules that do not trigger many statutory overrides. Where political divergence within the legislature is moderate, then it is more likely that enactable preferences are uncertain, but statutory overrides remain possible. One would thus expect courts to be more likely to use preference-eliciting default rules that trigger more statutory overrides. But once political divergence is great between the House and Senate, then the odds of legislative correction are probably too low to merit use of a preference-eliciting default rule. One would thus expect statutory overrides to be low again. All this is consistent with the inverted U curve we in fact see.

In short, statutory overrides (1) do not increase with political divergence between judges and legislatures, (2) are usually neither partisan nor controversial, and (3) do not simply decrease the more that intralegislative conflict disables the legislature from overriding the courts. Further, courts knowingly use statutory canons that are especially prone to eliciting statutory overrides, and often even expressly call for statutory overrides. None of this evidence is consistent with the assumption that judges just try to further their own preferences to the extent they can while avoiding override, nor with the notion that they provoke overrides only by mistake. But all this evidence is entirely consistent with the theories in this book.

Prior interpretations of these statistics have been misled by the premise that there is only one alternative to the assumption that judges directly or strategically further their own preferences. That sole alternative is that judges follow mechanical legal rules that bear no relation to maximizing political preferences.[31] Given that premise, this prior work sensibly asks which of those two possibilities best fit the data. But the same statistics support a quite different conclusion when one also entertains the theory of this book—that where statutes are unclear, legal default rules call on judges to estimate or elicit current political preferences when that would maximize political satisfaction.

The Attitudinal Model

Rather than assuming that judges make decisions that take legislative reactions into account, the "attitudinal" model posits that judges decide based on their own preferences, without considering the law, legislative preferences, or legislative reactions.[32] This model is normatively unattractive, for reasons already stressed. Moreover, it is even less consistent with the statistical evidence on statutory decisions, for the following reasons.

1. The attitudinal model cannot explain the fact that statutory interpretations do vary with changing congressional preferences, and that 70% of conference discussions refer to political actors' preferences or likely reactions.
2. Because the attitudinal model assumes that judges just vote their own political preferences without considering legislative views, it clearly predicts that statutory overrides will increase with increased political divergence between the judges and the legislature. In fact, as we have seen, this does not happen.
3. The attitudinal model is also inconsistent with the empirical evidence that judges often invite statute overrides.[33] If judges were just voting

in whatever way advanced their own interests, they would never invite override. The fact that they invite override also dispels the attitudinal assumption that judges are not even considering legislative reactions.

4. The attitudinal model would predict that statutory overrides should decrease with increasing political divergence between the House and Senate. Such intralegislative divergence should increasingly disable the legislature from overriding courts, which by hypothesis are just voting judicial preferences without considering the possibility of legislative reaction. Instead, the relationship between statutory overrides and intralegislative conflict exhibits the inverted U curve noted above.[34]

Further, the affirmative evidence to support the attitudinal model is much weaker than one might think. Consider the recent influential empirical study of *Chevron* by Professors Miles and Sunstein, one of the best-done studies in support of the attitudinal model.[35] They find that conservative justices were more likely to invalidate Clinton agency decisions than Bush ones, that conservative appellate judges have been more likely to invalidate liberal agency decisions than conservative ones, and that liberal justices and judges have the opposite tendencies. They conclude that these data prove their attitudinal (or realist) hypothesis: that judges decide based on their own political preferences rather than based on the *Chevron* doctrine.

One might think this study conflicts with my theory of *Chevron*. But it doesn't, for several reasons. First, this study does not measure whether judges follow the default rule provided by *Chevron*. Rather, the study measures whether judges affirm agency actions, and thus collapses the question of how judges ascertain whether statutory meaning exists with the question of whether judges follow the right default rule when statutory meaning is unclear. In fact, almost all the judicial invalidations of agency actions that the study found were decisions holding that the agency action had deviated from the clear statutory meaning. Where judges determined that statutory meaning was unclear, they almost always did defer to the agency decision under *Chevron*. Nor did the study find any significant ideological difference in whether the justices applied *Chevron* in cases when statutory meaning was unclear. Thus, even if the study picked up any tendency toward ideological decisionmaking by judges, it would only be in how those judges decide whether statutory meaning is clear—a topic about which *Chevron* offers no guidance—and not on what default rule to apply when statutory meaning is unclear.

Second, a difference in preferred legal methodology rather than ideology can explain some or all of the results of this study. Republican or conservative agency decisions are more likely to share the methodological views of conservative judges, particularly the view that statutory meaning should be ascertained purely from the text of the statute. Democrat or liberal agency decisions are more likely to share the methodological view of liberal judges that statutory meaning should be ascertained by some combination of text, purpose, and legislative history. Even if all judges apply their preferred methodologies for ascertaining statutory meaning without any political bias, it is more likely that they will invalidate decisions that have applied the opposite methodology. But here a difference in agency methodology correlates with a difference in agency political views. Thus, even if every judge neutrally applied that methodology, conservative judges are more likely to invalidate Democratic or liberal agency decisions, and liberal judges are more likely to invalidate Republican or conservative agency decisions. In short, some or all of the difference that Miles and Sunstein find could be explained by differences in preferred legal methodologies, rather than by differences in political ideologies.

The third problem is the biggest, because it is shared by just about every study that purports to establish the attitudinal model. Like these other studies, this study concludes that, if the data show that judges' political ideology influences their decisionmaking, then the attitudinal hypothesis is true and the hypothesis that judges follow legal doctrine is false. But this is a highly biased way of testing the hypotheses, because it applies two very different empirical tests to the two hypotheses. It deems the attitudinal hypothesis true as long as it has more than 0% influence, but deems the doctrinal hypothesis true only if it has 100% influence. To see the bias this creates, suppose that judges decide 10% based on political ideology and 90% based on legal doctrine. Then, this and other similar attitudinal studies would find that ideology does influence judicial decisionmaking, and then conclude that the attitudinal hypothesis is true and the doctrinal hypothesis is false, even though in fact the doctrinal hypothesis explains a lot more of judicial decisionmaking than the attitudinal hypothesis does.

For example, although Miles and Sunstein conclude that, for judicial review of agency decisions, they have disproven the doctrinal hypothesis and established the attitudinal hypothesis, what they actually find is that 6–30% of the variance in judicial decisions can be explained by whether the agency shares the judges' political persuasion. Even if we assume, contrary to the above, that all of this variance reflects ideological differences, rather than differences in legal methodology, it means that 70–94% of judicial decision-making is *not* accounted for by political differences. The conclusions of this study are thus entirely consistent with another study (by prominent proponents of the attitudinal model) that found that 68% of Supreme Court decisions were the opposite of what the ideological model predicted.[36]

In short, legal doctrine can meaningfully constrain judicial decisions, and even dictate most decisions, without eliminating all ideological influence. Thus, even if these studies accurately measure the extent of ideological decisionmaking, they do not at all disprove the theory that *Chevron* provides a default rule that helps maximize political satisfaction. They merely prove that this default rule does not determine 100% of decisions reviewing agency action.

It is also worth noting that the findings by Miles and Sunstein conflict with two other empirical studies that found no ideological divergence in judicial review of agency decisions.[37] A third study by Professor (now Dean) Revesz might seem more supportive of Miles and Sunstein because it found that D.C. Circuit judges are less likely to affirm agency decisions that conflict with the judge's ideology. However, this study found that this effect came entirely from votes on procedural issues, and that "following the Supreme Court's *Chevron* decision, there were no statistically significant differences in the way in which Democratic and Republican judges voted on statutory issues."[38]

Fourth, one must keep in mind that ideological variances in votes by individual conservative or liberal justices are likely to be muted in any multimember court that spans ideologies. The reason is that actual outcomes will be determined by the votes of the median justices, and they are the least likely to be voting ideologically. In the Miles and Sunstein study, the median justices were O'Connor and Kennedy, and they did not exhibit an ideological difference in their willingness to invalidate agency action, and were the most strongly influenced by whether *Chevron* deference applied. One thus cannot leap from the observation that some or even most justices do vote ideologically to the conclusion that *court outcomes* are ideological. Here, precisely the contrary is true, given the behavior of the median justices; and it is court outcomes (rather than individual justice votes) that determines legal doctrine.

We see a similar pattern in preemption cases. As noted in Chapter 13, the overall pattern of case results fits the theory of this book well. However, Greve and Klick's impressive study did also find that the odds of a preemption vote varied with the justice, with Justice Stevens at the low end (41%) and Justice Scalia at the high end (56%). But neither extreme was really that far from the Court's 52% odds of preemption result. Moveover, their study also showed that the votes of the median justices were the ones who determined the results, and that the identity of the median justice changed from case to case.[39]

This is one reason it makes sense to have more judges the higher the court. Because higher courts deal with more ambiguous legal issues (that have split lower courts), they have greater discretion to engage in ideological decisionmaking. This can to some extent be offset by increasing the number of judges.

CHAPTER 16

Interest Group and Collective Choice Theory

A different sort of objection is not descriptive, but normative. The objection is that satisfying political preferences is not a desirable goal, because the political process itself is defective. Some stress that the political process is distorted by interest group politics. They argue that, rather than maximize the satisfaction of enactable preferences, judges should interpret any statutory ambiguity against interest groups.[1] Others stress that the political process is beset by irrationalities and arbitrary results like cycling and path dependence, which apply in any process of aggregating votes into collective choices. They argue that judges should thus be less deferential to political preferences, including when interpreting statutes.[2]

I have already laid out one response to this critique. As Chapter 2 observes, this critique cannot really justify treating cases where statutes are unclear differently from cases where statutes are clear. Thus, even if this critique were valid, it would provide a basis for reforming the political process to change what statutes are enacted, not a theory for interpreting the results of a political process that is treated as valid.

In this chapter, I will turn to a more foundational response. Namely, neither of these critiques of the political process can establish defects in that process that can be separated from controversial normative premises about which outcomes are best. Applying these critiques to justify deviation from enactable preferences thus amounts to imposing those normative premises on the political process. It thus cannot really be separated from having judges impose their substantive normative views on the political process. Moreover, both critiques apply to the litigation process as well as to the political process, and thus fail to establish that lawmaking by the litigation process would be any less susceptible to the same problems.

Any Interest Group Theory Condemnation of Process Is the Same as Condemning the Outcome

Interest group theory argues that some groups are disproportionately able to organize about certain issues, because they have relatively high per member stakes in those issues, and have few enough members that they can police the free rider problems that otherwise plague efforts to contribute to collective political efforts.[3] Legislators are thus disproportionately influenced by these interest groups and underrepresent large diffusely-interested groups.

This picture of the political process is hardly uncontroversial. Other scholars have convincingly demonstrated that noneconomic factors, such as altruism and ideology, play at least some role in political participation and decisionmaking, and that the preferences of regulators and the general public sometimes prevail over the preferences of interest groups.[4] Still, these scholars do not disprove the point that the economic benefits and costs of political organization play a strong role, nor the point that special interest groups often take advantage of these economic factors to exercise disproportionate political influence. In any event, I do not wish to enter the empirical debate about the extent to which economic versus noneconomic factors play a role in political decisionmaking. My purpose is rather to address the normative question whether, to the extent one accepts its empirical claims, interest group theory justifies changing statutory interpretation.

The Dependence on a Normative Baseline

To the extent that it is empirically valid, interest group theory identifies the factors that make certain groups more willing than others to expend resources on seeking governmental action. However, identifying those factors cannot alone demonstrate which groups' political efforts are normatively disproportionate. Such a normative conclusion is possible only if we have some baseline for determining what level of political effort is normatively proportional to each group's interest. Interest group theory does not itself provide such a normative baseline. Rather, implicit normative baselines are adopted, usually without any discussion, when analysts draw normative implications from the degree of political influence predicted by interest group theory.

Often, the starting point for the implicit baseline is that a group's influence should be proportional to the number of individuals represented by the group. For example, when Mancur Olson talks of the "disproportionate power" of small groups with intensely interested members, he means that they will often have more political influence than the "large groups . . . normally supposed to prevail in a democracy."[5] But while one might expect large groups to prevail in a democracy, there are no grounds for concluding that the majority always should prevail over the minority, particularly when the majority's per person interest is lukewarm and the minority's per person interest is intense. Rather, under any plausible measure of social desirability, it will in some instances be desirable for the intensely interested minority to win.

To illustrate, suppose that we had no constitutional restriction on racist legislation, and that a racist majority in a particular community would derive a diffuse sense of satisfaction by retaining legislation that oppresses a racial minority. The racial minority is smaller, but more intensely interested in overturning the oppressive legislation than the majority is in passing it. These factors, it turns out, enable the racial minority to organize more effectively than the racial majority, and secure new legislation overturning the old law.[6] Under ordinary normative standards of racial justice, this seems entirely desirable. Here, it seems, the small intensely-interested group should win because its interest "outweighs" the diffuse (and presumably illegitimate) interest of the majority. But this conclusion follows only because we have a normative policy view supporting the conclusion that the majority's political preference does not deserve any more influence than it has achieved.

In other situations, the normative baseline will be less clear. Take, for example, the issue of affirmative action. Assume that the members of the racial minority are intensely interested in affirmative action, whereas the majority's members have a weaker per capita interest in avoiding it. Because of this, the racial minority succeeds in getting the government to adopt an affirmative action statute. Does this prove that the affirmative action statute represents the rent-seeking product of interest group politics? So some might argue.[7] But while the racial minority has, in this case, achieved an influence disproportionate to its numbers, one needs to posit a baseline standard of social desirability to conclude that its influence is disproportionate to the influence it "should" have had.

If, for example, one's normative standard of racial justice mandates equality of results, then (as in the racial oppression example) the minority's interest in having affirmative action normatively "outweighs" the majority's in avoiding it. The minority's organizational advantage does not, under this stipulated measure of social desirability, enable the minority to achieve an influence that is "disproportionate" to its interest. Rather, it simply enables the minority to achieve a political influence commensurate with the level of interest that should be ascribed to the minority.

Now instead assume that one's normative standard of racial justice mandates a view of equality of opportunity that is violated by the particular affirmative action statute under consideration. In that case, the racial minority's organizational advantage has enabled it to achieve a political influence disproportionate to its "true" interest in affirmative action. And the majority's structural disorganization has prevented it from fully expressing the interest of its members in equal job opportunity.

In short, even if interest group theory can explain, in all the above cases, how the racial minority was able to achieve an influence disproportionate to its numbers, by itself the theory cannot generate any normative conclusion about whether the group's influence was disproportionate to the influence it should have had. Such a normative conclusion requires some normative baseline about which levels of influence were appropriate for the minority and the majority. But once one has such a baseline, interest group theory provides no additional normative insight. The normative standards used to derive the baseline could simply be applied directly to the governmental action to reach the same conclusions, without the detour through interest group theory.

These examples may seem tendentious because they involve race relations, an area where some "interests" (such as venting prejudice) can justifiably be deemed unconstitutional or otherwise unworthy of satisfying, and where concerns about majoritarian exploitation are especially serious. But I begin with them only because they illustrate the problem most clearly and graphically. The same problem exists if we limit our analysis to the realm of economic regulation.

Suppose, for example, that our Constitution had no takings clause and that a majority wished the government to take the property of a wealthy minority without providing any compensation. The members of the wealthy minority, however, are intensely interested in avoiding the taking of their property, while the majority's members have a more diffuse interest in dividing up the minority's wealth. This organizational advantage enables the minority to block the uncompensated taking. Is this undesirable? The answer would seem to be no under the actual takings clause of the U.S. Constitution. The answer is also no to most economists, including public choice economists, because uncompensated takings produce allocative inefficiency and undermine productive incentives.[8]

One thus cannot say that, in the realm of economic regulation, it is generally undesirable for the minority to exercise political influence in disproportion to its numbers. How, then, do we know when a group has exercised "disproportionate" influence? The economist's apparent answer is that a group's political clout is disproportionate when it exceeds the group's economic interest in the matter. Thus, the arbitrary confiscation of property is categorized as majoritarian exploitation, and any minority success in preventing it is applauded and not regarded as the product of disproportionate interest group influence.[9] On the other hand, the enactment of the Sherman Act, which took monopoly profits away from cartelists to benefit consumers, is not viewed as majoritarian exploitation. The reason is that prohibiting cartels eliminates a dead weight loss, which is another way of saying that the aggregate economic gain to consumers exceeds the economic loss to cartelists. Similarly, where producers succeed in getting price floors enacted, their success is not hailed as preventing majoritarian exploitation. Rather, their success is regarded as interest group politics, because the price floors impose economic costs on consumers that exceed the economic gain enjoyed by producers.[10]

But using a group's economic interest as the baseline measure of the degree of political influence it should possess is appropriate only if one believes that economic efficiency should be our governing normative standard. Whenever groups comply with the baseline norm, and the political process is thus operating "correctly," the side with the largest economic interest at stake will win. Whenever the side with the smaller economic interest triumphs, the political process can always be condemned as reflecting either majoritarian exploitation or the exercise of "disproportionate" influence by a special interest group. It follows that, under this baseline, no governmental decision will be regarded as properly influenced unless it favors the side with the largest economic stake—that is, unless it maximizes the aggregate economic wealth in society. Because wealth maximization is the standard generally used to measure economic efficiency, this amounts to the conclusion that the only governmental actions that are properly influenced are those that advance economic efficiency.[11]

This should hardly be surprising because, after all, economic efficiency is what economists consider to be in the public interest. Indeed, as economists themselves explain, their entry into public choice theory was motivated largely by a desire to explain why the political and regulatory process was not producing the economically efficient laws and regulations that economists believed would advance the public interest.[12] But wealth maximization is hardly an uncontroversial measure of social desirability. It is not even an uncontroversial measure of efficiency. Many instead believe that Pareto's test is the true measure of efficiency, or that utility maximization is a more appropriate measure of social efficiency. Under both those measures, the distribution of wealth can be as important as its maximization.[13]

More important for present purposes, interest group theory provides no reason for changing whatever view one holds about the attraction of wealth maximization (i.e., economic efficiency) as a normative standard. If one believes that economic efficiency should be the normative standard for assessing the desirability of laws, one gains no additional insight by examining whether the groups backing a law exercised influence disproportionate to their economic interest, for in the end that examination replicates the assessment of the regulation's economic efficiency. And if one does not believe economic efficiency is the appropriate normative standard, one should not be misled into implicitly applying precisely that standard by using an interest group theory that condemns influence as disproportionate when it exceeds a group's economic interest.

To illustrate the controversy that can result from this implicit normative baseline when applying interest group theory, suppose that the issue is whether the state will enact a statute repealing city rent control ordinances. Suppose further that landlords are better organized than tenants because landlords have greater per capita stakes in repealing rent control than tenants have in maintaining it. As a result, the rent control ordinances are repealed. Does this reflect disproportionate influence (or capture) by a special interest group, namely landlords? Or have the landlords merely undone prior capture by tenants, who were a special interest group that initially got the rent control ordinance enacted because incumbent tenants had far more votes than landlords, and much higher per capita interests than prospective tenants?

The answer under economic interest group theory would seem to depend on whether rent control is economically inefficient. If, as most economists believe, rent control is inefficient,[14] then the tenant group's influence was "disproportionate" to its economic interest, and the landlords have undone interest group politics. If rent control is efficient, then the landlords have exercised disproportionate influence and the repeal reflects (rather than undoes) interest group politics. Again, the use of interest group theory seems gratuitous. If one is willing to make normative judgments about rent control based on its efficiency, there is no particular value in using the same normative judgment to assess the political influence that led to the enactment or repeal of rent control. One might as well immediately move to the issue of whether the resulting law is efficient.

Efficiency is not, however, the only implicit normative baseline used in assessing interest group influence over economic regulation. For example, Cass Sunstein, in his writings decrying interest group influence, argues that courts should invalidate governmental actions that reflect "naked preferences" for distributing wealth to politically powerful groups at the expense of others. But defining which preferences are "naked" requires some normative baseline. As Sunstein himself has stressed, the existing distribution of wealth in part reflects existing legal entitlements, which are themselves the product of governmental action. One thus cannot condemn all governmental decisions that redistribute wealth—unless, that is, one adopts the status quo as one's normative baseline. Sunstein rejects the status quo as a baseline, asserting that some governmental decisions to redistribute wealth are not "naked" because they promote the public good rather than reward "raw" political power.[15] But distinguishing the redistributions that are nakedly based on raw political power from those that promote the public good requires a theory of distributive justice. Sunstein nowhere articulates such a theory, but one can infer that his implicit baseline norm involves a more equal distribution of wealth. The political power of an interest group, under this interpretation, is only disproportionate (or raw) when it exacerbates inequalities in wealth. Interest group influence that results in redistributions that reduce inequality is apparently not raw or naked, but clothed with a public interest justification.

Such an egalitarian baseline can lead to conclusions about the excessiveness of interest group influence that differ significantly from the conclusions derived using an efficiency baseline. The differences are often present when efforts are made to change or reinstate the common law. To the economist who believes the common law is generally efficient, attempts to alter the common law will likely appear to be a manifestation of interest group influence. Under an egalitarian baseline, however, social welfare is not maximized by retaining or reinstating a common law regime that is wealth maximizing, but does not redistribute wealth. Efforts to retain or reinstate the common law may thus seem to manifest the disproportionate influence of a certain group—namely, the most economically productive members of society. To be sure, the economically less productive might be worse off if the law redistributed wealth more equitably, because the resulting decrease in incentives to produce might leave little wealth to redistribute. But this may not always be true, and one cannot be sure what empirical conclusions those implementing an egalitarian baseline are likely to draw.

One thus cannot apply interest group theory to condemn the political process without some independent normative baseline. One might object, however, that this normative baseline need not turn on the substance of outcomes. Imagine, for example, a baseline that accepts any political outcome that would have been reached under circumstances where each person had full information and equal political influence. Such a baseline might seem purely process based. However, because interest group theory assumes that each participant acts solely in her self-interest, applying such a baseline is identical to applying a standard that only upholds an outcome if the outcome benefits a greater number of persons than it hurts. This standard, which I call the majoritarian baseline, turns on the substance of outcomes. It is just one more alternative to other substantive standards such as wealth maximization, utility maximization, or distributive justice, each of which weighs outcomes by factors other than the sheer number of persons benefited and hurt. In any event, whether substantive or procedural, purely majoritarian baselines are normatively unattractive because they do not account for the varying intensity of individual preferences.

Indeed, interest group theory suggests that organizational activity may, in a rough way, offset the tendency a democratic government would otherwise have toward majoritarian exploitation. A perennial problem with a system of majority rule is that voting generally takes no account of how intensely different voters feel about the issues. Under a system of majority rule, informed voting by everyone would underweigh the interests of an intensely interested minority. Interest group theory, on the other hand, suggests that such intensely interested minorities will face less severe free rider problems in forming a political organization. This collective action advantage should sometimes enable the intensely interested minority to achieve political success that is socially desirable. The minority might block the enactment of laws that would undesirably cause much more harm than good (under a stipulated measure of social desirability) by distributing small benefits to a large number of persons and inflicting huge injury on a small number. Or the minority might secure the enactment of laws that will desirably cause much more good than harm (under the stipulated measure) even though these laws confer huge benefits on a small number of persons and impose minor costs on a large number. Such political success by the minority might be regarded as not only desirable, but necessary for the legitimacy of majoritarian rule.

Thus, democratic bias and the concern about majoritarian exploitation may roughly tend to offset the free rider problem and the concern about minorities exploiting the majority. A group's observed willingness to expend the political resources necessary to achieve political success could be taken as evidence of the group's "revealed intensity," much as economics takes a person's observed willingness to buy a good at a given price as evidence of that person's "revealed preference" for that good. One might accordingly deem whatever outcomes result from this political system as presumptively desirable.

To be sure, given the way the distribution of voting power and organizational advantage can bias the outcome, this measure of "revealed intensity" is rough indeed. But there is no clear reason to think this measure is any rougher than the measure of revealed preference commonly used in private markets, which is obviously heavily biased by individual variance in ability to pay. In both cases, relying instead on what groups/persons claim as their intensity/preference seems more likely to result in overclaiming than in increased accuracy. Just as the revealed preferences used in our economic markets free us from making impossible interpersonal utility comparisons, so, too, revealed intensity could be said to free us from making equally impossible intergroup utility comparisons in the political market.

Nor does the revealed intensity definition of socially desirable political outcomes seem inherently worse or rougher than other definitions, like wealth maximization, majority preference, or egalitarianism. Each of these seems to be an imperfect reflection of what individuals value: wealth maximization ignores the distribution of wealth; majoritarianism ignores the varying intensity of individual preferences; and egalitarianism undermines incentives to produce and comes in many conflicting versions, varying mainly on how much of a priority they give to benefiting those who are worse off. Each normative standard thus has its limits. Although revealed intensity has its own limitations, it at least has the attractive features of

being somewhat self-correcting and of providing an outlet for intense opposition to governmental laws.

In any event, if normative standards such as efficiency or egalitarianism
or majoritarianism are attractive, the basis for their attraction does not lie in
interest group theory. They must be independently justified. Individually,
we can each use interest group theory in conjunction with our own normative beliefs to reach individual conclusions about how the political process
reaches undesirable outcomes. But interest group theory cannot generate
the normative baselines necessary to draw these conclusions.

Nor can interest group theory demonstrate that the polity, however ideally defined, *shares* the normative standards used in these baselines. If we
believe that we have an independent basis for deriving collective normative
standards, interest group theory does not help us—for we or our judges
could apply those independent normative standards directly. If we instead
believe that only the polity can define the normative standards of society,
interest group theory leaves us with no solid ground for collective condemnation at all.

The Implications for the Proposals to Alter Statutory Interpretation

The above analysis explodes the claim that one can effectively limit aggressive judicial interpretation of statutes to a subset of cases by permitting it to
be triggered only where courts make a threshold finding that interest groups
have exercised excessive political influence. Whether courts will find any
given level of influence excessive depends on the normative baseline they
use. The problem is not just that judges, being mortal, will likely succumb to
the temptation to use implicit normative baselines. Even an ideally conscientious and knowledgeable judge will be unable to separate judicial findings
about whether interest group influence is excessive from normative conclusions about how much influence that interest group should have. Thus, in
making the threshold finding that supposedly narrows their normative discretion, judges will be making precisely the sort of normative judgment that
the proposals seek to limit to a subset of cases. The result is no different than
if the judge applied that normative standard to all cases.

For example, suppose a proposal suggests that, where a judge finds that a
statute resulted from disproportionate interest group influence, the judge
should be more willing to find statutory ambiguities, and then interpret
them against the interest group. The judge must adopt some baseline to de-

termine when a group's influence is disproportionate. A judge whose view of proper policy is economic efficiency will likely adopt that view as her baseline, finding interest group influence disproportionate whenever a statute is inefficient, and then interpreting any plausible ambiguities to make the statute more efficient. A judge who has an egalitarian view of proper policy will likely adopt that view as her baseline, finding interest group influence disproportionate whenever a statute exacerbates inequality, and then interpreting any plausible ambiguity to achieve a more just redistribution of wealth.

The result is precisely the same as if the proposal suggested that a judge should be more willing to find statutory ambiguities, and then resolve them in accord with the judge's own view of proper policy. In either case, statutes conforming to the judge's normative view will be left untouched, and other statutes will be interpreted to bring them into closer conformity with the judge's views. Worse, there may be no telling what normative baselines a judge will use.

Of course, one could imagine proposals that specify both the normative baseline to be used in assessing interest group influence and the normative policy views to be used when interpreting statutes. Moreover, one could imagine that the normative baseline used in assessing interest group influence might differ from—and be more limited than—the normative policy view that is applied when interpreting statutes. For example, one might argue that narrow judicial interpretation of an inefficient statute is appropriate only when an interest group's influence is disproportionate to both its numbers and its economic interest. Wouldn't such a proposal effectively limit the expansion of judicial lawmaking power?

Although such proposals do limit the likelihood that judicial action will aggressively interpret statutes, they do so by weakening the normative judgment courts are authorized to apply, not by limiting which statutes are subject to normative adjustment by judges. The proposal sketched in the preceding paragraph, for example, would have more limited results than a proposal to interpret all inefficient statutes narrowly. But the proposal would have precisely the same effect as a proposal to have judges narrowly construe any statute that is both inefficient and harms more persons than it helps. The normative judgment condemning inefficiency that harms the majority is less sweeping, and perhaps more attractive, than the normative judgment condemning any inefficiency. But one should recognize that the proposal nonetheless calls for judges to review all statutes under the stipulated normative policy view. If judges should expand their lawmaking role in interpreting statutes, it would be better (and certainly less misleading) for scholars to make the normative argument directly and for judges to apply the stipulated normative view openly, rather than smuggling it into a seemingly factual and process-based determination of whether interest group influence was disproportionate.

One could of course imagine proposals that embody even more narrow (and thus more attractive) normative judgments. For example, a proposal might authorize expanded judicial lawmaking power only when interest group influence is disproportionate to its numbers and its economic interest *and* results in regulation that exacerbates inequality. Such a proposal, however, simply embodies the normative judgment that it is undesirable to take action that is inefficient, exacerbates inequality, and harms more persons than are helped. Such a normative judgment may often be justifiable, but not necessarily always. Consider the fact that the U.S. social security program is quite popular, even though it probably violates all three of these standards. In any event, the point here is that the justification—and its limits—must be derived from some normative theory, not from interest group theory.

In short, any defects in the political process identified by interest group theory depend on implicit normative baselines, and thus do not stand independent of substantive conclusions about the merits of particular political outcomes. Accordingly, proposals for more aggressive judicial interpretation of statutes cannot meaningfully be limited by requiring threshold findings of excessive interest group influence. Nor can we be sure that an "undistorted" polity would share any normative judgments used in the baseline necessary to measure interest group distortion. Instead, the use of interest group theory to narrow the influence of the political process reflects normative views that are contestable, and may not reflect the views of the polity at all.

Interest Group Theory Cannot Show That the Litigation Process Is Any Better Than the Political Process

Those advocating more aggressive judicial interpretation of statutes rarely address the comparative question: whether interest group theory provides any sound basis to expect the litigation process to be any better than the political process. Instead the tendency is to emphasize the flaws of the political process and then assume, without analysis, that the litigation process will operate better.

But the litigation process cannot be treated as exogenous to interest group theory: it, too, is susceptible to interest group influences. Just as with political efforts to secure legislative outcomes, individual members of groups that would benefit from favorable judicial precedent have free rider incentives not to contribute toward the costs of establishing that precedent, because they must share the benefits with other group members. Large diffuse groups unable to organize effective efforts to influence the political branches, where they at least have the advantage of more votes, are also likely to be unable to organize effective efforts to influence the litigation process. Accordingly, the same interest groups that have an organizational advantage in collecting resources to influence legislators and agencies generally also have an organizational advantage in collecting resources to influence the courts. Indeed, because special interest groups have fewer voting members, one might predict that their relative influence over the political branches would actually be lower than with the courts, where the number of votes doesn't matter. Increasing the lawmaking power of the courts may only exacerbate the influence of interest groups.

We thus need to examine whether there is any reason to believe that the litigation process is less susceptible to interest group influence than the political process, and whether any factors that make it less susceptible are likely to make it better at lawmaking. Although rarely delving directly into these comparative assessments, the literature taken as a whole suggests four reasons for having greater faith in the litigation process. First, some argue that the common law process of lawmaking allows the law to evolve toward efficiency. Second, class actions help groups overcome the free rider problem in litigation. Third, the adversarial structure of litigation guarantees that at least two viewpoints are represented. Finally, the litigation process is more insulated from political influence and thus from interest groups. I address each of those arguments in turn in the following sections.

1. The "Evolutionary" Common Law Process

One commonly cited advantage of judicial decisionmaking is that, under the common law process, judges cannot set their own agenda. Judicial lawmaking authority must be triggered by a party's decision to litigate, and is generally incremental and subject to appellate review. Using the same assumption of self-interested behavior that underlies interest group theory, the field of law and economics has developed an evolutionary theory, which argues that rules formed through such a common law process will naturally tend to evolve toward efficiency. At least for those who believe that laws should be efficient, this would suggest that forming and changing legal rules through a common law process has a comparative advantage over lawmaking through the political process.

First articulated by Paul Rubin, the basic thrust of this evolutionary theory is that litigation challenges to inefficient precedents will be more frequent and skillful than challenges to efficient precedents.[16] Assuming that efficiency is defined as wealth maximization, those aggrieved by an inefficient rule suffer costs that, by definition, exceed the benefits to those who profit from the rule, and an inefficient rule imposes greater net costs than would a more efficient rule. Further, the theory notes, litigation is costly, and will only be pursued to the extent that the benefits parties derive from litigation exceed its costs. Because the benefits from overturning a precedent are greater if the precedent is inefficient, parties are more likely to pursue litigation (to trial or on appeal) when it challenges inefficient precedents than when it challenges efficient precedents. For similar reasons, parties challenging inefficient precedents (or defending efficient ones) will tend to expend more resources than their opponents on making skillful legal arguments.

This difference in the frequency and skill of litigation will, evolutionary theory concludes, create a tendency for the law to evolve toward efficiency regardless of whether judges generally have the ability or desire to make the law more efficient. Even if judges randomly decide which side wins in litigation, the increased frequency of litigated challenges to inefficient rules will make those rules more likely to be reexamined, and overruled, than efficient rules. And assuming that judges respond favorably to skillful legal arguments, the generally greater skill of legal arguments for efficient rules will, on balance, give challenges to inefficient rules a higher probability of success than challenges to efficient rules. Thus, over time, and without any conscious design, the common law process of making law through litigation will tend to displace inefficient rules in favor of efficient ones.

However, this analysis faces serious problems under interest group theory. Namely, as Paul Rubin himself came to acknowledge,[17] the collective action problems described by interest group theory undermine evolutionary theory's premise that those with the greater economic interest will invest in more frequent and skillful litigation. Just as with laws enacted by statute or regulation, so, too, laws (or precedents) adopted through adjudication tend to confer benefits on a class of persons, whether or not they contribute to efforts to get that law adopted. This creates the same free rider problems that face groups in lobbying political actors; the groups that enjoy organizational advantages in collecting resources to petition the political branches should also enjoy the same advantages in collecting resources to petition the courts. Groups that are less susceptible to free rider problems, or better able to curb them, should fund more frequent and more skillful litigation than their counterparts.

Thus, far from explaining why the litigation process should be less susceptible to interest group influence than the political process, evolutionary theory explains the very mechanisms by which interest groups are likely to exert their "disproportionate" influence over the litigation process. This suggests not only that the litigation process is susceptible to interest group influence, but that increasing the lawmaking power of courts will simply encourage interest groups to invest more resources in litigation and thus exacerbate their influence over the litigation process.

Moreover, to the extent it has force, evolutionary analysis could just as well be applied to the political process. Inefficient statutory and regulatory rules, like inefficient common law rules, confer fewer benefits and impose greater costs than do efficient rules. Parties aggrieved by an inefficient statute or regulation thus gain more from its repeal or nonenactment than their opponents gain from its retention or enactment. Parties who profit from an efficient statute or regulation gain more from its retention or enactment than their opponents gain from its repeal or nonenactment. Applying the same analysis, one might thus expect that efforts to repeal or block inefficient statutes or regulations (and efforts to retain or enact efficient statutes or regulations) will be more frequent and successful than counterefforts. If so, statutes and regulations will also tend to evolve toward efficiency. And, in fact, the literature arguing that the common law tends to evolve toward efficiency has a parallel in the statutory and regulatory world: Gary Becker's work arguing that, in the political arena, competition among interest groups will tend to lead to efficient laws, or at least to more efficient means of subsidizing the groups that have disproportionate influence.[18]

In both the judicial and political processes, a mixed picture is more accurate. Where efficient rules benefit organized groups at the expense of less organized groups, those rules are likely to become law in either forum. Where inefficient laws benefit organized groups at the expense of disorganized groups, the result is more uncertain. Sometimes the increased frequency and intensity of petitioning associated with better organization will exceed the increased frequency and intensity associated with opposition to inefficient laws. Sometimes the opposite will hold true. In any event, evolutionary theory provides no reason to believe that any disproportionate influence associated with better organization will be more pronounced in the political process than in the litigation process.

2. Class Actions

William Eskridge has argued that one structural factor making the judicial process less susceptible to interest group influence than the political process is the availability of class actions in litigation. Class actions, he argues, help curb free rider problems because they allow "entrepreneurial counsel" to organize a group, which collectively finances the litigation through fees payable out of class action awards.[19] In this way, large diffusely-interested groups that go unrepresented in the political process can get represented in litigation.

Class actions, however, are by no means always feasible whenever free rider problems regarding lawmaking exist. Such free rider problems exist when numerous persons cannot be excluded from the benefits of a favorable law produced by successful petitioning. But bringing a class action requires more than showing that class members share common interests in a particular legal issue; it also requires other factual demonstrations, most typically a showing that common legal or factual issues "predominate" their lawsuits. And even if a class action is legally possible, it may not be feasible. To bring a class action seeking monetary relief, normally someone must incur the costs of notifying the class and preparing the case, and lawyers must incur the risk that they will not earn any fees if they lose or fail to get the class certified. These costs and risks often suffice to discourage anyone from bringing or pursuing class actions. Moreover, where the class action seeks nonmonetary relief that does not create a common fund—which will often be the case when statutory interpretation is the issue—class action lawyers will get no recovery unless a fee-shifting statute is in place.[20]

A more fundamental problem is that class members have little choice in selecting who represents them in a class action.[21] For class actions under Federal Rule of Civil Procedure 23(b)(3), the only effective choice available to diffusely interested members is whether or not to opt out of the class. If the class action proceeds under Rule 23(b)(1) or (b)(2), class members may not even have this choice. Although, where applicable, the right to opt out certainly gives class members some say, it is difficult to see why the right to opt out should be regarded as more effective than the right to vote in general elections. The exercise of both rights seems likely to be marked by rational ignorance because, for each right, the costs of absorbing, analyzing, and acting on the available information will often exceed the expected benefit from exercising the right in an informed manner.[22]

Indeed, the ability to select "political entrepreneurs" through voting seems, in many respects, more effective than the right to select "entrepreneurial counsel" through opting out. In voting, individuals at least have a choice between candidates. In class actions, however, members can choose only between accepting or rejecting the representative the court has approved. Because of their small individual stake, it will not be feasible for them to fund their own representative; and because most of the class will not opt out, another lawyer is unlikely to come forward to represent the members who opted out. The opt-out choice thus has some similarities to voting with only one candidate on the ballot. And where class actions are not possible, diffusely-interested persons get no representation at all in the litigation process, whereas in the political process they can at least be represented to some extent through voting.

There is also a coercive element to the opt-out choice. The voter who votes against the only candidate on the ballot will not be excluded from whatever collective benefits that candidate provides. But the class member who opts out of an action seeking monetary relief will be excluded from the benefits of the litigation (which will almost certainly proceed) and will usually find it infeasible to collect those benefits through a separate class action. Class members may thus decline to opt out of the offered representation—even though they would prefer a different representative—because they would likely receive no representation, and no recovery, if the class action goes forward without them.

All of this means that, in class action litigation, diffusely-interested members have little ability to select or influence the attorney who acts on their behalf. The class action attorney may have policy views that differ from the views of class members. Worse, the attorney often has financial incentives to litigate in ways that do not advance the net interests of the class. In particular, lawyers may bring claims that offer a significant chance of recovery (in which the lawyer can share) even though the claims will increase each member's indirect or future costs by more than the recovery is worth. The attorney also has strong incentives to agree to settlements with favorable fee arrangements, even though the class members would prefer other settlements or further litigation.

To be sure, a court must approve any class action settlement and may have to find that the lawyer adequately represents the interests of the class. But judicial review of these issues is widely regarded as ineffective.[23] In any event, it would be bootstrapping to rely on the necessity of judicial approval to conclude that the judicial process has an advantage over the political process. Unless we have some independent reason for thinking that judicial decisionmaking is more reliable than political decisionmaking, requiring judicial approval cannot make the selection of litigation representatives more reliable than the selection of political representatives. Moreover, even if the attorney does fulfill her fiduciary duty to maximize the class members' recovery, the attorney has little if any financial incentive to use class action litigation to set favorable precedent that will confer benefits outside of the class action recovery.

None of this means that class actions have no useful role. They permit the adjudication of small claims that otherwise could not feasibly be adjudicated at all, and avoid duplicative litigation of issues common to a class. But the question here is not whether class actions should be permitted. Rather, the question is whether class actions make litigation a more suitable forum for lawmaking than the political process. The observation that class actions can be better than no litigation is no more dispositive of that question than the counter-observation that providing public goods through the political process can be better than not providing public goods at all.

Finally, if the coercive financing of collective representation is litigation's advantage, then reforming the political process to allow such financing would appear to be a more attractive reform than expanding the lawmaking power of courts. Indeed, some examples of similar financing already exist: our current government financing of presidential campaigns and our financing of mailings by congressional incumbents. But, as many already object, such financing raises serious problems because it may unduly favor the incumbent parties or representatives. Not surprisingly, the problem parallels the difficulties inherent in our method of funding class action litigation.

Of course, funding candidates in general elections does not tailor the representation to a subset group in the same way that class actions can. But one could imagine using a procedure similar to class actions to unbundle issues in the political arena. Organizations could petition courts to be recognized as the official political representatives of defined subgroups and could, if judicially approved, be given a portion of the subsidies received (or income taxes paid) by any of their subgroup's members. We could, in other words, have class action lobbyists. Currently, such a scheme would—unless it allowed members to opt out—apparently run afoul of First Amendment case law, which has prohibited unions and bar associations from using legal coercion to force their members to finance the group's petitioning efforts.[24] And one might expect that members would take advantage of any opportunity to opt out because, unlike in class action litigation, they would not be any worse off if the group lobbying goes on without them. But if we were truly convinced that coercive financing is advantageous, we could adopt a constitutional amendment to allow it without an opt out in the political arena.

I suspect, however, that most persons would oppose such a scheme for coercively financing political lobbying. The likely reason would be the same one that prompted the Supreme Court to adopt the current First Amendment doctrine: the possibility that such laws will help us avoid free rider problems in political lobbying does not justify the risk that such laws will coerce us into funding political positions that we do not support. Interest group theory does not alleviate concerns about the latter risk, for it suggests that the same groups that generally have excessive political power will also gain influence over decisions about which groups receive public financing. But if the hostility to coercive financing of political petitioning is justified, it suggests that we should not expand the coercive financing currently used in class actions by transferring more of the lawmaking function to class action litigation. More generally, the analysis suggests that any scheme to cure under-representation by appointing a group representative, be it a class action lawyer or a class action lobbyist, does little more than shift the problem to a new level, because it cannot solve the problem of who represents the disorganized group in choosing and guiding its group representative.[25]

3. Adversarial Structure

Another argument frequently made is that the adversarial structure of the litigation process renders it less susceptible to interest group influence. This structure means that at least two opposing views are usually represented in litigated cases. Thus, judges are less likely than legislators and agencies to make law having heard only the arguments supporting the resulting law.

This is an important advantage of the litigation process. Unfortunately, it does not offset an interest group's ability to exercise any disproportionate influence it has. Small intensely-interested groups are still likely to spend more on their litigation efforts than any large diffuse groups opposing them. The former will on balance be able to hire more skilled lawyers and experts, and thus have more influence on the information presented to the court about the social desirability of the parties' conduct and any legal rule under consideration. And the very fact that they can fund more frequent litigation will ultimately tend to lead to more decisions favoring small intensely-interested groups.

Moreover, the adversarial structure has offsetting disadvantages. First, courts generally only hear (or pay attention to) the arguments of the actual litigants. Other persons interested in the precedential implications of the case, but not in the judgment itself, generally lack standing and receive inadequate consideration. Nor, assuming that there are more possible policy positions or legal rules than there are litigants, will the courts necessarily be presented with the full array of policy arguments and regulatory options. Each party may argue only for the policy or rule that is best for it; none may argue for the policy or rule that is best for society. To be sure, courts can accept amicus briefs from nonparties. But amicus briefs are generally supplied either by the very interest groups that are best positioned to fund them, or by the political branches on which those interest groups have supposedly had a disproportionate influence.

Indeed, if large diffusely-interested groups really suffer such extensive free rider problems that they are unlikely to make any appearance in a political forum, they are also unlikely to make any appearance in litigation—unless they do so via a class action or public interest representative, which raises the problems discussed in the previous section. Cases that do not involve such problematic representation are thus likely to present only the opposing viewpoints of intensely-interested persons. The interests of the members of large diffusely-interested groups can remain under-represented or malrepresented.

A second, and related, problem is that courts tend to underweigh, or be underinformed about, the systemic and prospective consequences of their decisions because they focus on the particular parties and adjudicated historical facts that are before them.[26] A trial record usually reveals less about the social and economic consequences of the court's possible decision than does the information presented to legislatures or administrative agencies. Even if a court is informed about the systemic effects on unnamed persons, those effects are unlikely to carry an emotional impact proportional to the plight of the identified human beings who will be bound by the court's judgment. Legislators and regulatory rulemakers, on the other hand, deal in systemic effects, and are less likely to be distracted by the idiosyncratic situations of particular persons.

The adversarial structure of litigation also creates a third serious problem: it permits parties to settle strategically in cases where the type of judge or set of facts seems likely to lead to unfavorable precedent. A trade association seeking a favorable regulatory ruling may, for example, choose to settle a case if it gets assigned to a judge hostile to regulation. Or the trade association may be willing to refrain from appealing contrary judgments until it has a good "test case," where the facts seem particularly sympathetic. Some courts have even allowed parties to vacate unfavorable precedent through post-judgment settlements.[27]

Small intensely-interested groups will be better positioned to pursue a policy of molding precedent through strategic settlement. Such groups are repeat players with a relatively large stake in the value of setting precedent, and a relatively low stake in how an individual case comes out. Large diffusely-interested groups will be harder pressed to collect the funds necessary to pay off litigants bringing worrisome cases. And isolated individuals, even if intensely interested in their case, have little interest in precedent, and thus a strong incentive to accept any settlement favorable in the case at hand.

In the political process, a policy of strategic settlement is, on the whole, harder to implement. An interest group cannot usually expect that settling with opposing petitioners will vacate unfavorable legislation or regulation; nor can a group normally hope that, if it settles today, an issue will get assigned to a different legislature or agency next time. Moreover, action taken by a legislature or agency is typically not aimed at specific individuals. This makes it both less likely that selective settlement will focus lawmakers on a more favorable set of facts and more difficult to pay off all the persons who might object to the lawmakers' actions.

In sum, the adversarial structure of litigation has offsetting advantages and disadvantages. Litigation guarantees that any decision takes into account at least two views and a particular factual situation, and that parties control the settlement of their own disputes. But litigation also means that decisions fail to consider the full range of views and societal facts, and that settlements do not reflect the entire spectrum of considerations. Litigation is thus likely to be more desirable where it is highly important to focus on the views, factual situations, and interests of a limited number of persons, and less important to have other views, facts, and interests fully represented. Or, to put the matter in more familiar terms, the adversarial structure of litigation generally makes it better suited for the adjudication of fact-specific disputes than for general rulemaking. The latter is what is required when interpreting a statute, as opposed to when just applying that interpretation to particular facts.

4. Political Insulation

Perhaps the most seriously pressed interest group argument for why judges make superior lawmakers is that they are insulated from political influence. U.S. federal judges have life tenure, salaries that cannot be reduced, and procedural rules that limit the standing and ex parte contact of interest groups. Because this general political insulation also shields federal judges from interest group pressure, the argument is that these judges are better able than legislators to fashion wise policy.

The political insulation of *judges*, however, does not ensure the insulation of the *litigation process* from interest group influence. Under the mechanisms already discussed, organized interest groups will still be able to litigate more frequently, to influence better the information tribunals receive, and to strategically settle cases that may produce unfavorable precedents. These methods do not require that the judge sympathize with any particular view; they depend solely on parties' (differential) decisions about when to litigate, what resources to devote to litigation, and when to settle.

In fact, these methods seem *more* effective for influencing courts than other lawmakers. Unlike courts, legislators and regulators do not have their lawmaking power triggered by party action: they can initiate lawmaking on their own and are not forced to make a decision when a party petitions. Legislators and agencies also usually have far more resources to conduct their own investigations, whereas courts must generally rely on the information the parties present to them. Further, while in the political process the organizational advantages of small groups are somewhat offset by the greater votes of large groups, no such offset exists in the litigation process.

Nonetheless, one might conclude that these disadvantages of litigation are not only reduced, but outweighed, by the greater political insulation of federal judges. This conclusion, however, faces two main difficulties. First, interest groups can influence judicial appointments, and are more likely to do so the more regulatory power we give judges. Second, interest group theory does nothing to demonstrate that greater political insulation is desirable. Let's take those propositions in turn.

Interest group influence over judicial appointments. Although federal judges need not run periodically for reelection, they do not reach their positions in a nonpolitical fashion. They must be nominated by the president and confirmed by the Senate. Nominations and confirmations are matters over which special interest groups can exercise any disproportionate political clout they possess. One might thus expect that interest groups would use their political influence to ensure that judicial appointments go to persons holding views favorable to the interest group. Interest groups might, in short, disproportionately influence and even "capture" the selection of judges. (The concern is even greater for state judges who often are elected.)

One objection to this might be that we do not in fact observe extensive interest group influence over judicial appointments, at least not by interest groups with an economic agenda. But if this is true, the reason likely lies in the fact that judges today are not major sources of economic regulation, at least not compared to elected and agency officials. If we changed that, by expanding judicial lawmaking authority, then economic interest groups would likely become far more active in the nomination and confirmation process. After all, before *Roe v. Wade,* we did not see major activity by pro-life and pro-choice groups regarding Supreme Court appointments. But after *Roe* made clear that the Court had become the country's main abortion regulator, both groups became highly active in attempting to influence who gets nominated and confirmed.

Thus, any expansion of judicial lawmaking authority that gives courts a larger role in economic regulation may—instead of curbing interest group influence over the political process—have the perverse effect of *exacerbating* interest group influence over judicial appointments. To the extent that we value political insulation for other reasons (such as facilitating the fair adjudication of facts or the neutral application of law), we undermine that insulation if we encourage interest groups to step up their participation in the appointment process, by converting courts into ordinary regulatory lawmakers.

Although judicial appointments are susceptible to interest group influence, it must be conceded that the lack of ongoing political accountability makes federal judges somewhat less susceptible to political influence than legislators. Ongoing accountability may not, however, be that relevant. We do not usually observe notable shifts in policy when a president enters his second term or when a legislator serves out her last term before a planned retirement.[28] By and large, the policy preferences that got them elected turn out to be the same policy preferences they carry out when they have no need to position themselves for reelection. Moreover, to the extent that judges are less subject to ongoing accountability, that factor may serve only to encourage interest group influence over the initial appointment, because it makes the fruits of successful interest group capture more durable and thus more valuable.[29]

A more significant difference between judges and politicians may lie in the length of their terms. Even if interest groups can "capture" the appointment or election process, they can only make sure that the current—and known—views of those they appoint or elect will favor the interest groups on the issues the groups can currently foresee. But persons change, unknown views surface, and unforeseen issues arise; the longer the term of service, the more likely such changes and unforeseen developments will be. Thus, influencing the appointment of judges to lifetime terms will have a less certain influence on the decisions that ultimately get made than will influencing the election of politicians to their final (shorter) terms. This raises the next question: does interest group theory provide any reason to think that this somewhat greater political insulation is desirable?

Interest group theory does not show that political insulation is desirable. This is not the place for an extended discussion of the benefits and dangers of a politically insulated judiciary. Fortunately, an extended discussion is unnecessary, because the issue here is whether interest group theory provides any affirmative reason to regard political insulation as desirable when exercising a power to broaden or narrow statutes, not whether political insulation is desirable for other reasons.

In answering this more limited question, we must remember that the critical bite of interest group theory comes from its claim that the political process inaccurately reflects the will of the polity. The theory demonstrates that group structure affects political influence in a way that can, under some normative baselines, distort how the political process aggregates the affected social interests or otherwise defines the public interest. In particular, the theory demonstrates that the political process can produce outcomes harmful to the majority, a result that is undesirable under a (crude) majoritarian baseline.

But this critique provides no reason to prefer lawmaking that is insulated from political pressure, for such insulation shields lawmakers not only from interest groups but from the rest of the polity as well. This insulated law-making can produce even *worse* distortions and results that are even *more* antimajoritarian. While the political process may disproportionately reflect the views of minority groups, an insulated judicial process can dispropor-tionately reflect the views of single individuals—namely, the views of judges who may make no effort to represent the views or interests of the polity. Even if judges do try to represent the polity, the very unresponsiveness to, and unfamiliarity with, the affected interests that creates political insulation also makes judges more likely to err in assessing, canvassing, weighing, or maximizing the affected interests. As inaccurate as the political process may be in reflecting the will of the polity, there is no reason to believe it is less ac-curate than judicial lawmaking.[30]

If politically insulated lawmaking does not represent the polity, what sort of predictions does interest group theory suggest about insulated lawmak-ing? Within the paradigm of interest group theory, it seems that consistency requires ascribing some sort of self-centered motivation to judges. Some suggest that judges seek to expand their own power. It is hard to see why this should be expected to improve decisionmaking. In specific cases, the motive to expand judicial power would often lead to undesirable results. More generally, the judicial power expansion likely to result from such a motive can be desirable only if we have some independent reason for be-lieving judicial lawmaking is better than political lawmaking.

Other possible public choice theories are that judges seek to maximize their salaries, their budgets, their jurisdiction, or their chances of promotion by pleasing legislators.[31] A Congress that is displeased with judicial decisions might effectively reduce judicial salaries by refusing to adjust for inflation, might make insufficient appropriations for judicial support staff, or might dilute judicial power by expanding the number of judgeships or shrinking a court's jurisdiction. Or it might single out individual judges by denying pro-motions, making adverse statements about them, holding hearings about their actions, or in extreme cases threatening impeachment. But to the ex-tent that these motives do operate, they suggest that judges are unlikely to be better decisionmakers than the legislatures they seek to please.

Another hypothesis is that courts seek the approval of lawyers and legal academics.[32] To the extent this is true, courts are accountable, but to a rather narrow segment of society. This creates its own distortion because lawyers and legal academics hardly represent a cross section of the polity. Moreover, interest groups who realize where the real power lies can exert influence on the bar or the academy, through hiring and foundation grants. In any event, a judge is unlikely to care about the approval of lawyers and academics unless they already share her political leanings. A conservative judge will not be swayed (and will probably be relieved) if her decision has been critiqued by a leftist law professor, and a radical judge will not lose much sleep if his decision garners the disapproval of the corporate bar.

Finally, judges might be motivated by the desire to impose their own values and policy preferences on society. But, at least within interest group theory, any differences between judicial views and the present balance of political influence can be traced to one of four things: (1) the dead hand of past political influence that is reflected in the initial, known views the judge held at the time of appointment and did not change; (2) the migration of the judge's views since appointment; (3) views that the judge did not reveal at appointment; and (4) the application of the judge's initial, known views to issues unforeseen at appointment. The first factor hardly suggests an improvement; the influence of previously powerful interest groups not only will be just as disproportionate as contemporary ones but also will reflect outdated factual circumstances. The other three factors seem to represent an essentially random package of views. One is reminded of the story about the newly appointed judge who, on meeting a U.S. Supreme Court justice, says: "I'm delighted to meet you in person because I have just taken an oath to support and defend whatever comes into your head."[33] Interest group theory gives us no reason to think that whatever comes into a justice's head (or was within that head but unknown or unappreciated at the time of appointment) will produce better social policy than a more politically responsive process.

In short, even if interest group theory succeeds in demonstrating defects in the political process, one cannot leap to the conclusion that a process of judicial decisionmaking would improve lawmaking. The litigation process cannot be treated as exogenous to interest group theory: it is itself subject to forms of interest group influence that will be exacerbated the greater the interstitial lawmaking power that is exercised by judges. Nor does interest group theory establish that overall the litigation process is less subject to interest group influence than, or is otherwise preferable to, the political process.

Increasing the Transaction Costs of Legal Change Provides No Justification

Even if interest group theory does not show that the litigation process is less defective than the political process, one might see another interest group justification for making judicial interpretation of statutes more aggressive— namely, that two obstacles are better than one. Because interest groups would have to influence two bodies of government, more aggressive judicial interpretation might be justified on the ground that it reduces the promulgation of legal changes favoring interest groups by increasing the transaction costs of interest group capture. However, this transaction-cost argument founders on the following scores.

1. Transaction Costs May Not Increase

The premise that more aggressive judicial interpretation will increase the transaction costs of interest group capture assumes that legal results favoring special interest groups come about only if the laws are first enacted by a legislature or agency and then upheld by a court. But if interest groups enjoy disproportionate influence over the judiciary, influencing the court may often be the only step necessary.

Suppose, for example, it is efficient to have laws that enforce the written terms of franchise agreements regardless of their "fairness," and that efficiency is our baseline standard for judging whether political influence is disproportionate. The legislature has enacted an efficient statute requiring the enforcement of franchise agreements as written. However, the franchisees have (under our posited normative baseline) a disproportionate influence on the courts. Because of this influence, the franchisees persuade a court to construe the statute narrowly, either under the court's generally expanded authority or on the ground that the statute must have been the product of capture by franchisors. Under this example, interest group capture is effectuated solely by influencing the judiciary.

Indeed, more aggressive judicial interpretation may sometimes *decrease* the transaction costs of interest group capture. Interest groups facing higher transaction costs in the legislature (or relevant agency) than in court may simply push for the result they want in the lower-cost forum. For example, suppose that in the last hypothetical the franchisees could have won in the legislature, but at a much higher cost. They may then simply decide to accept their defeat in the legislature, relying on their ability to influence the courts at a lower cost. Or, if the transaction costs in the legislature are so high that the franchisees could not have met them at all, the increased scope of matters left to judicial interpretation may make possible a capture that otherwise could not have happened. Instead of erecting two obstacles, more aggressive judicial interpretation may simply provide two bites at the apple.

2. Increasing Transaction Costs Can Encourage Interest Group Activity

Now assume that we have a case where more aggressive judicial interpretation has increased the transaction costs of capture. The interest group must first induce the legislature to enact the statute and then persuade a court to refrain from construing it narrowly. Does it follow from this that interest group activity will be discouraged? Not necessarily, for the simple reason that increasing transaction costs may also increase the benefits of interest group capture by making that capture harder to undo. Where these increased benefits outweigh the increased transaction costs, expanded judicial lawmaking power over statutes will actually encourage interest group activity.

To illustrate, suppose that the issue is again what law should govern franchise agreements. The franchisees must incur certain costs in order to (disproportionately) influence the legislature to enact an inefficient statute making certain "unfair" terms unenforceable. The expansion in judicial authority means that the franchisees must now also incur extra costs and risks to get judges not to narrowly interpret the statute. If, however, the franchisees incur these costs and succeed in getting the statute enacted and neutrally interpreted, the franchisors cannot overturn the law by incurring only the costs of getting the legislature to enact a new statute making unfair terms enforceable. The franchisors must also be willing and able to incur both the extra costs of persuading the court not to narrowly interpret the new statute and the heightened risk that it will not. Those increased costs and risks will often make an otherwise feasible franchisor attack unfeasible. Accordingly, the increased transaction costs of a complete legal change make the initial statute favoring franchisees less vulnerable to franchisor attack, and thus more durable and valuable.

3. Increasing Transaction Costs Can Increase the
Relative Advantage of Interest Groups

The previous two sections establish that making judicial interpretation more aggressive would sometimes not increase transaction costs and that, even when it did, doing so would sometimes encourage interest group activity. It remains possible that, in other cases, more aggressive judicial interpretation would discourage interest group activity. But even in such cases, the promulgation of laws favoring interest groups might not decline. The reason is that, if increased transaction costs would discourage interest group activity, they should also discourage opposition to it. The net effect might well be an increased promulgation of laws favoring organized interest groups.

Under interest group theory, the likelihood that the government will promulgate a requested legal change turns not on the absolute level of a group's petitioning efforts, but on whether those efforts exceed the efforts made by other groups. It does not matter how many votes one can deliver so long as one can deliver more votes than anyone else. Indeed, the theory's basic deduction from the free rider problem rests on this premise. The theory observes that free rider problems will cause all groups—small and large—to invest less in petitioning than would be optimal for the group. But the theory concludes that, because greater free rider problems plague large diffuse groups, the large groups' level of petitioning will fall farther short of optimal than the small groups' level, and that this will increase the likelihood that the government will rule in the small groups' favor. Thus, the free rider problem itself discourages interest group activity but, because it discourages opposition activity more, increases the likelihood of laws favoring special interest groups.

Increasing the transaction costs of legal change can have a similar effect. Even when such an increase discourages interest group activity, it should also discourage political activity by the opposition. The opposition, after all, must incur both the costs of pursuing litigation as far as the interest group is willing to take it, and the risk that the interest group will be able to salvage any defeats it suffers in agencies, legislatures, or lower courts by taking the issue to the next stage.

Worse, if the costs rise equally, the impact on the opposition will generally be greater than the impact on the organized interest group. After all, organized interest groups are, by definition, groups that are especially able and willing to expend resources on seeking or opposing legal change. Their opponents are less organized (otherwise the interest groups would not be exerting disproportionate influence) and thus less able to organize the expenditure of petitioning resources. Organized interest groups will thus be better positioned to meet increased transaction costs than will their disorganized opponents. One might accordingly expect that an increase in transaction costs would often decrease the opposition's level of activity more than the interest group's, and that the interest group's chances of success will increase instead of decrease.

4. Discouraging All Legal Change Favors a Status Quo That Is Equally Affected by Interest Group Influence

Let us now assume that the above arguments have been rejected or deemed inapplicable, and that one accordingly believes that more aggressive judicial interpretation will increase transaction costs, discourage interest group activity, and retard the promulgation of legal rules favoring special interest groups. Even then, however, the transaction-costs argument faces a serious problem—namely, that increasing transaction costs discourages not only legal changes favoring organized interest groups but also legal changes benefiting the general public. Such an effect is desirable only if one has grounds for preferring the status quo to the mix of legal changes that is likely to result under our present system. Interest group theory, however, provides no persuasive grounds for believing the status quo is preferable to the mix of likely legal changes.

Under interest group theory, the laws embodied in the status quo are just as likely to reflect the past influence of organized interest groups as current legal changes are likely to reflect their present influence. The legislation and regulation in place will reflect which groups used to have political influence. The judge-made law in place will, as argued above, reflect either past political influence or a politically insulated lawmaking that interest group theory gives no reason to prefer over lawmaking that does reflect political influence. Interest group theory thus provides no grounds for believing that the mix of laws present in the status quo is more desirable than the mix of legal changes that the current system is likely to produce.

Of course, one might regard the laws embodied in the status quo as desirable on independent normative grounds. For example, the common law still forms much of our current law, and Richard Posner, who argues that the law should be efficient, regards the common law as generally efficient.[34] But not everyone believes the common law is efficient or otherwise desirable. More important, this is a fundamentally different kind of argument—that we should increase the transaction costs of legal change because we pretty much like the law the way it is. Such an argument may be persuasive to some, but it is not an argument supported by interest group theory. Nor is it an argument that the current *process of lawmaking* is worse than the past one. It thus seems to be an argument that should have its persuasiveness tested by presenting it to our current lawmakers, rather than an argument for making it harder for those lawmakers to make law.

A different sort of argument is that we should discourage legal changes because they generally interfere with a private market ordering that, under the Coase Theorem, is presumptively better than any mix of legal changes. The Coase Theorem provides that no matter how the legal rule assigns initial rights or liabilities, the efficient outcome will always result if private bargaining is unimpeded by transaction costs or other obstacles.[35] Although the Theorem is obviously persuasive only if one accepts economic efficiency as the best normative standard,[36] the ordering produced by Coasean bargaining does not appear to depend on any claims about the desirability of past legal decisions. To an adherent of efficiency, then, the Coase Theorem seems to provide a reason to think that our current system of interest-group-influenced lawmaking is likely to worsen the status quo—not because that status quo reflects better laws or a better process of lawmaking, but because it reflects the efficient private ordering created by the process of Coasean bargaining.

An initial problem with this argument is that Coasean bargaining often fails to occur. Even if transaction costs are zero, bargaining may break down because each party wants a larger share of the gains created by an efficiency-enhancing bargain. Moreover, the transaction costs of bargaining are frequently large enough to block the Coasean bargaining necessary to avoid inefficient outcomes, with the result that a wrong assignment of legal rights will stick, producing inefficiency.[37]

Even without such obstacles to bargaining, the Coase Theorem does not—despite appearances—establish that the resulting private ordering will be independent of the legal entitlements recognized. To begin with, the assignment of initial entitlements can affect a party's ability or willingness to pay (or to accept payment) in order to change outcomes. Parties that are allocated initial entitlements tend to demand more to sell those entitlements than those same parties would (or could) pay to buy the same entitlements were they allocated to someone else.[38] Accordingly, rights will not only tend to stay where they are initially allocated, but the initial allocation can actually determine *which* outcome is regarded as efficient under a wealth-maximization standard.[39] The Coase Theorem thus does not actually show that unimpeded bargaining will produce *the* efficient outcome regardless of how the legal right is assigned; it shows only that *an* efficient outcome will result whose identity may depend on the legal assignment made. Because one of these efficient outcomes may be more desirable than the other, the Coase Theorem cannot assure that the most desirable efficient result occurs.

Coasean bargaining thus often fails to achieve the most efficient or desirable result because of bargaining obstacles or assignments of initial legal rights. But the problem with relying on Coasean bargaining is not simply that it leaves a neutral mix of Coasean failures. A more pointed problem is that the same collective action problems that afflict the lawmaking process also afflict the past legal correction of Coasean failures, the initial distribution of those failures, and the conduct of Coasean bargaining. Large diffuse groups are thus disproportionately likely to be harmed both by Coasean failures and by Coasean bargaining itself.

To see this, first assume that the initial mix of Coasean failures is neutral. Even under this assumption, the mix of *uncorrected* Coasean failures would not be neutral under interest group theory, because small intensely-interested groups have an advantage in legally correcting Coasean failures. Small intense groups are more likely than large diffuse ones to secure legal changes (from the legislature or the courts) that alter the initial assignment of property rights to benefit themselves; they are also more likely to block legal changes that would harm them. As a result, large diffusely-interested groups are, at any given time, more likely to be afflicted with legally uncorrected Coasean failures.

Further, the initial distribution of Coasean failures will also be affected by collective action problems. Because greater free rider problems plague large diffuse groups, they will be less successful than small groups in overcoming the transaction costs necessary to complete Coasean bargains that avoid inefficient property assignments that harm them. Suppose, for example, that the state has assigned a right to pollute (free of a claim for nuisance) and that in two towns pollution would be inefficient, given the effect on the surrounding residents. In the first town, the surrounding residents are numerous, not very wealthy, and each owns a small house. Here, the individual harm from the pollution is relatively modest, though the collective harm is great. In the second town, the surrounding residents comprise a few very large vacation resorts. These resorts suffer high per capita harm from the pollution, but no more collective harm than the residents of the first town. Obviously collective action problems are more likely to plague the large diffuse group harmed by the first polluter than the small intense group harmed by the second polluter. The small intense group will face lower organization costs and will be less susceptible to free riding. It will thus be more able and willing to negotiate with the polluter, to pay the polluter enough to conclude a Coasean bargain, and to monitor and enforce any Coasean bargain that is struck. Accordingly, Coasean bargaining is more likely to protect the small intense group than the large diffuse group from inefficient pollution.

More generally, assume (as seems appropriate if one places one's faith not in the legal regime but in Coasean bargaining) that the legal regime has randomly distributed initial rights: some assignments are efficient and some inefficient, some harm small groups and some large groups. Where the property assignment is efficient, the Coase Theorem predicts that neither small nor large groups will be able to shift that assignment through bargaining. Where the property assignment is inefficient, the right will be transferred if the groups can overcome the transaction costs of bargaining. But where successful bargaining to avoid an inefficient outcome will confer benefits on the group as a whole, large groups' greater susceptibility to free riding means that they will have a harder time overcoming these transaction costs than small groups will. Thus, even if initial rights are randomly distributed, and even if large groups did not have a disadvantage in securing legal corrections, they would still be more likely to be harmed by inefficient assignments of rights that are uncorrected by Coasean bargaining. Coasean failures afflicting large diffuse groups are not only more likely to go legally uncorrected, but more likely to exist in the first place.

Finally, sometimes Coasean bargaining can exploit the collective action problems of large groups and actually increase inefficiency. This is true when a monopolist engages in anticompetitive conduct that excludes its rivals. For such conduct to succeed, the monopolist must get buyers to agree to do business with it, even though its anticompetitive conduct will harm buyers. The main reason buyers agree is that they have collective action problems, which the monopolist can exploit because it is a unitary actor.[40] Typically the monopolist can secure each buyer's agreement for some nominal discount from the monopoly price that is being inflated by its conduct. Although each buyer may realize that all of them would be better off if none of them agreed to do business with the anticompetitive monopolist, each also realizes that individually it would be better off if the others refused and it did not: it would gain a discount that is unavailable to other buyers on the downstream market. Further, each buyer also knows that its individual refusal to agree would make little difference to the ultimate market structure if the other buyers did not refuse. In other words, each of a numerous set of buyers has an incentive to free ride, because it benefits from other buyers' antimonopoly efforts whether or not it contributes to those efforts, and because any contribution it offers would make little difference to the chances of blocking the monopoly. In this way, an initial situation that was more efficient is not (as one might expect under the Coase Theorem) converted by bargaining into an outcome that is efficient, but rather into an outcome that lowers efficiency.

More generally, whenever avoiding an inefficient injury requires a collective refusal to bargain by the potentially injured members of a group, a well-organized bargainer can exploit the members' incentives to free ride by offering a bribe that is worth less than the per capita injury that will result when all of them agree to the bargain. The bargains are Coasean in the sense that each bargain not only benefits the well-organized bargainer but also benefits each member of the group, acting individually, because each rationally realizes that its individual agreement will have little impact on whether the more general market injury ultimately results. But the overall result is decreased efficiency. Small intense groups are not only less susceptible than large diffuse groups to being exploited by such bargaining, but can sometimes use such bargaining to directly exploit larger, more diffusely interested groups.

In summary, the same sort of collective action problems that plague large diffuse groups in political effort also plague them in correcting and conducting Coasean bargaining. There thus seems to be no persuasive ground for believing that the process of Coasean bargaining will produce better results than the process of lawmaking. This suggests that the private ordering is more likely to reflect the undesirable exercise of rights by small intense groups than the undesirable exercise of rights by large diffuse groups, and that there are thus more potential legal changes that will benefit the general public than there are potential legal changes that will profit organized interest groups. Accordingly, interest group theory, even when coupled with the Coase Theorem, does not support the conclusion that it would be desirable to decrease the likelihood of legal change by increasing the transaction costs of such change.

Collective Choice Theory Doesn't Justify Aggressive Judicial Interpretation Either

A critique of politics that is distinct from interest group theory concerns logical problems in forming collective social choices. This collective choice theory demonstrates that no method of aggregating individual preferences into a social choice function can guarantee "a consistent social ranking of policy alternatives."[41] The most common illustration of the problem is that majority rule can be intransitive: policy A could command a majority against policy B, which commands a majority against policy C, which commands a majority against policy A.[42] Such intransitive situations will produce a perpetual cycle unless the voting process is structured to lead to a final vote, the winner of which cannot be challenged by any losers of prior votes. When the voting process has this finality, the policy alternative chosen will turn on how the voting agenda is ordered. If the order in which alternatives arise is random, the final choice may seem arbitrary. If instead some person or entity, such as a legislative committee, consciously orders the agenda, that agenda setter will have significant influence on the final outcome. More generally, Arrow's Impossibility Theorem proves that it is impossible to construct any process of collective decisionmaking that will always (1) avoid intransitivity, (2) be nondictatorial, (3) adopt Pareto preferences, (4) impose no restriction on how individuals order their preferences, *and* (5) decide between two policy alternatives without regard to independent alternatives.[43]

Although these cycling and inconsistency problems cannot theoretically be eliminated, they are probably not that empirically significant, for reasons already explored in Chapter 6. However, even to the extent that they are empirically significant, collective choice theory would not justify more aggressive judicial interpretation of statutes. Because the three main reasons for this answer parallel the reasons explicated above regarding interest group theory, I hope you will forgive me if I go through them in somewhat abbreviated fashion.

The Dependence on Controversial Normative Premises

To begin with, it is not at all obvious that the problems identified by collective choice theory establish that the political process is normatively defective. Two of Arrow's conditions, transitivity and the irrelevance of independent alternatives, have proven to have a particularly controversial normative content.

The requirement that social choices between alternatives be unaffected by independent alternatives (the independence condition) in effect excludes information that is relevant to the intensity of voters' views, from which one might derive voters' cardinal, interpersonally comparable utilities.[44] That Arrow chose a condition having this implication is not surprising: he believed that interpersonal utility comparisons were meaningless, and aimed to develop a social welfare function that did not rely on them. But the normative superiority of purely ordinal preference rankings is hardly clear. Indeed, Arrow himself has ironically provided perhaps the most convincing argument against a purely ordinal aggregation: its instability.

Nor is it obvious that intransitivity should be condemned normatively. To be sure, intransitivity implies either cycling, path dependence, or strong influence by the agenda setter. But the normative deficiency of each of those possibilities is contestable.

Some scholars argue that cycling enhances, rather than undermines, the democratic process, because cycling prevents a fixed majority from permanently subordinating the policy views of a fixed minority.[45] The minority that loses one vote always has the possibility of winning the next vote by reframing the issue. Cycling thus empowers the minority in a way that may be integral to distinguishing democracy from a dictatorship by the majority. Consider, for example, Robert Post's argument that democracy does not mean majority rule but self-determination, and that self-determination requires giving the minority some opportunity to engage in a public discourse that may influence governmental decisionmaking.[46] Collective choice theory suggests that this public discourse can have real bite even if it does not change anyone's mind, because it may allow the minority to reframe issues along lines that give it a chance of forming a winning coalition.

To the extent that cycling is terminated (at least temporarily) by a final vote, intransitivity implies path dependence. This need not be devastating. It might be nice, in some abstract sense, if we could achieve path independence without sacrificing other decisionmaking values. But where no majority favors one alternative over all the others, and an arbitrarily chosen path is the only way to resolve the social choice, path independence is an unrealistic ideal against which to measure the desirability of the democratic process. Indeed, in other decisionmaking processes, path independence is not commonly regarded as essential. Sports leagues and tournaments routinely crown champions who might have lost to teams or players that lost earlier playoff rounds. As long as the method for determining the sequence of play is fair—and here fair means unbiased and sometimes random—this path dependence does not seem to detract from the acceptability of the process. Rather, such processes, and the champions they produce, appear to be accepted on the quite sensible ground that the process is the best we can do.

A more significant problem may arise if agenda setters can utilize their agenda-setting power to influence the final outcome. Such an agenda setter, typically a legislative committee, will possess "the lion's share of influence over what alternative is chosen from among those that can beat the status quo."[47] But this is problematic only if the mechanism for choosing the agenda setter is somehow flawed. The collective choice theory critique of the democratic process here thus piggybacks somewhat on the argument that interest groups disproportionately influence committee members; the critique is therefore susceptible to the lines of argument developed above. Further, if the method of selecting the agenda setter were the root problem, the logical avenue of reform would appear to be changing that method, not making judicial interpretation more aggressive.

More fundamentally, even if the decision about which of the alternatives the majority prefers to the status quo is arbitrary or is influenced by the agenda setter, at least majority rule helps assure that a majority does in fact prefer the alternative to the present state of affairs.[48] That much certainly appears desirable, as is evidenced by the painful consequences that follow when tyrannies can ignore majority preferences. Cycling among alternatives may occur in a democracy, but at least the cycle will stay within relatively acceptable bounds.

The Comparative Question

Even if one concedes that collective choice theory demonstrates that majority rule is defective in some meaningful normative sense, this does not prove that more intrusive judicial review would be an improvement. As multimember bodies, the Supreme Court and other appellate courts are also subject to the aggregation problems of cycling or path dependence.[49] Like legislatures, courts have adopted a set of institutional responses to deal with those issues.[50] But the judicial problems may even be worse than those faced by legislatures, because under prevailing ethical norms judges cannot engage in the sort of logrolling that legislators commonly employ. Because logrolling can sometimes avoid cycling and path dependence (by violating the independence condition), a decisionmaking body that does not engage in logrolling is, all other things being equal, more likely to promulgate inconsistent or path-dependent decisions than one that does.

One might try to avoid these aggregation problems by having a one-member court. But that would violate one of Arrow's conditions for rational social choice that is far more fundamental than the condition of transitivity: the "nondictatorship" condition.[51] Majority rule may aggregate individual preferences inconsistently, but dictatorial decisionmaking need take no cognizance of it at all. Nor does there seem much attraction to the oligarchic rule of multi-member courts, even assuming they could avoid aggregation problems.

More generally, judicial decisionmaking is, as a matter of collective choice theory, worse than intransitive majority rule in two important respects. First, in cases where a policy alternative does exist that commands a majority against all others, judges may refuse to choose it. Second, although committees may manipulate the choice among those policy alternatives that can defeat the status quo, judges can choose alternatives that could not beat the status quo.

To be sure, in the long run the Supreme Court can successfully impose an alternative only if it chooses one that is immune from reversal. In statutory interpretation cases, this requires that at least one of the three principal political actors—the House, the Senate, or (where his veto would be sustained) the president—prefers the judicially-chosen alternative to any alternative that is considered preferable by both of the other two principal political actors. But even this gives the Court substantial power to choose alternatives that could not defeat the status quo, especially when coupled with the scarcity of legislative time and the power of legislative inertia. If the Court is satisfied to impose its policy preference over the short run, then even these limited restrictions would not restrain its (short run) power to choose alternatives that could not beat the status quo.

Protecting Markets or the Status Quo

Perhaps those who advocate expanded judicial lawmaking power based on collective choice theory are operating on the premise that such expanded judicial power will be limited to narrowing deviations from the status quo and, in particular, from the free market. But it is plain that judicial interpretation can and often does cause deviations from the status quo and the free market. This is especially true when courts interpret regulatory statutes, which often involves filling in or extending the meaning of market regulation.

Even if judicial review were limited to policing deviations from a free market, collective choice theory would not demonstrate the desirability of more intrusive judicial review. The reason is that the free market is itself a method of aggregating preferences to make collective social choices, most notably choices about how to allocate labor and resources. Thus, as Kenneth Arrow made clear in his seminal work, the free market is just as susceptible to the problems identified by his theorem as is majority rule or any other method of making collective social choices.[52] Arrow's Theorem describes the logical problems in forming any collective decision out of a diverse set of individual views. The problem does not lie in the particular method used for making social choices, for none can satisfy his conditions.

CHAPTER 17

Protecting Reliance or Avoiding Change or Effect

Some scholars say courts shouldn't be trying to maximize political satisfaction. Instead, they should be protecting reliance interests, or minimizing legal change or regulatory effects. These arguments form the basis for alternative default rules that protect reliance, minimize change, or reduce effects.

While each of these alternative default rules has its own problems, one significant problem is common to all of them: they consider only the direct effects of legal interpretations. Although switching to these alternative default rules would, by definition, reduce the legal change or regulatory effect directly created by interpretations, it is not at all clear that these default rules would reduce *overall* legal change or regulatory effect. The reason is that using these default rules, rather than those that maximize political satisfaction, will by definition increase political dissatisfaction. That is more likely to trigger new legislation, which may come less often than new judicial opinions, but when it comes will likely create more violent change and more sweeping regulatory effects. Ironically, then, these alternative default rules might on balance discourage reliance, and increase legal change and regulatory effect.

In short, these alternative default rules depend on an empirical premise that is quite uncertain. Thus, the case for them is empirically ambiguous, even if one (mistakenly) thought that protecting reliance, or avoiding legal change or regulatory effect, were more important than satisfying political preferences. In the analysis that follows, however, I assume, for the sake of argument, that these alternative default rules would on balance actually encourage reliance, or reduce legal change and regulatory effect. Even granting that unclear empirical assumption, adopting these alternative default rules should not be permitted to trump those that maximize political satisfaction. However, reliance concerns may sometimes inform estimates of what is likely to maximize political satisfaction.

The Alternative of a Default Rule That Protects Reliance

Generally my recommended statutory default rules will not defeat reliance interests, even if one limits consideration to the direct effects of statutory interpretations. After all, such statutory default rules do not call for any change in interpretation over time if the statutory meaning is clear. Further, where recent legislative action has consciously allowed an existing interpretation to stand, then (as Chapter 4 shows) a current preferences default rule *increases* the ability of parties to rely on existing interpretations, by eliminating the risk that a later court will conclude that the first interpretation misread enactor preferences. In addition, for reasons detailed in Chapter 12, my default rules affirmatively support a strong presumption of statutory *stare decisis*, absent affirmative evidence of a change in legislative conditions or factual circumstances.

Still, my default rule analysis does support the judicial practice of changing statutory interpretations if there is evidence of changed enactable preferences, embodied in reliable official action like a changed agency interpretation or recent legislative action. Some have argued instead that all statutory ambiguities should be resolved to protect reliance interests.[1] They thus effectively argue for the alternative default rule of protecting reliance, rather than maximizing political satisfaction.

In addressing these sorts of reliance arguments, one must be careful to avoid the tendency toward circularity. Whether people will rely on something depends on whether the law tells them they can rely on it. Likewise, reliance on something cannot be considered reasonable if the law has made it plain that people should not rely on it or that it is subject to change. In the end, then, the question is what degree of reliance we *want* people to place in the thing under consideration. Generally, there are powerful reasons to conclude that the law should not encourage people to believe that their reliance will bar application of default rules that maximize political satisfaction.

Reliance on What?

One cannot really rely on a statutory ambiguity. The reliance argument thus would seem to pose no limit on using preference-estimating or supplemental default rules to fill in the *initial* statutory interpretation. But one might imagine the following sort of reliance objection to using a preference-eliciting default rule to provide that initial statutory interpretation. That objection would claim that, where meaning is ambiguous, parties are entitled to rely on their assessment of the interpretation that most likely reflects legislative preferences. However, the conditions for using a preference-eliciting default rule apply only when legislative preferences are uncertain. Further, this reliance claim begs the question whether statutory interpretation doctrine does and should entitle parties to the interpretation that most likely reflects legislative preferences in such a case, even when those preferences are uncertain and that interpretation ultimately results in less overall legislative preference satisfaction. If I am right that current statutory canons already adopt a preference-eliciting approach, parties cannot claim that current doctrine entitles them to assume the contrary. If I were wrong in this descriptive claim, then the normative claim would remain that such preference-eliciting default rules should be adopted prospectively, so that they would affect what future parties are entitled to assume. While parties may have made interpretation-specific investments relying on another interpretation, such reliance investments should only affect future doctrine when they are the sorts of investments we want parties to make.

Nor would it be reasonable to argue that reliance on an initial statutory interpretation bars a *higher* court from changing that interpretation. This is not because such reliance does not occur, for it surely does. But a default rule that protected that sort of reliance would change the interpretation that is legally binding from whichever one is authoritative, under the current system, to whichever interpretation comes first. Indeed, the very first interpretation that parties are likely to receive will be from their own attorneys. Unless each attorney's interpretations are to become binding on the legal system, clients must rely on them at their own risk. The same goes for lower court interpretations. If the first court interpretation became binding because parties relied on it, then ordinary notions of appellate review would be turned upside down by making the lower court rulings binding on the upper courts. Further, statutory interpretation would turn on whatever happenstance (or party strategy) produced the first decision. This would exacerbate incentives for manipulation, and bias the process toward the groups that are organized and wealthy enough to game the process by forum shopping and settling cases that begin in a bad forum. Accordingly, parties who rely on lower court interpretations must do so recognizing that they are taking the risk that they will be overturned by higher courts.

Reliance on Prior Decisions of the Same Court

A more reasonable claim might be that reliance interests should prevent a court from deviating from its own prior statutory interpretations. Such a limited pro-reliance default rule would provide no guidance in cases that do not involve such reliance on a court's own statutory precedent, and thus cannot be a full-fledged alternative to my default rules. However, such a proreliance default rule would at least support a rule of *stare decisis* that is stronger than the one described in Chapter 12. This would be unadvisable for several reasons.

To begin with, as this book shows, statutory interpretations are *in fact* changing with subsequent legislative or agency action. It would thus respect reliance interests far more to make that reality explicit, rather than to mislead people into relying on old precedent that in fact is subject to change.

One might nonetheless think that, in order to protect reliance interests, we should change existing law to overturn its prevailing regime of current preferences default rules. However, for the current preferences default rule to warrant changing an interpretation, there would have to be some subsequent legislative or agency action. Any such modern legislative or agency action is likely to alter the reasonableness of relying on the judicial precedent that precedes it. It could not, for example, be said to be reasonable to rely on statutory precedent that Congress had overridden by statute. Likewise, subsequent legislative or agency action that rebuts the *stare decisis* presumption (given our current preferences default rule) indicates that it is unreasonable to continue relying on an older judicial interpretation.

Another way to put the point is this: the question is *not whether* to protect reliance, but *on what* we prefer to have parties rely. Do we want them to rely exclusively on old judicial interpretations? Or is it better for them to rely on current agency interpretations and reasonable inferences drawn from modern legislation? A generic desire to promote reliance does not answer the question. So we might as well encourage parties to rely on the sources that will lead their behavior to comport best with current enactable preferences, especially given that, for reasons explained in Chapter 3, such a default rule will also maximize the political satisfaction of the enacting legislature.

One might object that, regardless of what statutory interpretation doctrine says, people will rely on old judicial precedent, not on current agency interpretations, nor on inferences drawn from recent legislative action that is not directly on point. But this empirical claim seems implausible. Consider the two possible sets of persons. (1) The advised set will have received legal advice before acting. If statutory interpretation doctrine says that they should rely on modern legislative or agency action, rather than on conflicting older precedent, then their lawyers will advise them about this. Thus, they will rely on the modern political action rather than on the older precedent. (2) The unadvised set of persons will not have sought legal advice before engaging in conduct. They are unlikely to know anything about the old judicial precedent, which will not be in the news and usually will be known only to lawyers. They are far more likely to know about modern legislative and agency action, which may well have produced news and public political statements about which they have some awareness.[2] Thus, they are also more likely to rely on modern agency and legislative action than on old judicial precedent.

Indeed, the fact that unadvised persons are more likely to rely on modern agency and legislative action than on old judicial precedent actually means that reliance arguments weigh affirmatively *in favor of* a current preferences default rule. That is, suppose we (implausibly) cared *solely* about reliance. The effects on advised persons would be neutral, because we could obtain adequate reliance with either doctrine. The reliance interests of the unadvised would, on the other hand, be protected more by a current preferences default rule than by sticking to old precedent that they never considered.

Another sort of objection is that a current preferences default rule leads to more frequent legal change, and that this discourages reliance that might take the form of desirable investments. This objection rests on an empirical premise that is debatable for reasons noted at the top of this chapter. But let's suppose that empirical premise is true. Even then, the argument falters because it has been shown that, if a legal change is otherwise desirable, the degree of reliance that parties place on the law will normally be more desirable if the relying parties bear the full risk that such a legal change might occur. Risk aversion could be a problem, but generally parties should be able to buy insurance against the risk of legal changes that do not compensate their reliance.[3]

Parties clearly understand, for example, that they bear the risk that any statutory interpretation might change if the legislature enacts an amendment to reflect new enactable preferences. If political satisfaction can also be enhanced by having courts change their interpretations when there are reliable official indications that enactable preferences have changed, then it would be more efficient to have parties consider the risk of such a change when they decide how much reliance to put on the initial interpretation. In short, if it actually does reduce the rate of legal change, a proreliance default rule would encourage *excessive* reliance on interpretations. To be sure, any judicial precedent will induce some reliance. But parties will invest in the socially optimal amount of reliance if they bear the risk that changing the initial interpretation turns out to be socially desirable. And any reliance that took account of such a risk cannot be said to be disappointed by the fact that the risk in fact materialized.

Deciding to instead adopt a default rule that protected this excessive reliance would also inflict the serious cost of freezing statutory interpretation, not only when current enactable preferences change but also when circumstances change in a way that means static preferences imply a new interpretation. This would reduce the satisfaction of political preferences for everyone, including the enacting and current polity. And it would do so to reward an unreasonable level of reliance that could have been avoided by a simple method: having interpretations instead signal that party reliance must take into account the risk that the interpreting court or agency may change that interpretation in the future.

This point is often misunderstood because people analogize the statutory situation to private law, where one party often must make a contractually-binding commitment in order to induce desirable reliance by the other.[4] But in contract law the problem is that, without the binding commitment, the first party has incentives to make changes that benefit itself even if they are socially undesirable. Here, by hypothesis, any change is socially desirable because it reflects enactable preferences. A commitment is thus unnecessary to avoid socially undesirable changes that ignore some of the relevant interests. Instead, the question is whether reliance should restrain our ability to adopt socially desirable changes. And the answer is that the reliance we get will be optimal if we do not restrain that ability.

Two important limitations should be emphasized. First, sometimes reliance can alter whether changing the interpretation does advance current enactable preferences. For example, suppose current enactable preferences would make it desirable to require new firms to install a new type of smoke scrubber, given how those preferences assess the relevant costs and benefits. These same preferences (and thus same assessments of costs and benefits) may make it undesirable to require an old firm that has the old smoke scrubber to switch to the new scrubber, because the costs would be higher and the incremental benefits lower. Under these assumptions, reliance on an old interpretation that required the old scrubber would mean that changing the interpretation (to require old firms to install the new scrubber) would not advance current enactable preferences. This helps explain why legislatures that enact new statutes themselves often conclude that their preferences can best be advanced by grandfathering those who relied on the prior legal rule.[5] Similarly, changing statutory precedent is usually more likely to advance current enactable preferences when it can be done prospectively.

Second, if courts were too quick to overturn statutory precedent, then their precedent would fail to have any behavioral effect. If, to take the extreme case, a court announced that it planned to change its past statutory interpretations daily, then parties would cease to pay any attention to those interpretations. And it cannot further any conception of political preferences to have interpretations that lack any behavioral consequences. Thus, an approach that changed interpretations daily would not maximize political satisfaction, even if every interpretation precisely reflected enactable preferences, because none of those interpretations would have any effect.

The point is not that reliance and stability offer independent normative grounds for deviating from the default rules that best maximize political satisfaction. The point is rather that the legislative polity itself would want some degree of stability and reliance, because it makes the interpretations that reflect its estimated preferences more effective. That is, the goal of maximizing political satisfaction itself requires statutory interpretations that are sufficiently stable to induce behavioral reliance. Thus, those factors should be considered but subordinated to the larger goal of maximizing the satisfaction of enactable preferences. For an interpretation to have any bite, and thus any ability to maximize political satisfaction, the interpreter must signal that, while it reserves the right to change its interpretations, it will exercise this power either rarely or only prospectively.

This analysis provides another reason why the enacting and current legislatures would prefer a current preferences default rule that included the limitation requiring reliable official indications of changed enactable preferences. This limitation helps assure sufficient stability in interpretations to make them meaningful. The analysis here further predicts that interpreters who render prospective interpretations will change those interpretations more freely than those who cannot, and that lower court interpreters will act more bound by their statutory precedent than will higher courts, who visit interpretive issues less often.

The above two limitations fit fairly well the contours of modern doctrine. The *Chevron* doctrine has established that, where statutory meaning is unclear, agencies must have the flexibility to change regulatory policy by altering statutory interpretations over time. Indeed, as Chapter 12 noted, the recent *Brand X* case established that an agency could even change those past interpretations that were statutory precedent rendered by a court. Any private party who reads the case law thus knows not to put too much reliance on judicial precedent about any topic administered by an agency, because that interpretation is subject to change. Because agencies are much more likely to render prospective interpretations than courts, which mainly adjudicate disputes about the legality of past conduct, it makes sense that the Supreme Court has signaled that agencies are especially free to alter interpretations over time. Such prospective agency interpretations are less likely to involve reliance that alters the desirability of the change, and will interfere less with behavioral reliance, because parties know that the changes will be announced well in advance. And if past reliance alters the desirability of applying a new rule to those who already relied, then an agency that is accountable to current enactable preferences has full incentives to include a grandfather clause in any new regulation.

As for judicial interpretations, the U.S. Supreme Court has encouraged reliance by often citing reliance as a reason for giving statutory precedent special *stare decisis* effect.[6] But in the Court's own practice, as Chapter 12 noted, this statutory *stare decisis* rule tends to be trumped when it conflicts with reliable evidence that current enactable preferences have changed. This has opened the Court up to charges of hypocrisy and inconsistency, because it has not lived up to the principles it itself has espoused. However, because the Supreme Court visits any particular interpretive issue infrequently, rarely more than once a decade, it makes sense for it to exercise more freedom to change statutory precedent than it is willing to give the lower courts. Thus, it can be consistent, rather than hypocritical, for the Court to announce a strong norm of following statutory precedent to guide lower courts, even though the high court's own practice does not conform with that norm. But because the Court tends to act retroactively, it also makes sense that it gives itself less freedom to change interpretations—by adopting a fairly strong presumption against change—than it is willing to give agencies.

Reliance on Prior Legislative Acts

Parties may rely not only on past interpretations, but on past statutes themselves where their language is clear. Such reliance does not bar legislatures from changing old statutes or from enacting a new statute with retroactive effect. Legislatures, however, generally do take such reliance into account by making their statutes purely prospective. But how should courts interpret a statute that fails to make clear whether it also applies retroactively?

In such cases, the default rule is that ambiguous statutes should be interpreted to be prospective.[7] The U.S. Supreme Court has in part justified this canon against retroactivity on the grounds that "[b]ecause it accords with widely held intuitions about how statutes ordinarily operate, a presumption against retroactivity will generally coincide with legislative and public expectations." Consistent with this, every state legislature to enact an interpretive statute on the subject has adopted a presumption against retroactive interpretations, unless a contrary legislative meaning or intent is clear.

In most applications, then, this canon against retroactive interpretations probably reflects a preference-estimating default rule. This understanding usually makes sense for most applications of the canon, given reasons already noted above. Statutes cannot retroactively change past behavior, and normally it is behavioral change that is sought. Further, past reliance can alter the desirability of a change and thus make it less likely that applying that change retroactively will advance enactable preferences. It thus makes sense to conclude non-retroactivity will generally advance political satisfaction, unless there is some specific contrary indication of enactable preferences.

However, the U.S. Supreme Court has also been willing to brush aside specific indications that Congress did favor retroactive application, which suggests that this is more than just a preference-estimating default rule. One might try to ground this approach in a constitutional norm disfavoring retroactive statutes. But the strength of such a constitutional rationale appears limited, because the Court recognized that "[r]etroactivity provisions often serve entirely benign and legitimate purposes," and that "the constitutional impediments to retroactive civil legislation are now modest."[8]

Another rationale cited by the Court suggests that it views its aggressive application of the canon as a preference-eliciting default rule. It has stressed that the canon "helps ensure that Congress itself has determined that the benefits of retroactivity outweigh the potential for disruption or unfairness." The Court elaborated:

> Requiring clear intent assures that Congress itself has affirmatively considered the potential unfairness of retroactive application and determined that it is an acceptable price to pay for the countervailing benefits. Such a requirement allocates to Congress responsibility for fundamental policy judgments concerning the proper temporal reach of statutes, and has the additional virtue of giving legislators a predictable background rule against which to legislate.[9]

The Court's emphasis on providing a "predictable background rule against which to legislate" suggests that this default rule is aimed at eliciting legislative preferences ex ante, in the original statutory drafting, rather than ex post, through a statutory override. This makes sense because usually the odds are low that the legislature would bother to override a judicial ruling that a statute applies only prospectively. The stakes are generally too small for the legislature to bother, given that the ruling does not affect the statute's application to current conduct. Further, by the time the retroactivity issue has been definitively resolved by the relevant high court, the old conduct will be in the relatively distant past, and probably hard to reach with a new statute without running into constitutional difficulties.

As a default rule to elicit preferences ex ante in the original statute, however, a strong presumption against retroactivity seems entirely sensible. To begin with, even if there are some indications that the legislature preferred retroactivity, a preference-estimating default rule will normally fail to provide a clear answer. This is because there is not just one form of retroactivity, but a myriad of possibilities. A statute might retroactively apply to preenactment conduct, or even further to litigation already initiated. Or it might not apply to preenactment conduct at all, but only to future conduct flowing from past transactions or vested rights. Or the statute might retroactively apply to preenactment conduct only if it does not upset justifiable reliance. Or it might apply to preenactment conduct as regards to procedural rules, but not as to substantive rules, or as to prospective injunctive relief, but not as to retroactive relief like damages. And there is always the tricky question of what to do with conduct that begins before enactment, but is completed (or inflicts harm) after enactment.

Thus, even if we think the legislature probably preferred some sort of retroactivity, preference-estimating analysis will rarely provide a confident answer about just what form that retroactivity should take. A preference-eliciting default rule can better ascertain precisely what sort of retroactivity a legislature desires, if it desires retroactivity at all. This is not the typical sort of statutory ambiguity that arises because of changed or uncontemplated circumstances. Political actors can anticipate that the question of retroactive application will arise in every statute. The issue is not some surprising future issue that legislators could not have anticipated. Rather, it concerns how to deal with concrete past cases that they (or other political participants) know about, cases that indeed probably prompted the legislation.

To be sure, instead of eliciting legislative preferences with a default rule of complete nonretroactivity, one could try to do so with a default rule of complete retroactivity. But that sort of default rule is undesirable, for three reasons. First, even in cases where we have reason to think legislatures would prefer some retroactivity, they will rarely prefer complete retroactivity to complete nonretroactivity, given the considerations noted above. Second, switching to complete retroactivity in such cases would require making difficult distinctions between the preference-estimating and eliciting cases, distinctions that could be avoided by simply sticking to a rule of complete nonretroactivity. Third, a default rule of complete nonretroactivity better serves the preference-eliciting function than its opposite, because the proponents of an enacted bill will normally have more control over what gets on the legislative agenda for a vote. The opponents, who are not the ones introducing the statutory text for a vote, may not be able to get the legislature to vote on an amendment making the statute nonretroactive. In contrast, the proponents will usually have sufficient control over the legislative drafting process to introduce statutory text on retroactivity, at least if they think they can (and want to) get it enacted. The normal reason statutory supporters would not introduce a retroactivity provision is because they find it undesirable or lack the votes to enact it.

In fact, the major Supreme Court case articulating the canon against retroactive application recited evidence that explicit retroactivity provisions were dropped during the drafting process.[10] This legislative history indicated that the retroactivity was fully anticipated, but that the attempts at retroactivity were not enactable. A preference-eliciting default rule against retroactivity thus helps make sure that the statutory result more accurately reflects enactable political preferences.

In short, the default rule against retroactive interpretations of statutes is typically a preference-estimating default rule, and when it isn't, it serves a preference-eliciting function. It is thus a default rule that maximizes political satisfaction, rather than a reliance-based exception that trumps political satisfaction.

The Alternative of Anti-Effect or Anti-Change Default Rules

Judge Easterbrook and others have advocated the alternative default rule that, where statutory meaning is unclear, it should have no effect.[11] Where such statutory uncertainty exists, one argument goes, we do not have a sufficiently considered legislative judgment to qualify as a binding statute. We should instead force the legislature to explicitly address the question in order to test the proposition of what could pass the legislature. This "no-effect" default rule also, other arguments add, helpfully maximizes private freedom from government legislation, and (for congressional statutes) furthers federalism by maximizing the extent to which matters are left to states.

My colleague David Shapiro advocates a related default rule, that "close questions of construction should be resolved in favor of continuity and against change."[12] This will generally mean giving a statute its minimal effect, but need not always mean that, because sometimes continuity may require giving the statute greater effect. To distinguish it from a "no-effect" default rule, I will call Shapiro's approach the "anti-change" default rule. It is similar to the protect-reliance default rule discussed above, but goes beyond it to interpret statutes against change even when there is no reliance.

Any position advocated by scholars as learned as Frank Easterbrook and David Shapiro commands our utmost attention. But careful attention, I think, reveals that their positions are ultimately unpersuasive. Several reasons follow.

Hidden Uncertainties and Baseline Problems

Because much of the attraction of these default rules rests in their apparent ease of application, it is worth noting that the seeming clarity of the no-effect and anti-change default rules dissolves on close examination. Often the option of giving no effect or creating no change will not be available, or will lie outside the range of plausible meanings produced by our interpretive methods. Most interpretive choices are about *which* effect or change to attribute to unclear statutory language, not about whether the statute will cause any effect or change at all. Applying these default rules thus requires ascertaining what gives a statute "less effect" or causes "less change," among two different sorts of effects or changes the statute might have. The problem is that there is no way to rank different sorts of effects or changes without some normative framework, which these default rules do not provide.

For example, it is not clear what the no-effect default rule would have meant in the Guantanamo detainees case. Would it have meant giving a broad meaning to the jurisdiction-stripping provisions, because that would minimize the effect of jurisdictional statutes on the president, or giving it a narrow meaning, because that would minimize the effect of the statutes on the Supreme Court? Nor are the implications of an anti-change rule clear. Would it have meant narrowly interpreting the statutes granting detainees adjudication rights, because that would minimize any change caused by the enactment of those statutes or to the president's practice since 2001, or broadly interpreting those statutes, because that would cause the least change from the practice between their enactment and 2001?

The general problem is that these default rules provide no clear baseline from which to measure an effect or change. If the baseline is (in the no-effect default rule) the common law free from regulation, then one needs to ask which precise version of the common law (from what era, and which state or nation), and what to do with many seemingly regulatory features of the common law. Do aggressive modern impositions of tort liabilities or affirmative duties become part of the common law baseline, even though they themselves may be regulatory or impinge on state autonomy? Likewise, what does one do with a deregulatory statute: should it be construed narrowly (to give as little effect as possible) or broadly (to give as much effect as possible to nonstatutory law)?

If the baseline is (in the anti-change default) the prior status quo, then one needs to know at what precise time to measure the status quo. Does an erroneous practice or statutory interpretation, if it lasts for years, become the new status quo, or should it be overruled to bring us back to the status quo before the statute was enacted? If the former, how many years are enough and does that depend on the issue? For example, in the sentencing guidelines case, the question was whether, given the constitutional ruling, Congress would have preferred (1) complete invalidation, (2) making the sentencing guidelines advisory, or (3) having juries find facts for sentencing. Would the anti-change default rule require complete invalidation, because the right baseline was the time before the sentencing guidelines were enacted? Or, because the sentencing guidelines had been operational for over 20 years, did the baseline become the practice over those 20 years? And if so, how could one determine which would create the greater change from that baseline: making the guidelines advisory or having juries find sentencing facts?

In short, to be operational, the anti-effect and anti-change default rules must specify some baseline from which to measure effects or change, and thus to define the halcyon state of affairs from which statutory deviation should be disfavored. But neither provides an adequate theory for specifying that baseline. The nature of the baseline that is required, moreover, just reveals what these default rules really do: impose a substantive preference for whatever particular state of affairs they define as the baseline.

Failing to Address Changed or Unforeseen Circumstances

Neither the no-effect nor the anti-change default rule deals well with the problem of changed or unforeseen circumstances. Changed and unforeseen circumstances are ubiquitous, and create ambiguities in statutory meaning that require judgment about how best to give effect to legislative preferences, given the change. A commitment to always narrowly interpret statutes in the face of changed or unforeseen circumstances would be a commitment to consistently thwart the enacting legislature's purposes and preferences. Yet this is what the no-effect default rule would do.

Changed circumstances also create definitional problems for the anti-change default rule. What best promotes continuity when changed circumstances indicate that a statutory purpose would be thwarted unless the meaning of the statute changes with it? One approach would be to continue the statutory purpose, but that requires a change in the scope of statutory interpretation and covered conduct. Another approach would be to continue the statutory interpretation and covered conduct, but that requires a change in the effectuation of the statutory purpose. A canon that favors continuity over change cannot tell us which approach to favor, for it favors a status quo that is irretrievably lost as soon as circumstances change.

A Policy Bias That Thwarts Likely Political Preferences

The more fundamental problem is that these alternative default rules, by definition, decline to embrace the default rule that maximizes political satisfaction. Thus, judges must be imposing interpretations that increase deviations from likely political preferences, which can only be justified on some implicit policy view unrelated to those political preferences. Absent some constitutional argument, which I address below, judges have no justification for imposing policy views that contradict political preferences.

Neither the no-effect nor anti-change default rule is politically neutral. To the contrary, each enforces a political preference for a particular set of laws. To give a statutory provision no effect is not to render a decision with no effect; it is to give effect instead to whatever other statute or common law would otherwise govern the issue. Likewise, interpreting against change just gives effect to whatever statute or common law happened to predate the legislation in question. As discussed in the previous chapter, there is no general reason for believing that the effect of these other laws will be preferable to the court's best estimate of the political preferences for the statute at hand.[13]

Nor is there any warrant for judges to further their own policy views by biasing statutory interpretation against regulation or change. Whether to favor regulation over common law or change over the status quo are fundamental questions of policy best left to the political process. Indeed, under all but the most simplistic policy views, it would seem that there would be no general preference: everyone is likely to think, on at least some occasions, that change from the status quo or from the common law is precisely what is called for to address some new or previously unsolved problem. We often do and should oppose regulation or change, but there is no reason to impose that judgment when, by definition, it conflicts with our reading of political preferences, given the reasons for regulation or change.

For parallel reasons, the default rule of giving no effect or minimizing change is not the approach taken in contract or corporate law. If the matter at issue is within the contractual or corporate relationship, courts adopt (and scholars argue for) either hypothetical consent default rules or penalty (preference-eliciting) default rules. They do not blindly adopt or favor whatever rule minimizes the restrictive effect of the contract or charter, or lessens the change in legal relations. For such a rule would systematically underenforce contracts and charters relative to our best estimate of the contracting parties' preferences.

Indeed, where the narrow conditions for a preference-eliciting default rule are not met, both the no-effect and anti-change default rules systematically thwart legislative preferences, compared to a default rule that reflects

the interpreter's best estimate of how to maximize the satisfaction of legislative preferences. A diagram might help.

Suppose statutory uncertainty leaves us with three possible interpretive
options that can be plotted on a line where the distance between options indicates the extent to which the preferences of a legislature desiring one option would be dissatisfied with the other option. Let's call the interpretive
options Narrow, Middle, and Broad, with each separated by 10 units of legislative preference dissatisfaction from each other. Suppose the narrow interpretation is the one that best fits the no-effect and anti-change default
rules. Suppose further that, while courts cannot be sure which option best
matches legislative preferences, courts can identify one option as 60%
likely, with the others each 20% likely. Further, no judicial interpretation is
likely to be revisited by the legislature, so a preference-eliciting default is
unwarranted.

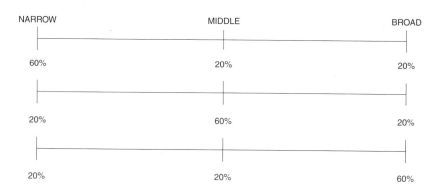

There are three cases, depending on which option the courts find 60%
likely to match legislative preferences. If it is the narrow option, then that
choice will be made under either a preference-estimating or narrow-
interpreting default rule, and there is no difference in legislative preference
dissatisfaction. If it is the middle option, then a narrow-interpreting default
rule will produce an expected preference dissatisfaction of $(0.2)(0) + (0.6)(10) + (0.2)(20) = 10$. A preference-estimating default rule would produce an expected preference dissatisfaction of $(0.2)(10) + (0.6)(0) + (0.2)(10) = 4$. If the
60% option is the broad option, then a narrow-interpreting default rule will
produce an expected preference dissatisfaction of $(0.2)(0) + (0.2)(10) + (0.6)(20) = 14$. The preference-estimating default rule will, in contrast, pro-

318 Statutory Default Rules

duce an expected preference dissatisfaction of only $(0.2)(20) + (0.2)(10) + (0.6)(0) = 6$. Thus, over the full range of cases, a narrow-interpreting default rule will systematically produce more legislative preference dissatisfaction than a preference-estimating default rule. This does not mean that judges when deciding cases should try to measure units of expected political dissatisfaction. I am rather using this analysis to explain why adopting the interpretation that most likely reflects legislative preferences will naturally lead to less political dissatisfaction than adopting the most narrow interpretation in all cases.

The same follows in cases where these alternative default rules would produce a broad interpretation that conflicts with our best estimate of enactable preferences. Consider *Cernauskas v. Fletcher*. There the Arkansas legislature enacted a statute giving municipalities the power to alter public streets and alleys that included a provision stating: "All laws and parts of laws . . . are hereby repealed."[14] Read literally, this provision repealed all Arkansas statutes. Even if one thought its words were ambiguous, an anti-effect default rule would require interpreting the statute to minimize the regulatory effect on private parties, and thus adopting the reading whereby the statute repealed all prior statutes. One suspects the proponents of the anti-effect default rule would not press it so far, but it is hard to know what basis there would be for refusing to apply the default rule if one did not rely on estimates of plausible legislative preferences. After all, the literal reading would not be absurd in any absolute sense: many people favor deregulation and would prefer to return to the simpler days when life was just regulated by the common law. Nor could the literal interpretation be rejected even on Dworkinian grounds of statutory coherence because if all prior statutes were repealed, there would be nothing left to cohere with.

Under a preference-estimating default rule, in contrast, the case is easily resolved. Given that this language came in a narrow statute authorizing municipal street regulation, it seemed clear such a wholesale repeal could not reflect the enactable preferences of this legislature. Such a reading would not be absurd in the absolute sense but rather (as discussed in Chapter 7) in the sense of being inconsistent with any plausible understanding of enactable preferences. Thus, the court correctly decided that the provision should be interpreted to repeal only laws in conflict with the new statute rather than "all laws."

Had the statutory context been different, the same interpretation of the same language would not have been appropriate. Imagine, for example, that precisely the same language came as part of a huge deregulatory movement that culminated in the "Return to the Common Law Act." Then, that very same language should be read to do just what it literally seems to do—repeal all prior statutes—for then that reading would reflect likely enactable preferences. Notice that the anti-change default rule would reach the right reading in *Cernauskas* but not in this hypothetical.

None of the above analysis denies that one factor to consider in estimating likely legislative preferences is that legislatures generally like to retain control over big social changes, and are unlikely to make what would be a large change at the time of enactment without ever having adverted to it.[15] But this is merely one factor to consider in the inquiry into meaning and choice of the best default rule, and should be subordinated to the larger question of (and broader set of evidence on) which interpretations will maximize political satisfaction.

Imposing a Preference-Eliciting Rule Regardless of Conditions

We come now to a more general problem with the no-effect or anti-change default rules. Their underlying theory is that, rather than trying to reflect likely legislative preferences, the default rule should force the legislature itself to resolve any statutory uncertainty. Where these default rules deviate from the preference-estimating ones, they effectively impose a preference-eliciting default rule regardless of whether the proper conditions for imposing such a default rule are met.

For reasons explained in Part III, a legislation-forcing default rule makes sense only in limited circumstances, where legislative preferences are unclear, significant differential odds of legislative correction exist, and any interim costs are acceptable. To instead expand preference-eliciting default rules wholesale to all legislation would be to have statutory results stick in a large range of cases where they would likely be contrary to legislative preferences.

Worse, the no-effect or anti-change default rules would often perversely put the burden of action on the political forces that are least able to get the issue on the legislative agenda. Such narrow interpretations will thus generally stick, with undesirable results.

Even when they do not stick, application of general legislation-forcing default rules will often be harmful. It will force legislatures to take up their scarce time with costly ex ante efforts to identify every conceivable contingency and specify a solution, or with ex post efforts to enact override statutes when such ex ante specification fails, even when eliciting such a legislative reaction is unnecessary to estimate legislative preferences. This needless ongoing burden to preempt or correct wayward judicial interpretations will take up legislative time that could have been better spent developing new statutory solutions to social problems.

Sometimes the costs of either providing the necessary specification or living with judicial interpretations that needlessly increase political dissatisfaction will dissuade the legislature from enacting the relevant statute at all, even though the polity would have considered the statute desirable if the judiciary were to take a more cooperative approach to its interpretation.[16] Further, where (as often) the enacting legislature did not anticipate the ambiguity, it could not have been corrected in the original statute, but will have to be corrected after the fact. This means that the result that conflicts with estimated legislative preferences will needlessly stick for at least the interim before any statutory override, imposing unnecessary interim costs.

What Legislatures Actually Want

To confirm that an anti-change or no-effect default rule would not maximize political satisfaction, we might look to the interpretive codes that legislatures promulgate. Given that courts have long interpreted ambiguous statutes to further the perceived legislative intent or purpose, one might have thought that a legislature that preferred that judges instead interpret all statutory ambiguity narrowly would have enacted a code of construction saying so. In fact, codes of construction generally direct courts to inquire into legislative purposes, and none of them direct a narrow construction of statutory ambiguities.

To the contrary, the state legislatures that have addressed the issue have expressly rejected the canon providing for narrow construction of statutes in derogation of the common law. True, New York nominally seems to have adopted the anti-change default rule by providing that "[a] change in long established rules of law is not deemed to have been intended by the Legislature in the absence of a clear manifestation of such intention."[17] However, this rule is limited by other statutory provisions that, as Chapter 14 notes, specify that legislative intent is the primary consideration, meaning that this rule is probably best viewed as supplying the supplemental rule where legislative preferences cannot be estimated. Further, the New York legislature has specified that statutory ambiguities should not be construed narrowly, but to further the leg-islative purpose or intent. Indeed, opposing any anti-change default rule is an-other New York statute providing that when the legislature enacts a change in statutory language, it intends "a material change in the law."[18] Thus, whatever grounds there might be for a no-effect or anti-change default rule, political sat-isfaction and legislative supremacy do not appear to be among them.

The U.S. Constitution Does Not Require a No-Effect or Anti-Change Default Rule

One might of course argue that, whether or not no-effect or antichange de-fault rules are desirable or advance political satisfaction, the U.S. Constitu-tion requires them. However, this claim generally has no applicability outside the United States. Further, it has so far been rejected by U.S. courts. Indeed, as noted above, the Court has not even recognized a constitutional basis for the one limited canon it does apply that reduces statutory effects or change—the canon against retroactive application of statutes. Nonetheless, it is a serious argument that requires attention.

One prominent textualist argument has been that, unless some clear meaning is provided by text that satisfies the constitutional process for statutory enactments (in the U.S., bicameralism and presentment), we have no authoritative legislative command that has satisfied constitutional re-quirements.[19] Thus, uncertain statutory text cannot be given effect, or be al-lowed to change the status quo, however desirable that might be. Although generally focused on the U.S. Constitution, the main argument is that the constitutional specification of a particular procedure for enacting statutes bars courts from relying on sources that have not gone through that proce-dure, an argument that presumably could be extended to most systems of constitutional government.

But, as already explained in Chapter 6, because no text can be interpreted without some resort to extrinsic evidence, one cannot really say that inter-pretive aids are limited to the text. Further, the Constitution simply leaves statutory interpretation to be resolved by the "judicial power" without spec-ifying how that interpretation should be conducted. To the extent we have evidence on the original understanding of this phrase, it appears to have conferred broad power on courts to go beyond the text in interpreting statutes when that helps courts advance legislative preferences.

Even if courts viewed themselves as prohibited from relying on sources outside the statutory text, that alone would not dictate a narrow interpretation. Courts could equally conclude they should adopt the broadest interpretation, or the one that made the most sense to the courts themselves. The textualist argument standing alone thus cannot explain the bias toward narrow interpretations. We thus need some other more affirmative rationale to explain this bias.

The main such argument appears to be that judges should adopt a bias against change or regulation because that was the U.S. framers' intent in specifying burdensome procedures for enacting statutes. Professor Manning, for example, argues that the U.S. framers thought the risk of ill-advised governmental action exceeded the risk of ill-advised inaction.[20] This theory does not explain why interpretation should (as Manning argues) turn on agency views or judicial precedent that seem equally likely to be ill-advised. But if valid, this theory would provide a legal basis for what I above denied was warranted: a substantive bias against change or regulation.

This is an intriguing possibility, but ultimately unpersuasive. The framers indeed set up certain obstacles to legislative action, but they did not impose those same obstacles on the interpretation of statutes. Nor, at the time of the framing or since, have judges adopted the philosophy that each statute must be given its most narrow possible interpretation. Nothing in the constitutional text, history, or precedent thus suggests that once legislation has gone through the hoops imposed for enactment, it should not, where ambiguous, be given the fairest reading of what would maximize legislative preferences.

Just because the framers had a sufficient bias against change to impose certain obstacles to legislative action does not mean they wanted judges to impose any additional obstacles to legislative action that the judges could imagine. To the contrary, the framers made a particular trade-off when they decided to impose only specified obstacles on legislative action (such as bicameralism and presentment) and not additional ones, such as mandating narrow interpretations of whatever was wrought by this legislative process. Likewise, the fact that contracts require consent of the contracting parties has never meant that courts should impose additional obstacles to advancing contracting party preferences, like narrowly interpreting whatever they wrote.

True, the Constitution specified a certain process for enacting legislative text because that process was thought desirable. But the argument that courts should thus do what they can to encourage specification in legislative text has no natural stopping point. In particular, it is hard to see why one would stop with a rejection of evidence regarding enactable preferences. Under this argument, interpreters should generally try to interpret statutory ambiguities in the most numbskulled way possible, because that is more likely to deviate from legislative preferences and provoke textual specification. No one would agree to such an approach, but the problem is that the goal of encouraging specification in legislative text by itself provides no self-limiting principle, especially if such encouragement is viewed as a constitutional requirement. Using preference-eliciting default rules only under conditions where they enhance legislative preference-satisfaction, in contrast, provides the necessary self-limiting principle.

To refrain from using those default rules that are best calculated to maximize the satisfaction of enactable preferences is necessarily to produce greater dissatisfaction of the legislative preferences that could satisfy the constitutional requirements of bicameralism and presentment. It is hard to see how the clauses requiring bicameralism and presentment, or vesting Congress with legislative powers, could dictate a judicial doctrine that would predictably thwart enactable legislative preferences more often than the alternative. For judges to thwart enactable legislative preferences in the name of legislative supremacy or separation of powers seems more perverse than persuasive. Nor does anything in the U.S. Constitution dictate such an undesirable result. While the Constitution surely leaves the power of interpretation to courts rather than Congress, nothing in it suggests courts should adopt interpretations that are more likely to thwart legislative preferences, and that has never been the judicial practice.

CHAPTER 18

Rebutting Operational and Jurisprudential Objections

I have argued that fashioning statutory default rules to maximize political satisfaction offers a positive theory of how courts actually interpret statutes, as well as a normative theory of why this pattern of judicial interpretation desirably maximizes the satisfaction of legislative preferences. But how would judges operationalize this theory? One might doubt that judges could practically estimate the enactable preferences of any government, or could determine whether current political influence produces the differential odds of legislative correction that are necessary to justify a preference-eliciting default rule.

To some extent, operationalization would be easy, for these theories largely offer a fuller explanation and justification for the statutory doctrines and distinctions that courts already employ, such as deferring to agency interpretations, the rule of lenity, and the presumptions against retroactivity, extraterritorial application, and antitrust and tax exemptions. For such doctrines, courts need not do anything different than they already do.

This does not mean that understanding the underlying theory is unimportant. An improved understanding can rebut common critiques that, viewed in this new light, turn out to be unjustified. This might help reduce some of the prevailing cynicism about statutory interpretation, and avoid harmful reforms. Further, a better underlying theory can help courts resolve cases at the margins of current categories in statutory construction doctrine.

Part of the goal is also to get courts to apply canons of statutory construction more consistently. This raises the question: should courts explicitly rely on estimates of political preferences or the likelihood of eliciting a legislative reaction in explaining why these canons are sometimes applied and sometimes ignored? My answer is affirmative. If judges are differentially applying canons on the basis of intuitions about legislative preferences or about the existence of a differential likelihood of legislative correction, then making these intuitions explicit helpfully makes their decisions more transparent and predictable. This suggestion must meet the usual trio of jurisprudential objections that are made whenever judges make their interstitial policy-making explicit: inappropriateness, inadministrability, and incompetence.

Appropriateness

One question is whether any political assessments required by my approach would be inappropriate because they do not reflect "law" or ordinary legal practice. I do not believe so. Political satisfaction analysis is merely a way of understanding the basis and application of traditional legal canons long employed by courts. As Chapter 15 observed, 70% of Supreme Court conference discussions in nonconstitutional cases already explicitly refer to the preferences or likely actions of current legislatures or other governmental actors, and 10% of their opinions openly invite legislative override. Even if courts are not explicit about their basis, Justice Holmes was right that law is a prediction of what judges will do.[1] If political satisfaction theory offers a sound prediction of judicial behavior, it should be understood as law.

An interpretation does not, after all, become more appropriate just because its basis is implicit rather than explicit. Nor can one say that (whether implicit or explicit) preference-eliciting default rules are not law because they take away the entitlement of parties to an interpretation that conforms to likely legislative preferences, for that begs the question of what entitlements parties do and should have. And even if judges never admitted to using political satisfaction theory in their opinions (just as they generally downplay their interstitial policymaking in interpreting legal ambiguities), lawyers advising clients should employ whatever theory helps them best predict to clients the likely outcome of statutory interpretations.

What we consider acceptable judicial practice has clearly changed over time. In the formalist age, it may have seemed unthinkable that courts would ever admit that formal legal materials were ambiguous and openly explain their policy grounds for resolving such ambiguity. But now that happens all the time. The once unthinkable became routine, because it was recognized that—whether they wanted to or not—formalist courts were making substantive judgments about policy in resolving inevitable legal ambiguities, and it was better for them to do so explicitly with reasoning, rather than implicitly by seat-of-the-pants judgments. The interpretation of antitrust statutes has, for example, been markedly improved by just such a shift, which has made antitrust doctrine correspond far better to economic realities.

Likewise, whether they want to or not, courts that interpret statutes necessarily have an impact on the political process, the satisfaction of political preferences, and the likelihood of explicit legislative reactions. Recognizing the preference-estimating or eliciting effects and analysis that are implicit in their cases merely requires courts to become as post-formalist about legislative process as they are about legislative policy and common law.

A quite different objection of inappropriateness might be leveled against preference-eliciting default rules in particular. This objection would be that such rules violate Kantian norms because they treat people as means rather than ends, by subjecting them to a result that likely deviates from legislative preferences in order to achieve the greater good of eliciting more precise legislative instructions. If valid, this concern would suggest that courts should instead always prefer a preference-estimating reading of the statute to make justice in the particular case more likely.

But the objection that persons are being used as means presumes precisely what is uncertain—that they deserve to be treated differently—and would block the default rule that is most likely to lead to statutory results that treat all persons as they deserve. When the elicited clarifications occurs ex ante, no person is ever treated other than she deserves, including in the short run. Indeed, more persons are treated as they deserve, assuming we take legislative preferences as our measure of desert, as this objection presupposes. When the only correction occurs ex post, there is an unavoidable trade-off, even on grounds of Kantian desert. Given actual uncertainty about enactable preferences, the alternative to subjecting the politically powerful side to a rule that may be wrong will be subjecting the politically powerless side to a rule that may be wrong. The former choice is more likely to inflict adverse ex post short-term consequences on the politically powerful side, but it can avoid any adverse long-term effects. The latter choice will inflict adverse effects less often on the politically powerless side, but those adverse effects will be inflicted in both the short and long run. Assuming that the long run is sufficiently longer than the short run, the latter choice will, even if all correction is ex post, overall result in persons being treated as they deserve more often. And taking into account ex ante correction makes this even more true, because such ex ante correction treats everyone as they deserve in both the short and long run.

Moreover, if taken seriously, such a Kantian objection would apply far beyond preference-eliciting default rules. It would apply *whenever* a legal doctrine is justified on institutional grounds, rather than based purely on the merits of the individual case. In particular, it would suggest that similar Kantian objections should prohibit the application of rules to any overinclusive case, because such cases are used as means to the end of preserving the precision of the rule. In the end, then, this is not an objection to preference-eliciting rules per se, but to rules generally. And there is no doubt that rules have long been considered appropriate in the law. Indeed, rules are generally jurisprudentially favored by rule-of-law norms.

Administrability

Wouldn't it be inadministrable for courts to take case-by-case testimony on the extent to which certain official action reflects enactable preferences, or on the differing political influence or preferences of various groups? Perhaps, but nothing in political satisfaction analysis requires that approach. Rather, assessments could continue to be made categorically, in a rule-like fashion for a given class of cases. Requiring particularized assessments of the influence of specific groups (rather than a general assessment for a given category of law) would likely prove unduly burdensome to courts and invite self-serving and unreliable testimony.

True, there will surely be hard decisions at the margins of any category. For example, should gun control laws benefit from the rule of lenity? While this seems a form of criminal law, gun enthusiasts are hardly an isolated group with little political influence, but rather are strongly represented through such groups as the National Rifle Association. A case-specific analysis thus suggests that applying preference-eliciting default rule against prosecutors may well be inappropriate in many gun control cases.[2] It might thus be desirable to define a standard-like exception, given the tension between the formal applicability of the rule of lenity and the underlying policy basis for the rule. Alternatively, one could consider the specific case just an overinclusive application of a generally sound rule, and apply the rule anyway. Or one could instead define some sort of exception to the rule, rather than shift to case-by-case analysis.

But these are the same sorts of issues that courts always face when defining rules or choosing between rules and standards. The decision basically turns on whether the error costs of the facial over- and under-inclusiveness of the rule are greater than the error costs of less precise application of a case-by-case standard.[3] Other relevant factors include the extent to which legal uncertainty might fail to provide fair warning, encourage behavioral compliance, or lower the costs of ascertaining the law. Such decisions will tend to be made at the highest court level for any jurisdiction, just as they are for other interstitial lawmaking that courts perform. Here, that is even more appropriate, because Supreme Court decisions are much more likely, when they erroneously estimate legislative preferences, to invite a legislative reaction. Such decisions are not made any less administrable because they are made explicitly.

Competence

Is it impossible for courts to acquire the expertise or information necessary to employ preference-estimating or eliciting analysis? I think not. After all, judicial use of these canons already follows such analysis, and does a fairly good job of it. If judges can be this accurate based on unspoken (and perhaps not even self-understood) intuition, then making such judgments expressly does not seem beyond their ability. Making such decisions is not inherently more difficult or information-intensive than the sort of interstitial policy decisions that courts now recognize they make all the time.

One must be careful not to overestimate the difficulties. Current preferences default rules require evidence of certain kinds of official action. It requires no special competence to defer to agency interpretations when statutory meaning is unclear. And although the doctrines that describe the various exceptions to *Chevron* are complex, using them does not require political polling. Indeed, understanding that they fit where the agency action is unlikely to reliably indicate current enactable preferences makes the doctrine much easier to understand. While estimating enactable preferences in an old legislature is often an uncertain task, in some cases it is obvious, and in closer cases it mainly requires inquiry into the same sort of legislative materials that judges already examine. In addition, these inquiries need only produce a probabilistic estimate that is better than random in order to reduce political dissatisfaction. Indeed, this understanding helps rebut the otherwise persuasive objection that no shared legislative intent can be divined.

Preference-eliciting default rules might seem more problematic because they require determining when differential odds of legislative correction exist. But, as noted above, these judgments will generally be categorical for the class of cases governed by a given statutory canon, and thus need not turn on case-by-case assessments of relative political influence. Further, to be a good candidate for a preference-eliciting default rule, the category of statutory interpretation must involve a persistent one-sided political demand for legislation. So, far from requiring nuanced political judgments and close monitoring over time, preference-eliciting analysis depends on a one-sidedness of political demand that tends to be structural and last a long time. Thus, the questions are not that hard or frequent, nor do they vary greatly over time.

One must also be careful not to implicitly judge this—or any other legal doctrine—by a Nirvana standard. It may not take great certainty to make a legal approach advisable: it need only be more accurate than the alternatives. In particular, it need not take a great deal of certainty to form the predicate for a default rule. Uncertainty may even be the justification, as in the case of supplemental or preference-eliciting default rules. Suppose courts have great uncertainty about which interpretation best matches legislative preferences. Then, a very slight expected advantage in provoking legislative reaction can justify choosing a preference-eliciting default rule, even when the overall odds of legislative reaction are small. That is, great uncertainty in estimating enactable preferences does not justify abandoning the goal of maximizing political satisfaction, but rather alters which default rules are most likely to do so.

Errors will be inevitable, as they are in any legal or policy standard applied by courts. But errors are likely to be smaller if the courts are at least thinking about the right questions. We are also likely to find, as with interstitial policymaking by judges, that being explicit about the underlying political analysis itself provokes the creation of better information for undertaking such analysis. For example, while cases overruling other cases are well reported and easy to find through traditional legal research tools, legislative overrides are not systematically collected in any source. Good empirical studies of the issue are thus highly labor intensive and few and far between. But if judges were being explicit about the extent to which application of their canons varied with the likelihood of legislative override, that would likely generate a far better database of information for use in the future. There seems to be no reason that Shepard's or Westlaw Keycite could not

make finding overriding statutes as easy as finding overruling cases. Likewise, both could easily be modified to turn up cites to the case not only in
subsequent cases but also in subsequent legislative history.

In the final analysis, though, claims of judicial incompetence require us to
answer the question: compared to what? Courts are the ones making decisions about how to resolve ambiguities in statutory interpretations. If courts
were to ignore the consequences of their decisions for political preference
satisfaction or the likelihood of legislative override, that would not mean
those consequences will not follow. It would merely mean that courts
would be making decisions that have those consequences without thinking
about them. There is no reason to think that judicial incompetence is so
great that judges make worse decisions when they estimate the consequences than they would if they ignored them. That would only be true if
judicial estimations were actually worse than random.

Claims of judicial incompetence can be persuasive only if it is possible for
courts to shift the relevant decision to a more competent branch. But that is
not a claim that can be made against political satisfaction canons, for their aim
is precisely to either (1) estimate political preferences where the statute is unclear, when possible by deference to agencies that are generally more competent at estimating current preferences, or (2) use preference-eliciting canons
to shift the decision to the legislative branch, which can best maximize the satisfaction of enactable political preferences by identifying what they are.

A recent book by Professor Vermeule poses two more subtle objections
about judicial capacity. *First*, he argues that judges face serious empirical uncertainty in applying not just a political satisfaction theory like mine, but
any of the modern tools of interpretive theory. He further claims that these
uncertainties make current judicial methods of interpretation so inaccurate
that switching to his particular version of formalism would create relatively
little additional inaccuracy, and relatively large savings in uncertainty and
decisionmaking costs.[4] Under his version of formalism, judges should follow
statutory meaning when it is clear, defer to agency interpretations when no
clear meaning exists, and follow statutory precedent when neither exists.[5]

Although our underlying theories differ, we share the same general conclusions where clear meaning, agency interpretations, or statutory precedent exist, although I track existing doctrine in recognizing various limited
exceptions to these rules, in cases when doing so increases political satisfaction.[6] The big difference is that, when none of those three sources exist,
Vermeule advocates having judges randomly pick some canon without con-

sidering its merits,[7] whereas I advocate that judges continue to employ the full range of default rules that maximize political satisfaction.

Professor Vermeule's book is important because it poses the best consequentialist defense of formalism to date. However, his consequentialist claim that switching to his brand of formalism would reduce decisionmaking costs more than it would increase inaccuracy costs is, ultimately, an empirical claim. By his own logic, judges lack the competence to assess the accuracy of his empirical claim, and thus cannot decide whether his claim should persuade them to overrule current doctrines on statutory interpretation. His empirical claim is also quite dubious. As Chapter 6 argued, judges can more accurately estimate legislative preferences if they consider the broader set of evidence that bears on those preferences, rather than restricting themselves to an arbitrary subset of that evidence. And while the decisionmaking costs of considering a broader set of evidence are hardly trivial to the few people who are involved in litigated cases, they are likely to be dwarfed by the benefits of accurately interpreting statutes that affect everyone.

Moreover, Vermeule offers no data to support his empirical claim. To the contrary, the only empirical evidence he musters is an analysis of one case, *Holy Trinity*, where he argues that the Court misread the legislative history. But his own analysis shows that, had the full set of legislative history been presented to the Court, the answer would have been clear.[8] This does not seem the sort of error that modern litigants are likely to replicate with regularity, given current databases on legislative history. More surprising, although his book stresses the importance of making comparative empirical assessments, Vermeule never empirically supports his comparative claim that formalism would produce similar levels of accuracy over the full range of cases. Rather he commits a version of the Nirvana fallacy he decries, by assuming that if nonformalist interpretation sometimes commits errors, then formalist interpretation cannot do much worse, even when it consists of a random choice of canons.

At root, Vermeule's claim rests on a optimistic view of formalism's relative accuracy and certainty, coupled with a jaundiced view of the extent to which judges will misapply other interpretive approaches, and an implicit assumption that judges would, for some reason, be less able or motivated to misapply formalism. But he supports none of those controversial premises with empirical data. As this book shows, the doctrinal patterns and available empirical data are precisely to the contrary. Not only are judicial decisions constrained by a doctrine that fits a system of default rules that maximize political satisfaction, but judicial decisions based on formalist notions of plain meaning are both more likely to deviate from legislative preferences and more likely to reflect judges' political ideologies.[9]

Vermeule's empirical claim would also seem to conflict with the empirical judgment of the legislatures themselves. The lion's share of them have enacted codes of construction that explicitly reject pure formalism, and all of them have failed to enact any codes restricting the current nonformalist methods that Vermeule finds objectionable.[10] Under Vermeule's thesis that courts should follow any clear statutory meanings, it would seem that courts would have to follow the clear meaning of those codes of construction, which dictate that courts should not restrict themselves to formalism when interpreting statutes. Thus, Vermeule's own formalist approach implies that courts should reject his formalist approach in the bulk of states. In the other states, one would think the empirical judgment of most legislatures, and the lack of any contrary empirical judgments by any other legislature, would suggest that his empirical claim is untenable.

None of this means that the sorts of concerns Vermeule points out are irrelevant. To the contrary, as the previous section indicated, uncertainty and decisionmaking costs should considered when deciding whether to adopt rule-like (rather than case-by-case) methods of implementing a political satisfaction approach. But preference-estimating or eliciting analysis should still drive legal choices among the set of rule-like canons that lower decision and uncertainty costs. Further, I myself cited the possibility of judicial inaccuracy to explain why legislatures should generally be able to opt out of the current set of default rules, and why we should understand statutes with clear meanings as constituting specific opt outs.[11] But absent such a legislative opt out, judges need to pick some default rules, despite the irreducible empirical uncertainty that besets this and all legal questions. And there is no persuasive reason to think that the problems with judicial interpretation are so pervasive that they justify the sort of wholesale change in default rules Vermeule advocates.

Second, Professor Vermeule raises a separate claim about judicial capacity, which he says undermines preference-eliciting default rules. He argues that courts lack the ability to use preference-eliciting default rules, because those default rules require coordination among multiple courts that courts are unable to achieve.[12] But his argument fails on multiple grounds.

To begin with, nothing in the theory of preference-eliciting rules requires coordination among multiple courts. If the three conditions for a preference-eliciting default rule are met, they would justify an individual court in adopting such a default rule, regardless of what the other judges are doing. This is clearly true when the relevant issue is eliciting ex post legislative correction. Nor does eliciting ex ante legislative reactions require that 100% of judges use preference-eliciting default rules. As long as some judges use them, that creates a risk that should induce some ex ante legislative reactions. After all, judges do not uniformly use legislative history, but there is no doubt that the fact that many do use it alters what legislatures put in that history.

For that matter, even if no other judge used preference-eliciting default rules, each individual judge who decided to do so would marginally increase the incentives for ex ante legislative clarifications, in a way that should exceed the marginal cost of deviating from a perhaps better (but uncertain) estimate of legislative preferences. If only one judge in a 100-judge system takes an eliciting position, then the legislature faces only a 1% risk that it will draw that judge when the statute is interpreted, but that risk should marginally increase the legislative incentive to resolve issues ex ante. While that marginal effect is small, it is also the case that the judge is only deciding 1% of the cases, so any deviation from what (without considering the eliciting effect) would be the best interpretation will only occur in 1% of cases, too. This risk-neutral calculation of net effects is no different for the individual judge than for all of them. Indeed, if we more reasonably assume legislative risk aversion, then a 1% risk would have more than a 1% effect on the legislature, so that eliciting will be even *more* attractive to a single judge than to multiple judges. At a minimum, adopting preference-eliciting default rules makes no less policy sense for individual judges than for the judiciary collectively.[13]

Even if coordination problems existed, they would easily be solved. The entire structure of appellate review restricts any coordination problems among multiple lower courts, because high courts can, and have, simply imposed the various preference-eliciting canons on lower courts as a matter of law. Moreover, as explained in Chapter 10, the usage of preference-eliciting default rules should generally be limited to the highest court in a jurisdiction, because it is the only one likely to elicit a legislative action. Such a unitary high court has no coordination problems. Professor Vermeule seems to think individual justices on the high court would have a coordination problem, but they don't, because their decisions only have any effect (eliciting or estimating) if the Court adopts them. Whether or not other justices agree will not alter any individual justice's assessment of whether an eliciting rule would have net positive effects; it only alters whether those net positive effects actually occur.

In any event, Professor Vermeule's argument ignores the basic point that current doctrine already has a raft of preference-eliciting default rules, and thus has in actual practice overcome the coordination problem he asserts is theoretically insuperable. If any coordination problem did remain, the relevant executive and legislature could solve it by declining to nominate or confirm judges with wayward views, or by enacting a code of construction imposing the desired rule of interpretation.

Conclusion

One might object that having judges use statutory default rules that estimate or elicit enactable preferences would be inappropriate, inadministrable, or beyond judicial competence. But these objections parallel the objections raised to the legal realist analysis that judges were implicitly using policy in resolving legal uncertainties. Recognizing the preference-estimating or eliciting effects and analysis that are implicit in their cases merely requires courts to become as post-formalist about legislative process as they are about legislative policy and common law. Nor does it require judges to employ open-ended case-by-case standards requiring testimony by political scientists on how best to estimate or elicit political preferences. It rather offers a way of explaining the set of doctrinal rules judges have been applying to accomplish those ends.

Finally, it is not a persuasive objection that judicial decisions about the best rules to advance those ends may be uncertain and often inaccurate. That is true for any sort of judicial decision, and here judges can take account of uncertainty by using elicting or supplemental default rules. Moreover, judges cannot avoid making decisions one way or the other about how to resolve uncertainties in statutory interpretations. Those interpretations will have consequences for the likelihood of political preference satisfaction whether or not judges consider them. Nor is there any reason to think judges make worse decisions when they estimate the consequences than when they ignore them; this would only be true if judicial estimations of such consequences were actually worse than random. In any event, a persuasive claim of judicial incompetence must be relative, and thus rest on a claim that courts should instead shift the relevant decision to a more competent branch. But that is precisely what the default rules that I have described aim to do.

NOTES

INDEX

Notes

Throughout these notes, a single note will, where convenient, be used to refer to multiple references in the same paragraph.

1. Introduction and Overview

1. Cass R. Sunstein, "Interpreting Statutes in the Regulatory State," 103 *Harvard Law Review* 405, 413, 438 (1989).

2. Why Courts Should Maximize Enactable Preferences

1. For theories that interpretation should follow the underlying "moral reality," see Heidi M. Hurd, "Challenging Authority," 100 *Yale Law Journal* 1611, 1620, 1667–1677 (1991); Heidi M. Hurd, "Sovereignty in Silence," 99 *Yale Law Journal* 945, 995–997, 1028 (1990); Michael S. Moore, "A Natural Law Theory of Interpretation," 58 *Southern California Law Review* 279, 353–358, 383–386 (1985). An alternative version of this objection might say that interpretation must vindicate people's "rights." But absent some claim of privileged insight into moral reality, to say there is a "right" is to presume we have some defined constitutional constraint or statutory meaning, and this book assumes we are operating in the realm where we have neither.
2. See Norberto Bobbio, *Democracy and Dictatorship,* trans. Peter Kennealy (Minneapolis: University of Minnesota Press, 1989), 137, 144–145; Hans Kelsen, *General Theory of Law and State,* trans. Anders Wedberg (New York: Russell & Russell, 1961), 284–286.
3. See Jeremy Waldron, *Law and Disagreement* (New York: Oxford University Press, 2001); Jeremy Waldron, *The Dignity of Legislation* (New York: Cambridge University Press, 1999), 147–148, 158–162.
4. See, e.g., Robert Dahl, *Democracy and Its Critics* (New Haven, Conn.: Yale University Press, 1989), chs. 4–5.
5. See Waldron, *Law,* 15.

6. In the original Condorcet jury theorem from which this point originates, it was assumed *each* voter made decisions that were better than random. However, more recent work establishes that the point also holds as long as the *average* voter is better than random. Bernard Grofman, Guillermo Owen & Scott L. Feld, "Thirteen Theorems in Search of the Truth," 15 *Theory & Decision* 261, 268–271 (1983). Further, although the original theorem was limited to choices between two options, it has been shown that the point also applies to plurality voting among multiple options. In particular, when choosing among multiple options, as long as voters are more likely to choose the correct option than any other option (even if their odds of choosing the correct option are less than 50% given the multiple options), then plurality voting is more likely to choose the correct option than any other. The odds that the correct option will be the plurality winner approach 100% the greater the number of voters. Christian List & Robert E. Goodin, "Epistemic Democracy," 9 *Journal of Political Philosophy* 277 (2001).

7. David Estlund, "Opinion Leaders, Independence, and Condorcet's Jury Theorem," 36 *Theory & Decision* 131, 131 (1994).

8. More precisely, suppose voters have a certain rate at which they defer to a common opinion leader, and a given accuracy rate given such deference. Then, voters will remain independent, in the requisite sense, as long as their accuracy rate exceeds their deference rate. Expressed more intuitively, voters will remain independent as long as they add some wisdom to the opinion leader, in the sense that they have a sufficiently better than random chance of choosing when to defer and when not to. Ibid., 151–152.

9. Ibid., 159; Bernard Grofman & Scott L. Feld, "Rousseau's General Will: A Condorcetian Perspective," 82 *American Political Science Review* 567, 571 (1988).

10. See, e.g. James Surowiecki, *The Wisdom of Crowds* (New York: Doubleday, 2004).

11. See Jonathan Baron, "Value Analysis of Political Behavior," 151 *University of Pennsylvania Law Review* 1135, 1142–1143 (2003).

12. Indeed, Baron argues that when voting is altruistic, rather than self-interested, it often leads to moralistic political decisions that decrease welfare. Ibid.

13. Amartya Sen, "Rationality and Social Choice," 85 *American Economic Review* 1 (1995).

14. See Bus. Elecs. Corp. v. Sharp Elecs. Corp., 485 U.S. 717, 732 (1988); Frank H. Easterbrook, "Statutes' Domains," 50 *University of Chicago Law Review* 533, 544 (1983).

15. Ronald Dworkin, *Law's Empire* (Cambridge, Mass.: Harvard University Press, 1986); David L. Shapiro, "Continuity and Change in Statutory Interpretation," 67 *New York University Law Review* 921, 938 (1992); Amanda Tyler, "Continuity, Coherence, and the Canons," 99 *Northwestern University Law Review* 1389, 1393, 1406 (2005).

16. See Cass R. Sunstein, "Interpreting Statutes in the Regulatory State," 103 *Harvard Law Review* 405 (1989).

17. Ibid., 330–333.

18. See Cal. Civ. Proc. Code §1859; Mont. Code Ann. §1–2–102; Or. Rev. Stat. Ann.

§174.020; Colo. Rev. Stat. §2–4–205; Iowa Code Ann. §4.7; Minn. Stat. Ann. §645.26(1); N.D. Cent. Code §1–02–07; Ohio Rev. Code Ann. §1.51; 1 Pa. Cons. Stat. Ann. §1933; Tex. Gov't Code Ann. §311.026; N.Y. Stat. Law §238.

19. Morton v. Mancari, 417 U.S. 535, 550–551 (1974).

20. See Thomas J. Miles & Cass R. Sunstein, "Do Judges Make Regulatory Policy? An Empirical Investigation of *Chevron,*" 73 *University of Chicago Law Review* 823, 867–868 (2006).

21. For work favoring deliberative democracy, see "Symposium: The Republican Civic Tradition," 97 *Yale Law Journal* 1493 (1988); Jon Elster, ed., *Deliberative Democracy* (Cambridge, UK: Cambridge University Press, 1998); Amy Gutmann & Dennis Thompson, *Democracy and Disagreement* (Cambridge, MA: Harvard University Press, 1996), 128–164; Jürgen Habermas, *Between Facts and Norms,* trans. William Rehg (New Baskerville: MIT Press, 1996), 287–328 ; Cass R. Sunstein, *The Partial Constitution* (Cambridge, MA: Harvard University Press, 1993), 133–145.

22. Estlund, "Opinion Leaders."

23. Surowiecki, *Wisdom of Crowds;* Cass R. Sunstein, "Deliberative Trouble? Why Groups Go to Extremes," 110 *Yale Law Journal* 71 (2000) (surveying literature); David Schkade, Cass R. Sunstein, & Daniel Kahneman, "Deliberating About Dollars: The Severity Shift," 100 *Columbia Law Review* 1139, 1139 (2000).

24. John Rawls, *A Theory of Justice* (Cambridge, Mass.: Harvard University Press, 1971), 348; Sunstein, "Deliberative," 73.

3. The General Theory for Current Preferences Default Rules

1. Friedrich v. City of Chicago, 888 F.2d 511, 514 (7th Cir. 1989) (Posner, J.); United States v. Klinger, 199 F.2d 645, 648 (2d Cir. 1952), aff'd per curiam, 345 U.S. 979 (1953) (Learned Hand, J.); Burnet v. Guggenheim, 288 U.S. 280, 285 (1933) (Cardozo, J.); Aristotle, *The Nicomachean Ethics,* trans. David Ross, ed. J. L. Ackrill & J. O. Urmson (New York: Oxford University Press, 1998), 133; Richard A. Posner, *The Problems of Jurisprudence* (Cambridge, Mass.: Harvard University Press, 1990), 270.

2. See Guido Calabresi, *A Common Law for the Age of Statutes* (Cambridge, Mass.: Harvard University Press, 1982), 2, 6–7; Ronald Dworkin, *Law's Empire* (Cambridge, Mass.: Harvard University Press, 1986), 347–354; William N. Eskridge, Jr., *Dynamic Statutory Interpretation* (Cambridge, Mass.: Harvard University Press, 1994), 5–7, 9–11, 69, 107–108, 120–121; Cass R. Sunstein, "Interpreting Statutes in the Regulatory State," 103 *Harvard Law Review,* 412, 433 & n.99, 495 (1989).

3. See David R. Mayhew, *Congress: The Electoral Connection* (New Haven, Conn.: Yale University Press, 1974), 49–73; Joseph Ignagni, James Meernik, & Kimi Lynn King, "Statutory Construction and Congressional Response," 26 *American Politics Quarterly* 459, 468–469, 477 (1998).

4. See Morris P. Fiorina, *Retrospective Voting in American National Elections* (New

Haven, Conn.: Yale University Press, 1981) 20–43; Linda Cohen & Matthew Spitzer, "Term Limits," 80 *Georgetown Law Review* 477, 487–488 (1992).

5. See Daniel A. Farber & Philip P. Frickey, "The Jurisprudence of Public Choice," 65 *Texas Law Review* 873, 890–901 (1987) (summarizing literature).

6. See Chapters 1 and 2.

7. See Amanda Tyler, "Continuity, Coherence, and the Canons," 99 *Northwestern University Law Review* 1389, 1411 (2005).

8. Consistent with this possibility, one study has shown that Supreme Court decisions interpreting civil rights statutes track the ideological preferences of the justices, and are not affected by the changing preferences of Congress or the president. See Jeffrey A. Segal, "Separation-of-Powers Games in the Positive Theory of Congress and Courts," 91 *American Political Science Review* 28, 39–42 (1997).

9. See, e.g., John A. Ferejohn & Barry R. Weingast, "A Positive Theory of Statutory Interpretation," 12 *International Review of Law & Economics* 263, 266–267 (1992); Matthew D. McCubbins, Roger G. Noll, & Barry R. Weingast, "Administrative Procedures as Instruments of Political Control," 3 *Journal of Law, Economics & Organization* 243, 248–253 (1987); Matthew D. McCubbins, Roger G. Noll, & Barry R. Weingast, "Structure and Process, Politics and Policy: Administrative Arrangements and the Political Control of Agencies," 75 *Virginia Law Review* 431, 445 (1989).

10. William Landes & Richard Posner, "The Independent Judiciary in an Interest-Group Perspective," 18 *Journal of Law & Economics* 875, 877–879 (1975); see also Terry Moe, "The Politics of Bureaucratic Structure," in John E. Chubb & Paul E. Peterson, eds., *Can the Government Govern?* (Washington, D.C.: Brookings Institution Press, 1989), 267–277. Bidding in their model should be understood to include not just providing money, but providing any means of political support useful to those legislators.

11. See Tyler, "Continuity," 1409.

12. Omri Ben-Shahar, "Legal Durability," 1 *Review of Law and Economics* 15 (2005).

13. Jacob Gerson, "Temporary Legislation," 74 *University of Chicago Law Review* 247 (2007).

14. See Calabresi, *A Common Law*, 2, 6–7, 100–104.

15. See Amanda Frost, "Certifying Questions to Congress," 101 *Northwestern Law Review* (2006).

16. Tyler, "Continuity," 1409 n.100.

17. See Calabresi, *A Common Law*, 2, 6–7; Dworkin, *Law's Empire*, 347–354; Eskridge, *Dynamic*, 5–7, 9–11, 107–108, 120–121; Sunstein, "Interpreting Statutes," 412, 495.

18. Lon L. Fuller, *The Morality of Law* (New Haven, Conn.: Yale University Press, 1969), 209–210.

19. See Dworkin, *Law's Empire*, 349; Eskridge, *Dynamic*, 10–11, 139, 156–159; William N. Eskridge, Jr., "Public Values in Statutory Interpretation," 137 *University of Pennsylvania Law Review* 1007, 1017–1061 (1989); Sunstein, "Interpreting Statutes," 495. Eskridge argues that courts must make sure not to adopt

interpretations that will be legislatively overridden, but does not claim that courts should adopt the interpretation most likely to be enactable. Indeed, he even argues in favor of statutory interpretations that are sometimes "counter- or nonmajoritarian." *Dynamic*, 7, 69, 151. Calabresi argues that courts should overrule old statutory meanings that are no longer enactable by the current leg- islature, but he would not require any evidence that the new meaning be the one most likely to be enactable. *A Common Law*, 2, 7.

20. See Dworkin, *Law's Empire*, 319 (arguing that interpretation should reflect judi- cial "opinions about the influence that the attitudes, beliefs, and ambitions of particular groups of officials and citizens ought to have in the process of legisla- tion" and about "whether lobbying, logrolling, and political action committees are a corruption of the democratic process"); Eskridge, *Dynamic*, 157–158.

21. Dworkin argues that the judge should act as the legislature's "partner" (rather than agent), developing the statutory scheme in "the best way," which will turn in part on the judge's "own judgment." He rejects the view that "statutes should be read, not according to what judges believe would make them best, but ac- cording to what the legislators who actually adopted them intended," and ar- gues that interpretive questions "must be answered in political theory, by taking up particular views about controversial issues of political morality." *Law's Em- pire*, 313–314, 316; see also 334 ("A judge must ultimately rely on his own opin- ions [and] [h]is own political convictions."); 347 (stating that interpretation should turn in part on the judge's "substantive opinion" about which statutory reading "would make it better from the point of view of sound policy"). Eskridge likewise regards it as unavoidable that courts must make "value choices," and ultimately supports his theory of dynamic interpretation with the argument that it is "normatively desirable" for courts to adopt a stance of criti- cal pragmatism that considers whether an interpretation will "unsettle existing practice," "reasonably accommodate a diversity of interests," and be "responsive to social needs and public values"; *Dynamic*, 174–176; see also Sunstein, "Inter- preting Statutes," 412–413 (rejecting the view that "controversial views about public policy . . . should never be part of statutory construction" and setting forth the "substantive norms" courts should follow and those it should reject).

22. Dworkin, *Law's Empire*, 313 (arguing that judicial interpretation will depend on judges' "best answer to political questions [like] how far Congress should defer to public opinion in matters of this sort."); also at 319 (arguing that judicial interpre- tation turns on judges' "views on the old question whether representative legisla- tors should be guided by their own opinions and convictions" rather than public opinion). For the other quotations in the textual paragraph, see 340–342, 349.

23. Eskridge, *Dynamic*, 151; see also 156–157, 159–161.

24. See Laurence H. Tribe, "The Puzzling Persistence of Process-Based Constitu- tional Theories," 89 *Yale Law Journal* 1063, 1072–1077 (1980).

25. See Stephen McG. Bundy & Einer Elhauge, "Knowledge About Legal Sanc- tions," 92 *Michigan Law Review* 261, 270–272 (1993).

26. See U.S. Const. arts. I & III; Reichelderfer v. Quinn, 287 U.S. 315, 318 (1932);

Manigault v. Springs, 199 U.S. 473, 487 (1905); Newton v. Comm'rs, 100 U.S. 548, 559 (1879); 1 Blackstone, Commentaries, *90; Thomas M. Cooley, *A Treatise on the Constitutional Limitations Which Rest Upon the Legislative Power of the States of the American Union* (Boston: Little, Brown, 1868), 125–126; Earl T. Crawford, *The Construction of Statutes* (St. Louis: Thompson Law Book Company, 1940), 171, 193; Laurence H. Tribe, *American Constitutional Law* (New York: Foundation Press, 2000), §§2–3 n.1.

27. Nicholas Rosenkranz, "Federal Rules of Statutory Interpretation," 115 *Harvard Law Review* 2085, 2104–2105 (2002).

4. Inferring Current Preferences from Recent Legislative Action

1. This issue also applies to legislative decisions to let stand agency interpretations that either were decided before *Chevron* or fall outside its scope. See generally Chapter 5.

2. United States v. Rutherford, 442 U.S. 544, 554 n.10 (1979); see also FDA v. Brown & Williamson Tobacco Corp., 529 U.S. 120, 155 (2000); Commodity Futures Trading Comm'n v. Schor, 478 U.S. 833, 846 (1986); Bob Jones Univ. v. United States, 461 U.S. 574, 599–602 (1983); Herman & MacLean v. Huddleston, 459 U.S. 375, 384–386 (1983); North Haven Bd. of Educ. v. Bell, 456 U.S. 512, 535 (1982); Merrill Lynch, Pierce, Fenner & Smith, Inc. v. Curran, 456 U.S. 353, 379–382 (1982); Haig v. Agee, 453 U.S. 280, 300–301 (1981); Cannon v. Univ. of Chi., 441 U.S. 677, 686 n.7, 702–703 (1979); Lorillard v. Pons, 434 U.S. 575, 580 (1978); United States v. Bd. of Comm'rs, 435 U.S. 110, 134–135 (1978); Runyon v. McCrary, 427 U.S. 160, 173–175 (1976); Red Lion Broad. Co. v. FCC, 395 U.S. 367, 381 n.11 (1969); Apex Hosiery Co. v. Leader, 310 U.S. 469, 488–489 (1940).

3. See Aaron v. SEC, 446 U.S. 680, 694 n.11 (1980); Monell v. Dep't of Soc. Servs., 436 U.S. 658, 696–699 (1978); Zuber v. Allen, 396 U.S. 168, 185 n.21, 192–194 (1969); Leary v. United States, 395 U.S. 6, 24–25 (1969); Girouard v. United States, 328 U.S. 61, 70 (1946).

4. See, e.g., *Brown & Williamson*, 529 U.S. 120, 143–156 (2000); Franklin v. Gwinnett County Pub. Sch., 503 U.S. 60, 78 (1992) (Scalia, J., concurring in the judgment).

5. Pension Benefit Guar. Corp. v. LTV Corp., 496 U.S. 633, 650 (1990); Mackey v. Lanier Collection Agency & Serv., Inc., 486 U.S. 825, 840 (1988); Consumer Prod. Safety Comm'n v. GTE Sylvania, Inc., 447 U.S. 102, 117–118 (1980); see also Pub. Employees Ret. Sys. v. Betts, 492 U.S. 158, 168 (1989); United States v. Southwestern Cable Co., 392 U.S. 157, 170 (1968); Haynes v. United States, 390 U.S. 85, 87 n.4 (1968).

6. Seatrain Shipbuilding Corp. v. Shell Oil Co., 444 U.S. 572, 596 (1980); see also Finkelstein, 496 U.S. at 628 n.8; Andrus v. Shell Oil Co., 446 U.S. 657, 666 n.8 (1980).

7. Morton v. Mancari, 417 U.S. 535, 549 (1974).

8. *Brown & Williamson,* 529 U.S. at 143; see also at 133; United States v. Fausto, 484 U.S. 439, 453 (1988); Bowen v. Yuckert, 482 U.S. 137, 149–152 (1987).

9. *Brown & Williamson,* 529 U.S. at 143.

10. *Bob Jones,* 461 U.S. at 593 n.20, 597–599.

11. Ibid., 599–602. The quotations in this paragraph are from pages 593 and 598. Although such an IRS interpretation might also ordinarily merit agency deference, that agency was under a Treasury Department that had announced its intent to revoke this interpretation. See Chapter 5.

12. Ibid., 585 n.9. See *Legislation to Deny Tax Exemption to Racially Discriminatory Private Schools: Hearing Before the Senate Comm. on Fin.,* 97th Cong. 225–226, 229–232 (1982) (statement of Hon. R. T. McNamar, Deputy Sec'y of the Treasury); and at 244, 247 (statement of Sen. Boren).

13. *Legislation to Deny Tax Exemption Hearing,* 234–35, 253. Chairman Dole stated that, while "legislation is going to be very difficult until there is a full understanding" of where the Supreme Court would leave the state of the law, if action were necessary, his assessment was that "there has been such an avalanche of feeling about racial discrimination. You are not going to get any votes in this committee for racial discrimination." Ibid., 254. Some statements also suggested that Senate Democrats were not eager to enact a bill that would get the Reagan administration off the political hook, at 244, 247, and that might imply that the prior IRS interpretation had been legally improper at, 241, 244. But notwithstanding this strategic political interest, there was no doubt that their enactable preference would, if necessary, have been for a statute that denied a tax exemption to racially discriminatory schools.

14. *Bob Jones,* 461 U.S., at 601.

15. *Morton,* 417 U.S., at 548–551 (collecting cases).

16. Minn. Stat. Ann. §645.16–645.17 (West 1946); 1 Pa. Cons. Stat. Ann. §1921–22 (West 1995); N.Y. Stat. Law §75(a) (McKinney 1971).

5. Inferring Current Preferences from Agency Action

1. Chevron U.S.A. Inc. v. Natural Res. Def. Council, Inc., 467 U.S. 837 (1984); Thomas W. Merrill & Kristin E. Hickman, "Chevron's Domain," 89 *Georgetown Law Journal* 833 (2001). Some areas, like labor and tax law, had longstanding deference doctrines similar to *Chevron* (838–839), and in practice, deference was extensive even before *Chevron.*

2. Colo. Rev. Stat. Ann. §2-4-203(1)(f) (West 2000); Iowa Code Ann. §4.6 (West 2001); Minn. Stat. Ann. §645.16; N.M. Stat. Ann. §12-2A-20(B)(4) (Michie 1978); N.Y. Stat. Law §129; N.D. Cent. Code §1-02-39 (1987); Ohio Rev. Code Ann. §1.49 (West 1994); 1 Pa. Cons. Stat. Ann. §1921; Texas Gov't Code Ann. §311.023 (Vernon 1998). Mexico's legislature even adds that the court can consider an agency's interpretation of a "similar statute."

3. Wayne Washington, "Ashcroft Supports Affirmative Action Rule—Files a Brief Backing Policy in Colo. Case," *Boston Globe,* August 11, 2001, A3.

4. See Elena Kagan, "Presidential Administration," 114 *Harvard Law Review* 2245, 2258 (2001); McNollgast, "The Political Origins of the Administrative Procedure Act," 15 *Journal of Law, Economics & Organization* 180–181, 185–186, 198–199 (1999). McNollgast elsewhere theorize that administrative procedures give interested groups the ability to raise a "fire alarm" to make sure an agency does not deviate from the preferences of the *enacting* coalition. Matthew D. McCubbins, Roger G. Noll, & Barry R. Weingast, "Structure and Process, Politics and Policy: Administrative Arrangements and the Political Control of Agencies," 75 *Virginia Law Review* 431–434, 441–442 (1989). But this theory fits poorly with the actual Administrative Procedure Act, which "gives exactly the same participation opportunity to groups that opposed the original legislation as to those who supported it . . . And when groups that oppose agency action trip legislative fire alarms, the fire will be doused (or fed or ignored) by the existing power balance in the legislature rather than by the coalition that existed at the time the legislation was enacted." Michael Asimov, "On Pressing McNollgast to the Limits," 57 *Law & Contemporary Problems* 127, 131 (1994).
5. See Kagan, "Presidential Administration," 2254–2260, 2264–2269, 2274–2319.
6. See David Epstein & Sharyn O'Halloran, "Legislative Organization Under Separate Powers," 17 *Journal of Law, Economics & Organization* 373, 375–379, 381–390 (2001).
7. See Kagan, "Presidential Administration," 2280–2281 n.142.
8. *Chevron*, 467 U.S. at 842–843, 865–866. For better flow, I have changed the order of the sentences in the first block quote from their original ordering.
9. Ibid., 842, 863–864.
10. Merrill & Hickman, "Chevron's Domain," 863–868, 870–871.
11. Ibid., 871; Antonin Scalia, "Judicial Deference to Administrative Interpretations of Law," 1989 *Duke Law Journal* 511, 517; *Chevron*, 467 U.S. at 865.
12. 5 U.S.C. §706 (2000); McNollgast, "The Political Origins of the Administrative Procedure Act," 189–192, 200, 203–204, 213–215.
13. 5 U.S.C. §559.
14. Merrill & Hickman, "Chevron's Domain," 868–870 & n.197. Merrill and Hickman also worry that this theory is hard to square with the APA, but they ultimately concede that understanding *Chevron* as a canon of construction avoids this problem (868).
15. Peter L. Strauss, "One-Hundred-Fifty Cases Per Year: Some Implications of the Supreme Court's Limited Resources for Judicial Review of Agency Action," 87 *Columbia Law Review* 1093, 1110–1113, 1118–1129 (1987). At the time Strauss wrote, the Supreme Court decided 150 cases a year. More recently, it has decided about half that, and most of those do not involve reviews of agency interpretations.
16. See Richard L. Revesz, "Congressional Influence on Judicial Behavior? An Empirical Examination of Challenges to Agency Action in the D.C. Circuit," 76 *New York University Law Review* 1100, 1103 (2001) (noting that the D.C. Circuit has

exclusive venue to review many agency decisions and hears one-third of appeals from federal agencies).

17. Richard B. Stewart, "The Reformation of American Administrative Law," 88 *Harvard Law Review* 1667, 1683 (1975).

18. Ibid., 1683–1684.

19. See Stephen Breyer, *Breaking the Vicious Circle: Toward Effective Risk Regulation* (Cambridge, Mass.: Harvard University Press, 1993), 61; Cass R. Sunstein, "Law and Administration After *Chevron*," 90 *Columbia Law Review* 2071, 2088–2090, 2094–2095 (1990).

20. See United States v. Mead Corp., 533 U.S. 218, 226–229, 233–237 (2001) (summarizing factors for deference articulated in Skidmore v. Swift & Co., 323 U.S. 134 [1944]). *Skidmore* is the backstop doctrine that applies when *Chevron* deference is unavailing; 220–221, 233–235.

21. *Chevron*, 467 U.S. at 865–866; National Cable & Telecom. Ass'n v. Brand X Internet Services, 125 S.Ct. 2688, 2699–2700 (2005).

22. See, e.g., Pub. Employees Ret. Sys. v. Betts, 492 U.S. 158, 174–175 (1989); Bowen v. Georgetown Univ. Hosp., 488 U.S. 204, 212 (1988). In contrast, the courts do give *Seminole Rock* deference to agency interpretations of their own regulations, even though those interpretations are only advanced in litigation briefing. See Auer v. Robbins, 519 U.S. 452, 461–463 (1997). Although, for Justice Scalia, *Auer* indicated a change in the law on *Chevron* deference, the Supreme Court rejected that view in *Mead*, 533 U.S. at 238 (denying *Chevron* deference to agency statutory interpretation that was reflected in litigation briefs).

23. See Smiley v. Citibank, 517 U.S. 735, 741 (1996).

24. See Dan M. Kahan, "Is *Chevron* Relevant to Federal Criminal Law?" 110 *Harvard Law Review* 469, 489–490, 495–496, 518–520 (1996).

25. Outside of criminal law, Department of Justice expertise and uniformity instead justify weaker *Skidmore* deference. See Kahan, "Is *Chevron* Relevant," 509. Inside criminal law, however, there are grounds for a preference-eliciting default rule that explains why, rather than deferring to the Department of Justice, the courts instead apply a rule of lenity that leans against it. See Part III.

26. *Mead*, 533 U.S. at 237 n.17; Christensen v. Harris County, 529 U.S. 576, 587 (2000). Nor would *Chevron* deference be triggered by more informal statements by agency officials in speeches, press releases, or press conferences. See Merrill & Hickman, "Chevron's Domain," 866.

27. *Mead*, 533 U.S. at 227–231; *Christensen*, 529 U.S. at 587.

28. See Merrill & Hickman, "Chevron's Domain," 837, 846–847, 881, 890–892.

29. *Mead*, 533 U.S. at 223–224, 229–231, 233; *Christensen*, 529 U.S. at 587. True, *Mead* left open a small residual category illustrated by one case that involved informal rulemaking, but it made clear that the most significant factor was the existence of a "notice-and-comment" procedure. 533 U.S. at 231.

30. Merrill & Hickman, "Chevron's Domain," 838 n.23, 890–892 (collecting cases).

31. See 5 U.S.C. §§556–557 (2000) (providing requirements for formal adjudication); Merrill & Hickman, "Chevron's Domain," 884–886. An alternative explanation is that when Congress authorizes agencies to formally adjudicate cases, it is expressly delegating to the agency the authority to make those statutory interpretations that are incident to that adjudication. Under this explanation, even if such agency adjudications would not by themselves fit within a current preferences default rule, Congress has opted out of that default rule by enacting the statutory provisions expressly providing for such adjudication. The Court cases finding *Chevron* applicable to agency adjudications have in fact involved strong evidence that Congress was delegating interpretive authority to the agency adjudications. See, e.g., INS v. Aguirre-Aguirre, 526 U.S. 415, 424–425 (1999).

32. See Envirocare of Utah, Inc. v. Nuclear Regulatory Comm'n, 194 F.3d 72, 79 (D.C. Cir. 1999) (suggesting that the cases collected in Kagan, "Presidential Administration," 2271 n.92, are no longer good law).

33. *Mead*, 533 U.S. at 221–222 (quoting 19 U.S.C. §1502(a) (2000) and 19 C.F.R. §177.9(a) [2000]).

34. *Smiley*, 517 U.S. at 742; see also *Chevron*, 467 U.S. at 863–864; Rust v. Sullivan, 500 U.S. 173, 186–187 (1991) (emphasizing that agencies "must" retain the power to change their interpretations over time).

35. See *Mead*, 533 U.S. at 223, 226–227, 232–235.

36. Ibid., 232–233.

37. Ibid., 256–257, 258 & n.6, 259–260 (Scalia, J., dissenting).

38. *Mead*, 533 U.S. at 228–231 & n.13 (citing NationsBank of N.C. v. Variable Annuity Life Ins. Co., 513 U.S. 251, 254–257 [1995]).

39. *Mead*, 533 U.S. at 253–254 (Scalia, J., dissenting) (citing Mead Corp. v. Tilley, 490 U.S. 714, 722 (1989) and Pension Benefit Guar. Corp. v. LTV Corp., 496 U.S. 633, 642–643, 647–648 [1990]). In *Tilley*, three agencies—the Pension Benefit Guaranty Corporation, the IRS, and the Department of Labor—all agreed on the relevant statutory interpretation in various opinion letters and guidelines written in advance of litigation. *LTV* involved a consistent uniform agency interpretation, evidenced by three separate opinion letters, before the notice of restoration challenged in the case. Moreover, the notice of restoration itself might be regarded as an agency adjudication within *Mead*.

    The only two other cases Justice Scalia cited as inconsistent with *Mead* also involved longstanding uniform agency positions. *Mead*, 533 U.S. at 252–253 (Scalia, J., dissenting) (citing FDIC v. Phila. Gear Corp., 476 U.S. 426 (1986), and Young v. Cmty. Nutrition Inst., 476 U.S. 974 [1986]). They also fell within the doctrine that courts should follow prevailing interpretations that Congress was aware of, and yet chose not to alter, even though Congress reenacted or amended the statute. See *Philadelphia Gear*, 476 U.S. at 436–439; *Young*, 476 U.S. at 983. As explained in Chapter 4, even if such an interpretation is not binding under *Chevron*, courts are still justified in adopting such an interpretation as the current preferences default rule based on inferences from the legislative action.

40. *Mead*, 533 U.S. at 229–233 & n.16. The Court tried to get around the "presumed

to be correct" provision by noting that other statutory provisions provided that the reviewing court could consider new grounds and facts (229–233 & n.16), but this did not offer any response to Justice Scalia's cogent critique that this statute provided no reason to deny deference on legal issues that had been considered by the agency. 257–258 (Scalia, J., dissenting).

41. Ibid. (Scalia, J., dissenting).

42. *Mead*, 533 U.S. at 232; see also *Christensen*, 529 U.S. at 587.

43. 5 U.S.C. §301 (2000). See generally Chrysler Corp. v. Brown, 441 U.S. 281, 308–312 (1979) (describing the history of the housekeeping statute).

44. 5 U.S.C. §558(b); *Chrysler*, 441 U.S. at 302–303, 308; Interstate Commerce Comm'n v. Cincinnati, New Orleans & Tex. Pac. Ry. Co., 167 U.S. 479, 494–495 (1897); Merrill & Hickman, "Chevron's Domain," 883.

45. See 5 U.S.C. §553; Merrill & Hickman, "Chevron's Domain," 903. Interestingly, there appears to be a chicken-and-egg phenomenon at work. The reason the 1946 APA. exempted interpretive rules from notice-and-comment requirements was that courts at the time did not defer to them. See ibid., 887 n.264. The important point is that the two go together: (1) some opportunity for political participation, like notice-and-comment procedures, and (2) deference to the result as likely tracking current political preferences.

46. *Mead*, 533 U.S. at 232. Procedural rules are also exempt from notice and comment—see 5 U.S.C. §553(b)(A)—and thus should be treated like interpretive rules for purposes of *Chevron* deference.

47. See United States v. Haggar Apparel Co., 526 U.S. 380, 391 (1999). See also Merrill & Hickman, "Chevron's Domain," 840–841, 871–872, 909. Merrill and Hickman argue that any presumption based on presumed congressional intent should be weak to avoid distorting legislative intent (888), which is also inconsistent with the doctrine because, in their view, *Haggar* reflects a strong presumption. See 840–841.

48. *Chevron*, 467 U.S. at 845, 864–866.

49. Bob Jones Univ. v. United States, 461 U.S. 574 (1983). Although *Bob Jones* was decided a year before *Chevron*, there were already tax cases providing for a similar rule of deference, and in any event, the case illustrates the point. The Treasury interpretation was a change from an IRS interpretation that had prevailed since 1970, but such changes in interpretation are perfectly proper under *Chevron*. Interestingly, the Court did suggest some willingness to defer to the IRS interpretation, which it stressed was consistent with current political views, even though it seemed blind to the contrary interpretation by the IRS's superiors in Treasury. Under the theory urged here, this variation in treatment is explainable because the latter's admitted lack of conformity to current political views gave them no resonance.

50. See William N. Eskridge, Jr., & John Ferejohn, "The Article I, Section 7 Game," 80 *Georgetown Law Journal* 523, 528–540, 547–551 (1992); Cynthia R. Farina, "Statutory Interpretation and the Balance of Power in the Administrative State," 89 *Columbia Law Review* 452, 501–526 (1989).

51. Eskridge & Ferejohn, "Game," 540–547; INS v. Chadha, 462 U.S. 919 (1983); Bowsher v. Synar, 478 U.S. 714 (1986).

52. See *Chevron*, 467 U.S. at 865 ("[A]n agency . . . may . . . properly rely upon the incumbent administration's views . . . While agencies are not directly accountable to the people, the Chief Executive is").

53. See Kagan, "Presidential Administration," 2250, 2290–2294, 2323 & n.308.

54. See *Chevron*, 467 U.S. at 853–859, 864. The Court also stressed that enactor preferences were unclear. See at 845 ("Congress did not actually have an intent [on the relevant question]"). The less clear enactor preferences are, the less reliable the evidence of correspondence with current preferences has to be to merit deference.

55. See Kagan, "Presidential Administration," 2347 (noting empirical evidence that independent agencies are more responsive to Congress than executive agencies are). Although more responsive to congressional preferences, independent agencies do remain responsive to presidential political preferences. See Terry Moe, "Regulatory Performance and Presidential Administration," 26 *American Journal of Political Science* 197, 220–221 (1982).

56. Rust v. Sullivan, 500 U.S. 173 (1991). Congress had passed a bill to overturn the interpretation, which President Bush vetoed.

57. See Kagan, "Presidential Administration," 2281–2319. I take no position here on whether such presidential authority over agencies is constitutionally protected or prohibited, or normatively desirable or not. See 2251, 2319–2363 (discussing these issues). My only point here is that, if such presidential authority is exercised in ways that mean agency action does not reflect current enactable preferences, then judicial deference based on likely agency correspondence to those preferences should be denied. Kagan takes the contrary view that presidential involvement should actually heighten, rather than weaken, *Chevron* deference; 2372–2380. But this is based on her adopting the premise I rejected in Chapter 2: the premise that where congressional intent is unclear, the default rule should reflect what she (or judicial judgment) regards as the wisest policy (2330–2363) even though that conflicts with enactable preferences; 2345 (acknowledging that "both Presidents [pursuing her approach] self-consciously put in place a set of policies that could not have succeeded in getting through Congress"). Kagan also acknowledges that her position does not fit the actual contours of the *Chevron* doctrine; 2373–2376.

58. See ibid., 2283.

59. FDA v. Brown & Williamson Tobacco Corp., 529 U.S. 120, 126, 137–138, 143–159 (2000).

60. Ibid., 183, 188–192 (Breyer, J., dissenting) ("Congress both failed to grant express authority to the FDA when the FDA denied it had jurisdiction over tobacco and failed to take that authority expressly away when the agency later asserted jurisdiction").

61. Ibid., 159 (citation omitted).

62. See Cass Sunstein, "*Chevron* Step Zero," 92 *Virginia Law Review* 187, 232 (2006).

63. See, e.g., Timothy Armstrong, "Chevron Deference and Agency Self-Interest," 13 *Cornell Journal of Law & Public Policy* 203, 261 (2004).
64. Miss. Power & Light Co. v. Mississippi ex rel. Moore, 487 U.S. 354, 381 (1988) (Scalia, J., concurring in judgment); see Ry. Labor Executives' Ass'n v. Nat'l Mediation Bd., 29 F.3d 655, 676–677 (D.C. Cir. 1994) (en banc) (Williams, J., dissenting); Quincy M. Crawford, "Comment, *Chevron* Deference to Agency Interpretations That Delimit the Scope of the Agency's Jurisdiction," 61 *University of Chicago Law Review* 957, 957 (1994). The concern motivating a scope of jurisdiction exception, although really applicable to all agency interpretations, is a real one: that agencies are biased in favor of expanding their own power. But the mechanisms for keeping this bias in check are the various forms of political accountability that make agencies relatively reliable determinants of current political preferences. See Daryl Levinson, "Empire-Building Government in Constitutional Law," 118 *Harvard Law Review* 915, 932–934 (2005) (arguing that agencies' political accountability will tend to curb any interest in expanding their jurisdiction).
65. *Brown & Williamson,* 529 U.S. at 159–161.
66. Dep't of Commerce v. U.S. House of Representatives, 525 U.S. 316, 334–341 (1999).
67. Ibid., 360–361 (Stevens, J., joined by Souter & Ginsburg, JJ., dissenting) (acknowledging that the use of samples had become a "partisan issue").
68. Ibid., 334–342. Three justices also relied on a general assessment that legislators would not prefer to change the method by which they are elected without some discussion: 342–343 (O'Connor, J., plurality opinion as to Part III.B, joined by Rehnquist, C. J., & Kennedy, J.).
69. 126 S.Ct. 904, 916–923 (2006).
70. On this point, the dissent by Justices Scalia, Roberts, and Thomas seemed more persuasive. Ibid., 926–939.
71. 126 S.Ct. 904, 913 (2006).
72. Ibid., 921.
73. Hamdan v. Rumsfeld, 126 S. Ct. 2749 (2006); Neal Kumar Katyal, "Comment—*Hamdan v. Rumsfeld,*" 120 *Harvard Law Review* 65, 105–114 (2006).
74. 126 S.Ct. at 2773–2775. Justice Kennedy's concurring opinion likewise stressed that the president's powers were at their lowest when he conflicted with congressional views. See also at 2800–2801.
75. Matthew Stephenson, "Legislative Allocation of Delegated Power," 119 *Harvard Law Review* 1035, 1043–1044 (2006).
76. Ibid., 1042, 1070.
77. See Matthew Stephenson, "The Strategic Substitution Effect," 120 *Harvard Law Review* 528, 537–549 (2006).
78. See Barnhart v. Walton, 535 U.S. 212, 221–222 (2002).
79. See Matthew C. Stephenson, *Optimal Political Control of the Bureaucracy* (July 26, 2007, draft presented at Harvard Law Faculty Workshop). In this draft, Stephenson calls the relevant political actors "the President" and the relevant

democratic preferences "majority preferences," but he is agnostic about which actors and preferences one considers relevant. The other debatable assumptions required for this result are the following.

First, he assumes a concave and symmetrical benefit curve, specifically that the relevant political actors suffer disutility that equals the square of the difference in policy units between their preferences and the agency position. However, on many (maybe most) issues, it is not clear there is any "unit" to determine the location of policy positions on a spectrum of policy views other than the utility divergence from the ideal points of others. For such issues, it would make no sense to say that disutility is an increasing function of utility deviation. On other issues, the symmetry assumption seems dubious. For example, political actors might think the optimal tax rate is 30%, but suffer much more disutility from going 1% above that rate than from going 1% below it. Finally, even if we have independent policy units, one might think that the marginal disutility of 1 unit of additional policy divergence from political preferences is the same whether the agency moves from 0 to 1 unit away, or from 999 to 1000 units away. For example, if one's optimal pollution standard for some pollutant were 1000 parts per million (ppm), it is not clear why a change from 1000 to 1001 ppm would be regarded as causing much less of a utility loss than a change from 1999 to 2000 ppm. Indeed, it might be that, past some threshold ppm, the bad effects of the pollutant are unchanged so that the latter change of 1 ppm causes less marginal disutility. Even if the disutility curve were an increasing function of policy distance, one might wonder about the extreme assumption that it varies with the square of the distance, which would mean that the latter change is 1999 times more harmful because the difference between 0^2 and 1^2 is 1, while the difference between 1000^2 and 999^2 is 1999. While his model predicts some insulation remains optimal even with lesser degrees of concavity, the degree of optimal insulation would be lower if the benefit curve were less steep.

Second, he assumes that the costs that political actors incur to influence agencies to change their positions turn only on the degree of agency insulation times the square of the distance the agency moves. Although a concave cost curve does strike me as likely because efforts to influence agencies will presumably first substitute for the least valuable alternative uses of political actor time, it seems to me this function should be multiplied by some factor reflecting the opportunity cost of that time. This wouldn't alter his conclusion that some insulation could be optimal, but would reduce the optimal degree of such insulation considerably. Further the opportunity costs of political actor time might be higher during some periods (say, wartime) than others, indicating the optimal degree of political insulation should also vary with these changing opportunity costs.

Third, in the case he argues is most plausible, he assumes that the costs that political actors incur to influence agencies to change their positions exceed the costs to voters from those efforts. But it is not clear this is true. Having to spend increasing amounts of time and effort bringing agencies into line with political views will necessarily substitute for other political activities like passing new legislation or planning wars, which will harm voters because Stephenson assumes that the expected views of the political actors match voter preferences. It seems plausible that the costs to voters from distracting political actors on other issues will typically exceed any costs to the political actors themselves. Stephenson anticipates and models this possibility, but considers it less plausible than I would. He concludes that, if this possibility is true, the optimal solution is either zero or total agency insulation, depending on whether the agency deviation from the relevant preferences exceeds the political variance from those preferences.

80. See Stephen M. Bainbridge & G. Mitu Gulati, "How Do Judges Maximize? (The Same Way Everybody Else Does—Boundedly)," 51 *Emory Law Journal* 83, 150–151 (2002) (arguing that self-interested judges will avoid issues or delegate them to law clerks to avoid the costs of analyzing the issues themselves); Frank B. Cross & Blake J. Nelson, "Strategic Institutional Effects on Supreme Court Decisionmaking," 95 *Northwestern University Law Review* 1437, 1481–1482 (2001) (discussing this theory for deference).

6. From Legislative Intent to Probabilistic Estimates

1. Colo. Rev. Stat. Ann. §2-4-201; Iowa Code Ann. §4.6; N.D. Cent. Code §1-02-39; Ohio Rev. Code Ann. §1.49; Minn. Stat. Ann. §645.16; N.J. Stat. Ann. §2A:58C-1; N.M. Stat. Ann. §12-2A-20; N.Y. Stat. Law §§124–125; 1 Pa. Cons. Stat. Ann. §1921; Tex. Gov't Code Ann. §311.023.

2. Ariz. Rev. Stat. Ann. §1-211(B); Ark. Code Ann. §1-2-202; Cal. Civ. Proc. Code §1859; Del. Code Ann. tit. 1, §301; Ga. Code Ann. §1-3-1(a); Haw. Rev. Stat. Ann. §1-15(2); Idaho Code §73-102(1); 5 Ill. Comp. Stat. Ann. 70/1.01; Ind. Code Ann. §§1-1-4-1, 1-1-4-5; Kan. Stat. Ann. §77-201; Ky. Rev. Stat. Ann. §446.080(1); La. Civ. Code Ann. art. 10; Mass. Ann. Laws ch. 4, §§6–7; Mich. Comp. Laws Ann. §8.3; Miss. Code Ann. §1-3-1; Mo. Ann. Stat. §1.010; Mont. Code Ann. §1-2-102; Neb. Rev. Stat. §§49-802, 49-806; N.H. Rev. Stat. Ann. §21:1; N.J. Stat. Ann. §1:1-1; N.C. Gen. Stat. §12-3; Okla. Stat. Ann. tit. 25, §29; Or. Rev. Stat. Ann. §174.020; R.I. Gen. Laws §43-3-2; S.D. Codified Laws §2-14-12; Utah Code Ann. §68-3-2; Vt. Stat. Ann. tit. 1, §101; Va. Code Ann. §§1–13, 8.2–5, 19.2–5; W. Va. Code Ann. §2-2-10; Wis. Stat. Ann. §§990.001, 990.01. In addition, the Washington legislature enacted a statute directing that its statutes be "liberally construed," Wash. Rev. Code Ann. §1.12.010, which probably was intended to authorize inquiries into legislative purposes and has been so read by the Washington courts. Dep't of Ecology v. Campbell & Gwinn, L.L.C., 43 P.3d 4, 9 (Wash. 2002). I include the New Jersey statute here because the statute cited in the preceding note concerned the legislative history of a particular act, whereas the statute in this note is the one that generally applies to all statutory construction. Because I counted it before, I omit counting it here to avoid double-counting.

3. Keifer & Keifer v. Reconstruction Fin. Corp., 306 U.S. 381, 389 (1939); John F. Manning, "Textualism as a Nondelegation Doctrine," 97 *Columbia Law Review*

673, 733–737 & n.253 (1997)(collecting cases); Archibald Cox, "Judge Learned Hand and the Interpretation of Statutes," 60 *Harvard Law Review* 370, 379 (1947); Felix Frankfurter, "Some Reflections on the Reading of Statutes," 47 *Columbia Law Review* 527, 539 (1947).

4. Rumsfeld v. FAIR, 126 S.Ct. 1297, 1304–1306 (2006).

5. See *Keifer,* 306 U.S. at 389; Frankfurter, "Some Reflections," 539.

6. See, e.g., FDA v. Brown & Williamson Tobacco Corp., 529 U.S. 120, 132–133 (2000); Pub. Employees Ret. Sys. v. Betts, 492 U.S. 158 (1989); United States v. Monsanto, 491 U.S. 600 (1989); United States v. Fausto, 484 U.S. 439, 453 (1988). However, the theory here (and doctrine just cited) is supplementary: it would not justify interpreting a statute contrary to legislative preferences in order to avoid an inconsistency that apparently did not bother the legislature. See Chapter 2.

7. Haw. Rev. Stat. Ann. §1-16; La. Civ. Code Ann. art. 13; Minn. Stat. Ann. §645.16; Colo. Rev. Stat. Ann. §2-4-203; Iowa Code Ann. §4.6; N.D. Cent. Code §1-02-39; Ohio Rev. Code Ann. §1.49; 1 Pa. Cons. Stat. Ann. §1921; Tex. Gov't Code Ann. §311.023; N.M. Stat. Ann. §12-2A-20; N.Y. Stat. Law §§221–223.

8. Max Radin, "Statutory Interpretation," 43 *Harvard Law Review* 863, 870–871 (1930); Easterbrook, "Statutes' Domains," 50 *University of Chicago Law Review* 533, 547–548 (1983); Kenneth A. Shepsle, "Congress Is a 'They,' Not an 'It': Legislative Intent as Oxymoron," 12 *International Review of Law & Economics* 239, 239 (1992).

9. Radin, "Statutory Interpretation," 870.

10. For sources supporting the propositions in this paragraph, see Einer R. Elhauge, "Does Interest Group Theory Justify More Intrusive Judicial Review?" 101 *Yale Law Journal* 31, 102 (1991); Alan Schwartz, "Statutory Interpretation, Capture, and Tort Law," 2 *American Law & Economics Review* 1, 13–15 (2000); Dennis Mueller, *Public Choice II* (New York: Cambridge University Press, 1989), 196–203; Daniel A. Farber & Philip P. Frickey, *Law and Public Choice* (Chicago: University of Chicago Press, 1991), 49–55; Matthew D. McCubbins, Roger G. Noll, & Barry R. Weingast, "Structure and Process, Politics and Policy: Administrative Arrangements and the Political Control of Agencies," 75 *Virginia Law Review* 431, 433–445 (1989); Kenneth Shepsle & Barry Weingast, "Structure-Induced Equilibrium and Legislative Choice," 37 *Public Choice* 503 (1981).

11. See Elhauge, "Interest Group Theory," 104–105.

12. See Manning, "Textualism as Nondelegation," 679–680 nn.22 & 27.

13. McNollgast, "Positive Canons: The Role of Legislative Bargains in Statutory Interpretation," 80 *Georgetown Law Journal* 705, 720–727 (1992). If the actors' political preferences lay on both sides of the status quo, then no legislation could be enacted, because some actor would veto any shift from the status quo in a direction unfavorable to it.

14. The veto point for each actor is the point at which the proposal has gotten so far away from its ideal point that it would prefer the status quo, and would thus veto the proposal. Ibid., 722–724. When one actor requires the concurrence of a second actor to make its veto stick, like a president who needs the political

support of one-third of the legislators to sustain his veto, the collective veto point of the two actors will be the furthest of their two veto points from the status quo (722–724).

15. See John F. Manning, "Textualism and the Equity of the Statute," 101 *Columbia Law Review* 1, 18, 20–22 (2001) (collecting sources).

16. Easterbrook, "Statutes' Domains," 548.

17. See Conroy v. Aniskoff, 507 U.S. 511, 518–528 (1993) (Scalia, J., concurring in the judgment); Radin, "Statutory Interpretation," 870–871.

18. See Daniel A. Farber & Philip P. Frickey, "Legislative Intent and Public Choice," 74 *Virginia Law Review* 423, 445 (1988); Matthew McCubbins, Roger G. Noll, & Barry Weingast, "Legislative Intent: The Use of Positive Political Theory in Statutory Interpretation," 57 *Law & Contemporary Problems* 3, 24–26 (1994). In one sense, legislative history is likely to be far more accurate than the extrinsic evidence commonly used to interpret unclear contracts. Precontract statements are often oral, or documented in only a fragmentary fashion, raising serious questions about the accuracy of any finding about what statements were made. For legislative history, there is usually little argument that some official documentary source accurately recorded what was stated. The dispute is just whether what was stated reflects correctly the legislature's views.

19. Stephen F. Ross, "Where Have You Gone Karl Llewellyn? Should Congress Turn Its Lonely Eyes To You?" 45 *Vanderbilt Law Review* 561, 575–576 (1992).

20. E.g., Clarke v. Sec. Indus. Ass'n, 479 U.S. 388, 407 (1987); Bd. of Governors, FRS v. Dimension Fin. Corp., 474 U.S. 361, 372 (1986).

21. See American Bar Association (ABA), *Report of the Task Force on Presidential Signing Statements and the Separation of Powers Doctrine* (2006).

22. Garber & Wimmer, "Presidential Signing Statements as Interpretations of Legislative Intent: An Executive Aggrandizement of Power," 24 *Harvard Journal on Legislation* 363 (1989).

23. ABA, *Report*, 26.

24. Hamdan v. Rumsfeld, 126 S.Ct. 2749, 2816 & n.5 (2006) (Scalia, J., dissenting).

25. United States v. Story, 891 F.2d 988, 994 (2nd Cir. 1989).

26. See Civil Rights Act of 1991, Pub. L. No. 102–166, §105(b), 105 Stat. 1071 (1991) ("No statements other than the interpretive memorandum . . . shall be considered legislative history.").

27. See Thompson v. Thompson, 484 U.S. 174, 191–192 (1988) (Scalia, J., dissenting); Manning, "Textualism as Nondelegation," 696–699 (collecting sources).

28. See Manning, "Textualism as Nondelegation," 702–705.

29. See William N. Eskridge, Jr., "Textualism, The Unknown Ideal?" 96 *Michigan Law Review* 1509, 1522–1532 (1998).

30. Manning, "Textualism and Equity," 8–9, 36–105. Manning's analysis consciously excludes the case of statutory ambiguities; 3 n.3. Indeed, the passages of the *Federalist Papers* that he cites in support of the faithful agent theory include statements that, in cases of statutory ambiguity, courts should follow the "pleasure" or "will" of the legislature, or "sense" of its provisions "apart from any technical rules"; 82–84 & n.325.

31. Eyston v. Studd, 75 Eng. Rep. 688, 699 (K.B. 1574) (Plowden's note); see also 1 Blackstone, Commentaries, 105, *62 (noting that equity of statute conferred a "power vested of defining those circumstances, which (had they been foreseen) the legislator himself would have expressed"). Other statements of the equity of the statute doctrine likewise stressed that it must be used to further the statutory "purpose," "cause," "sense," "reason," "spirit," "motive," "object," or "intentions." Manning, "Textualism and Equity," 8, 32–36, 101 n.390–392 (collecting sources).

32. See Bank One Chi., N.A. v. Midwest Bank & Trust Co., 516 U.S. 264, 279–280 (1996) (Scalia, J., concurring in part and concurring in the judgment); Manning, "Textualism as Nondelegation," 675–676, 699–737. This argument should be distinguished from the argument, also made by Scalia and others, that relying on legislative history violates the general nondelegation doctrine that limits the legislature's ability to delegate its legislative powers to anyone else. The general nondelegation doctrine has little if any bite, and in any event would not explain why courts should reject legislative history but rely on dictionary or treatise writers, agencies, or judicial precedent. Here, the objection is to legislative self-aggrandizement, rather than to legislative self-abnegation.

33. See Manning, "Textualism as Nondelegation," 675 n.9, 725.

34. See ibid., 679–680, 683–684, 721.

35. Manning, "Textualism as Nondelegation," 706–707.

36. See Nicholas Quinn Rosenkranz, "Federal Rules of Statutory Interpretation," 115 *Harvard Law Review* 2085, 2136–2137 (2002); Jonathan R. Siegel, "The Use of Legislative History in a System of Separated Powers," 53 *Vanderbilt Law Review* 1457, 1479–1480 (2000).

37. Colo. Rev. Stat. Ann. §2-4-201 (West 2000); Iowa Code Ann. §4.4 (West 2001); Minn. Stat. Ann. §645.17 (West 1946); N.M. Stat Ann. §12-2A-18 (Michie 1978); N.D. Cent. Code §1-02-38 (1987); Ohio Rev. Code Ann. §1.47 (West 1994); 1 Pa. Cons. Stat. Ann. §1922 (West 1995); Tex. Gov't Code Ann. §311.021 (Vernon 1998); Hooper v. California, 155 U.S. 648, 657 (1895); United States v. Booker, 543 U.S. 220, 245–65 (2005).

38. 543 U.S. at 248.

7. Moderation, Unforeseen Circumstances, and a Theory of Meaning

1. There might also be positive odds that legislative deadlock or preferences would have prevented either interpretation from being enacted. In that event, though, minimizing the dissatisfaction of enactable preferences would involve figuring out the relative likelihood of each interpretive option being enacted, if the legislative polity had made a choice. For example, if the first option is 30% likely to be what the legislature would have enacted, and the second option is 20% likely, the first is more likely to minimize political dissatisfaction, and the relative probabilities (as I am using the term) of enactability among the two options would be 60% and 40%. Sometimes the odds of deadlock might be so high that there is no relevant enactable preference for a particular legislative polity. In such cases, where neither current nor enactor preference default rules provide

any answer, the court must turn to the preference-eliciting or supplemental default rules described in Parts III and IV.

2. Because the probabilities are relative, they add up to 100%, even though there might also be positive odds that legislative preferences or deadlock would have prevented any of the interpretive options from being enacted. For example, if the odds of deadlock were 50%, and the odds of options 1, 2, and 3 being enacted were, respectively, 20%, 15%, and 15%, then the relative odds of enactment if the government had made a choice would, respectively, be 40%, 30%, and 30%.

3. See Ian Ayres, "Default Rules for Incomplete Contracts," in Peter Newman, ed., 1 *The New Palgrave Dictionary of Economics and the Law* (New York: Stockton Press, 1998), 585–586; Ian Ayres, "Making a Difference: The Contractual Contributions of Easterbrook & Fischel," 59 *University of Chicago Law Review* 1391, 1402 (1992); David Charny, "Hypothetical Bargains: The Normative Structure of Contract Interpretation," 89 *Michigan Law Review* 1815, 1816–1817 (1991).

4. Note that these percentages do not correspond to the share of persons who hold that view, but rather to the relative odds that this position would be enactable. Intensely interested persons often have more influence than their numbers alone would suggest, making the odds that their favored position is enactable exceed their numbers.

5. Einer Elhauge, "Preference-Estimating Statutory Default Rules," 102 *Columbia Law Review* 2027, 2079–2080 (2002). In contracts and corporate charters, the problem arises in a somewhat different guise. There the usual question is what to do when the population entering into contracts or corporate charters differ in what default rule they would prefer, but the court cannot tell them apart, and no single default rule seems likely to command a majority. Thus, for contracts and corporate charters, this question would normally be framed as which of the "minority" options to choose as a general default rule, in a case where tailoring seems impossible. Here, in contrast, I am assuming that courts are tailoring, and the percentages do not refer to the share of the population that favors a particular statutory interpretation. Rather, the percentages here refer to the estimated odds that the interpretation could have been enacted, if the enactors had been required to make a choice. But the same answer is appropriate. The parallel is even clearer if the issue concerns tailored contract or corporate default rules, where the court is tailoring the default rule and is uncertain what the parties would have wanted.

6. Univ. of Cal. Bd. of Regents v. Bakke, 438 U.S. 265, 269–320 (1978).

7. See Robert Charles Clark, *Corporate Law* (Boston: Little, Brown, 1986), 29, 219–221, 234–262, 761–800.

8. See ibid., 234–262 (collecting cases that fit this account).

9. Sinclair Refining Co. v. Atkinson, 370 U.S. 195, 207 (1962).

10. Boys Markets, Inc. v. Retail Clerks Union, Local 770, 398 U.S. 235, 243 (1970).

11. Ibid., 244–249. In the alternative, the Court also concluded that the 1962 decision was wrongly decided because it failed to take into account the fact that by 1962 congressional policy had shifted from its 1932 preference for protecting the labor movement from federal courts that were then promanagement to a

preference for "administrative techniques for the peaceful resolution of industrial disputes"; 249–253. That is, the Court faulted the 1962 decision for applying an enactor preferences default rule rather than a current preferences default rule. See Part I.

12. See Guido Calabresi, *A Common Law for the Age of Statutes* (Cambridge, Mass.: Harvard University Press, 1982), 2, 6–7, 82, 100–104, 163–166; Ronald Dworkin, *Law's Empire* (Cambridge, Mass.: Harvard University Press, 1986), 348–350; William N. Eskridge, Jr., *Dynamic Statutory Interpretation* (Cambridge, Mass.: Harvard University Press: 1994), 167–170; Richard Posner, *Overcoming Law* (Cambridge, Mass.: Harvard University Press, 1995), 231; Daniel A. Farber, "Statutory Interpretation and Legislative Supremacy," 78 *Georgetown Law Journal* 281, 282–283, 306–317 (1989); Lawrence Lessig, "Fidelity in Translation," 71 *Texas Law Review* 1165, 1166–1173 (1993); Cass R. Sunstein, "Interpreting Statutes in the Regulatory State," 103 *Harvard Law Review* 405, 412, 439, 493–496 (1989).

13. See People v. Barnett, 319 Ill. 403 (1925); Commonwealth v. Welosky, 276 Mass. 398 (1931).

14. See Commonwealth v. Maxwell, 271 Pa. 378 (1921).

15. See, e.g., United States v. X-Citement Video, Inc., 513 U.S. 64, 68–69 (1994); Pub. Citizen v. Dep't of Justice, 491 U.S. 440, 454 (1989); Church of The Holy Trinity v. United States, 143 U.S. 457, 459 (1892).

16. U.S. v. Kirby, 74 U.S. 482, 487 (1868); see also 1 Blackstone, *Commentaries*, *60.

17. See Brogan v. United States, 522 U.S. 398, 406 (1998) (Scalia, J., opinion for the Court); Rotella v. Wood, 528 U.S. 549, 560–561 (2000) (opinion joined by Scalia & Thomas, JJ.); Frank H. Easterbrook, "The Case of the Speluncean Explorers: Revisited," 112 *Harvard Law Review* 1913, 1913–1914 (1999); John F. Manning, "Textualism and the Equity of the Statute," 101 *Columbia Law Review* 1, 113–114 (2001).

18. Easterbrook, "Speluncean Explorers," 1913–1914; Manning, "Textualism and Equity," 113–115.

19. United States v. Ron Pair Enters., Inc., 489 U.S. 235, 242 (1989) (quoting Griffin v. Oceanic Contractors, Inc., 458 U.S. 564, 571 [1982]); Mova Pharm. Corp. v. Shalala, 140 F.3d 1060, 1068 (D.C. Cir. 1998).

20. Sturges v. Crowninshield, 17 U.S. (4 Wheat.) 70, 107 (1819) (Marshall, C. J.).

21. John F. Manning, "The Absurdity Doctrine," 116 *Harvard Law Review* 2387 (2003); Adrian Vermeule, *Judging Under Uncertainty* (Cambridge, Mass.: Harvard University Press, 2006), 43.

22. See Steve Shavell, "On the Writing and the Interpretation of Contracts," 22 *Journal of Law, Economics & Organization* 289 (2006).

23. This is the only form of opt-out Professor Shavell considers. See ibid., 292, 305–306.

24. See Green v. Bock Laundry Machine Co., 490 U.S. 504 (1989); Cernauskas v. Fletcher, 211 Ark. 678 (1947).

25. Haw. Rev. Stat. Ann. §1-15; La. Civ. Code Ann. art. 9; Minn. Stat. Ann. §645.17; 1 Pa. Cons. Stat. Ann. §1922; N.M. Stat. Ann. §12-2A-18; N.Y. Stat. Law §145.

8. Eliciting Legislative Preferences

1. The parallel theory of penalty default rules for contract law, which inspires this theory of preference-eliciting statutory default rules, was first developed by Ian Ayres and Robert Gertner, who in a brief aside were also the first to suggest that it might be extended to statutory interpretation. See Ian Ayres & Robert Gertner, "Filling Gaps in Incomplete Contracts: An Economic Theory of Default Rules," 99 *Yale Law Journal* 87, 129–130 (1989).

2. See, e.g., W. Va. Univ. Hosps., Inc. v. Casey, 499 U.S. 83, 113–115 (1991) (Stevens, J., dissenting) (supposing so); Michael E. Solimine & James L. Walker, "The Next Word: Congressional Response to Supreme Court Statutory Decisions," 65 *Temple Law Review* 425, 431–433 (1992) (collecting legal scholarship asserting that the existence of statutory overrides shows that the plain meaning canon is mistaken).

3. Ayres & Gertner, "Filling Gaps," 93, 97–98, 127–128.

4. This should be distinguished from the case where the legislature correctly understood the degree of ambiguity, but did not think the cost of legislative resolution was worthwhile. In such a case, a preference-eliciting default rule is not merited because it would impose costs on the legislature that, in the legislature's own judgment, exceed the benefits of resolving the ambiguity. Such a legislature would thus prefer to have the ambiguity resolved by courts or agencies, preferably the latter because they are more responsive to prevailing political preferences.

5. Easterbrook, "Statutes' Domains," *University of Chicago Law Review* 533, 540–543 (1983).

6. See William N. Eskridge, Jr., "Overriding Supreme Court Statutory Interpretation Decisions," 101 *Yale Law Journal* 331, 334–336, 338–340, 344–345, 397 (1991). Congress overrode 121 Supreme Court statutory interpretations in the period 1967–90, and 98 in 1975–90 (338). This amounts to five to six decisions a year, which is 6–8% of the 80 statutory interpretations the Court on average issued a year during this period (339 n.15).

7. Ibid., 336 n.7.

8. Elhauge, "Preference-Eliciting Statutory Default Rules," 102 *Columbia Law Review* 2162, 2181–2183 (2002). For extensions to cases where there are interim costs, or where the aim is to elicit a third option C that is not a plausible interpretation available to the interpreter, see 2286–2290.

9. See Eskridge, "Overriding," at 348, 351, 410; see also Harry P. Stumpf, "Congressional Response to Supreme Court Rulings: The Interaction of Law and Politics," 14 *Journal of Public Law* 391–392 (1965) (collecting data showing that Congress overrides Supreme Court decisions when interest groups are on only one side of the issue).

10. See Kay Lehman Schlozman & John T. Tierney, *Organized Interests and American Democracy* (New York: Harper & Row, 1986), 314–315, 395–396, 398.

11. Jonathan Macey, "Promoting Public-Regarding Legislation Through Statutory Interpretation: An Interest Group Model," 86 *Columbia Law Review* 223, 236–240 (1986).

12. Ibid., 228 n.29, 252. Under default rules that maximize political satisfaction, the canon against derogations from the common law has a far more limited role. See Chapter 14.

13. Neal Kumar Katyal, "Comment—*Hamdan v. Rumsfeld*," 120 *Harvard Law Review* 65, 95–96 (2006).

14. Hamdan v. Rumsfeld, 126 S. Ct. 2749, 2764 (2006). Having cited this canon, the Court went on to resolve the case on the basis of a linguistic canon that, we shall see in Chapter 10, tends to be applied more often when it furthers a preference-eliciting function.

15. See Michael T. Hayes, *Lobbyists and Legislators* (New Brunswick, N.J.: Rutgers University Press, 1981), 93–126; Eskridge, "Overriding," at 365–367, 377; Stumpf, "Congressional Response," 377, 391–392 (collecting data showing that Congress rarely overrides or changes Supreme Court decisions that provoke interest group activity on both sides).

16. Eskridge, "Overriding," 345 (finding that almost half the statutory overrides were within two years); Solimine & Walker, "The Next Word," 445 (finding that 56% were within two years).

17. See Stephen McG. Bundy & Einer Elhauge, "Knowledge About Legal Sanctions," 92 *Michigan Law Review* 261, 267–279 (1993).

9. Canons Favoring the Politically Powerless

1. United States v. Bass, 404 U.S. 336, 347–348 (1971).

2. Dan M. Kahan, "Lenity and Federal Common Law Crimes," 1994 *Supreme Court Review* 345, 354–356, 368–369.

3. William N. Eskridge, Jr., "Overriding Supreme Court Statutory Interpretation Decisions," 101 *Yale Law Journal* 331, 344 tbl.4 (1991). Moreover, Eskridge's exhaustive study understated this phenomenon because it missed those legislative overrides of rule of lenity decisions that were not explicitly flagged in the legislative history. See, for example, Hughey v. United States, 495 U.S. 411, 422 (1990) (interpreting statute not to allow restitution for harms caused by conduct for which no conviction was obtained in plea bargain), a case partially overridden by the Crime Control Act of 1990, 104 Stat. 4789, 4863 (codified at 18 U.S.C. §3663(a)(3) [2000]) (allowing restitution for harms caused by conduct for which no conviction was obtained if agreed to in plea bargain).

4. Eskridge, "Overriding," 348 tbl.7, 362.

5. Ibid.

6. 470 P.2d 617, 618–619 (Cal. 1970).

7. Some legislative history suggested a desire to adopt common law standards, and some old common law limited "murder" to killing a person born alive. However, this common law reflected older medical technology that meant an unborn fetus was not viable. Further, other common law (without calling it "murder") nonetheless imposed the death penalty on those who killed a "quickened" fetus before birth, thus suggesting no practical difference at common law. Ibid. at 624; at 630–631, 633 (Burke, J., dissenting).

8. Cal. Penal Code §187 (West 1999). Although consensual abortion was defined not to be murder, it was then punishable by two to five years in prison under California Penal Code §274. *Keeler*, 470 P.2d at 627, 631 n.2 (Burke, J., dissenting) (Cal. 1970).

9. 1 Blackstone, *Commentaries*, *88.

10. See, e.g., Ratzlaf v. United States, 510 U.S. 135 (1994), overruled by Pub. L. No. 103–325, §411, 108 Stat. 2160 (1994), codified at 31 U.S.C. §5321; McNally v. United States, 483 U.S. 350 (1987), overruled by Pub. L. 100–690, Title VII, §7603(a), 102 Stat. 4508 (1988), codified at 18 U.S.C. §1346.

11. Moskal v. United States, 498 U.S. 103, 108 (1990); NOW v. Scheidler, 510 U.S. 249, 262 (1994); Reno v. Koray, 515 U.S. 50, 65 (1995). The state courts have made similar statements. See Zachary Price, "The Rule of Lenity as a Rule of Structure," 72 *Fordham Law Review* 885, 904–905 (2004).

12. E.g., United States v. Lanier, 520 U.S. 259, 265 n.5 (1997); United States v. Aguilar, 515 U.S. 593, 600 (1995); Dowling v. United States, 473 U.S. 207, 213–214 (1985); *Bass*, 404 U.S. 336, 348 (1971); *Keeler*, 470 P.2d at 620–622.

13. See John Calvin Jeffries, Jr., "Legality, Vagueness, and the Construction of Penal Statutes," 71 *Virginia Law Review* 189, 203 n.40 (1985); Kahan, "Lenity," 348–349, 351–356, 367–381.

14. See, e.g., 15 U.S.C. §§78w(a), 78ff (2000) (giving agencies power to create rules governing securities).

15. See, e.g., *Bass*, 404 U.S. at 347–348; *Dowling*, 473 U.S. at 213–214. A variant of this argument might be that the "beyond a reasonable doubt" standard, which applies to establishing the facts of a crime, should also apply to establishing the law. See Gary Lawson, "Legal Theory: Proving the Law," 86 *Northwestern University Law Review* 859, 894–896 (1992); Richard Friedman, "Standard of Persuasion and the Distinction Between Fact and Law," 86 *Northwestern University Law Review* 916, 938–942 (1992). But once a court resolves a statutory ambiguity with a given interpretation, there is no longer any doubt about what the law is, just as any legal doubt is removed by a legislature's decision resolving its own ambiguous political preferences. The argument must thus rest on a claim that judicial lawmaking to resolve legal doubts is less appropriate than legislative lawmaking, which is a claim I already addressed above.

16. See Eskridge, "Overriding," 413; Kahan, "Lenity," 349 n.16 (collecting articles).

17. See generally Chapter 16.

18. E.g., United States v. Lanier, 520 U.S. 259, 265–266 (1997); United States v. Aguilar, 515 U.S. 593, 600 (1995); *Bass*, 404 U.S. at 347–348; McBoyle v. United States, 283 U.S. 25, 27 (1931); *Keeler*, 470 P.2d 617, 626.

19. Isaac Ehrlich & Richard A. Posner, "An Economic Analysis of Legal Rulemaking," 3 *Journal of Legal Studies* 257, 262–263 (1974).

20. See Stephen McG. Bundy & Einer Elhauge, "Knowledge About Legal Sanctions," 92 *Michigan Law Review* 261, 308–309, 323–327 (1993).

21. Lanier, 520 U.S. at 266–268; Wainwright v. Stone, 414 U.S. 21, 22–23 (1973). For these reasons, I would reject the suggestion, by some, that the rule of lenity might be required by the due process clause. See William N. Eskridge, Jr., &

Philip P. Frickey, "Quasi-Constitutional Law," 45 *Vanderbilt Law Review* 593, 600 (1992); Nicholas Quinn Rosenkranz, "Federal Rules of Statutory Interpretation," 115 *Harvard Law Review* 2085, 2093–2094 (2002). Any due process concerns would be fully vindicated by a judicial decision that adopts a clear evenhanded interpretation for prospective application (and thus provides the requisite notice to future criminals), but holds that the past statutory ambiguity means the statute cannot be applied to past cases under the void-for-vagueness doctrine. Further, the relevant notice concerns are weak, for reasons discussed in the following text.

22. A similar point is made by Jeffries, "Legality, Vagueness," 220–223.

23. Ibid., 205–212.

24. See Nash v. United States, 229 U.S. 373, 376–378 (1913). Criminal violations do require proof either of an anticompetitive intent or of knowledge that anticompetitive effects were probable and in fact ensued. United States v. United States Gypsum, 438 U.S. 422, 444 & n.21 (1978). However, criminal enforcement is not limited to per se violations, and indictments have even been sustained against conduct that other district courts found legal under the rule of reason. Phillip E. Areeda, Roger D. Blair, & Herbert Hovenkamp, 2 *Antitrust Law*, 2d ed. (New York: Aspen Law & Business, 2000), ¶303, 29–30.

25. Carpenter v. United States, 484 U.S. 19 (1987).

26. See United States v. O'Hagan, 521 U.S. 642, 650 (1997); 680 (Thomas, J., concurring in the judgment in part and dissenting in part).

27. For works arguing that many antitrust violations should be legal, see, e.g., Robert H. Bork, *The Antitrust Paradox* (New York Basic Books, 1978), 288–298. For works arguing that insider trading may be desirable, see, e.g., Stephen M. Bainbridge, *Securities Law: Insider Trading* (New York Foundation Press, 1999), 127–139; Frank H. Easterbrook & Daniel R. Fischel, *The Economic Structure of Corporate Law* (Cambridge, MA: Harvard University Press, 1991), 256–259. The federal mail and wire fraud statutes, have also been given expansive readings in the face of ambiguous statutory language, covering not only misappropriation but a range of other ambiguously defined misconduct. See *Carpenter*, 484 U.S. at 28; Jeffries, "Legality, Vagueness," 199 n.26; Kahan, "Lenity," 373–381. Moreover, although common law fraud seems to be *malum in se*, statutory fraud extends far beyond to include all acts by which undue advantage is taken of another, and the particular line to draw about what counts as fraud is highly regulatory and *malum prohibitum*, extending for example to misuse of confidential information and depriving another of the intangible right of honest services. Kahan, "Lenity," 374–375. Scholarly opinion is split on whether many forms of statutory fraud should be criminal at all. See, e.g., John C. Coffee, Jr., "Paradigms Lost," 101 *Yale Law Journal* 1875, 1878–1879 (1992).

28. See William N. Eskridge, Jr., *Dynamic Statutory Interpretation* (Cambridge, Mass.: Harvard University Press, 1994), 153 (reporting study showing that business lobbies have more ability than typical criminal defendants to get adverse statutory interpretations reversed in Congress).

29. See Michael T. Hayes, *Lobbyists and Legislators* (New Brunswick, N.J.: Rutgers University Press, 1981), 93–126; Eskridge, *Dynamic,* 365–367 (noting that both the U.S. Department of Justice and business interests were able to secure considerable legislative attention and support for efforts to overturn adverse interpretations of antitrust or RICO, but conflict between them meant neither could succeed in securing legislative override of adverse decisions).

30. In an illuminating article, Dan Kahan advocates wholesale repudiation of the rule of lenity as an interference with legislative delegation to courts, but this rests on his implicit premise (wrong in my view) that all cases of ambiguity in criminal statutes involve intentional delegations. Kahan, "Lenity," 348–349, 353–354.

31. Price, "The Rule," 902–903; Cal. Penal Code §4.

32. Jeffries, "Legality, Vagueness," 198. Recognizing this distinction was a Senate Report that proposed a statute with similar "fair import" language. See S. Rep. No. 96–553, at 22 (1980). The avowed aim was to repeal whatever vestiges remained of the doctrine of strict construction of criminal statutes. S. Rep. No. 95–605, at 23 (1977). But the Senate Report recognized that this differed sharply from "lenity," which applied only if ambiguity persisted after reference to all extra-textual sources of meaning (24).

33. E.g., Nat'l Gerimedical Hosp. & Gerontology Ctr. v. Blue Cross, 452 U.S. 378, 388–389 (1981); Group Life & Health Ins. Co. v. Royal Drug Co., 440 U.S. 205, 231 (1979); S. Motor Carriers Rate Conference, Inc. v. United States, 471 U.S. 48, 57, 60–61, 62–63 (1985); United States v. Wells Fargo Bank, 485 U.S. 351, 354–359 (1988).

34. See Eskridge, "Overriding," 348 (organized business groups are second only to the U.S. Government in their success rate at getting statutory interpretations overridden by Congress); Michael E. Solimine & James L. Walker, "The Next Word: Congressional Response to Supreme Court Statutory Decisions," 65 *Temple Law Review* 425, 446 (1992) (cases that interpret taxation and economic regulation against business interest groups are overridden at a higher rate). For example, the decision denying a tax exemption in United States v. Hendler, 303 U.S. 564 (1938), was legislatively overridden in 1939. See Gen. Couns. Mem. 34,483 (Apr. 21, 1971), available at 1971 WL 28973.

35. See Kay Lehman Schlozman & John T. Tierney, *Organized Interests and American Democracy* (New York: Harper & Row, 1986), 314–315, 395–396, 398.

36. United Dominion Indus. v. United States, 532 U.S. 822, 838–839 (2001) (Thomas, J., concurring) (collecting cases); 839–841 & n.1 (Stevens, J., dissenting) (collecting cases).

37. See, e.g., May v. Heiner, 281 U.S. 238, 245 (1930) (applying canon that "doubt must be resolved in favor of the taxpayer"), overridden by Act of Mar. 3, 1931, ch. 454, 46 Stat. 1516 (1931) (codified at 26 U.S.C. §2036(a) [2000]).

38. United Dominion, 532 U.S. at 838–839 (Thomas, J. concurring) (stating that the canon favoring taxpayers only applied when the "provision of the Code and the corresponding regulations are ambiguous").

39. Zadvydas v. Davis, 533 U.S. 678 (2001); Clark v. Martinez, 543 U.S. 371 (2005).

40. Graham v. Richardson, 403 U.S. 365, 372 (1971) (concluding that "[a]liens as a class are a prime example of a 'discrete and insular' minority").

41. 543 U.S. at 386 & n.8; Senate bill S.2611, §202; House bill, H.R. 4437, §401.

42. INS v. St. Cyr, 533 U.S. 289, 298–300 (2001), overridden by Pub. L. 109–13, Div. B, Title I, §106, 119 Stat. 304 (May 11, 2005).

43. Fong Haw Tan v. Phelan, 333 U.S. 6, 9–10 (1948).

44. See United States v. Carolene Prods. Co., 304 U.S. 144, 153 n.4 (1938); John Hart Ely, *Democracy and Distrust: A Theory of Judicial Review* (Cambridge, Mass.: Harvard University Press, 1980), 75–77.

45. See Laurence H. Tribe, "The Puzzling Persistence of Process-Based Constitutional Theories," 89 *Yale Law Journal* 1072–1077 (1980).

46. Bruce A. Ackerman, "Beyond Carolene Products," 98 *Harvard Law Review* 713, 722–731 (1985).

47. Rust v. Sullivan, 500 U.S. 173, 190–191 (1991).

48. Bryan v. Itasca County, 426 U.S. 373, 392–393 (1976); Worcester v. Georgia, 31 U.S. (6 Pet.) 515, 552 (1832).

49. Choate v. Trapp, 224 U.S. 665, 675 (1912).

50. South Carolina v. Catawba Indian Tribe, Inc., 476 U.S. 498, 506 (1986).

10. Linguistic Canons of Statutory Construction

1. Karl N. Llewellyn, "Remarks on the Theory of Appellate Decision and the Rules or Canons About How Statutes Are to Be Construed," 3 *Vanderbilt Law Review* 395, 401–406 (1950). Of the 28 canon pairs that Llewellyn asserted were in conflict, canon pairs 2–11, 13–19, 21, and 23–27 are of this variety, and arguably canon pair 28 is as well, depending on the meaning given to a statute's "equity."

2. Ibid., 397–401.

3. Ibid., 405 (canon 20); 2A Norman J. Singer, *Sutherland Statutory Construction* §47.23, 216–217 (5th ed. 1992); Hawkeye Chem. Co. v. St. Paul Fire & Marine Ins. Co., 510 F.2d 322, 326–327 (7th Cir. 1975).

4. See Llewellyn, "Remarks," 405 (canon 20); Singer, *Sutherland Statutory Construction*, §47.25, at 234.

5. City of Detroit v. Township of Redford, 235 N.W. 217, 218–219 (Mich. 1931), overridden by Act of May 29, 1931, No. 233, §2250, 1931 Mich. Pub. Acts 408, 408.

6. Act of June 2, 1909, No. 279, §14, 1909 Mich. Pub. Acts 509, 509.

7. Springer v. Philippine Islands, 277 U.S. 189, 200, 206–208 (1928).

8. See Organic Act, ch. 416, 39 Stat. 545 (1916).

9. Hamdan v. Rumsfeld, 126 S. Ct. 2749, 2765 (2006).

10. See City of Columbus v. Ours Garage, 536 U.S. 424 (2002).

11. Llewellyn, "Remarks," at 405 (canon 22); Singer, *Sutherland Statutory Construction*, §47.17, at 188; Hull Hosp., Inc. v. Wheeler, 250 N.W. 637, 638 (Iowa 1933).

12. Llewellyn, "Remarks," 405 (canon 22); Singer, *Sutherland Statutory Construction*, §47.22, at 210.

13. Hull Hospital, 250 N.W. at 639, overridden by Act of Mar. 10, 1934, ch. 131, §1, 1934 Iowa Acts 255, 255–257 (codified at Iowa Code Ann. §582.1–582.4).

14. Texas v. United States, 292 U.S. 522, 534 (1934).

15. Grosjean v. Am. Paint Works, 160 So. 449, 452–453 (La. Ct. App. 1935).

16. Llewellyn, "Remarks," 401–403 (canons 1 & 12).

17. In Newhall v. Sanger, 92 U.S. 761, 766 (1875), the only tangential reference to the plain meaning rule did not bear on the statute actually being adjudicated, and thus did not invoke a plain meaning rule in any way that might trigger a legislative reaction.

18. First Nat'l Bank of Webster Springs v. De Berriz, 105 S.E. 900, 901 (W. Va. 1921), overridden by W. Va. Code Ann. §44–8–7 note (Michie 1997).

19. Ronald Dworkin, *Law's Empire* (Cambridge, Mass.: Harvard University Press, 1986), 15–23, 313–354.

20. Tenn. Valley Auth. v. Hill, 437 U.S. 153, 160, 163–64, 167, 170–171, 173, 194–195 (1978); Dworkin, *Law's Empire,* 313.

21. Riggs v. Palmer, 22 N.E. 188, 189 (N.Y. 1889).

22. 437 U.S. at 165, 173–187.

23. Ibid., 189–193.

24. See ibid., 187–188, 194.

25. 437 U.S. at 195 (majority); 210 (dissent). For the statutory overrides, see Endangered Species Act Amendments of 1978, Pub. L. No. 95–632, 92 Stat. 3751, 3755–3760, 3761 (codified as amended at 16 U.S.C. §§1531–40 [2000]); Energy and Water Development Appropriation Act, Pub. L. No. 96–69, 93 Stat. 437, 449 (1979) (codified as amended at 16 U.S.C. §1539 [2000]).

26. *Riggs,* 22 N.E. at 189.

27. More precisely, the clear exception was for heirs who intentionally murdered unwilling victims. More difficult questions would be raised by mercy killings or if the killer were insane or negligent, or if the issue were whether the blameless children of the murderer could inherit. But none of those complications was raised by the broad set of cases that *Riggs* considered.

28. William N. Eskridge, Jr., "Overriding Supreme Court Statutory Interpretation Decisions," 101 *Yale Law Journal* 331, 350 tbl.8 (1991) (Congress overrode 13.4% of plain meaning interpretations, and 4.4% of interpretations using legislative history or statutory purpose); Michael E. Solimine & James L. Walker, "The Next Word: Congressional Response to Supreme Court Statutory Decisions," 65 *Temple Law Review* 425, 448 chart 3 (1992) (over 60% of overridden cases invoked plain meaning canon, whereas less than 20% of all statutory construction cases did); see also 431 & n.41 (collecting other sources noting that textualist opinions are frequently overturned by Congress). Decisions that relied on other canons of construction were overturned at a rate of 12%, also around three times the rate of opinions resting on legislative history or statutory purpose. Eskridge, "Overriding," 350 tbl.8.

29. See, e.g., Pub. Employees Ret. Sys. v. Betts, 492 U.S. 158, 164, 168 (1989) (inviting override of plain meaning interpretation of the Age Discrimination in Employment Act); Teleprompter Corp. v. CBS, 415 U.S. 394, 414 & n.16 (1974)

(inviting override of an interpretation of the Copyright Act, that Court acknowledged did not take into account changes in technology).

30. See Pepper v. Hart, 1993 App. Cas. 593, 594 (appeal taken from Eng.); T. St. J. N. Bates, "The Contemporary Use of Legislative History in the United Kingdom," 54 *Cambridge Law Journal* 127–128 (1995).

31. See Adrian Vermeule, "Legislative History and the Limits of Judicial Competence," 50 *Stanford Law Review* 1833, 1836 & n.15 (1998).

32. See Robert G. Vaughn, "A Comparative Analysis of the Influence of Legislative History on Judicial Decision-Making and Legislation," 7 *Indiana International & Comparative Law Review* 1, 6–7 (1996).

33. Eskridge, "Overriding," 337 n.12. One study found that congressional staff were generally unaware of even D.C. Circuit statutory interpretations, whose importance and proximity would seem to make it the most likely federal appellate court to trigger congressional attention. See Robert A. Katzmann, *Courts and Congress* (Washington, D.C.: Brookings Institution Press, 1997), 69–76. This may be because Congress relies on Supreme Court review of lower court decisions for the very narrow set of cases at issue—those where meaning and preferences are unclear, and the other conditions for a preference-eliciting default rule are met—especially because such conditions seem the ones most likely to generate circuit splits necessitating Supreme Court review.

11. Interpretations That May Create International Conflict

1. Murray v. Schooner Charming Betsy, 6 U.S. 64, 118 (1804); Restatement (Third) of Foreign Relations Law §§114–115 (1987).

2. EEOC v. Arabian Am. Oil Co. (Aramco), 499 U.S. 244, 248 (1991); Hartford Fire Insur. v. California, 509 U.S. 764, 796 (1993); Restatement (Third) of Foreign Relations Law §402 (1987); Einer Elhauge & Damien Geradin, *Global Antitrust Law & Economics* (Foundation Press 2007), ch. 8.A.

3. F. Hoffmann-la Roche Ltd. V. Empagran S.A., 542 U.S. 155, 164–169 (2004); Restatement (Third) of Foreign Relations Law §403 (1987); Elhauge & Geradin, *Global Antitrust,* ch. 8.A.

4. 499 U.S. at 248, 250–251.

5. Larry Kramer, "Vestiges of Beale," 1991 *Supreme Court Review* 179, 201–202, 216–217 & n.136; Jonathan Turley, "When in Rome," 84 *Northwestern University Law Review* 598, 618–627 (1990).

6. 499 U.S. at 248, 255.

7. Civil Rights Act of 1991 §109(a), 105 Stat. 1071, 1077 (codified at 42 U.S.C. §§2000e(f), 2000e-1 [2000]).

8. See Older Americans Act Amendments of 1984 §802, 98 Stat. 1767, 1792 (codified at 29 U.S.C. §623(f)–(h) [2000]) (overriding Cleary v. United States Lines, Inc., 728 F.2d 607, 610 [3d Cir. 1984] and Thomas v. Brown & Root, Inc., 745 F.2d 279, 281 [4th Cir. 1984]). Professor Bradley makes a similar argument about *Aramco* but on separation-of-powers grounds rather than preference-

eliciting analysis, and thus does not limit the argument to cases where the three conditions necessary for a preference-eliciting default rule are met. See Curtis A. Bradley, "Territorial Intellectual Property Rights in an Age of Globalism," 37 *Virginia Journal of International Law* 505, 552–553 (1997).

9. See William N. Eskridge, Jr., "Overriding Supreme Court Statutory Interpretation Decisions," 101 *Yale Law Journal* 331, 348 tbl.7 (1991); Phillip R. Trimble, "The Supreme Court and International Law," 89 *American Journal of International Law* 53, 57 (1995).

10. See Jack L. Goldsmith, "The New Formalism in United States Foreign Relations Law," 70 *University of Colorado Law Review* 1395, 1414, 1419–1420, 1433–1436 (1999). Professor Goldsmith ultimately argues for a preference-estimating approach rather than a preference-eliciting one.

11. One can make a similar preference-eliciting argument in favor of the act-of-state canon. That canon provides that unclear statutes should be interpreted to be inapplicable if application would require second-guessing the validity of foreign acts of state. See Banco Nacional de Cuba v. Sabbatino, 376 U.S. 398 (1964); Restatement (Third) of Foreign Relations Law §443 (1987). Indeed, *Sabbatino* elicited congressional override in the "Hickenlooper Amendment," now codified at 22 U.S.C. §2370(e)(2) (2000).

12. *Hartford,* 509 U.S. at 796; Restatement (Third) of Foreign Relations Law §402 (1987); Elhauge & Geradin, *Global Antitrust,* ch. 8.A.

13. Timberlane Lumber Co. v. Bank of America, 549 F.2d 597, 610–615 (9th Cir. 1976); Elhauge & Geradin, *Global Antitrust,* ch. 8.A.

14. *Empagran,* 542 U.S. 155, 164–169.

15. Restatement (Third) of Foreign Relations Law §403(3) (1987).

16. See United States v. Baker Hughes, 731 F. Supp. 3, 6 n.5 (D.D.C. 1990), aff'd, 908 F.2d 981 (D.C. Cir. 1990). See also First National City Bank v. Banco Nacional de Cuba, 406 U.S. 759, 768–770 (1972) (opinion of Rhenquist, J.) (advocating such a rule for the act-of-state doctrine).

17. *Hartford,* 509 U.S. at 798–799; A. Ahlström Osakeyhtiö v. Commission (Wood Pulp), Joined Cases 89, 104, 114, 116, 117, and 125 to 129/85, ECR, [1988] 5193; Gencor Ltd v. Commission, T-102/96.ECR, [1999] II-753.

18. Elhauge & Geradin, *Global Antitrust,* ch. 8.F.

19. See Andrew T. Guzman, "Antitrust and International Regulatory Federalism," 76 *New York University Law Review* 1142, 1151–1162 (2001).

20. Elhauge & Geradin, *Global Antitrust,* ch. 8.

21. Ibid., ch. 8.B.

12. Explaining Seeming Inconsistencies in Statutory *Stare Decisis*

1. See, e.g., Square D Co. v. Niagara Frontier Tariff Bureau, 476 U.S. 409, 424 n.34 (1986); City of Oklahoma City v. Tuttle, 471 U.S. 808, 818 n.5 (1985) (plurality opinion); William N. Eskridge, Jr., "Overriding Supreme Court Statutory Interpretation Decisions," 101 *Yale Law Journal* 362–363 (1991).

2. See e.g., NLRB v. Int'l Longshoremen's Ass'n, 473 U.S. 61, 84 (1985); *Tuttle,* 471 U.S. at 818 n.5.

3. I here put aside the possibility that cycling problems may mean that both *A* and *B* are enactable, so that either might be overturned in favor of the other. If that is the case, a preference-eliciting default rule still makes sense, because the enactability of either option means that there is no reliable ground for a preference-estimating default rule, and putting the burden on the party that can best command the legislative agenda helps test the proposition that either is enactable or that a third option is no more enactable than either. Moreover, if such cycling actually occurred in the legislative process, then the issue about sticking to precedent that has not been overridden would not arise, because any precedent would have been subject to legislative override already.

4. See Michael E. Solimine & James L. Walker, "The Next Word: Congressional Response to Supreme Court Statutory Decisions," 65 *Temple Law Review* 429–430 (1992) (collecting sources).

5. See National Cable & Telecom. Ass'n v. Brand X Internet Services, 125 S.Ct. 2688, 2700–2702 (2005).

6. Eskridge, "Overriding," 331, 397–400 & n.218 (1991)(noting that 38% of cases overruling federal statutory precedent relied on indications of current congressional preferences).

7. Ibid., 399.

8. Boys Markets, Inc. v. Retail Clerks Union, Local 770, 398 U.S. 235, 249–253 (1970); Monell v. Dep't of Soc. Servs., 436 U.S. 658, 664–701 (1978).

9. Patterson v. McLean Credit Union, 491 U.S. 164, 174 (1989).

10. 407 U.S. 258, 282 (1972); Fed. Baseball Club v. Nat'l League of Prof'l Baseball Clubs, 259 U.S. 200, 208–209 (1922); Eskridge, "Overriding," 380–381 (collecting authorities).

11. 15 U.S.C. §§1291, 1294 (2000); 407 U.S. at 281–282. The Court acknowledged that this baseball exemption was inconsistent and illogical because other sports had subsequently been held to be subject to antitrust scrutiny (282–284). But as Chapter 2 noted, there is no requirement that political preferences conform to judicial notions of consistency. Moreover, given that neither the baseball exemption nor the other sports' nonexemptions conflicted with any affirmative indication of current enactable preferences, it was not illogical to differentiate the sports on the basis of their reliance on different precedent, which is what the Court did. See 283–284. While such reliance interests should not trump ascertainable enactable preferences, they do form a sensible basis for interpretation when no contrary enactable preference can be ascertained. See Chapters 2 and 17.

12. See Eskridge, "Overriding," 404–406.

13. On the other hand, sometimes intervening events might persuade the court not only that the precedent is no longer a good preference-eliciting default rule but also that the precedent is now more likely to match legislative preferences than the other interpretive options. In such a case, the court might stick to the precedent even though the underlying rationale for it has shifted.

14. William N. Eskridge, Jr., *Dynamic Statutory Interpretation* (Cambridge, Mass.: Harvard University Press, 1994), 253, 316–322.

15. See, e.g., N. Haven Bd. of Educ. v. Bell, 456 U.S. 512, 530–535 (1982); United States v. Rutherford, 442 U.S. 544, 554 n.10 (1979); see also Shearson/American Express Inc. v. McMahon, 482 U.S. 220, 237–238 (1987); Bob Jones Univ. v. United States, 461 U.S. 574, 599–602 (1983); Herman & MacLean v. Huddleston, 459 U.S. 375, 384–386 (1983); Merrill Lynch, Pierce, Fenner & Smith, Inc. v. Curran, 456 U.S. 353, 379–382 (1982); Haig v. Agee, 453 U.S. 280, 300–301 (1981); Cannon v. Univ. of Chi., 441 U.S. 677, 686 n.7, 702–703 (1979); United States v. Bd. of Comm'rs, 435 U.S. 110, 134–135 (1978); Lorillard, Inc. v. Pons, 434 U.S. 575, 580 (1978); Apex Hosiery Co. v. Leader, 310 U.S. 469, 488–489 (1940) (Roberts, J., dissenting).

13. Tracking the Preferences of Political Subunits

1. See Richard H. Fallon, Jr., Daniel J. Meltzer, & David L. Shapiro, *Hart and Wechsler's The Federal Courts and the Federal System,* 4th ed. (Westbury, N.Y.: Foundation Press, 1996), 820–823.

2. Ibid., 768–770.

3. Medtronic, Inc. v. Lohr, 518 U.S. 470, 485 (1996).

4. Roderick M. Hills, Jr., "Against Preemption," 82 *New York University Law Review* 1 (2007); Jack Goldsmith, "Statutory Foreign Affairs Preemption," 2000 *Supreme Court Review* 175, 186; Note, "New Evidence on the Presumption Against Preemption," 120 *Harvard Law Review* 1604, 1610–11 (2007).

5. Note, "New Evidence," 1612–1613.

6. Note, "New Evidence," 1611, & n.49, 1613 & n.54.

7. Goldsmith, "Statutory Foreign Affairs Preemption," 178; Caleb Nelson, "Preemption," 86 *Virginia Law Review* 225, 232 (2000); Note, "New Evidence," 1604.

8. See Catherine Sharkey, "Products Liability Preemption" (draft presented to Harvard Law Faculty Workshop, March 13, 2007).

9. Michael S. Greve and Jonathan Klick, "Preemption in the Rehnquist Court: A Preliminary Empirical Assessment," 14 *Supreme Court Economic Review* 43, 52 (2006) (preemption rate is 62.5% for state common law and 47.9% for other state laws).

10. Samuel Issacharoff and Catherine M. Sharkey, "Backdoor Federalization," 53 *UCLA Law Review* 1353, 1368–1369, 1390 (2006).

11. Greve and Klick, "Preemption," 67, 71.

12. See City of Columbus v. Ours Garage, 536 U.S. 424, 439–440 (2002); Dellmuth v. Muth, 491 U.S. 223, 228 (1989); Atascadero State Hosp. v. Scanlon, 473 U.S. 234, 240 (1985); Pennhurst State School and Hosp. v. Halderman, 451 U.S. 1, 16–17 (1981).

13. See Education of the Handicapped Act Amendments of 1990, Pub. L. No. 101–476, §103, 104 Stat. 1103, 1106 (1990) (overriding *Dellmuth*); Rehabilitation Act Amendments of 1986, Pub. L. No. 99–506, §1003, 100 Stat. 1807, 1845

(1986) (overriding *Atascadero*); Copyright Remedy Clarification Act, Pub. L. No. 101–553, §2, 104 Stat. 2749, 2749 (1990) (overriding case that applied *Atascadero*, BV Eng'g v. UCLA, 858 F.2d 1394 [9th Cir. 1988]).

14. William N. Eskridge, Jr., *Dynamic Statutory Interpretation* (Cambridge, Mass.: Harvard University Press, 1994), 153, 288; William N. Eskridge, Jr., "Overriding Supreme Court Statutory Interpretation Decisions," 101 *Yale Law Journal* 331, 348 (1991).

15. Eskridge, "Overriding," at 409–410.

16. Bennett v. Ky. Dep't of Educ., 470 U.S. 656, 670 (1985); Cal. State Bd. of Optometry v. FTC, 910 F.2d 976, 981–82 (D.C. Cir. 1990).

14. Tracking High Court Preferences

1. Ariz. Rev. Stat. Ann. §1-211 (West 1995); Cal. Civ. Proc. Code §4 (West 1982); Idaho Code §73-102 (Michie 1999); Iowa Code Ann. §4.2 (West 2001); Ky. Rev. Stat. Ann. §446.080 (Michie 1999); Mo. Ann. Stat. §1.010 (West 2000); Mont. Code Ann. §1-2-103 (2001); N.M. Stat. Ann. §12-2A-18 (Michie 1998); N.D. Cent. Code §1-02-01 (1987); Okla. Stat. Ann. tit. 25, §29 (West 1987); 1 Pa. Cons. Stat. Ann. §1928 (West 1995); S.C. Code Ann. §§14-1-60, 15-1-10, 18-1-170, 19-1-10 (Law. Co-op. 1977); S.D. Codified Laws §2-14-12 (Michie 1992); Tex. Gov't Code Ann. §312.006 (Vernon 1998); Utah Code Ann. §68-3-2 (2000); Wash. Rev. Code Ann. §1.12.010 (West 2001).

2. David L. Shapiro, "Continuity and Change in Statutory Interpretation," 67 *New York University Law Review* 921, 938 (1992). As with many canons, the canon for liberally construing remedial statutes is justifiable only if applied selectively. Applying it to identify appropriate cases for negating the canon against interpretations in derogation of the common law makes sense. Applying it to adopt the broadest plausible interpretation of any civil statute does not. See Antonin Scalia, "Assorted Canards of Contemporary Legal Analysis," 40 *Case Western Reserve Law Review* 581, 583–586 (1990).

3. N.Y. Stat. Law §301 (McKinney 2001).

4. Ibid., §§91–92, 95–96, 111, 120, 124, 191.

5. Ibid., §321.

6. See, e.g., Solid Waste Agency of N. Cook County v. United States Army Corps of Eng'rs, 531 U.S. 159, 172–173 (2001); Pub. Citizen v. Dep't of Justice, 491 U.S. 440, 455 (1989); Edward J. DeBartolo Corp. v. Fla. Gulf Coast Bldg. & Constr. Trades Council, 485 U.S. 568, 574–575 (1988); NLRB v. Catholic Bishop, 440 U.S. 490, 500 (1979).

7. United States v. Monsanto, 491 U.S. 600, 611 (1989) (describing the canon against constitutional doubts as "useful in close cases, *or* when statutory language is ambiguous" [emphasis added]); George Moore Ice Cream Co. v. Rose, 289 U.S. 373, 379 (1933) ("[A]voidance of a [constitutional] difficulty will not be pressed to the point of disingenuous evasion" by applying the canon where "the intention of the Congress is revealed . . . distinctly.").

8. Rumsfeld v. FAIR, 126 S.Ct. 1297, 1306–1313 (2006).
9. Cass R. Sunstein, "Law and Administration After *Chevron*," 90 *Columbia Law Review* 2071, 2113 (1990).
10. Dep't of Commerce v. United States House of Representatives, 525 U.S. 316, 343 (1999) ("If there is one doctrine more deeply rooted than any other in the process of constitutional adjudication, it is that we ought not to pass on questions of constitutionality . . . unless such adjudication is unavoidable.").
11. Sunstein, "After *Chevron*," at 2111–2113.

15. The Fit with Prior Political Science Models and Empirical Data

1. William N. Eskridge, Jr., *Dynamic Statutory Interpretation* (Cambridge, Mass.: Harvard University Press, 1994), 167–170; Eskridge, "Overriding Supreme Court Statutory Interpretation Decisions," 101 *Yale Law Journal* 378–385 (1991); William N. Eskridge, Jr., & John Ferejohn, "Making the Deal Stick," 8 *Journal of Law, Economics & Organization* 165, 168 (1992); Eskridge & Ferejohn, "The Article I, Section 7 Game," 80 *Georgetown Law Journal* 523, 549–551 (1992); John A. Ferejohn & Barry R. Weingast, "A Positive Theory of Statutory Interpretation," 12 *International Review of Law & Economics* 263, 267–268 (1992); Edward P. Schwartz, Pablo T. Spiller, & Santiago Urbiztondo, "A Positive Theory of Legislative Intent," 57 *Law & Contemporary Problems* 51, 56–57 & n.23 (1994). See also Linda R. Cohen & Matthew L. Spitzer, "Solving the *Chevron* Puzzle," 57 *Law & Contemporary Problems* 65, 69–76 (1994) (assuming there is a best statutory interpretation but that courts are free to deviate from it across an infinite continuum of views about policy and process); Rafael Gely & Pablo T. Spiller, "A Rational Choice Theory of Supreme Court Statutory Decisions With Applications to the *State Farm* and *Grove City* Cases," 6 *Journal of Law, Economics & Organization* 263, 268–283 (1990) (basing most of their analysis on the assumption of infinite continuum but also considering the possibility that a court can make only a yes-or-no choice). A slightly different take is offered in Pablo T. Spiller, "Rationality, Decision Rules, and Collegial Courts," 12 *International Review of Law & Economics* 186, 188–190 (1992), which assumes that judges always have interpretive discretion to choose any point in a policy space, and would generally prefer to do so, but are sometimes driven by cycling problems to decide instead on a yes-or-no basis in order to achieve stable agreement on the point that is most likely to come close to the judicial policy preferences. None of these articles considers the possibility that legal methodology might reduce the interpretive choices to, say, two or three possibilities.
2. Eskridge, *Dynamic,* 167–170; Eskridge, "Overriding," 378–385; Eskridge & Ferejohn, "Deal," 183–186; Eskridge & Ferejohn, "Game," 549–551; Gely & Spiller, "Rational Choice," 267–268; Schwartz et al., "Positive Theory of Legislative," 57–58, 72; Spiller, "Rationality," 187–190. See also Cohen & Spitzer, "Puzzle," at 71–76 (assuming that judicial views incorporate preferences about both policy and legal process).

3. Frank B. Cross & Blake J. Nelson, "Strategic Institutional Effects on Supreme Court Decisionmaking," 95 *Northwestern University Law Review* 1437, 1459–1473 (2001); McNollgast, "Politics and the Courts," 68 *Southern California Law Review* 1631, 1634–1635, 1641–1665, 1675–1683 (1995) (showing that political branches can and do expand lower courts to make it harder for a politically wayward Supreme Court to obtain lower court compliance with its wayward doctrines).

4. See, e.g., Eskridge & Ferejohn, "Game," 548; Matthew McCubbins, Roger G. Noll, & Barry Weingast, "Legislative Intent," 57 *Law & Contemporary Problems* 5–6 (1994).

5. Ferejohn & Weingast, "Positive Theory of Statutory," 268–274.

6. Eskridge, *Dynamic,* 164–170; Cohen & Spitzer, "Puzzle," 68; Eskridge & Ferejohn, "Deal," 168; Eskridge & Ferejohn, "Game," 549. Often this assumption is not explicit, but is just an implicit premise of how the model is drawn and applied. See, e.g., Ferejohn & Weingast, "Positive Theory of Statutory," 267–276; Gely & Spiller, "Rational Choice," 270–283; Spiller, "Rationality," 187–190.

7. Eskridge, *Dynamic,* 164–170 (1994); Cohen & Spitzer, "Puzzle," 65, 69–70, 72–76; Eskridge & Ferejohn, "Deal," 165, 176–178; Eskridge & Ferejohn, "Game," 528–540, 547–551. The text in these articles sometimes acknowledges that the legislature also exerts some influence on agencies but argues it is small, and then in the actual models, the articles assume agency action reflects only presidential preferences.

8. Eskridge, *Dynamic,* 167–170; Cohen & Spitzer, "Puzzle," 69–70, 73–76; Eskridge, "Overriding," 378–385; Eskridge & Ferejohn, "Deal," 167–171; Eskridge & Ferejohn, "Game," 528–551; Ferejohn & Weingast, "Positive Theory of Statutory," 267–276; Gely & Spiller, "Rational Choice," 267–283.

9. Cohen & Spitzer, "Puzzle," 65, 69; Gely & Spiller, "Rational Choice," 263, 268 & n.15; Schwartz et al., "Positive Theory of Legislative," 51, 55, 59, 72.

10. Schwartz et al., "Positive Theory of Legislative," 56–57, falls within the latter category. All the other articles cited in note 1 fall within the former category.

11. Pablo T. Spiller & Emerson H. Tiller, "Invitations to Override: Congressional Reversals of Supreme Court Decisions," 16 *International Review of Law & Economics* 503 (1996).

12. Given their model, any result between the ideal points of the House and Senate is a possible one, because all are in the core of the legislative bargaining game (ibid., 506–507 & n.18), and the authors give no explanation of how judges could ascertain which one of those possible results will actually occur.

13. Ibid., 510–511. They also ignore ex ante effects, and the possibility that interpretations that do not reflect enactable preferences might have differential likelihoods of override; but within their driving assumption of judicial preference satisfaction, it is not clear that those factors would cause any change in their analysis. They also implicitly assume that all results that deviate from enactable legislative preferences are reversed and that, although judges vote to advance

personal preferences, they have no preference regarding the interpretations that prevail in the interim before reversal.

14. Ibid., 510.

15. Schwartz et al., "Positive Theory of Legislative," 55–61, 64–71.

16. Ibid., 64–70.

17. See, e.g., Pablo T. Spiller & Rafael Gely, "Congressional Control or Judicial Independence: The Determinants of U.S. Supreme Court Labor-Relations Decisions, 1949–1988," 23 *RAND Journal of Economics* 463, 481–482 (1992); Lee Epstein & Jack Knight, *The Choices Justices Make* (Washington, D.C.: CQ Press, 1998), 149–150.

18. Frank B. Cross & Blake J. Nelson, "Strategic Institutional Effects on Supreme Court Decisionmaking," 95 *Northwestern University Law Review* 1437, 1455–1457 (2001).

19. See, e.g., Gely & Spiller, "Rational Choice," 266 ("Congressional inaction will follow Supreme Court decisions, as these have already taken the composition of Congress into account.").

20. Another possibility is that courts try to make interpretations that avoid override, but legislative views later drift. However, half or more of statutory overrides occur within only two years of a Supreme Court decision.

21. Joseph Ignagni, James Meernik, & Kimi Lynn King, "Statutory Construction and Congressional Response," 26 *American Politics Research* 459, 473–477 (1998).

22. Ibid., 478.

23. Michael E. Solimine & James L. Walker, "The Next Word: Congressional Response to Supreme Court Statutory Decisions," 65 *Temple Law Review* 449, 453 (1992).

24. Ibid., 449.

25. W. Va. Univ. Hosps., Inc. v. Casey, 499 U.S. 83, 113–115 (1991) (Stevens, J., dissenting). Congress overruled *Casey* with the Civil Rights Act of 1991 §113, 42 U.S.C. §§1988, 2000e-5(k) (2000).

26. Lori Hausegger & Lawrence Baum, "Inviting Congressional Action: A Study of Supreme Court Motivations in Statutory Interpretation," 43 *American Journal of Political Science* 162, 164 n.4, 165–167, 178 n.21 (1999). The figures in the text only include invitations in majority opinions. If one includes invitations in concurring or dissenting opinions as well, then 11 percent of Supreme Court statutory interpretations contained strong invitations for Congressional override.

27. Ibid., 174–177, 180–182.

28. Ibid., 170–174, 180–181.

29. Spiller & Tiller, "Invitations," 509, 519–520.

30. Ibid., 509.

31. See Hausegger & Baum, "Inviting," 168–177; Spiller & Tiller, "Invitations," at 507–511, 519–520.

32. Frank B. Cross, "Political Science and the New Legal Realism: A Case of Unfor-

tunate Interdisciplinary Ignorance," 92 *Northwestern University Law Review* 251, 265–279 (1997) (reviewing literature).

33. Hausegger & Baum, "Inviting," 168, 181–182.
34. Spiller & Tiller, "Invitations," 509, 519–520.
35. See Miles & Sunstein, "Do Judges Make Regulatory Policy? An Empirical Investigation of *Chevron*," 73 *University of Chicago Law Review* 823 (2006).
36. Frank B. Cross, "Political Science," 294 n.259, 303–304, citing Jeffrey Segal & Harold Spaeth, *The Supreme Court and the Attitudinal Model* (New York: Cambridge University Press, 1993), 259.
37. See Jerome Nelson, "The *Chevron* Deference Rule and Judicial Review of FERC Orders," 9 *Energy Law Journal* 59, 82 (1988); Orin S. Kerr, "Shedding Light on *Chevron*:: An Empirical Study of the *Chevron* Doctrine in the U.S. Courts of Appeals," 15 *Yale Journal on Regulation* 1, 35–37 (1998).
38. Richard L. Revesz, "Congressional Influence on Judicial Behavior? An Empirical Examination of Challenges to Agency Action in the D.C. Circuit," 76 *New York University Law Review* 1100, 1104–1115 (2001). Professor Revesz hypothesizes this is true because the Supreme Court is more likely to reverse statutory interpretations. Ibid., 1113. However, given the actual low odds of Supreme Court review, the more plausible explanation is that judges are following the default rule in the interpretive cases. In any event, the fact that appellate review is what enforces a legal doctrine hardly makes the doctrine meaningless.
39. See Michael S. Greve and Jonathan Klick, "Preemption in the Rehnquist Court: A Preliminary Empirical Assessment," 14 Supreme Court Economic Review 43, 57, 80–84 (2006).

16. Interest Group and Collective Choice Theory

1. See Frank H. Easterbrook, "The Supreme Court, 1983 Term-Foreword," 98 *Harvard Law Review* 4, 15–18 (1984); William N. Eskridge, Jr., "Politics Without Romance: Implications of Public Choice Theory for Statutory Interpretation," 74 *Virginia Law Review* 275, 279, 298–299, 303–309, 324–325 (1988); Jonathan R. Macey, "Promoting Public-Regarding Legislation Through Statutory Interpretation," 86 *Columbia Law Review* 223, 228 n.29, 252 (1986); Cass R. Sunstein, "Interpreting Statutes in the Regulatory State," 103 *Harvard Law Review*, 405, 471, 486 (1989).
2. See Frank H. Easterbrook, "Statutes' Domains," 50 *University of Chicago Law Review* 533, 533, 547–548 (1983); John F. Manning, "Textualism and the Equity of the Statute," 101 *Columbia Law Review* 1, 19 (2001); Kenneth A. Shepsle, "Congress Is a 'They,' Not an 'It': Legislative Intent as Oxymoron," 12 *International Review of Law & Economics* 239 (1992); William H. Riker & Barry R. Weingast, "Constitutional Regulation of Legislative Choice," 74 *Virginia Law Review* 373, 374–375 (1988); Richard M. Pildes & Elizabeth S. Anderson, "Slinging Arrows at Democracy," 90 *Columbia Law Review* 2121, 2124–2126 (1990).
3. See, e.g., Mancur Olson, *The Logic of Collective Action*, 2d ed. (Cambridge, Mass.:

Harvard University Press, 1971); David R. Mayhew, *Congress: The Electoral Connection* (New Haven, Conn.: Yale University Press, 1974), 39–41; George Stigler, "The Theory of Economic Regulation," 2 *Bell Journal of Economics & Management Science* 3 (1971); William M. Landes & Richard A. Posner, "The Independent Judiciary in an Interest-Group Perspective," 18 *Journal of Law & Economics* 875, 877 (1975); Sam Peltzman, "Toward a More General Theory of Regulation," 19 *Journal of Law & Economics* 211 (1976).

4. See Steven P. Croley, *Regulation and Public Interests* (Princeton, N.J.: Princeton University Press, 2007); Daniel A. Farber & Philip P. Frickey, "The Jurisprudence of Public Choice," 65 *Texas Law Review* 887–890, 893–901 (1987); Herbert Hovenkamp, "Legislation, Well-Being, and Public Choice," 57 *University of Chicago Law Review* 63, 88 & n.56 (1990); Mark Kelman, "On Democracy-Bashing," 74 *Virginia Law Review* 199, 214–223 (1988); Edward L. Rubin, "Beyond Public Choice," 66 *New York University Law Review* 1, 2 & n.3, 12–45 (1991).

5. Olson, *Logic,* at 127–128.

6. As Bruce Ackerman has pointed out, discrete and insular minorities should be more, rather than less, equipped to police free rider problems in organizing political effort. See Bruce A. Ackerman, "Beyond Carolene Products," 98 *Harvard Law Review* 713, 723–731 (1985).

7. See Jennifer Roback, "The Separation of Race and State," 14 *Harvard Journal of Law & Public Policy* 58, 59, 62 (1991). Roback does not single out minority interest groups or affirmative action, but rather argues against rent seeking by groups of any ethnicity or interest.

8. Riker & Weingast, "Constitutional Regulation," 374 & n.2; James D. Gwartney & Richard E. Wagner, "Public Choice and the Conduct of Representative Government," in James D. Gwartney & Richard E. Wagner, eds., *Public Choice and Constitutional Economics* (1988) 3, 17–18; William A. Fischel & Perry Shapiro, "Takings, Insurance, and Michelman," 17 *Journal of Legal Studies* 269 (1988); Susan Rose-Ackerman, "Progressive Law and Economics—And the New Administrative Law," 98 *Yale Law Journal* 341, 342 n.5 (1988) (collecting sources).

9. See also Gordon Tullock, *The Economics of Special Privilege and Rent Seeking* (Springer Press, 1989), 32 & n.3 (arguing that small group aims should be implemented where "it would cost society less than the benefit to the small group"); at 4 (concluding that lobbying by the company he represented was not rent seeking, because it sought to remove a market restriction rather than impose one).

10. See, e.g., Olson, *Logic,* 47, 74 ("On balance, special-interest organizations and collusions reduce efficiency and aggregate income."); Tullock, *Economics,* vii, 20 (1989) (describing rent seeking as situations of net economic loss that benefit a minority); Gary Becker, "Public Policies, Pressure Groups, and Dead Weight Losses," 28 *Journal of Public Economics* 329, 343–345 (1985) (arguing that condemnation of interest group influence is justified only when that influence reduces social output).

11. Economic analysts sometimes use efficiency to mean Pareto "efficiency." How-

ever, because just about any regulatory decision harms some persons and benefits others, Pareto efficiency is usually a useless standard for judging governmental action. Compare Guido Calabresi, "The Pointlessness of Pareto," 100 *Yale Law Journal* 1211, 1215–1221 (1991) (arguing that any Pareto optimal change already would have been achieved). Breaking up a price-fixing cartel, for example, is not Pareto efficient because it harms the cartelists. Thus, in judging regulatory decisions, economists usually employ the Kaldor-Hicks test of efficiency, under which a change is efficient if the winners gain enough that they could compensate the losers. See Nicholas Kaldor, "Welfare Propositions of Economics and Interpersonal Comparisons of Utility," 49 *Economic Journal* 549 (1939); J. R. Hicks, "The Valuation of the Social Income," 7 *Economica* 105 (1940). Because the Kaldor-Hicks test does not require that the winners actually compensate the losers, it is identical to defining efficiency as wealth maximization if (as is typical) gains and losses are measured monetarily.

12. Robert E. McCormick & Robert D. Tollison, *Politicians, Legislation, and the Economy* (Kluwer: Boston, 1981), ix, 3–5; George J. Stigler, *The Citizen and the State,* (University of Chicago Press, 1975), ix; Peltzman, "Toward," 211–212; Richard Posner, "Theories of Economic Regulation," 5 *Bell Journal of Economics & Management Science* 335, 336–337 (1974).

13. The traditional response is, of course, that regulatory policy should strive for economic efficiency, because wealth redistribution can usually be accomplished more efficiently and precisely through general taxation and welfare programs. See, e.g., A. Mitchell Polinsky, *An Introduction to Law and Economics,* 2d ed. (Boston: Little, Brown, 1989), 124–127; Louis Kaplow & Steven Shavell, "Why the Legal System Is Less Efficient Than the Income Tax in Redistributing Income," 23 *Journal of Legal Studies* 667 (1994). Although this claim often has merit, it rests on contestable empirical assumptions. As Richard Posner has pointed out, there is no a priori reason to believe that the inefficiencies created by redistributive taxes are lower than the inefficiencies caused by a redistributive regulatory regime. Richard A. Posner, "Taxation by Regulation," 2 *Bell Journal of Economics & Management Science* 22, 41–45, 47 (1971). In any event, the traditional response does not demonstrate the desirability of any legal change that increases wealth but is not coupled with further tax redistribution.

14. See Bruno S. Frey et al., "Consensus and Dissension Among Economists: An Empirical Inquiry," 74 *American Economic Review* 986, 987 (1984).

15. Cass R. Sunstein, "Interest Groups in American Public Law," 38 *Stanford Law Review* 49–55 (1985); Sunstein, "Naked Preferences and the Constitution," 84 *Columbia Law Review* 1689–1695 (1984).

16. Paul H. Rubin, "Why Is the Common Law Efficient?" 6 *Journal of Legal Studies* 51 (1977). See also John C. Goodman, "An Economic Theory of the Evolution of Common Law," 7 *Journal of Legal Studies* 393 (1978); George L. Priest, "The Common Law Process and the Selection of Efficient Rules," 6 *Journal of Legal Studies* 65 (1977).

17. See Paul H. Rubin, "Common Law and Statute Law," 11 *Journal of Legal Studies* 205, 211–214 (1982).

18. See Gary S. Becker, "A Theory of Competition Among Pressure Groups for Political Influence," 98 *Quartery Journal of Economics* 371 (1983).

19. Eskridge, "Politics," 303–304; see also Peter Aranson, *American Government* (Cambridge, Mass.: Winthrop, 1981), 512–513.

20. See Alyeska Pipeline Serv. Co. v. Wilderness Soc'y, 421 U.S. 240, 260–271 (1975).

21. In securities class actions, a court does review who is selected as the lead plaintiff, who in turn selects the class counsel. See 15 U.S.C. §78u-4. But the class itself does not get to pick the representatives.

22. For both rights, the expected individual benefits from becoming sufficiently informed to exercise the right intelligently are far less than the collective benefit. This is because the individual discounts from her expected benefit (1) the share of group benefits she does not receive; (2) the likelihood that absorbing the information will not change her decision; and (3) the likelihood (which approaches 100% as the group grows large) that any individual member's vote (or opt out) will not make any difference to the collective outcome. Compare Dennis Mueller, *Public Choice II* (New York: Cambridge University Press, 1989), 205–206 (describing "rational ignorance" problem in voting).

23. The underlying problems are (1) judges have little incentive to oppose settlements, and (2) the lawyers effectively control the court's access to information about the merits of the case and about the quality and quantity of legal representation. See John C. Coffee, Jr., "Understanding the Plaintiff's Attorney," 86 *Columbia Law Review* 669, 714 n.121 (1986); Jonathan R. Macey & Geoffrey P. Miller, "The Plaintiffs' Attorney's Role in Class Action and Derivative Litigation," 58 *University of Chicago Law Review* 1, 45–47 (1991).

24. Keller v. State Bar of Cal., 496 U.S. 1 (1990); Abood v. Detroit Bd. of Educ., 431 U.S. 209 (1977).

25. Similar problems afflict efforts to represent underrepresented groups in litigation through government financing of public interest advocates. See Richard B. Stewart, "The Reformation of American Administrative Law," 88 *Harvard Law Review* 1667, 1763–1770 (1975).

26. Donald Horowitz, *The Courts and Social Policy* (Washington, D.C.: Brookings Institution, 1977), 45–56; R. Shep Melnick, *Regulation and the Courts: The Case of the Clean Air Act* (Washington, D.C.: Brookings Institution, 1983), 14, 347–348, 350, 352; Gordon Tullock, *Trials on Trial* (Columbia University Press, 1980), 202–203.

27. Jill E. Fisch, "Rewriting History," 76 *Cornell Law Review* 589 (1991).

28. John R. Lott, "Political Cheating," 52 *Public Choice* 169, 183 (1987); Mark A. Zupan, "The Last Period Problem in Politics," 65 *Public Choice* 167 (1990).

29. Omri Ben-Shahar, "Legal Durability," 1 *Review of Law and Economics* 15 (2005).

30. See Jesse Choper, *Judicial Review and the National Political Process* (Chicago: University of Chicago Press, 1980), 4–59 (concluding, partly on the basis of numerous earlier empirical studies, that despite various defects, the political process reflects the will of the majority of voters more accurately than the Supreme Court does).

31. See Robert D. Tollison, "Public Choice and Legislation," 74 *Virginia Law Review* 339, 345–346 (1988).

32. See, e.g., Richard A. Posner, *The Problems of Jurisprudence* (1990), 194–196; Robert Cooter, "The Objectives of Private and Public Judges," 41 *Public Choice* 107, 129–130 (1983).

33. Robert H. Bork, *The Tempting of America* (New York: Free Press, 1990), 171.

34. Richard A. Posner, *The Economics of Justice* (Cambridge, Mass.: Harvard University Press, 1981), 60–103.

35. See R. H. Coase, "The Problem of Social Cost," 3 *Journal of Law & Economics* 1, 2–8 (1960).

36. If one adopts a definition of efficiency (or social desirability) that turns on utility maximization or the distribution of wealth, the efficient (or desirable) outcome will not (even with zero transaction costs) occur independently of how the legal issue is decided. See Herbert Hovenkamp, "Marginal Utility and the Coase Theorem," 75 *Cornell Law Review* 783, 798–809 (1990).

37. See R. H. Coase, *The Firm, The Market, and the Law* (Chicago: University of Chicago Press, 1988), 26, 174; Robert Cooter, "The Costs of Coase," 11 *Journal of Legal Studies* 1, 16–29 (1982); Robert C. Ellickson, "The Case for Coase and Against 'Coaseanism,'" 99 *Yale Law Journal* 611, 614–615 (1989); Varouj A. Aivazian & Jeffrey L. Callen, "The Coase Theorem and the Empty Core," 24 *Journal of Law & Economics* 175 (1981).

38. Initial allocations of rights can affect a party's ability or willingness to pay or to accept payment by (1) altering that party's wealth or (2) creating an endowment effect that alters subjective valuations even when wealth effects are trivial. See, e.g., Daniel Kahneman et al., "Experimental Tests of the Endowment Effect and the Coase Theorem," 98 *Journal of Political Economy* 1325 (1990); Jack L. Knetsch, "The Endowment Effect and Evidence of Nonreversible Indifference Curves," 79 *American Economic Review* 1277 (1989); Richard Thaler, "Toward a Positive Theory of Consumer Choice," 1 *Journal of Economic Behavior and Organization* 39, 43–47 (1980).

39. See Cooter, "The Costs," 15; Hovenkamp, "Marginal Utility," 785. For example, if people have a right to pollute, a party who has $30,000 in wealth may be unwilling to pay more than $15,000 to have her neighbor stop polluting, but if people have a right to be free from pollution, the same party may refuse to take less than $25,000 to sell it. Suppose that, because stopping pollution is costly, polluters value the right to pollute at $20,000. If the regime recognizes a right to be free from pollution, the efficient outcome that will occur is no pollution (because the holders of rights to no pollution value it by $5,000 more than those desiring a right to pollute). If the regime recognizes a right to pollute, the efficient outcome that will occur is allowing pollution (because the holders of rights to pollute value it by $5,000 more than those desiring a right to be free of pollution).

40. Einer Elhauge, "Defining Better Monopolization Standards," 56 *Stanford Law Review* 253, 284–288 (2003).

41. Riker & Weingast, "Constitutional Regulation," 381.

42. See, e.g., Mueller, *Public Choice*, 63–65, 197–198; Riker & Weingast, "Constitu-

tional Regulation," 382–385. To illustrate, assume three voters with the following preference orderings: (1) voter 1 prefers A > B > C; (2) voter 2 prefers B > C > A; and (3) voter 3 prefers C > A > B. In a vote between A and B, A wins 2 to 1. In a vote between B and C, B wins 2 to 1. And in a vote between C and A, C wins 2 to 1.

43. Mueller, *Public Choice,* 385–387.

44. See Kenneth J. Arrow, *Social Choice and Individual Values,* 2d ed. (New York: Wiley, 1963), 9–11, 31–33, 59; Mueller, *Public Choice,* 393–395, 398–399, 406–407.

45. See Pildes & Anderson, "Slinging," 2166–2167, 2171–2175.

46. See Robert C. Post, "Racist Speech, Democracy, and the First Amendment," 32 *William & Mary Law Review,* 267, 279–285 (1991).

47. Riker & Weingast, "Constitutional Regulation," 386–387.

48. A technical caveat is necessary here. If the agenda setter can require a series of votes in which winning alternatives replace the initial status quo, and are then challenged in subsequent votes, then theoretically an agenda setter who knows the preferences of all voters can (where their aggregate preferences are intransitive) induce them to adopt any feasible policy alternative—including an alternative that would lose to the initial status quo. See Richard D. McKelvey, "Intransitivities in Multidimensional Voting Models and Some Implications for Agenda Control," 12 *Journal of Economic Theory* 472 (1976).

However, the informational conditions necessary to reach McKelvey's theoretical conclusion are extreme and somewhat odd. The agenda setter must be remarkably well informed about the preference ordering of each voter in order to schedule an agenda that will produce a certain result. Further, the voters must be well informed about policy issues but oddly uninformed about agenda issues. They must be well informed about policy issues; otherwise their preference ordering may be probabilistic and not susceptible to cycling. But they must also be sufficiently uninformed about agenda issues that they reveal their true preference ordering to the agenda setter, and cast each vote without foreseeing the sequence of votes to come. Whether any real-world voters possess such sophistication and ignorance simultaneously is dubious. Certainly if any agenda setter actually pursued the series of votes necessary for McKelvey's theoretical result, that would likely alert even the most obtuse of voters to take the possibility of subsequent iterations into account in future votes.

Moreover, real-world political processes do not permit the repeated iterations and unified agenda control that is required for McKelvey's theoretical conclusion. Legislative committee chairs, the typical agenda setters, might be able to hold a series of votes to determine which bill comes out of committee to face the status quo. If, however, that bill wins, they would have difficulty convincing the legislature to devote further time to consider replacing the enacted bill with another, let alone to consider replacing the second enacted bill with a third, and so forth. Legislative time and effort is a scarce commodity, and legislatures are unlikely to be willing to spend the time necessary to go through the iteration of votes that will maximize the influence of the agenda setter. The House, for example, usually considers bills under a closed rule that allows no amendments from the floor. Agenda-setting power is further limited by bicameralism, because an agenda-setting legislator in one chamber cannot control the voting agenda in the other chamber. At most, the convener in one chamber shares (with the convener of the other) agenda-setting influence over the conference committee, but any product of the conference committee must be able to beat the initial status quo in both chambers. Agenda-setting influence is thus generally limited to influencing the alternative chosen from the set that can beat the status quo. Accord Riker & Weingast, "Constitutional Regulation," 386–387, 394, 397.

49. See Frank H. Easterbrook, "Ways of Criticizing the Court," 95 *Harvard Law Review* 802, 813–832 (1982).

50. See Maxwell L. Stearns, *Constitutional Process* (University of Michigan Press, 2000).

51. See Arrow, *Social Choice*, 30.

52. See ibid., 5 ("[T]he distinction between voting and the market mechanism will be disregarded, both being regarded as special cases of the more general category of collective social choice."). Similarly, social decisionmaking that comports with the Kaldor-Hicks criteria also fails to satisfy Arrow's conditions. See 31–32, 38–47 (the same holds for utility maximization and Pareto efficiency based solely on consumption).

17. Protecting Reliance or Avoiding Change or Effect

1. See William N. Eskridge, Jr., *Dynamic Statutory Interpretation* (Cambridge, Mass.: Harvard University Press, 1994), 138–140 (considering this possibility); Amanda Tyler, "Continuity, Coherence, and the Canons," 99 *Northwestern University Law Review* 1389, 1393, 1414 (2005).

2. For a similar point, see Ronald Dworkin, *Law's Empire* (Cambridge, Mass.: Harvard University Press, 1986), 349–350.

3. Louis Kaplow, "An Economic Analysis of Legal Transitions," 99 *Harvard Law Review* 509, 522–536 (1986); Daniel Shaviro, *When Rules Change* (University of Chicago Press, 2000).

4. See Jonathan Masur, "Administrative Law Re-*Branded*," *Vanderbilt Law Review* (forthcoming). Masur's concern might be that a new political party could take office and change the standards of social desirability. If so, his proposal, that agencies be able to commit not to alter their regulations, would allow the agency to commit not only itself, but a future agency with different views. Then, the right private law analogy would be to a contract that tried to bind nonconsenting third parties. In any event, such agency action would raise all the legislative entrenchment problems discussed in Chapter 3 regarding statutes that try to bar repeals by future legislatures, even though the future legislature went through the same enactment process as the first legislature.

5. See Steven Shavell, "On Optimal Legal Change, Past Behavior, and Grandfathering," Harvard John M. Olin Center for Law, Economics, and Business, Discussion Paper No. 570 (Dec., 2006).

6. See, e.g., Helvering v. Griffiths, 318 U.S. 371, 402 (1943); William N. Eskridge,

Jr., "Overruling Statutory Precedents," 76 *Georgetown Law Journal* 1361, 1367–1369, 1382–1384 (1988).

7. Landgraf v. USI Film Prods., 511 U.S. 244, 261, 272–273, 280 (1994); Alaska Stat. §01.10.090 (Michie 2000); Ariz. Rev. Stat. Ann. §1-244 (West 1995); Cal. Civ. Proc. Code §3 (West 1982); Colo. Rev. Stat. §2-4-202 (2000); Ga. Code Ann. §1-3-5 (2000); Haw. Rev. Stat. Ann. §1-3 (Michie 1998); Idaho Code §73-101 (Michie 1999); Iowa Code Ann. §4.5 (West 2001); Ky. Rev. Stat. Ann. §446.080 (Michie 1999); Minn. Stat. Ann. §645.21 (West 1946); Mont. Code Ann. §1-2-109 (2001); N.M. Stat. Ann. §12-2A-8 (Michie 1998); N.D. Cent. Code §1-02-10 (1987); Ohio Rev. Code Ann. §1.48 (West 1994); 1 Pa. Cons. Stat. Ann. §1926 (West 1995); S.D. Codified Laws §2-14-21 (Michie 1992); Tex. Gov't Code Ann. §311.022 (Vernon 1998); Utah Code Ann. §68-3-3 (2000); W. Va. Code Ann. §2-2-10(bb) (Michie 2002).

8. *Landgraf,* 511 U.S. at 267–268, 272.

9. Ibid., 268 , 272–273.

10. Ibid., 262 & n.14.

11. See Frank H. Easterbrook, "Statutes' Domains," 50 *University of Chicago Law Review* 533, 544–552 (1983); Earl M. Maltz, "Rhetoric and Reality in the Theory of Statutory Interpretation: Underenforcement, Overenforcement, and the Problem of Legislative Supremacy," 71 *Boston University Law Review* 767, 788–789 (1991).

12. David L. Shapiro, "Continuity and Change in Statutory Interpretation," 67 *New York University Law Review* 921, 925 (1992). Agreeing with him is Tyler, "Continuity," 1393, 1415, 1422.

13. See Chapter 16 (explaining why interest group and collective choice theory provide no basis for preferring the status quo).

14. 211 Ark. 678 (1947).

15. The Supreme Court often relies on "the dog that did not bark," Chisom v. Roemer, 501 U.S. 380, 396 & n.23 (1991), which is the unlikelihood that Congress intended a major change without ever discussing it; FDA v. Brown & Williamson Tobacco Corp., 529 U.S. 120, 159–160 (2000).

16. McNollgast, "Positive Canons: The Role of Legislative Bargains in Statutory Interpretation," 80 *Georgetown Law Journal* 705, 715–716 (1992).

17. N.Y. Stat. Law §153.

18. N.Y. Stat. Law §193.

19. See Easterbrook, "Statutes'," at 537–539, 548–549.

20. John F. Manning, "Textualism and the Equity of the Statute," 101 *Columbia Law Review* 710 (2001).

18. Rebutting Operational and Jurisprudential Objections

1. Oliver Wendell Holmes, "The Path of the Law," 10 *Harvard Law Review* 457, 457–458 (1897).

2. Courts often define the conduct that gun control statutes criminalize without adverting to the rule of lenity because the adjudicated issue is whether to revoke a

gun dealer's license—see, for example, Dickerson v. New Banner Inst., Inc., 460 U.S. 103 (1983); but the statutory definition applies when imposing criminal punishment as well. This can produce expansive statutory interpretations that themselves are subject to legislative override because the gun lobby has far more influence than those who are burdened by ordinary criminal law. See Firearm Owners' Protection Act, 100 Stat. 449, 459 (1986) (codified at 18 U.S.C. §921 [2001]) (overriding *Dickerson*). In another case, the Supreme Court applied the rule of lenity to a gun control statute, but that case involved the effect of the statute on the politically isolated group of convicted drug dealers who wanted to possess guns, and was strongly influenced by constitutional federalism issues. United States v. Bass, 404 U.S. 336, 338 & n.2, 347–351 (1971).

3. See Stephen McG. Bundy & Einer Elhauge, "Knowledge About Legal Sanctions," 92 *Michigan Law Review* 261, 267–272 (1993).

4. Adrian Vermeule, *Judging Under Uncertainty* (Cambridge, Mass.: Harvard University Press, 2006), 10, 186–187, 192–197.

5. Ibid., 1, 4, 11, 183–229.

6. See Chapter 7 (explaining when absurdities are and should be deemed to make meaning unclear); Chapter 5 (explaining *Mead* and other exceptions to *Chevron* deference); Chapters 12 and 17 (explaining the pattern of exceptions to statutory *stare decisis*).

7. See Vermeule, *Judging*, 179–180, 201–202.

8. Ibid., 86–117.

9. See Chapters 10 and 15.

10. See Chapters 6–7.

11. See Chapters 3 and 7.

12. Vermeule, *Judging*, 118–148.

13. In contrast, Professor Vermeule's own theory does seem to require coordination among judges because its purported benefits are minimizing uncertainty and decision-making costs. If some judges try to adopt his recommendations, while others continue to apply traditional statutory default rules, then results will be even more uncertain (because they will depend more on which judge is drawn) and litigants will have to incur even more costs (because they will have to argue cases both ways). See Caleb Nelson, "Statutory Interpretation and Decision Theory," 74 *University of Chicago Law Review* 329, 345–347 (2007); Jonathan Siegel, "Judicial Interpretation in the Cost-Benefit Crucible," 92 *Minnesota Law Review* (fothcoming) (finding that Scalia's campaign against using legislative history has not reduced the rate of citations to legislative history). Thus, even if Vermeule were right both that minimizing uncertainty and decision-making costs should be our only goal and that his proposal would best achieve that goal if followed by the judiciary as a whole, any individual judge should not adopt his proposal unless he can get the other judges to make the change at the same time, because individual adoption would increase uncertainty and decision-making costs.

Index